THE JOHNS HOPKINS UNIVERSITY STUDIES
IN HISTORICAL AND POLITICAL SCIENCE
125TH SERIES (2007)

1. A. Katie Harris, *From Muslim to Christian Granada: Inventing a City's Past in Early Modern Spain*

Eruente nube
Heylan sculp.

Tanquam lapides in calcem

Ædificauit Dominus murum Hierusalem ex lapidibus de aceruis puluteris, qui com: busti sunt. 2 Esdr. 4. v. 2.

Conuersi sunt sunt iölino.

From Muslim to Christian Granada

Inventing a City's Past in Early Modern Spain

A. KATIE HARRIS

The Johns Hopkins University Press
Baltimore

This book was brought to publication with the generous assistance
of the Program for Cultural Cooperation between Spain's Ministry
of Education and Culture and United States' Universities.

The Johns Hopkins University Press
2715 North Charles Street
Baltimore, Maryland 21218-4363
www.press.jhu.edu

Library of Congress Cataloging-in-Publication Data
Harris, A. Katie, 1969–
From Muslim to Christian Granada : inventing a city's past
in early modern Spain / A. Katie Harris.
p. cm. — (Johns Hopkins University studies in historical
and political science ; 125th series, no. 1)
Includes bibliographical references and index.
ISBN-13: 978-0-8018-8523-5 (hardcover : alk. paper)
ISBN-10: 0-8018-8523-X (hardcover : alk. paper)
1. Granada (Spain)—History. 2. Granada (Spain)—History—
Sources. 3. Granada (Spain)—Church history. 4. Granada (Spain)—
Church history—Sources. 5. Group identity—Spain—Granada.
I. Title. II. Series: Johns Hopkins University studies in historical
and political science ; 125th ser., 1.
DP402.G6H36 2007
946'.8204—dc22
2006017417

A catalog record for this book is available from the British Library.

Frontispiece: Francisco Heylan, "Archbishop Pedro de Castro Ascends the Sacromonte by
Night to Venerate the Relics." Ca. 1611–28. Author's collection.

Contents

Illustrations

Acknowledgments

In the years it has taken to research and write this book, I have incurred many debts of gratitude. Thanks are due first and foremost to Richard L. Kagan, who directed the dissertation upon which this book is based, for his able supervision and unflagging encouragement. In Granada, I was aided by Antonio Luis Cortés Peña, Amalia García Pedraza, Miguel José Hagerty, and by the archivists and staffs of the cathedral and municipal archives and of the rare books collection of the library of the University of Granada. Special thanks are due to don Vicente Redondo Toro, canon and archivist of the Abbey of the Sacromonte, who welcomed me into his archive when I least expected it. His kindness, intelligence, and good humor alone were worth the trek from the city. In Madrid, the staffs of the libraries of Francisco de Zabalburú and of Bartolomé March Severa were kind enough to facilitate my access to the remarkable collections under their care. In the United States, the knowledgeable personnel of the Houghton Library at Harvard University and the rare book room of the Library of Congress were very helpful, as were the staffs of the interlibrary loan offices of the Milton S. Eisenhower Library of the Johns Hopkins University and of the Georgia State University Library.

I received generous financial support for the research and writing of the dissertation from the Fulbright Program, the Program for Cultural Cooperation between Spain's Ministry of Education, Culture, and Sports and United States Universities, and Oberlin College. Aid for additional study came from the American Historical Association, the National Endowment for the Humanities, the Office of the Vice President for Research of Georgia State University, and the Department of History of Georgia State University. The first fruits of my investigations were published in *Sixteenth Century Journal, Al-Qanṭara,* and the proceedings of the III Congreso de Historia de Andalucía. I completed the revisions at the American Academy in Rome.

Along the way and at different stages, many people read the manuscript in whole or in part, and I have benefited from their criticisms and suggestions: James Amelang, David Bell, Jodi Bilinkoff, Michelle Brattain, William Christian,

David Coleman, Mercedes García-Arenal, Walter Melion, Helen Nader, Sara Nalle, Harry Sieber, Bill Maclehose, Eric Rice, Walter Stephens, Elizabeth Wright, and the members of the Johns Hopkins University seminar in early modern Spanish history. I also learned a great deal from the comments of audiences at the Universidad Autónoma de Madrid, Georgia State University, and John Cabot University and at meetings of the American Historical Society, the International Congress on Medieval Studies, the Mediterranean Studies Association, the Sixteenth Century Studies Conference, the Society for Spanish and Portuguese Historical Studies, and the III Congreso de Historia de Andalucía. Henry Tom, of the Johns Hopkins University Press, gave patient guidance to a novice author.

The intellectual, financial, and emotional support provided by my family sustained me. Above all, Eric Forsman made the whole thing possible. This book is for him.

Introduction

On March 19, 1588, laborers working on the demolition of a tower known as the Torre Turpiana uncovered a parchment and a collection of saintly remains. These remarkable finds received an enthusiastic response from the citizens of Granada, who believed that the discoveries documented the ancient Christian origins of their city, the emblematic last stronghold of Iberian Islam. Their excitement intensified in February 1595, when treasure hunters digging on the Sacromonte, a nearby hillside, unearthed lead books and sacred relics that further confirmed the city's Christian roots. Though some doubted their authenticity, the saintly remains soon became the focus of intense devotion. Granadinos' pious hopes were fulfilled on April 30, 1600, when Granada's archbishop authenticated the relics and declared them worthy of veneration.

Few of the onlookers to the festivities in April 1600 could have guessed that the ceremonies celebrating the apotheosis of the relics marked not the end of the affair but the beginning of a long and complicated struggle over the authenticity of the relics and the documents that accompanied them. The discoveries in the Torre Turpiana and on the Sacromonte created a considerable controversy among scholars in Spain. Critics quickly pointed to the dubious doctrinal content and obvious anachronisms of the parchment and the lead books, which came to be known collectively as the *plomos* of Granada. As the debate continued, it became increasingly clear that the *plomos* were imaginative forgeries. After being shipped to Rome in 1642 for examination, the *plomos* were eventually condemned in 1682 by Pope Innocent XI as the creations of Muslims intent on undermining the Catholic faith. Despite their confiscation and condemnation by Rome, however, they remained a favorite topic among Spanish scholars, attracting both detractors and, especially in Granada, defenders and advocates.[1] The Collegiate Church of the Sacromonte (also commonly called the Abbey of the Sacromonte), an institution founded in 1609, continued to produce arguments in favor of the *plomos* until quite recently. In 1883, for example, José de Ramos López, a canon of the Sacromonte, published a short and credulous history of the affair, and the many works of the indefatigable Zótico Royo Campos, abbot of the Sacromonte from 1956 until his death in 1971, continued to advance the cause in the twentieth century.[2]

Since the middle of the nineteenth century, however, most historians of the Sacromonte have taken a more critical view of the *plomos*. Most prominently, José Godoy Alcántara's *Historia crítica de los falsos cronicones* (1868) investigated the documents' anachronisms and revealed the details of their syncretistic theology.[3] Godoy Alcántara's erudite and prize-winning critique established the themes and the tone for several generations of scholarship on the *plomos*. His influence is evident in the treatment given the issue by nineteenth-century scholars Vicente de la Fuente and Marcelino Menéndez y Pelayo, both of whom bemoaned the pernicious superstition and historical confusion caused by the forgeries.[4] In the twentieth century, Carlos Alonso's invaluable study of the affair reasserted Godoy Alcántara's conclusions while focusing on the diplomatic exchanges among Granada, Madrid, and Rome. Similarly, the late anthropologist Julio Caro Baroja's examination of the *plomos* within the wider context of forgeries in and of Spanish history reiterated the conventional interpretation.[5]

Some recent scholars of the *plomos* have built upon Godoy Alcántara's conclusions to produce more balanced treatments, which consider the *plomos* to be the theologically unorthodox expressions of Granadino Moriscos, the nominally Catholic descendants of Muslim converts. Arabist Darío Cabanelas Rodríguez's several studies on the subject of the *plomos* characterized them as attempts at "spiritual survival."[6] In a recently reissued edition of the *plomos'* texts, Miguel José Hagerty echoed Cabanelas's conclusions and noted that "these 'apocrypha' constitute, then, an attempt to institutionalize the *jofor* [a Morisco literary genre of prophecies or predictions], implanting it within a liturgy and a doctrine that, in the main, corresponded to those of Islam."[7]

Other scholars have taken still another approach, setting aside questions of theological orthodoxy and heterodoxy in order to examine the *plomos* within the contexts of Spanish national mythology and Counter-Reformation ideals. T. D. Kendrick claimed that the creators of the *plomos* intended not only to create a "compromise faith," an amalgam of Islam and Christianity, but also to "exalt Granada above all the cities in Spain in holiness and antiquity."[8] In a 1981 article, Antonio Bonet Correa noted that the *plomos* gave Granada "titles of nobility and authority to proclaim its historically Catholic genealogy," while the development of the Sacromonte "constituted a moral-didactic discourse of marked Counter-Reformation stamp." He proposed that the discoveries and the religious complex formed around them should be considered as part of an ambitious program of urban reforms to remake Granada into a "paradigmatic Counter-Reformation city" and a "New Jerusalem."[9] José Luis Orozco Pardo further refined this image, describing seventeenth-century Granada as a "Christianopolis," a baroque city of the Counter-Reformation in which the relics of the Sacromonte "rewrite the history of the city, which is founded . . . on a theophanic subsoil."[10]

Over the past twenty years, growing interest in the *plomos* has revitalized both the "Morisco school" and the "Christian school" of interpretation as an ever-increasing number of scholars has worked to analyze the *plomos* and their broader cultural context. Recent scholarship has deepened understandings of the *plomos'* place in both Morisco and non-Morisco culture. Barbara Fuchs, for example, has reread the *plomos* as a Morisco exercise in strategic mimesis that remade Spanish identity around a Muslim core, while L. P. Harvey has recently suggested that the forgers sought to transform basic Christian doctrine along Muslim lines.[11] David Coleman's discussion of the affair grounds initial responses to the *plomos* in a broad cross section of non-Morisco Granadino society, and Francisco Javier Martínez Medina has explored the overlap between the *plomos* and the cult of the Immaculate Conception fostered by the Tridentine Church.[12]

The approach to the *plomos* as part of a larger process of Christianization suggested by Kendrick, Bonet Correa, Orozco Pardo, and others provides a point of departure for my own consideration of the Sacromonte. In my understanding, the *plomos* created historical links to a mythical Christian past for a city that had been for centuries a stronghold of Islam and played a key role in its transformation into a model of continuous, steadfast Christianity. To date, most approaches to Granada's Christianization have focused on the key players and policies active in the programmatic effort to transform Muslim Granada into a Catholic and Castilian city after 1492. Some scholars have attended to strategies of urban renewal—the demolition of mosques and baths, for example, and the erection of churches and plazas—and to the extension of royal and ecclesiastical power into the city—the establishment of Castilian and Catholic institutions such the Chancery, a tribunal of the Inquisition, and an archiepiscopal see.[13] Others have investigated how Granada's new leaders legislated changes of language, dress, customs, and, of course, religion for the city's Muslim inhabitants, transforming *mudéjares*, Muslims living under Christian rule, into Moriscos. Orozco Pardo has examined how civic and ecclesiastical officials organized the city and its inhabitants into parishes and confraternities and converted the city's public spaces into ritual centers with processions and religious festivals.[14] These changes, together with the persistent and officially encouraged influx of immigrants from all over the Iberian Peninsula, contributed greatly to the postconquest Christianization and Castilianization of Granada, and the studies that examine them are indispensable to an understanding of this transformation.

My investigation of the *plomos* builds upon these studies by considering the hitherto underexamined symbolic and mythological aspects of Granada's transformation. The chapters that follow explore how Granada's new leaders constituted and articulated a new, Christianized communal identity through the textual, ritual, and cultic discourses surrounding the *plomos* and the Sacromonte that were current in Granada through the seventeenth century. Through the discourses that developed around the *plomos*—as represented in sermons, ceremonies, histories, maps, and devotions—Granadinos came to locate their city upon a new historical terrain, refiguring their civic identity and imagining themselves as the legitimate heirs of an ancient Christian heritage.

Inventions of Memory

Contemporary sources on the finds describe their discovery as an *invención*—the vernacular form of the medieval hagiographical *inventio*. Like its Latin parent, *invención* is a flexible word, encompassing the sense of discovery or finding, as well as that of creation or devising. Sebastián de Covarrubias Orozco's *Tesoro de la lengua castellana, o española* (1611) offers dual definitions for the related verb, *inventar*. He writes that sometimes it means "to create a new thing never seen before and that has no imitation," but "sometimes it means to lie."[15] The *plomos* are thus *invented* in multiple meanings of the word: exhumed from the Torre Turpiana and the Sacromonte, they are both innovative human creations and clever forgeries devised to give substance to a mythic past. Similarly, Granadino civic identity is itself a kind of invention, newly created around a historical fiction. I understand civic identity as a symbolically constituted sense of belonging to a deep-rooted community. Granadino identity was sustained by remembrance—by the collective memory of a communal past constituted and made present in the *plomos*. In ceremonies, sermons, histories, and devotions, Granadinos bound themselves together through the retelling of the story of their city's unique religious inheritance.

Of course, memory and identity depend upon each other, and, like so many other human constructions, both are subjective and inconstant, liable to change with shifting contexts. My study considers the intersections of communal memory and communal identity, grounding them in time and place in order to explore how one community defined itself through the recovery and retelling of its past.

In doing so, I do not aim to define early modern Granadino communal identity. Identities are plural, heterogeneous, and unbounded. "For any imaginable social group," notes Richard Handler, ". . . there is no definitive way to specify 'who we are,' for 'who we are' is a communicative process that includes many voices and varying degrees of understanding and, importantly, misunderstanding."[16] While the Sacromonte, the *plomos,* and the discourses to which they gave rise are perhaps the most prominent loci of early modern Granadino identity, other sites were available. The heroic deeds and royal service of Granada's founding families; the city's nationally notable institutions, like the Chancery or the Royal Chapel; its relationship to its royal "founders," Ferdinand and Isabella; its annual Corpus Christi celebration; its vote in the Castilian parliament, the Cortes; the municipal banner; the famous medieval fortress of the Alhambra—all were possible and to some degree actual alternative loci of Granadino self-definition.[17] In exploring the narratives constructed around the *plomos,* I have focused on the most noteworthy of the religious aspects of communal identity.

The enthusiastic response given the *plomos* and the important role they subsequently played in the transformation of Granada did not represent a public endorsement of the intentions of the forger(s), which remain a matter of speculation. Rather, they reflected the fact that Granadinos found in the story of the *plomos* means for the satisfaction of some desires or needs of their own. Given Granada's particular dilemma, burdened with an emblematically Islamic past in a Catholic territory, it is easy to see how the *plomos* could have been seen to fill the need for an appropriate past. In this regard, it may be helpful to consider the *plomos* in light of David Lowenthal's distinctions between history and heritage: "History seeks to convince by truth, and succumbs to falsehood. Heritage exaggerates and omits, candidly invents and frankly forgets." Heritage depends upon myth and fabrication, because heritage, not history, is essential to communal cohesion; heritage marks out the boundaries of membership at the divide between those who believe and those who do not. "Heritage everywhere not only tolerates but thrives on historical error. Falsified legacies are integral to group identity and uniqueness."[18]

Since the sixteenth century, critics of the *plomos* of the Sacromonte have agreed that the forgers were most likely members of Granada's Morisco community. It seems probable that, at least in part, their intention was to create a new and acceptable past for Granadino Moriscos, a heritage that would have guaranteed Morisco cultural survival by merging the separate pasts of the two communities, minority and majority, into a single unified narrative. Ironically, however, although the *plomos* themselves project this inclusive communal identity, their discursive elaboration in local culture undergirds a Granadino identity that is largely antagonistic toward the Morisco community. Granada's newfound past, especially as it was reconstructed and recollected in city histories and ritual, marginalized Moriscos in the civic community.

As well as leaving Moriscos at the community's edge, these constitutive discourses of Granadino identity were articulated by a limited sector of the city's urban population. Like the corporate constitutionalism that animated the early modern Spanish sense of national affiliation, the discourses created around the *plomos* were "the preserve of the dominant social and vocational groups"— namely, "nobles and gentry, urban patriciates, the lawyers, the clergy, the educated."[19] This elite group constituted Granada's dominant "memory community"; its interpretation of the past became the authorized, official version of the city.[20] Granada's leaders were far from being a single, unified block, however. A heterogeneous group of varied origins and differing institutional affiliations, the city's power elite frequently fought out its internal disputes upon the arena of the *plomos* and the Sacromonte. I argue that the discourses that developed around the *plomos* were not simple enactments of an idealized civic harmony and a shared communal identity, but also sites upon which Granada's patricians contested for power and influence.

Just as they dominated their city's political institutions, Granada's oligarchs dominated the discourses of communal memory and identity that developed around the *plomos*. While their vision of Granada's past is the primary focus of this book, the voices of humbler Granadinos are not wholly silent here. Men and women of all social stations participated in the rituals and devotions through which key aspects of civic identity were articulated, and their actions offer precious glimpses into the civic self-consciousness of average Granadinos. Still, the evidence presented here is more suggestive than definitive, and much work remains to be done to uncover the contours and historical currents of communal memory and identity outside the ranks of the city's elite.

Sources and Discourses

The *plomos*, the controversy that surrounded them, and their vital role in the Christianization and Castilianization of Granada gave rise to a wealth of manuscript and print material. I have drawn the bulk of the sources that form the foundation of this book from archives and libraries—both secular and ecclesiastical, public and private—scattered throughout Spain. In Granada, the rich holdings of the archive of the Abbey of the Sacromonte provided invaluable manuscript materials, including the dossier of witness depositions before the panel of inquiry into the discoveries, as well as letters, treatises, and other unique sources.[21] The records of chapter meetings and other documents preserved in the archive of the cathedral of Granada have offered important evidence, as have documents from Granada's municipal archive. I have made particular use of the holdings of the rare books section of the library of the University of Granada, especially the hard-to-find sermons that are included in the library's excellent Montenegro Collection.

Beyond Granada, I found a variety of letters, petitions, and other materials in the Patronato Real and Estado sections of the state archives at Simancas. Madrid's National Historical Archive yielded an assortment of documents from the Supreme Council of the Inquisition, as well as a large collection of papers generated by the Council of Castile's standing committee on the Sacromonte. I have used many print and manuscript sources held in the National Library in Madrid, while other materials have been drawn from the Royal Academy of History, the Archive of the Indies, the library of the Royal Monastery of El Escorial, and the private libraries of Bartolomé March Servera and of Francisco de Zabálburu. In the United States, the Houghton Library of Harvard University, the New York Public Library, and the Library of Congress provided important printed sources. I found additional materials in London at the British Library and in Rome at the archive of the Congregation for the Doctrine of the Faith.

The abundance of available sources is matched by a wealth of studies on the discourses of communal identity. The past several decades have witnessed an explosion of studies considering the development of communal identities in modern Europe, especially on the development of national identities, and much of it generated by cultural historians. The hallmark of this new attention has been a focus on the imaginary or mythological dimension of national genealogies, and many of the authors working in this area have drawn sustenance from a handful of widely influential works. Notable among these are the essays on the "invention of tradition" collected by Eric Hobsbawm and Terence Ranger, which elaborate the process by which industrial societies, immersed in transitional upheaval, fabricated historical semi-fictions or forgeries in order to create political or historical continuity with a meaningful real or invented past.[22] Likewise a landmark of work in this area, Benedict Anderson's study of the origins of nationalism characterizes nations as "imagined communities," symbolically constructed cultural artifacts.[23] In his monumental study of French national identity, *Les lieux de mémoire,* Pierre Nora and his collaborators have explored the symbols of nationhood as "sites" or "realms of memory," which range from actual geographical and physical places to more metaphorical sites, around which the French have constituted their national identity.[24]

In exploring the religious dimensions of the constitution of Granadino civic identity, my study of the *plomos* and their milieux participates in this ongoing conversation about the origins and development of communal identities in modern Europe. In examining the cultural constitution of Granadino identity, however, the present study seeks to bring the growing body of work on cultural constitution to bear on local and regional affinities, which are underexamined in the existing literature. This local take on the recent focus on the cultural constitution of communal identities contributes importantly to the overall discourse in that these "lower" level affinities often complement but sometimes conflict with national identities, and attention to them may highlight the contingent character of communal self-constitutions. Complication of the picture of relations among national, regional, and local identities fits perhaps better with a case such as that of Spain, where a "composite" monarchy—a hybrid of "localism and centralization; representation and autocracy; traditional aristocracy and modern state-builders; order and improvisation"—accommodated and encouraged loyalty to multiple communities, local, regional, and national.[25] Indeed, as Peter Sahlins has demonstrated in his work on the Spanish and French Pyrenees, subnational identities thrived during the ascendance and dominance of the nation-state and nationalism.[26] It may be that, as I. A. A. Thompson has argued, Spain's local communities responded to the Habsburg monarchy's triumphalist rhetoric with a heightened sense of collective identity.[27]

Whereas my local approach on the cultural constitution of communal identities is somewhat at variance with the national focus of the larger scholarly discourse, the local focus of my treatment of Granadino religiosity fits well with a growing body of work on the impact and implementation of Tridentine Catholicism, which attends closely to phenomena at the local and regional levels. In recent years, investigation into the subject has boomed, spawned by ground-breaking studies such as William Christian's examination of "local" Spanish religion and a general dissatisfaction with older, Rome-centric approaches.[28] This locally and regionally attentive current of work on the Counter-Reformation revises the prevailing interpretive paradigm of an increasingly dominant Rome and progressively weakening local churches and traditions by emphasizing the elements of compromise and cooperation that often prevailed in relations between center and periphery.[29]

While this book speaks to these studies, it differs in emphasis and intent. Rather than examining the implementation of reformed Catholicism in the

Granadino context, I focus on the intersections between local religion and local identity. In both Protestant and Catholic Europe, communal identity—local, regional, and national—came to be closely tied to confession. Similar to the Burgundian worthies examined by Mack Holt, the people of Granada viewed their Catholic belief and practice as an essential aspect their self-identification, both as Granadinos and as Spaniards.[30] In particular, the saints, devotions, and liturgies specific to Granada helped foster communal feeling by preserving and commemorating the shared past and spiritual allegiances that knit together the community. In spite of the allegedly homogenizing effects of social discipline and confessionalization, Catholic practices often retained a regionally heterogeneous, locally specific quality. The Tridentine Church's renewed emphasis on the cult of saints encouraged a receptive climate for the *plomos* in Granada and fostered the characteristically particularist devotion to the Sacromonte and to St. Cecilio, Granada's patron, that was so important to the local community.

Overview of the Book

The historian who focuses his studies on a specific place in time runs the risk of becoming lost in Marc Bloch's "maze of little local facts"; but it is local facts that inform and shape local identities. Accordingly, it is with local facts that I begin.[31] Following the prologue, "Old Bones for a New City," which describes the events that surrounded the discovery of the *plomos*, the first chapter examines the reforms and changes contributing to the Christianization of the city of Granada over the course of the sixteenth century, sketching in the process a profile of Granada as it was when the *plomos* first entered the scene. In the decades that followed the conquest in 1492, Granada's new civil and ecclesiastical leaders, governing through a collection of recently established institutions, enacted a package of policies designed to reshape both the brick-and-mortar infrastructure and the flesh-and-blood inhabitants of the city along Christian and Castilian lines. I consider these Christianizing policies, the institutions and elites that enacted them, and their effects on the Muslim city.

The finds in the Torre Turpiana and the Sacromonte provoked strong reactions, and supporters and detractors struggled to discredit or to defend the *plomos*. A vital issue in this debate was the *plomos'* connections to the culture of Granada's despised Morisco minority. The second chapter, "Controversy and Propaganda," explores the *plomos'* roots in Morisco culture and the critical responses they elicited from scholars throughout Spain and from Church authorities in Rome. The defense and promotion of the *plomos* by supporters like Pedro de Castro, the city's archbishop, fostered their appropriation and transformation into the founding monuments of Christian Granada.

The third, fourth, and fifth chapters explore the textual, ritual, and cultic discourses of Granadino civic identity to which the *plomos* gave rise. "Forging History: Granadino Historiography and the Sacromonte," considers how Granadino historians used the *plomos* as the documentary foundation for a new interpretation of Granada's past. Local scholars used the relics and lead books to create historical links to a mythical Christian past, recasting modern Granada as the heir to the antique Christian republic of Iliberis, and thus transforming what had been for centuries a Muslim city into a model of steadfast Christianity. Through close readings of several city histories dating from the late sixteenth century and the first half of the seventeenth century, I show how these writers elaborated new narratives of Granadino history that maintained continuity as their central principle.

In refiguring their city as the modern incarnation of an ancient Christian republic, Granadino historians provided a solid foundation for imagining Granada as a new Jerusalem—an exemplary Counter-Reformation city. This image was one of several developed in the sermons delivered as part of the annual festival commemorating the fall of Muslim Granada to the Catholic forces of Ferdinand and Isabella in 1492. The fourth chapter, "Civic Ritual and Civic Identity," examines this festival, known as the Toma, or capture of the city. As a key component of the civic ceremonial cycle, the Toma rehearsed the origins of modern Granada and reasserted the meanings and values associated with them. The procession, the high mass, the ceremonial waving of the city standard before the tombs of Ferdinand and Isabella, and the sermons themselves all reveal how the Toma confirmed and promoted the constitution of a new collective memory that was instrumental to the construction of Granadino civic consciousness. The Toma ceremony publicly reaffirmed Granada's faith, ritually reconstituting the city as a Christian community through the reenactment of its modern origins in the conquest, while the sermons, by invoking the Christian heritage documented by the *plomos,* stretched the boundaries of remembrance to encompass the city's ancient beginnings.

The public and collective qualities of early modern Catholic religiosity revealed in the Toma are likewise represented in the devotional and cultic expressions developed around the *plomos*. In the fifth chapter, "The *Plomos* and the Sacromonte in Granadino Piety," I examine the intersection between Granadino communal identity and the devotional activity engendered by the *plomos* and the Sacromonte. The first part of the chapter considers the reconfiguration of Granada's symbolic landscape effected through the human and supernatural responses to the discoveries on the Sacromonte. As revealed in a collection of maps created in the years following the discoveries, the hillside, once sacred to the Morisco community, became a principal symbol of the religious identity of Christian Granada and a geographic center of Granadinos' communal memory of their city's ancient past. The second and third sections of the chapter examine how Granada's municipal government endorsed and upheld that communal past through the official cult of St. Cecilio and the defense of the *plomos* and how, through the historical traditions supported by the *plomos,* Granadinos transformed the generic veneration of the Immaculate Conception of the Virgin Mary into a particularist devotion, deeply rooted in the city's invented antiquity.

Though removed to Rome in 1642 and condemned some forty years later, the discoveries from the Torre Turpiana and the Sacromonte remained embedded in local Granadino culture and civic identity. In the epilogue, I take up the *plomos'* continuing repercussions from the eighteenth century to the present and explore the possible identities of their authors.

From Muslim to Christian Granada

Old Bones for a New City

The Torre Turpiana, 1588

At seven o'clock on the morning of March 19, 1588, Francisco Cano, a construction worker in the southern Spanish city of Granada, took up his tools and set to work. His task for the day was to break up and remove a large section of a building that had been pulled down the previous afternoon. Though common opinion held the Old Tower to be very ancient, perhaps Phoenician in origin, the authorities had deemed it to be out of keeping with the new, modern cathedral under construction on the site of what had been medieval Granada's main mosque.[1] The building project was but one of many under way throughout the city. Since its fall in 1492 to the forces of Isabella of Castile and Ferdinand of Aragon, Granada, the final outpost of Iberian Islam, had undergone dramatic changes. Over the course of the century, the city's new rulers forced the indigenous Muslim community to abandon its faith and customs, becoming Moriscos, or Catholic converts from Islam. At the same time, settlers from throughout the Iberian Peninsula flocked to Granada, drawn by the economic and social opportunities it afforded. Changes in the outward structure of Granada accompanied the transformations wrought on the city's human face by conversion, acculturation, and immigration. Everywhere, medieval palaces were transformed into monasteries and convents, and mosques were replaced by hospitals and parish churches. The Old Tower, from which muezzins had once called Muslim Granadinos to prayer, had served for some decades as a makeshift bell tower. Now, however, the ancient structure was to be destroyed and its site to be incorporated into the new cathedral, the most conspicuous marker of Granada's new Christian regime.

As he labored in the rubble, Cano uncovered among the debris a small lead box, sealed with bitumen.[2] "What a treasure I have found!" he exclaimed.[3] While his companions crowded around, he pried open the box to reveal its strange contents: a folded parchment, a triangular piece of delicate fabric, a small bone, and some blue-black dust or sand, all wrapped within a piece of rough cloth. A tussle over the parchment quickly broke out among the excited workmen, and, alerted by the hubbub, the officials overseeing the construction site confiscated the strange objects and notified the members of the city's cathedral chapter.

Later that afternoon, the cathedral canons assembled in the chapter house to inspect the finds.[4] The parchment, they observed, was written in Arabic and Castilian. According to a Latin inscription across the bottom, in the first century A.D. Cecilio, Granada's first bishop, had entrusted the box to a follower in order that its precious contents—a new and unknown apocalypse of St. John the Evangelist, a bone from the arm of the martyr St. Stephen, and half of the handkerchief used by the Virgin Mary to dry her tears at the Crucifixion—be hidden from the "Moors."[5] The Arabic portion of the parchment revealed further marvels, describing how both the relics and the prophecy were gifts from St. Dionysius the Areopagite to St. Cecilio, who translated the prophetic text from Hebrew into Castilian and wrote a brief commentary in Arabic for the benefit of Spanish Christians. The prophecy, inscribed on a checkerboard grid in alternating letters of black and red with Greek letters interspersed, foretold the coming of both Mohammed, a "very obscure darkness" arising "in the eastern parts," and Luther, a "second darkness" or "dragon" from whose mouth "will spew forth a seed that will take root" and "the faith will divide into sects." These evil portents, together with coming epidemics, persecution of the clergy, and other "prodigious signs that Heaven will show," announced the imminent advent of the Antichrist and the Last Judgment.[6]

Predictions like these found a ready audience in the nervous climate of late sixteenth-century Spain. Although Spanish power and influence extended around the globe from Italy to the Americas and beyond, everywhere infidels and heretics seemed to threaten Catholic Christendom and its self-appointed defender. Despite the famous victory achieved in 1571 at Lepanto, the Muslim Ottoman Empire remained a potent presence in the Mediterranean. In northern Europe, Spanish troops struggled for decades to bring to heel the Calvinist Dutch rebels. Spain's interventions in France's civil wars between Catholics and Calvinists were proving increasingly costly, and tensions with Elizabeth I's England deepened as the "Invincible" Spanish Armada prepared for departure against the Protestant English—and a devastating defeat. For some Spaniards, attacks by Berber corsairs and English privateers on towns and villages along Iberia's southern coasts had brought these distant contests terrifyingly close to home. Indeed, only one year before the discoveries in the tower, Sir Francis Drake, commander of the English pirates, had burned much of the Spanish fleet in a daring raid on Cádiz. Many experienced directly the costs of Spanish global imperial might in the form of crushing taxes that exacerbated the financial distress provoked by economic recession and ever-climbing inflation. These woes, coupled with the arrival of poor harvests and waves of epidemic disease, fueled the popularity of street seers and inspired dreamers, and of the prophetic texts that circulated throughout Spanish society.[7]

Word of the astonishing finds in Granada spread quickly around the country, arousing devotion, curiosity, and skepticism. For Granadinos, the Old Tower's parchment and the astonishing relics that accompanied it held additional attraction because of the light they shed on their city's ancient Christian past. Because it had been a Muslim city for centuries, Granada possessed no remains of its legendary first bishop and evangelist, and Granadinos responded with excitement to the seemingly miraculous discovery of a document signed by St. Cecilio himself as "episcopus Granatensis," as well as important relics of such powerful saints as St. Stephen and the Virgin Mary. The public clamored to see and to venerate the relics. "It is a great thing to see the desire of all [the people of] this province that they show them this great treasure in public," wrote Juan Méndez de Salvatierra, Granada's archbishop.[8] He reported the discoveries to Philip II (r. 1556–98), a monarch known for his interest in saintly relics, and sent a copy of the parchment to the internationally acclaimed linguist and biblical scholar Benito Arias Montano (1527–98) for analysis and inspection.[9] While he waited for a reply from the king, the archbishop opened the formal process of investigation into the authenticity of the relics and the parchment by calling a meeting of local scholars, jurists, and theologians to consider the matter.[10] He also dispatched letters to the Vatican to request papal approval for the inquiry he had already begun, but in May 1588 he died suddenly, before there was any reply from Rome.

Archbishop Salvatierra's unexpected death left the investigation into the finds from the minaret in the hands of the cathedral chapter, which sent a copy of the parchment to Philip II, together with a fragment of the triangular handkerchief for his relic collection at the Escorial.[11] While most of the canons were enthusiastic about the relics and the parchment, a few were not. The opposition included lectoral canon Francisco Aguilar Terrones del Caño (1551–1613), who openly expressed his doubts about the authenticity of the finds and was threatened with sanctions as a result. The scholaster, Luis Ortega de Monsalve (d. 1596), harbored similar sentiments. It was possibly these tensions that persuaded the chapter to abandon the investigation until the arrival of the new archbishop, Pedro Vaca de Castro y Quiñones (1534–1623), in 1590.[12]

Within a year of his arrival in Granada, Archbishop Castro resumed the investigation into the relics. He ordered new translations of the parchment and consulted several eminent scholars, including the erudite royal almoner Pedro García de Loaysa Girón (1542–99), the Granadino historian Luis del Mármol Carvajal, and Benito Arias Montano. These shrewd critics raised difficult questions about the language, origins, and authenticity of the finds, and the archbishop was moved to shelve the inquiry in 1593, "until the time when God may grant more light."[13]

The Sacromonte, 1595

A few years later, a group of treasure hunters uncovered a series of underground caves on a hillside to the east above the city in an area called the Valparaíso, or Valley of Paradise. In the hopes of finding lost Moorish gold, they labored in secret over several months to clear the caves of the loose rock and dirt that filled them. On February 21, 1595, the searchers discovered not buried treasure, but a small lead plaque inscribed with strange and illegible letters. The text, which was eventually found to be Latin, recorded that in A.D. 56, during the reign of Nero, a certain Mesitón had suffered martyrdom on the hillside and was buried nearby.[14] Archbishop Castro, anxious to find new relics, ordered the excavation of the site, and by March 21, workers uncovered a second plaque that recorded the execution of Hiscio, a disciple of St. James, the patron saint of Spain, together with four companions in the caves of the Sacromonte, the name by which the hill soon became known. In the following weeks the excavation team unearthed the cremated remains of these martyrs and a third lead plaque that recounted the martyrdom of Tesifón, another disciple of St. James. The hillside also yielded even more peculiar objects. Alongside the ashes and plaques, workers found two curious books that consisted of several thin, round sheets of lead "the size of hosts for celebrating mass," bound together with lead thread, and inscribed on both sides with oddly distorted Arabic letters.[15] Report of the strange finds on the hillside spread quickly through the city, and the Sacromonte soon swarmed with crowds of the devout and the curious. Some visitors came to pray in the caves, while others scrabbled in the dirt and uncovered more of the mysterious lead books. Granadinos' hopes were finally fulfilled on April 30, when a young girl found a fourth plaque that stated that St. Cecilio himself had suffered martyrdom in the caves of the Sacromonte, and that his commentary on the prophecy of St. John the Evangelist was hidden with other relics in the upper part of the "Torre Turpiana"—a reference to the 1588 finds.

The discovery sent the city of Granada into paroxysms of joy. Primed by their experience of the discoveries in the minaret seven years before, the people of Granada responded to the relics recovered from the Sacromonte with enthusiastic devotion. Granadinos of all social stations jammed the city streets and flocked to the hillside to venerate the newly discovered saints.[16] "The people were so excited with joy," recorded a notary, "that because of the crowds one could pass through the streets only with difficulty."[17] Penitent Granadinos made barefoot pilgrimages to the caves, where they kept silent vigils. Some even climbed the hill on their knees, kissing the rocks and weeping with contrition.[18] Felipe Navarro, a beneficed parish priest of the Church of St. Peter and St. Paul, declared himself astonished at the "modesty and devotion" of the people "who go to visit the Sacromonte . . . with the greatest devotion, both men and women, and many of the women go barefoot."[19] Other officials stressed the deportment of the faithful, who, despite the dangerous mingling of the sexes in the streets, behaved very modestly, and they marveled at the silence and weeping of the devout penitents in the caves. "In Madrid they neither see nor know," Archbishop Castro told the papal nuncio, "the devotion and tears of the people, or the piety with which they venerate these saints, or the great mass of people who come to these caverns barefoot and weeping, without there ever having been any disturbance."[20]

The first of the crosses on the Sacromonte appeared on April 12, put there by persons unknown. Granada's institutions, guilds, and confraternities soon followed suit: the weavers, chandlers, ironmongers, tavern keepers, milkmen, officials of Granada's royal appellate court, or Chancery, cathedral choir boys, and notaries all carried crosses to the mountain in elaborate processions, accompanied by musicians, military honor guards, and candle-bearing friars. The city's ethnic minorities organized their own processions—on May 7, "the black men and women, the men dressed in the attire of soldiers, and with their own music and rejoicing, brought and erected their cross," and on May 28, "the mulattoes made their station in military fashion."[21] Within a few weeks of the first finds, the Sacromonte was a forest of crosses; one contemporary claimed that 800 were erected in just over a week.[22] Nearby communities and distant cities alike brought crosses and made pious donations to the newly revealed saints. The neighboring city of Guadix, for example, erected a cross on the hillside, and in 1599 the municipal council of Seville donated a costly silver lamp in fulfillment of a vow made to the Sacromonte saints in exchange for their intervention in an outbreak of plague.[23] Eventually, so constant was the traffic to the Sacromonte that, at the request of the king, Archbishop Castro reluctantly closed the caves to pious visitors. His efforts were apparently in vain, however, as the authorities posted to police the site were overwhelmed by the tide of popular devotion.[24]

For a few, prayers and pilgrimages received a miraculous response. Inexplicable cures of bodily and mental illness, supernatural rescues from peril, and other eruptions of the divine into worldly existence testified to the authenticity of the finds and the sanctity of the site. The miracles began with the discovery of the plaque documenting St. Cecilio's martyrdom. On that same day, a crippled young girl invoked the intercession of the saint and left the caves healed.[25] In another instance, thirteen witnesses testified to the miraculous cure worked on Leonor Bravo, the sister of an official in the Royal Chancery. Bedridden and unable to walk for four years, Leonor was carried to the Sacromonte on May 9, 1595. After praying in the caves, she rose and walked home. In another case occurring a few days later, washerwoman María Rodríguez and her child fell into a millstream and were swept into the wheel. She cried out for the aid of St. Cecilio and his companions, and both mother and child were miraculously preserved from death.[26]

Together, more than twenty individuals from a broad range of social backgrounds reported miraculous cures and rescues attained through the intervention of the Sacromonte saints. Some, like Leonor Bravo or Florencia de Calvache, were relatives of members of the Chancery or the cathedral chapter; others, like María Rodríguez, the artisan Ginés Tomás, or the Muslim slave Fátima, came from humbler circumstances.[27] Their testimony formed an important part of Archbishop Castro's investigation into the new discoveries. His vicars-general interviewed dozens of witnesses, from day laborers to prominent worthies. Doctors and priests gave testimony on the miraculous healings, while soap makers, silversmiths, and other specialists reported on the material of the ashes and the antiquity of the lead books and tablets. Some of these experts conducted experiments on the human remains found in the caves, grinding and mixing small samples to determine their composition. In one case, a former ash carrier tested the mysterious finds by tasting them.[28] Perfumers and pharmacists examined the documents and ashes to discover the source of their sweet odor (a traditional feature of a holy relic), and silversmiths examined the lead books to assess their antiquity and manner of fabrication.[29] Others specialists, including Miguel de Luna (d. 1615) and Alonso de Castillo, two Morisco interpreters who had previously deciphered the Arabic portion of the parchment from the Torre Turpiana, labored to translate the strange Arabic texts.[30]

The translations and the testimony became important parts of Archbishop Castro's efforts to authenticate the finds. Despite a papal decree issued in January 1596 that prohibited judgment on the books, on two occasions—September 28, 1596, and February 21, 1597—Castro convoked meetings of local theologians and asked them to examine the discoveries. Their positive assessments of the authenticity and orthodoxy of both the relics and the lead books encouraged the archbishop to convene a provincial council to meet in September 1598 in order to consider the relics' authentication. The death of King Philip II and a major outbreak of plague delayed the meeting for more than a year and a half, but finally, after citywide fasting, processions, and a pontifical mass, the provincial council began deliberations on April 16, 1600. The main role of the council, which included representatives from Spain's many dioceses and archdioceses, members of Granada's secular and regular clergy, and judges and other officials of the Royal Chancery, was primarily one of consultation. Because the decrees of the Council of Trent charged local prelates with the task of authentication of newly discovered saintly remains, the final decision lay with the archbishop alone. Pronouncement on the lead books and the parchment, however, rested with the authorities in Rome. After consideration of the evidence, the provincial council unanimously recommended the approbation of the relics. On April 30, 1600, cathedral canon Pedro Guerrero wept for joy as he read aloud Archbishop Castro's declaration that the relics from the Torre Turpiana and the Sacromonte were authentic and worthy of veneration.[31] Pealing church bells and artillery salvos announced the glorious news to the gathered crowds, "leaving all the people with great devotion and pleasure to have seen the end of this affair so successful and fortunate for their city and for all Christendom."[32]

CHAPTER ONE

Granada in the Sixteenth Century

The city that enthusiastically greeted the discoveries in the Torre Turpiana and on the Sacromonte was one in the throes of upheaval and transition. The construction boom was but the most immediately visible element of a tumultuous, century-long process by which Granada, the ultimate outpost of Islam in western Europe, was slowly transformed into a Christian and Castilian city. The metamorphosis began in January 1492, when the once-powerful emirate and its capital city fell to the forces of Isabella and Ferdinand, rulers of Castile and Aragon. News of the conquest traveled quickly and was greeted with joy throughout Christian Europe. In 1494 Pope Alexander VI rewarded Ferdinand and Isabella for their achievement with the title of "Catholic Monarchs." Their success marked both the end of the so-called Christian Reconquest—a centuries-long struggle for dominance between the Muslim kingdoms of Al-Andalus, in the southern portion of the Iberian Peninsula, and the Christian kingdoms to the north—and the extension of the crusading spirit of that conflict beyond Iberia, into North Africa and the Americas. It also signaled an important landmark in the growing power of the Crown of Castile. Yoked together in 1479 through the marriage of the two monarchs, the confederation of the Aragonese and Castilian crowns was an asymmetrical union. Castile—larger, wealthier, and more populous than the federation of kingdoms that made up the Crown of Aragon—was the dominant partner in the new Spanish monarchy. The annexation of Granada to the Crown of Castile was a signal event, indicative of Castile's ascendancy and of Spain's growing dominance both within the Iberian Peninsula and beyond.

A City Transformed

On January 6, 1492, four days after the formal handover, Ferdinand and Isabella entered the newly captured city. With perhaps some 50,000 inhabitants,
Granada was one of Spain's most populous urban centers.[1] Spread out on two
hills and a plain at the foot of the Sierra Nevada and intersected by the Darro and
Genil rivers, the city comprised several distinct and identifiable neighborhoods
or zones. Hieronymus Münzer, a German merchant who visited Granada in
1494, described it as composed of several "cities": the fortress of the Alhambra;
the Antequerela, which sat below it; and the Albaicín, the oldest and most heavily populated part of the city. To Münzer's eyes, the Albaicín was a confusing maze
of cramped and crooked streets, some so narrow that two donkeys could not
pass.[2] The paths, said Münzer, stank of refuse and sewage, "though the people
are, nevertheless, very clean." The houses of the Muslim inhabitants were
labyrinthine and tiny, one-fourth to one-fifth the size of those of the Castilians,
but they enjoyed running water, an unheard-of luxury.[3] On the plain below the
Albaicín and Antequerela lay the city's main mosque and commercial district.
Five times a day, the calls of the muezzins echoed across the city, exhorting the
faithful to pray in Granada's hundreds of mosques.[4] "So great was the clamor
coming from the towers of the mosques, that it was difficult to believe," said
Münzer.[5]

Above the city rose the Alhambra, the famous fortress so named for the red-
dish color of its walls (in Arabic, *al-qalᶜ al-ḥamrāʾ*, or red castle). Since the thirteenth century the Nasrid rulers of Granada had made their residence within the
confines of the citadel, and the conquering Christians marveled at the exotic
beauty of the Alhambra's palaces. After visiting the Alhambra in 1526, Andrea
Navagiero, ambassador of the Venetian Republic to the court of Charles V, noted
that "most of the space is occupied by a lovely palace that belonged to the Moorish kings. In truth, it is very beautiful and very sumptuously made, with fine marbles and all other things. The marbles are not on the walls, but on the floor . . .
the decoration is partly stucco, generously gilded, and partly of gilded ivory. In
truth, all very beautiful, especially the ceiling of the lower salon and all the walls."[6]
The size of the complex alone provoked surprise: "It is very large; it looks like a
small city," commented Antoine de Lalaing, a French nobleman who visited
Granada in 1501.[7] The conquering monarchs made the Alhambra their own, shut-
tling between lodgings in the stronghold above the defeated city and in their encampment at Santa Fe, to the west of the city. At both locations Ferdinand and Is-

abella pursued the business of state, meeting in Santa Fe with the hopeful explorer Christopher Columbus, and issuing from the Alhambra on March 31 the fateful decree that expelled the Jewish community from its domains.

The monarchs also oversaw the initial steps in the transformation of Granada. Because the capture of the city, so long desired, was central to their pious and political aspirations, they sought to convert Granada both in appearance and in fact. Soon after the royal victory, the process of Christianization and the restructuring of the city along Castilian lines began with the seizure of palaces and other lands for conversion into monasteries and government offices. The monarchs donated a house and a garden that had belonged to the city's Muslim rulers for the establishment of a Hieronymite monastery, and Crown officials transformed the Maristán, a hospital for the mentally ill, into a royal mint. The terms of the surrender agreement guaranteed that the majority of Granada's mosques would remain centers for Muslim worship. Shortly after the conquest, however, the monarchs ordered the al-Ṭayyibīn mosque—a religious center frequented by the city's *elches,* or Christian converts to Islam—be consecrated to St. John the Baptist and St. John the Evangelist. Catholic priests sang the first mass in the city in the main mosque of the Alhambra, which served as the city's first cathedral.[8]

During the first few years after the fall of Granada, however, despite the appropriation of some mosques and palaces by the victors, the city and its Muslim population remained in many ways substantially unchanged. The terms of the surrender treaty explicitly affirmed the religious and cultural traditions of the indigenous residents. Ferdinand and Isabella promised, for example, that Granadino Muslims would continue to live under *sharia,* Islam's legal code. In the case of a dispute between a Christian and a Muslim, justice would be rendered by two judges, one from each faith. They also pledged to respect the rights of the conquered Granadinos "to live in their own religion, and not permit that their mosques be taken from them."[9] Two years after the conquest, German visitor Hieronymus Münzer marveled at the devout crowds who flocked to Friday prayer services at Granada's main mosque. Hieronymite friar Hernando de Talavera, Granada's popular first archbishop, respected the treaty's guarantees against coerced conversions, preferring persuasion to force. Talavera made efforts to learn Arabic and sought to attract Muslims to Catholicism by incorporating a traditional Granadino dance, the *zambra,* into the festivities for Corpus Christi. Such methods garnered him the respect of Granadino Muslims, who called him the "Holy Alfaqui."[10] Unfortunately, however, Talavera's efforts won him few converts, and in 1499 the Crown turned to the hard-line tactics of Cardinal Francisco Jiménez de Cisneros.[11] Over the objections of Talavera, Cisneros enacted a pro-

gram of forced baptisms directed primarily at the hated *elches* and members of
the Muslim leadership. Cisneros's new tactics—a direct violation of the terms of
the treaty—provoked an armed revolt centered in the Alpujarras, a mountainous
and isolated area located to the southeast of the city and inhabited almost exclusively by Muslims. In response to the rebellion, the Crown rescinded the treaty
and demanded conversion as a condition of pardon. In 1501 Granada's entire
Muslim population either emigrated or underwent mass baptisms to become
Moriscos, Catholics of Muslim descent. Though the order to convert or leave was
extended the following year to the whole of the kingdom of Castile, *mudéjares* in
the territories of the kingdom of Aragon remained free to practice Islam until
early 1526.

In the decades that followed the conversion of the Moriscos, several large-
scale construction projects further changed the face of the city. Consecrated as
churches after the establishment of a parish system in 1501, most of Granada's
mosques suffered dramatic changes in form as well as function, as over the
course of the sixteenth century the city's new leaders constructed new church
buildings less immediately evocative of Islam.[12] In order to make space for a hospital and a church, officials demolished Granada's Jewish neighborhood.[13] The
site of a major cemetery located just outside the Elvira Gate and described by
Münzer as "twice the size of Nuremburg" came to be occupied by the Royal Hospital (1511), a Mercedarian monastery (1530), the Church of St. Ildefonso (1553),
and other structures.[14] The monarchs reinforced their strong personal attachment to the city by designating Granada as the site of their final resting place. In
1504 construction commenced on the Royal Chapel, which was to house both
their tombs and those of their successors, Philip "the Handsome" and Juana "the
Mad." These changes gained momentum in 1523 as workers began building a
new cathedral. Until the dedication of the new building in 1561, the adjacent main
mosque served as the city's religious center, reconsecrated as the Sagrario (the
parish church affiliated with the cathedral), under the advocation of St. Mary of
the O.[15]

In 1526 the visit of Charles V and his new bride, Isabella of Portugal, renewed
the ties between the city and the Crown. Honeymooning in the Alhambra—the
physical representation of the power of the Muslim emirs—the young king ordered the construction of a Renaissance palace in the heart of the fortress, thus
preserving the complex as a trophy of the conquest while converting it into a
Christian and royal stronghold and an emblem of Habsburg Spain's ascendant
imperial power.[16] In the city below, civic and ecclesiastical leaders superscribed
Castilian urban norms onto the Moorish metropolis by enforcing new building

regulations, widening and straightening streets, and creating plazas. In a second wave of urban reforms beginning in the 1570s and 1580s, urban planners embarked upon the wholesale destruction of mosques, the most visible reminders of Islam, and the erection of churches and religious houses on their foundations.[17]

The abrogation of the surrender agreement marked the beginning of Granada's construction boom and the first real wave of Christian immigration. Prior to 1499, the treaty's protections of Muslim property hindered immigrant efforts to acquire land within Granada, and most settlers established themselves in villages around the city and in other towns and villages of the kingdom of Granada.[18] After the uprisings, properties abandoned by Muslim emigrants and Crown tax provisions proved such attractive incentives that by 1561 Granada's immigrant residents numbered around 30,000, a population perhaps twice the size of the much diminished Morisco community, whose numbers continued to decline through surreptitious flight to North Africa.[19]

Within the city, the streets bustled as Moriscos and newcomers pursued a broad range of trades and occupations. While most Moriscos lived and worked within the confines of the Albaicín, the streets below were dominated by the thousands of merchants, artisans, servants, and other working-class immigrants of diverse social and geographical origins who settled in Granada during the sixteenth century. Samplings in the municipal records of persons petitioning for *vecindad,* or city citizenship, reveal that the majority came from cities in Andalusia and Old and New Castile.[20] Immigrants who earned their livings as peasant farmers, gardeners, and agricultural laborers dominated parishes like St. Ildefonso and St. Mary Magdalen, located on the margins of the city near the fields of Granada's immensely fertile plain. Merchants and high-status artisans like silversmiths were concentrated in the center of the city in the parish of the Sagrario, around the silk market and the main shopping street, the Zacatín; other artisans and craftsmen could be found nearby. Parishes such as St. Anne were home to builders, bricklayers, and other construction specialists who found ample employment in the many major building projects then transforming the appearance of the city. Many Moriscos too worked as skilled carpenters and masons, often specializing in plastering, roofing, and tile work.[21] Construction also provided temporary work for poor and unskilled immigrants.[22] Other workers, Granada's shearers and dyers, plied their trades along the banks of the Darro, preparing raw wool for export in bulk to the industrial cities of Castile and to Flanders.[23] A large Genoese colony dominated the local wool trade, though many religious communities and wealthy individuals owned huge flocks.[24]

Though wool accounted for a significant portion of the local economy, Granada's best-known and most lucrative product was silk. "Almost all the common people of the city earn their living from silk," noted one observer in 1548.[25] Perhaps a fifth of the city's population earned its living in the silk industry.[26] Around the city, gardeners cultivated the mulberry trees that were the exclusive feed for the silkworms. Morisco peasants, especially those in the more isolated areas of the kingdom of Granada, dominated silkworm cultivation and spinning, while many urban Moriscos worked as silk dyers.[27] Silk weaving, however, quickly became the province of urban-dwelling immigrants concentrated in the Antequerela neighborhood. At each level of production—spinning, cutting, dying, and the different styles of weaving—workers were organized into guilds, which were themselves overseen by the officials of the Casa del Arte de la Seda. Merchants sold the finished product in Granada's famous silk market, the Alcaicería. Located in the lower city, adjacent to the Zacatín, the Alcaicería was a warren of small shops that served as a clearinghouse for woven silks of all kinds. The Crown ensured its own profits through taxation, requiring 10 percent on all sales and 15 percent on silk to be exported outside the kingdom of Granada. A seventeenth-century annalist of Granada noted that

> today, all commerce in silk is there, with its great customshouse for the whole kingdom, with its merchants and exchange runners. By right, it gets fourteen and a half *reales* per pound, in bundles or bolts, which is all the same. And this is due from the first merchant [to sell the goods], and by this right [the goods] are [then] duty free, even though they are bought and sold many times, and with all this [the Alcaicería] is one of the biggest sources of income His Majesty has, since in all the kingdom more than thirty thousand ducats may be generated.[28]

Genoese exporters sold the raw silk to Castile and shipped the more finished cloth via the port at Málaga eastward to markets in Catalonia, Italy, and points beyond, southward to North Africa, and westward to Seville, Flanders, and the Indies.[29]

New Institutions for a New City

While land and commercial opportunities attracted farmers, artisans, and other workers, a different class of immigrants was drawn by the chance for advancement in the host of new governing institutions founded in postconquest Granada after the abrogation of the surrender treaty. The creation of Castilian and Christian administrative bodies in the conquered city was integral to the process of conversion and acculturation. The new institutions cemented the city's ties to the emerging Spanish monarchy and established Granada as one of the principal urban centers of the Spanish kingdoms, a peer to cities like Toledo, Valladolid, Barcelona, Valencia, or Seville. A quartet of institutions—the Royal Chancery, the city council, the Captaincy General, and the Church—governed Granada and its province, and their members dominated the local social and political scene.[30]

In 1505 the monarchs transferred one of Castile's two permanent high courts, or chanceries, from Ciudad Real to Granada, in order to establish the city as an important legal center and to strengthen the new ties between Granada and the royal government. The Royal Chancery's jurisdiction encompassed all towns and cities south of the Tajo River in central Castile. Judges ruled on appellate cases from within the wider jurisdiction, and, as Granada's *audiencia,* or royal court of first instance, the court heard civil and criminal trials originating from throughout the kingdom of Granada. The Chancery, housed in an impressive building on the Plaza Nueva, was headed by a president and sixteen powerful judges (*oidores*), followed by four criminal prosecutors (*alcaldes del crimen*), three prosecutors of nobility claims (*alcaldes de hijosdalgo*), and two *fiscales,* who represented royal interests in criminal and civil suits.[31] A highly cohesive and prominent group, the officials of the Chancery represented an important faction within local politics and society. Around them swarmed a multitude of lesser court personnel and hangers-on, such as sheriffs, notaries and scribes, lawyers, and jailers. The Chancery itself supported a major sector of the local economy by sustaining industries like printing and hostelry for the crowds of litigants and petitioners pursuing cases in the courts.[32]

The political and social prominence of the officials of the Royal Chancery was rivaled by that of the members of Granada's city council.[33] Created in the years following 1492, this governing body originally included representatives of both conquerors and conquered. By 1497, however, the city council was dominated by immigrants, as emigration to North Africa caused the city's indigenous leadership to dwindle.[34] After the 1499 uprising, Muslim representation was eliminated, and the council was restructured to resemble city councils found in most Castilian cities. The *corregidor,* the Crown's local representative, presided over the council, which met across from the cathedral and next door to the Alcaicería, in the Palace of the Madraza, a fourteenth-century building that previously had housed medieval Granada's *madrasa,* or Muslim college.[35] The *corregimiento* of Granada was one of the largest and most important in southern Spain, second only to that of Seville. An anonymous traveler in 1607 noted of the *corregimiento* that, "if it were not for the Chancery that resides there, it would be like the office of viceroy, both because the city is very big and populous and because of the many towns and villages and other large jurisdictions that are subordinate to it."[36] The city council itself comprised twenty-four voting councilmen, called *regidores* or *veinticuatros;* twenty *jurados,* nonvoting councilmen representing different neighborhoods; several scribes; and a number of lesser officials. Both *veinticuatrías* and *juraderías* were originally Crown appointments. During the sixteenth century, as a perpetually cash-strapped Crown expanded the number of seats on the council, councilmen increasingly came to their positions by purchase as well as inheritance.[37] The city council's responsibilities were broad, ranging from public safety to the regulation of prostitution. Councilmen and their agents oversaw the city's markets and guilds, stocked the city granary, arranged street repair, and organized festivities. From this body came the city's two *procuradores,* or representatives at the Castilian parliament, the Cortes, in which the city enjoyed voting rights. Granada's entry as the eighteenth member of the Cortes, effected by royal decree shortly after the conquest, established and enhanced the city's rank as one of the most important urban centers of the Spanish kingdoms.

Rounding out the secular governmental institutions in Granada was the Captaincy General. In 1492 Granada's status as a outpost on the frontier between Christendom and Islam and the perceived threat of its large, unassimilated *mudéjar* community prompted the creation of a captain general, or military governor, of the kingdom of Granada. Headquartered in the Alhambra, the captain general commanded all troops in the province, including the coastal guards, as well as the Alhambra garrison. Through the sixteenth and most of the seventeenth centuries, the office of the captain general was controlled by the counts of Tendilla (who were also the marquises of Mondéjar), members of the powerful Mendoza family and highly prominent figures on the local political and social scene. Like a modern military base, the Alhambra functioned as a separate city within the city. Ordinary Granadinos were denied entry into the Alhambra, which remained the exclusive preserve of the captain general, soldiers, and administrators attached to the presidio, and their families. Inhabitants of the Alhambra worshiped in a separate parish, and justice, both civil and criminal, was administered by the captain general in his capacity as governor of the fortress.[38]

Although the Royal Chancery, city council, and Captaincy General were all charged with the task of Christianization as well as that of maintaining order and justice in the city and kingdom, the labor of converting the Morisco population fell primarily to the institutions of the Catholic Church. Together with the city council, the Granadino Church took shape shortly after the fall of the city, in the early months of 1492. Granada was raised to the level of an archdiocese, with Guadix, Málaga, and Almería as its suffragan sees and Hieronymite friar Hernando de Talavera as its first archbishop. The monarchs also helped the new prelate establish a cathedral chapter, comprising a handful of ecclesiastical dignitaries and a fixed number of canons, prebendaries, chaplains, acolytes, and other personnel. The Royal Chapel, founded in 1504, functioned as a separate and rival institution, staffed by twenty-five chaplains charged with the care of the royal mausoleum. Appointments to positions within the Granadino Church were made by the Crown, which was empowered by the *Real Patronato,* a papal grant of 1486 entitling the Crown to the right of nomination and a portion of Church rents.[39] Together, the archbishop and the chapter took responsibility both for tending to the spiritual needs of Catholics who settled in the city and for converting the conquered Muslim population.[40] New demands for indoctrination, education, and ministry followed the forcible conversion of Granada's *mudéjares* after the 1499 revolt. In 1501 the city's mosques were consecrated to become part of a new system of parish churches, staffed by a parish clergy that, by 1591, consisted of approximately 220 priests, distributed unequally throughout the city's twenty-three parishes.

The regular clergy also played an active role in Granada's spiritual life. Perhaps as a counter to the city's symbolic status as the last stronghold of Islam, Christian monasteries and convents were founded at a rapid rate; by the end of the sixteenth century, Granada had nearly thirty religious houses, home to some 1,207 monks and nuns.[41] In their capacity as preachers, teachers, and confessors, both the city's Dominican and Franciscan friars and its Jesuit priests played an especially active role in ministry to and conversion of Moriscos. Their efforts were reinforced by the Holy Office of the Inquisition, established in Granada in 1526. From the Inquisition's chambers, located in a warren of buildings near the cathedral, three inquisitors and their numerous staff sought to enforce doctrinal orthodoxy and moral behavior within the entire kingdom of Granada, including the cities of Málaga and Almería.[42]

The formal authority of Granada's archbishop also extended to the city's university, which was founded by royal decree in 1526. Located directly across from the cathedral and adjoining the archiepiscopal palace, the university consisted of five faculties: Arts, Theology, Civil Law, Canon Law, and Medicine. By the 1550s, the university matriculated as many as 600 students each year.[43] After 1570 enrollments declined, but Granada's university remained an important regional center for education of local clergy and lawyers. Of the several colleges linked to the university, the oldest was the Seminary College of St. Cecilio, founded in 1492 by Archbishop Talavera for the education of the clergy.[44]

The presence of so many important institutions, many with overlapping areas of jurisdiction, led inevitably to competition and conflict, as the city council, Chancery, Captaincy General, and Church continually jockeyed for dominance. As early as 1505, municipal authorities opposed the Chancery's transfer to Granada, fearing a loss of political influence.[45] Rivalry between competing institutions often found expression in quarrels and lawsuits. In the latter decades of the sixteenth century, a particularly bitter struggle broke out between the cathedral chapter and the Royal Chancery concerning competing jurisdictions over criminals, the right of sanctuary, and the archbishop's claim to the privilege of a chair in the annual Corpus Christi procession.[46] Likewise, the captain general and the municipal council regularly fought over the issue of responsibility for coastal defense.[47] In 1563 a jurisdictional dispute between the captain general and the Chancery turned scandalous when the angry judges arrested Luis Hurtado de Mendoza, the Count of Tendilla's son.[48] In many cases, only intervention by the Crown could resolve the disputes. In 1602, for example, a royal decree only temporarily ended a long-standing quarrel between the cathedral chapter and the city council over seating of the municipal council during festival-day masses.[49]

Contests over power and precedence within institutions were likewise frequent. Over the course of the sixteenth century, *veinticuatros* and *jurados* sued each other repeatedly over participation of *jurados* on city council committees.[50] Within the Church, conflict between the regular and secular clergy and between different monastic orders was endemic. During Lent in 1558, for example, intense competition among Jesuit, Dominican, Franciscan, and Hieronymite preachers for sermon audiences required the intervention of the archbishop.[51] Contests within the secular clergy were equally common. In 1646 canons of the Collegiate Church of San Salvador sued a canon of the Collegiate Church of the Sacromonte, accusing him of usurping their exclusive privilege of preaching in a black choral cape.[52]

Contours of Granada's Ruling Elite

Competitions and contests like these were common among the elite groups that dominated the urban centers of early modern Spain. Granada's elite differed from that found in many other communities, however, in its high degree of permeability. The newness of Granada's institutions and the constant influx of immigrants lent a notable fluidity to Granadino society, making the local elite "a world in constant renovation."[53] The Royal Chancery, for example, attracted well-educated and ambitious men from across Castile. Some moved on relatively quickly without setting permanent roots into the community; others formed local ties through strategic marriages into established families. One such individual was the Madrid native Gregorio López Madera, a prosecutor in the Chancery. He married into the Porcel de Peralta clan, a prominent family with strong ties to the city council, and his son-in-law was Mateo Lisón y Biedma, a *procurador* to the Cortes for the city of Granada best known for his energetic opposition to the policies of Philip IV's favorite, the Count Duke of Olivares.[54] Strategic marriages also enabled foreign wool traders and bankers to integrate themselves into the local elite. In 1582, for example, Bartolomé Lomelín Veneroso, a Genoese trader who first settled in Granada in 1563, married Juana Messia y Alarcón, the sister of a city councilman. He soon obtained a post of his own on the city council, and the permanent office of *alguacil mayor* of the Chancery. His relative, Esteban Lomelín, had acquired a *veinticuatría* some years before, in 1559.[55]

Such alliances reflect the prestige and power associated with the city council, which, while it struggled with the other institutions for dominance, remained at the forefront of Granada's local social and political scene.[56] Likewise, these marriages highlight the heterogeneity and the permeable quality of the municipal council's membership, and Granada's ruling elite in general.[57] Such openness was not wholly unusual in Spanish cities at the turn of the sixteenth century. In Valladolid, for example, increasing immigration, sales of offices by the Crown, and admission of distant relatives broke the hold of two long-established family factions over distribution of offices within the municipal council, and in Ciudad Real, as in Granada, wealth and careful marriage making could gain social climbers membership in the city's elite.[58] Granada's particular historical circumstances, however, made its leadership exceptionally diverse. Drawn from cities throughout Andalusia, New Castile, and beyond, the city council's member families were varied in their social origins. Some of the council's most powerful families, like the Maza de Lizana y Mendoza clan or the Arósteguis, claimed as their founders armed participants in the conquest, while others pointed to their ancestors' service to the Crown as administrators and bureaucrats. A few, like the Zegrí and Hermes families, were Morisco descendants of the pre-Christian aristocracy or Morisco families who came to prominence in the social upheaval that followed the fall of the city. One powerful Morisco clan, the Granada Venegas family, claimed descent from Granada's Nasrid royalty.[59] The council included few active merchants or traders, though some did come from families whose wealth originated in commerce.[60] While most were *cristianos viejos*, "Old Christians" who claimed bloodlines free of Muslim or Jewish ancestry, some families associated with the city council, like the Bobadilla clan, were Conversos, descendants of converted Jews, who found in Granada greater opportunities for social advancement than were commonly available to them in the more established cities in the north.[61] Indeed, by the first decade of the sixteenth century, Granada's reputation as a haven for Conversos earned it the epithet of "Little Judea" from rogue inquisitor Diego Lucero.[62] In 1570 the prominence of Moriscos and Conversos within the city council prompted Granada's representatives at the Cortes to reject a measure calling for all municipal councilmen in Spain to be not only nobles but Old Christians as well.[63] While Converso councillors were certainly not unknown in other cities, the rather motley membership of Granada's city council highlights the unusual degree of social opportunity and mobility to be found in postconquest Granada.

While not all city councillors were members of the nobility (*hidalgos*), over the course of the sixteenth and seventeenth centuries, as in other cities throughout the Spanish kingdoms, the city council, and Granada's social and political elites in general, took on an increasingly patrician cast. *Veinticuatros* and *jurados,* officials of the Chancery, prosperous merchants, and other prominent citizens sought upward social mobility through the acquisition of patents of nobility (*hidalguía*) and knighthoods in the prestigious military orders and the purchase of estates and jurisdictions from land alienated by the ever-impecunious Crown.[64] It was arguably easier than elsewhere in Spain to claim nobility in Granada, where one's neighbors were less likely to know much about the newcomer's family reputation or background. Though increasingly aristocratic in appearance, Granada's elite also differed from that found in most other large cities in Andalusia in that, aside from the powerful Count of Tendilla, it had few members of the titled nobility resident in the area.[65] "There are not many very wealthy people in Granada," noted visitor Andrea Navagiero in 1526, "except for a few lords who have estates in this kingdom."[66] This situation was the product of Ferdinand and Isabella's policies governing distribution of lands after the fall of Granada in 1492. To prevent the domination of the newly conquered kingdom by Castilian grandees, land grants were usually small and geographically dispersed, consisting mainly of small villages or uninhabited common lands. Disappointed with their share of the spoils, most of the great noble houses of Castile sold or transferred their holdings in the kingdom of Granada to Andalusian noble families or to members of Granada's urban oligarchy.[67]

Such purchases—often the foundation of a family *mayorazgo,* or entailed estate—were important elements of family strategies for acquisition and consolidation of power. Elite families employed an arsenal of tactics, from strategic marriages and godparenthood to networks of clientelage, in order to enmesh and advance themselves in Granada's ever-changing social and political scene. A list of transfers of municipal office reveals the extensive family connections created by councilmen to preserve family possession of *veinticuatrías* and *juraderías*. For example, Francisco de los Cobos, city councilman and secretary to Charles V, renounced his municipal office in 1523 in favor of his niece's husband, Fernando de Zafra. The following year Cobos was designated for a second *veinticuatría*, which he later resigned and transferred to Pedro de Rojas, the husband of another niece. In 1556 Rojas himself retired, ceding his office to Fernando de Zafra, son of Fernando de Zafra, his fellow city councilman and relative.[68] The institutions of the Church, too, provided opportunities for family advancement—aspiring families of median social status sent sons into the parish priesthood, while the monasteries and convents filled with elite children ineligible for marriage and inheritance.[69] Unlike many other cities, Granada's cathedral chapter offered little attraction to elite families. Royal control over Church appointments and rents in Granada left the funding of both the chapter and the archbishop open to the depredations of the Crown. In practice, this meant that for a city of Granada's size and importance, the chapter was both unusually small and poorly paid. Only a handful of canons were noble or had family ties to the city council. Most appear to have hailed from middling, even humble backgrounds—the family of one member, chapter secretary Martín de Maldonado, included day laborers from a village near the Castilian town of Soria. The majority came from Granada or from other parts of southern Spain.[70]

Thus, Granada's elite minority was a heterogeneous group, divided internally by institutional affiliations and bound together both by familial ties and by a common allegiance to its adopted city.[71] The groups that constituted this small society engaged with the finds on the Sacromonte in diverse ways and to differing degrees. Sponsors, authors, audiences, and critics of the constitutive discourses of Granadino memory and identity, Granadino elites worked out in text, ritual, and cult their overlapping and competing loyalties to the city and to the different corporate bodies to which they belonged. As we will see, the discourses elaborated around the *plomos* divided Granada's elites as much as they unified them.

The Revolt of the Alpujarras and Its Repercussions

The integration of several elite Morisco families into the ruling oligarchy is indicative of both the character and the limits of sixteenth-century Granada's developing multicultural society. Although most studies have characterized the Morisco population as uniformly unfriendly to the Christian newcomers and their culture, recent investigations in local archives have uncovered a far more complex set of relations between the two populations and within the Morisco community itself.[72] Some Moriscos readily embraced Castilian customs and habits. In 1567 the Morisco leader Francisco Núñez Muley noted that most Morisco men (but not women) "have switched to dress and clothes in the Castilian manner, very different from what they used to wear."[73] Nor were all Moriscos hostile to Christianity. While many remained loyal Muslims, concealing their faith under a thin veil of Catholic practices, other Moriscos became convinced Christians. Some, like Dr. Diego Martín, scholaster of the cathedral chapter of Almería, and the Jesuit Juan de Albotodo, even became priests.[74] Investigations in Granada's notarial archive reveal that, over the course of the sixteenth century, a slowly growing minority of Morisco testators left provision in their wills for masses for their souls, a practice that may indicate their sincere Catholicism.[75] A small number of bicultural Morisco "collaborators" facilitated exchanges between the two peoples. Although most immigrants and Moriscos preferred to seek spouses within their own communities, intermarriage, especially among elite families, was not unknown. In the latter years of the century, for example, the Morisco *jurado* Alonso Hermes married his daughter Isabel to Rodrigo de Luna, an Old Christian advocate in the Chancery.[76]

However, these assimilated Moriscos—prosperous professionals and office-holders, wealthy merchants and landowners—remained a small, elite minority. While Moriscos could be found throughout the Spanish kingdoms, those of Castile and Aragon were comparatively more acculturated than those of Valencia and Granada—areas where Muslims had been less subject to interaction with and influence of Christian neighbors. Many Granadino Moriscos rejected the culture of the conquerors and struggled to sustain the identity of their community by retaining their language, dress, and customs. Some, though not all, invoked the Muslim idea of *taqiyya,* or religious dissimulation, and continued to practice in secret the faith of their ancestors.[77] In 1498 Granada's Christian and Muslim leaders agreed to partition the city into two separate zones. While the separation of the two communities was never absolute—Moriscos could be found residing in all parts of the city, and parish records list Christian immigrant residents in areas nominally reserved for Moriscos—the city's Morisco residents lived predominantly in the remote parishes of the Albaicín, far from the acculturating influences of their immigrant neighbors.[78] The segregation of the two groups both stemmed from and contributed to persistent tensions between them. Though after 1501 Granada was nominally a wholly Christian city, sharp divisions—social, cultural, and especially religious—continued to split the immigrant and Morisco communities.

Perhaps the most visible sign of persistent Morisco resistance to the culture of the Christian immigrants was the endurance of traditional dress. Morisca women continued to wear in public the *almalafa,* a long, white, pleated garment that veiled the wearer from head to toe. Foreign visitors found this attire particularly disquieting. "I find the dress of the women of Granada very strange," commented one early visitor in 1501, "because they wear nothing more than white sheets that trail to the floor . . . and they seem like ghosts when one encounters them at night."[79] (Not all of these ghosts were Moriscas, however—in the early decades of Christian rule, the city council was repeatedly forced to prohibit the adoption of this and other Morisco customs by immigrant women.)[80] Beneath their veils, Moriscas continued to prefer their traditional tunics and leggings to Castilian dresses, and to adorn themselves with tattoos and designs drawn in henna.[81] Local and Crown authorities repeatedly legislated against these and other markers of religious and community identity by issuing decrees prohibiting Morisco clothing and jewelry, the use of Arabic, and cultural and religious practices such as circumcision and the ritual slaughter of animals.

The Christian population reciprocated the ambivalence of the Moriscos toward their new neighbors. Whereas elite Granadinos welcomed Moriscos with wealth or noble blood into their ranks, most immigrants mistrusted Moriscos. Despite repeated prohibitions by both Crown and ecclesiastical officials, Old Christians regularly referred to Moriscos as *perros moros,* or Moorish dogs.[82] Morisco landowners found themselves the object of unwanted attention from land-hungry newcomers, who used both legal and extralegal means to acquire the Moriscos' intensively cultivated and irrigated small plots. In 1559, for example, a commission headed by a Dr. Santiago, a judge of the Valladolid Chancery, levied fines and confiscated properties of Moriscos unable to produce deeds. More than 100,00 hectares were resold to powerful members of Granada's immigrant elite.[83] Moriscos, like Conversos, technically were excluded from many offices and professions by the statutes of *limpieza de sangre,* or purity of blood. While in practice these requirements were often ignored, even Morisco elites ran into difficulty, especially toward the end of the sixteenth century, when observation of the rules became increasingly punctilious.[84] Many suspected that the Moriscos were in league with the Berber corsairs, who plagued the coastal areas, and worried that they might aid a possible invasion by Habsburg Spain's principal rival in the Mediterranean, the Ottoman Empire. These fears of a Muslim "fifth column" led to repeated efforts by the Crown to ban the ownership and carrying of weapons by Moriscos.[85]

Such prohibitions undercut royal efforts to achieve the cultural and religious assimilation of Granadino Moriscos. The Crown further distinguished its Morisco subjects from their immigrant neighbors by extracting from them both frequent cash "services" and a separate tax, the *farda*, part of which paid for the defense of the coast against North African pirates.[86] Abusive officials placed additional pressures on the Morisco community by overcollecting the *farda* and illegally appropriating Morisco lands. During his 1526 visit to Granada, Charles V called an assembly of civil and ecclesiastical officials to explore more effective ways to Christianize and Castilianize the resistant Moriscos. The assembly reprimanded the immigrants for their abuse of the Moriscos but also reiterated previous bans of Morisco cultural practices. Although a substantial payment of 90,000 ducats into Charles's ever-empty treasury helped win the Crown's benign neglect of the edicts against Morisco language and customs, the establishment of the Inquisition in Granada a few months after the meeting presented a new threat to the struggling minority.[87]

Despite its presence in the city, the Holy Office did not become very active in Granada until midcentury; between 1526 and about 1550, the Morisco and immigrant communities coexisted in a tense and uneasy truce. During this period, attempts to indoctrinate the Moriscos continued, but success was limited. Despite such measures as frequent Franciscan and Dominican missions to Morisco-dominated rural regions and special Jesuit schools for Morisco children, the majority of the indigenous population remained largely unassimilated.[88] With the accession of Philip II to the throne in 1556, the climate of relative tolerance for Morisco difference began to change. In the 1550s and 1560s, the number of Moriscos penanced by the Inquisition began a precipitous rise, as tensions between the Morisco and immigrant communities escalated. Repeated bad harvests added to the stresses already evoked in the immigrant population by persistent Turkish and Berber attacks along the coast and rising incidents of Morisco banditry in the interior, while Moriscos felt the pinch of massive land confiscations, increased taxation of silk, and Castilian penetration into the Morisco-dominated industry of silkworm cultivation.[89] A provincial synod, convoked in 1565 by Granada's archbishop, Pedro Guerrero (1546–76), expressed the Catholic authorities' impatience with the irreducible Moriscos and called once again for a total repression of Morisco customs.[90] Following a review by an assembly of theologians in Madrid, the synod's recommendations were issued in 1567 and were strictly enforced.

After two years of remonstrations, maneuvering, and plotting, Granada's Moriscos finally rose in revolt. The uprising, which began on December 24, 1568, was based in the Alpujarras—the same remote region that had been at the heart of the uprising of 1499—and quickly spread throughout the rural areas of the kingdom of Granada. Within the capital city, however, the uprising attracted only limited Morisco support, and the inhabitants of the Albaicín failed to respond to the call to arms. In the Alpujarras, the resumption of traditional cultural practices accompanied the restoration of Islam, as many rebels discarded their Castilian names for Arabic ones and resumed wearing traditional dress. The Moriscos directed their anger against the sites, objects, and persons representative of the faith of their oppressors, burning churches, destroying sacred images, and murdering priests and friars. Parishioners—including some Moriscos—who refused to renounce Christianity were also killed.[91]

The Crown's response more than matched the violence of the Morisco insurgents. The forces under the command of Juan de Austria, Philip II's half brother, put down the revolt in two years with great difficulty and even greater brutality. After the war, the Crown opted to neutralize the lingering threat of renewed violence by forcibly resettling huge numbers of Granadino Moriscos in Castile. Between 1569 and 1574, officials sent an estimated 80,000 Moriscos from the kingdom of Granada (nearly 15,000 of them from the city of Granada) on forced marches to Castile. Many died along the way of typhus and exposure. The approximately 10,000 to 15,000 Moriscos who stayed in the kingdom—4,000 to 5,000 of them within the city of Granada—were mostly prominent worthies, artisans, single women and widows, and children.[92] Many others, captured in the course of the fighting, remained behind as slaves. Like many European cities, Granada had a sizable population of enslaved people. Most were Africans from Portuguese "Guinea" (i.e., Senegal); others came from the Magreb or (especially after 1568) from the kingdom of Granada itself.[93]

The Revolt of the Alpujarras and the subsequent expulsions had devastating consequences for Granada. The demographic effects of the deportations were enormous: the city lost at least a third of its population to the expulsions. Between 1561 and 1591 the kingdom of Granada's overall population, already in decline, dropped almost 30 percent, while Morisco-dominated areas like the Alpujarras and the Valle de Lecrín lost up to 69 percent of their inhabitants. Whole villages stood abandoned; many disappeared from the map entirely.[94] The expulsions ravaged the all-important silk industry, leaving it with a severe shortage of raw goods and a dearth of workers experienced in the cultivation and spinning stages of production. "In the matter of silk," lamented an official, "without Moriscos the whole business is lost, because there is no one who knows how to cultivate it or to spin it. It used to cost fifteen *maravedís* to spin a pound of silk from the cocoon, made by the Morisco man or woman who would spin it, and now it costs two or three *reales.*"[95] Individuals and institutions that had invested in *censos* (annuities) and rents on land worked by Moriscos saw their incomes evaporate. Granada's religious houses were particularly hard hit. The canons of the Collegiate Church of San Salvador, located in the heart of the Albaicín, complained to Philip II in 1572 that not only had the expulsions deprived them of an annual rent of 250,000 *maravedís,* but the soldiers sent to put down the revolt had destroyed the church's rented houses.[96] While in principle the Crown assumed responsibility for payment of *censos,* in practice many years of litigation and petition passed before investors saw their incomes restored.

The Crown's program for rural repopulation failed to halt continued population decline in the kingdom of Granada. After the expulsions, tax exemptions and distributions of confiscated Morisco lands, houses, and other properties enticed approximately 35,000 settlers into the kingdom. By 1591 the population of the city numbered more than 8,000 *vecinos* (heads of household), or approximately 33,000 persons.[97] Recruited primarily from Andalusia and New Castile, the settlers were often unskilled or unwilling to undertake a precarious living farming on formerly Morisco lands.[98] Pedro de León, a Jesuit priest who in 1590–91 ministered to the immigrants established in the Alpujarras, described them as "an almost outlaw people, lowlifes, people who could not be tolerated in their native lands, murderers and criminals of wild and crude customs."[99] Unfamiliar with the agricultural techniques that had made the land productive for the now-vanished Moriscos, the settlers often abandoned their stakes or fell victim to the epidemics and crop failures that throttled Granada and all of Spain in the last decades of the sixteenth century. Locusts ate the crops in the northern part of the kingdom in 1572 and 1573, and a decade later, bad harvests led to an outbreak of *landres,* an unspecified epidemic disease. Continued poor crop returns throughout the Spanish kingdoms during the 1580s and 1590s were also felt in Granada; nor did the city escape the major outbreak of plague that swept across the peninsula, afflicting Granada in 1599 and 1600.[100]

In the wake of the revolt and the deportations, tensions between Moriscos and immigrants remained high. In addition to the usual difficulties of agrarian life, settlers in coastal areas continued to be subject to the depredations of Morisco bandits and Berber corsairs. The Old Christian majority viewed the few remaining Moriscos with suspicion, fed by rumors of new revolts and alliances with Ottoman Turks and French Huguenots. In 1572 Pedro de Deza, the president of the Council for Repopulation of the Kingdom of Granada, bemoaned the deleterious effects of persistent reports of Morisco-Turkish plots: "It is so well known that it has been enough to worry the new settlers, who suspect that if it is true they will take away their holdings, and therefore they cease to work and to improve [their plots] as they were accustomed to, until they see what results from the news."[101] These problems persisted—in 1588 Fernando Niño de Guevara, president of the Royal Chancery, described Granada's populace as "terrified."[102]

Within the city, the lingering effects of the revolt and the expulsions were still visible decades later. The Albaicín, which had harbored the majority of Granada's Morisco population, remained deserted. What had been a "living body" was now, lamented the celebrated poet Luis de Góngora, a "pitiful cadaver."[103] A 1587 census shows that while the city as a whole had lost approximately 35 percent of its total population, the losses in the Albaicín amounted to more than 55 percent. Rather than taking over abandoned Morisco homes in the Albaicín, many immigrants preferred to move into the neighborhoods of the lower city, the center of Granada's ongoing construction boom.[104] The empty houses were left to fall in on themselves or were demolished to make the enclosed gardens called *cármenes*, for which Granada later became famous.[105]

The crisis provoked by the expulsion of the Moriscos exacerbated the impact of the economic recession, inflation, and population decline that afflicted all of Spain in the last decades of the sixteenth and throughout the seventeenth centuries. By 1608 the number of looms active in the city had regained the levels reached in 1548—some 1,200 looms and 200 spinning machines—far from the prerevolt figures of 4,000 looms and 300 to 500 spinning machines. Although the silk and other industries had rebounded somewhat by the late seventeenth century, the 83,000 pounds of silk registered by the Alcaicería in 1677 in no way matched the 117,000 pounds exported in 1562.[106] Seventeenth-century visitors noted the continued depopulation in both the city and the kingdom of Granada. "It may be the least populated part of Spain at the present," claimed Antoine Jouvin, a French traveler who visited the region in 1669.[107] Granada's evident decline contrasted sharply with the rise of Seville to preeminence as the largest and most prosperous city in Spain. Fed by the wealth generated by the American silver trade, even during the difficult 1590s Seville's population increased, reaching approximately 120,000, a level it maintained until the 1640s.[108] Over the course of the sixteenth century, Seville, the gateway to the Americas, surpassed Granada in wealth, population, and power. Though still an important urban center, Granada—the treasure of the Catholic Monarchs, the symbol of the ascendant Habsburgs and Charles V—increasingly found itself relegated to the status of regional capital of eastern Andalusia.

The discoveries in the Torre Turpiana and the Sacromonte burst into this depressed and nervous city, energizing Granadinos with the promise of saintly power and an exalted Christian past. Created in and responding to the tense climate that prevailed during the decades that followed the Revolt of the Alpujarras, the *plomos* combined the culture and concerns of Granada's vulnerable Morisco remnant with the religious idiom of the immigrant majority. The strong reactions they provoked among both critics and defenders helped lay the groundwork for their appropriation and metamorphosis into the founding charter of an ancient Christian community.

CHAPTER TWO

Controversy and Propaganda

In 1588, the year of the strange discoveries in the Torre Turpiana, Granada was still a multicultural, multiethnic city. Although the majority of the city's Morisco inhabitants had disappeared into exile, the streets and structures of the urban landscape still recalled their presence. The cathedral rising on the plain at the foot of the two hills made manifest the city's new commitment to Christianity, but one had only to turn one's eyes upward to the Alhambra or to the Albaicín to recall the absent Moriscos and the heritage of nearly eight centuries of a culturally vibrant and politically powerful Iberian Islam. The *plomos* reflected Granada's tense and precarious diversity, blending the cultural traditions of the Morisco and immigrant Christian populations into a bold new amalgam. Through the documents and relics from the Torre Turpiana and the Sacromonte, the forgers, probably members of Granada's endangered Morisco minority, bolstered their community's increasingly perilous status by reaffirming traditional Morisco culture while recasting it into a Christian mold. The *plomos'* Morisco roots and historical anachronisms quickly won them denunciation by some of Spain's leading scholars and critics, and the forgers' efforts did not succeed in preventing the expulsion of nearly all of Spain's Morisco population between 1609 and 1614. As the city continued its metamorphosis into a Christian preserve, Granadinos' enthusiastic response to the finds, together with the promotional activities of devotees like Archbishop Pedro de Castro, helped sustain the *plomos'* transformation into the foundational remains of Christian Granada.

The *Plomos* in Morisco Culture

Between 1595 and 1599, between nineteen and twenty-two lead books were re-covered from the hillside.[1] Together, these remarkable documents appeared to substantiate the medieval legend of St. Cecilio and his six companions, the Seven Apostles of Spain, and cemented the relationship between the saint and the city of Granada. According to the Mozarabic calendars, martyrologies, and liturgies that retold the story, the Seven Apostles—Torcuato, Segundo, Indalecio, Eufrasio, Hiscio, Tesifón, and Cecilio—came to the Iberian Peninsula to continue the work of evangelization begun by St. James. Ordained as bishops in Rome by SS. Peter and Paul, the Seven arrived in Acci (Guadix), a city some forty miles to the east of Granada, and spread out to pursue their missionary labors in major Andalusian towns. According to the medieval texts, St. Cecilio's destination was Granada's Roman predecessor, a town called Eliberri, Iliberri, Iliberia, or Iliberis (or other variations).[2] The Arabic texts discovered on the Sacromonte fleshed out this bare-bones *vita* with surprising new details. One of the books, the *Book of the Famous Acts of Our Lord Jesus and of the Virgin Mary, His Mother,* revealed SS. Tesifón and Cecilio to be Aben Athar and Aben Alradi, twin sons of Saleh, an Arab of noble lineage. Carried from the Arabian Peninsula to Galilee by their father, the boys—born blind and deaf-mute, respectively—were miraculously healed of their in-firmities by Jesus himself, who then assigned them to the care of St. James. According to another of the texts, *On the Famous Deeds of the Apostle St. James and on His Miracles,* the brothers traveled with St. James to Spain and Granada, where Cecilio later became the city's first bishop and martyr.[3]

Even more surprising than these new hagiographic facts were the other con-tents of the lead books, which ranged from theological treatises and biographies to prayers and religious instruction by the Virgin Mary and SS. Peter and James, as transcribed by SS. Cecilio and Tesifón. In one text, *Book of the Enigmas and Mys-teries That the Virgin St. Mary Saw, by the Grace of God, on the Night of Her Collo-quy,* an Arabic-speaking Virgin Mary tells the assembled apostles how, seated on a mare and accompanied by the angel Gabriel, she flew by night to Heaven, where she witnessed the marvels of Paradise. Continuing her journey, she passed through Hell and Purgatory and entered into the presence of Jesus, who prom-ised to send her the book *Certainty of the Gospel.*[4] According to another of the lead books, *History of the Certainty of the Holy Gospel,* Gabriel presented the Virgin with the book, "written by the hand of power, with resplendent light, on tablets of precious stone," together with a copy on lead tablets, sealed with the seal of

Solomon.[5] The Virgin hid the book inside the Mount of Olives, which opened miraculously to receive the heavenly text, and gave the copy to St. James, with instructions to bury it on the Sacromonte. She prophesied that God would reveal the lead copy "by the hand of the holy priest" in a time in which the world will be rent by heresy and dissent about Jesus and the Gospel.[6] The revelation of the *Certainty of the Gospel* and the other lead books will cause a revival of faith, brought about by the Arabs and their language, "one of the most excellent peoples, and their language one of the most excellent languages."[7] The Arabs, ruled by a "king of the Arabs, who is not an Arab," will lead an ecumenical church council on Cyprus.[8] The assembled nations will accept the veracity and the supremacy of the *Certainty of the Gospel,* and all will be converted to the divine law it contains. Shortly thereafter, the Antichrist will appear.

Stories such as these are characteristic of the *plomos'* unique combination of Islam and Christianity. The theology they offer combines the two faiths, making concessions to Christian concepts but preserving certain key Muslim beliefs. They offer, perhaps, less a complete synthesis than a redefinition of Christianity along Muslim lines. For example, though the *plomos* define God as both one and three persons, Father, Son, and Holy Spirit, the Trinity does not include Jesus. Instead, the Jesus of the *plomos* is similar to the Jesus of the Quran—he is designated the Messiah, the Spirit of God, or the Word, but never God or Son of God.[9] (The texts do not offer a full explanation of the Trinity or the identity of the Son.) Throughout the *plomos,* Mary, St. James, and others repeatedly stress the fundamental unity and uniqueness of God, and the important but separate role of Jesus. In the *Book of the Famous Acts of Our Lord Jesus and of the Virgin Mary, His Mother,* St. Cecilio thanks Jesus for relieving his muteness with the words, "I testify that there is no other god but God, and you are his true spirit." This statement is a variation on the *Shahāda,* the Muslim statement of faith that testifies to the unity of the divinity and the role of Muhammad as prophet.[10] In general, the *plomos* combine the synoptic Gospels' account of the life of Jesus with a Quranic Christology. Born of the Virgin Mary, Jesus is both miracle-working prophet and intercessor for mankind before God. Unlike the Quranic ʿĪsā, however, the *plomos'* Jesus is crucified and resurrected. Those who would attain salvation must believe

> that he was condemned to death, and that he spilled his blood for the redemption of mankind, and that he descended to Limbo and freed the souls that awaited him, and that he was resurrected, and that he ascended to Heaven, and that he is seated at the right hand of the Father, and that there will be a day of the resurrection of the

body, and that he will come to judge in order to grant glory to the good and fire to the evil.[11]

Despite his prominent role in human redemption, this Jesus is most emphatically *not* divine—on the occasion of Jesus's baptism in the river Jordan at the hands of his cousin John, the voice of God does not claim him as his son but is heard to say, "You are my beloved spirit, and my repose."[12] As in the Quran, Jesus is his mother's son—he has no father, human or otherwise. The forgers of the lead books appear to have been willing to compromise on the sensitive question of the Crucifixion, the Resurrection, and Jesus's role in salvation, but remained firm on the fundamental Muslim objection to the doctrine of the Incarnation as imposing impossible limits on an illimitable God—an insistence also characteristic of Muslim polemic literature.[13]

Like Jesus, the figure of Mary in the *plomos* is influenced both by her place in the Quran and in Muslim myth and legend and by the Christian Gospels. As in both the Muslim and Christian traditions, she is forever virgin, devout, obedient, and the object of intense veneration. She appears much as she does in the book of Acts, at the center of the emerging Church; in her home, the assembled disciples receive her prophetic teachings. As the recipient of the divine revelation of the book *Certainty of the Gospel,* Mary prefigures and parallels the prophet Muhammad's reception of the Quran. Her marvelous nocturnal horseback visit to Heaven, Hell, and Purgatory closely resembles Muhammad's famous "night journey" to Heaven on the back of the fabulous beast al-Burāq.[14] The texts also reflect both Christian and Muslim traditional views on Mary's state of purity by emphasizing her freedom from original sin. As we will see in chapter 5, the Immaculate Conception of the Virgin was an increasingly popular doctrine in early modern Catholic Christianity. The *plomos'* avowal that the Virgin was exempt from original sin was sure to win them the enthusiastic support of immigrant Christian Granadinos—and Moriscos as well. Although orthodox Islam does not include a notion of a transmissible original sin, some traditional accounts assert that, of all humankind, only Jesus and Mary were exempt from the devil's touch that causes all newborns to cry.[15]

The lead books supplement their syncretic theological vision, potentially attractive to both immigrants and Moriscos, with ritual and devotional prescriptions that blended Christian and Muslim practices. For example, the mass—which, according to the *plomos,* was first performed by St. James upon the Sacromonte itself—should be said by a priest who has first completed ablutions similar to those performed by Muslims, washing not only his hands, but also his face and mouth. The service is to be celebrated not with wine but with water. Similarly, according to the lead books, faithful people must seek the sacraments of baptism and confession for forgiveness of sin, but so too should women avoid becoming the occasion to sin by keeping themselves veiled and hidden from prying eyes.[16]

Other aspects of the *plomos* belong more wholly to traditional Morisco culture. Each of the Arabic texts inscribed onto the lead tablets bore complex patterns made of six-pointed stars, which the books described as the "seal of Solomon." This biblical king occupied a prominent place in *mudéjar* and Morisco mythology as a wizard-like sage whose powers extended to both the natural and the supernatural worlds. Solomon's ring or seal—an emerald brought from Paradise by the archangel Gabriel—symbolized his wisdom and magical powers, and was commonly used as a talisman by Muslims of the Iberian Peninsula and beyond.[17] The seal of Solomon had similar resonances among Old Christians, who associated it with ritual magic and hermetic wisdom.[18] The seal often appears on Morisco charms or talismans known in sixteenth-century Spain as *herçes*—usually small slips of paper inscribed in Arabic with magical words, invocations of the names of God, and pious expressions drawn from the Quran. These were placed in small sacks of fine fabric and worn around the neck or in one's clothing as a means of protection against illness, wounding, the evil eye, or other maladies, and also as a sign of religious and ethnic identity.[19] The use of the seal in the *plomos* suggests that the forgers may have sought to evoke (and perhaps invoke) the wisdom and magical powers associated with Solomon, endowing their texts with greater authority. In one of the lead books, the Virgin Mary relates a version of the story, well known among Moriscos, of how Solomon was granted the ring by God, but temporarily lost it through the machinations of his pagan wife. According to the Virgin's gloss on the tale, the seal represents Jesus, God's divine law, and "the predestination of whom God chooses, and the gracious fulfillment of this by his grace after the Judgment."[20] In the *plomos*, the Solomonic six-pointed star effectively supplants the cross as symbol of power and protection.[21]

There is some evidence to suggest that *herçes* and other such textual objects were sometimes inscribed on lead tablets or plaques similar to those found on the Sacromonte. In 1571 the Holy Office of Granada punished a Morisco for possession of documents in Arabic and a "plaque of lead with Arabic letters that included some of the sayings of Mohammad."[22] The script used on some *herçes* offers another intriguing connection to the *plomos*. The "pseudo-Cufic" Arabic writing used on some talismans—letters joined to a horizontal straight line, with no diacritic marks—is remarkably similar to the Arabic lettering etched on the lead tablets. The lead books themselves describe this script as "Solomonic"—a name that would have bolstered the implied supernatural power of the texts and their resonance within the Morisco community.[23] The use of Arabic letters on the *plomos* also would have enhanced their status among Moriscos, who often viewed the written Arabic word as inherently sacred and as a marker of their cultural identity.[24]

More generally, Morisco cultural and ethnic identity found reinforcement and recognition in the lead books' radically revised vision of Granada's past, present, and future. The *plomos* transformed St. Cecilio and his followers into "Arabs," and the Moriscos—the descendants of the Arabic-speaking inhabitants of ancient Iliberis converted to Catholicism by St. Cecilio—into Old Christians with a pedigree more exalted than that claimed by most of the postconquest immigrants to Granada. Such genealogical manipulations were not unknown in the Morisco community. The noble Granada Venegas family devised a lineage stretching back to Christian Visigoths, while in the rural Alpujarras some individuals, called "of the miter," claimed descent from an unnamed bishop.[25] The Christian ancestry established by the lead books, however, was the patrimony of all Moriscos, rich and poor, Granadinos and non-Granadinos, and the future they prophesied assured the Moriscos—here integrated into a larger Arab world—a place of singular importance and honor in the divine plan for human salvation.[26] This hopeful vision of a coming vindication resembles the promised future described in *alguacias* or *jofores*—prophetic texts immensely popular among Moriscos—but with a twist: whereas most *jofores* prophesied the final victory of Islam, the *plomos* promised the triumph of a new Christianity, one refigured according to Muslim belief and practice.[27]

Despite their near universal approbation in Granada, controversy surrounded the *plomos* from the moment of their appearance. Archbishop Castro sent letters to some of Spain's most eminent theologians and scholars, such as the Jesuit historian Juan de Mariana (1536–1624) and the noted Hellenist Antonio de Covarrubias y Leyva (1524–1601), soliciting from each of them their opinions on the finds.[28] Some, like Pedro García de Loaysa Girón (d. 1599), tutor to the future king Philip III, or royal confessor Diego de Yepes (1529–1613), expressed enthusiasm; others, like Mariana, urged caution in coming to conclusions on the authenticity of the *plomos*. Many expressed doubts about the texts, noting such difficulties as their anachronistic vocabulary and problems of chronology.[29] Benito Arias Montano, for example, noted that the Sacromonte martyrial inscriptions in Latin called each martyr *divus* instead of the more correct *sanctus*, and he pleaded illness in order to avoid having to travel from Seville to Granada to ex-

amine the *plomos* in person.[30] Harsher appraisals of the *plomos* came from scholars like Juan Bautista Pérez (1534–97), the bishop of Segorbe and a renowned
specialist in ecclesiastical history. Shortly after their discovery on the Sacromonte,
he pronounced the lead books as "good for nothing but laughs" and circulated
through the royal court an erudite treatise on the discoveries that noted, among
other things, their poor Latin and strange script.[31]

In Madrid, a circle of opponents of the *plomos* gathered around Pedro de Valencia (1555–1620), a student of Arias Montano and one of the preeminent humanists of the age.[32] In 1607, at the request of Inquisitor General Bernardo de
Rojas y Sandoval, cardinal-archbishop of Toledo (1546–1618), Valencia turned his
expert philological skills to the finds from the Torre Turpiana and the Sacromonte.
Based on a careful linguistic and doctrinal analysis, Valencia concluded that, "It
is all an imposture and a fraud of recent vintage, composed by men who perhaps
are alive today, men uneducated in ecclesiastical history and doctrine and in hu-
mane letters and in ancient letters."[33] Critics also drew attention to the *plomos*'
close ties to Islam and to Morisco culture. The Morisco Jesuit Ignacio de las Casas
(1550–1608) told Pope Paul V that his translations of the *plomos* had led him to
believe that "the authors of all this have been various, a mix of eastern schismat-
ics, heretics, and Muslims, of whom all frequently come to Spain, and especially
to this kingdom of Granada."[34] Other commentators, like the ex-Jesuit Martín de
Berrotarán y Mendiola and Francisco de Gurmendi, a member of the household
of the president of the Council of Orders, Juan de Idiáquez, circulated through
the royal court critical expositions of the *plomos*' Islamicizing theology and very
contemporary Morisco Arabic vocabulary and style.[35]

For these scholars, the forgeries clearly indicated the ethnicity, if not the precise identity of their creator(s). One early modern commentator, however, took
his criticism so far as to suggest some names. In 1593 Luis del Mármol Carvajal,
the author of a well-known history of the Morisco uprising of 1568, commented
on the similarities between the Torre Turpiana parchment and Morisco *jofores*,
noting that Alonso de Castillo—a Morisco member of the *plomos* translation
team—had lent him copies of several popular prophetic texts for use in writing
his history. Moreover, said Mármol, Castillo had informed him that several years
before the Revolt of the Alpujarras, "a Morisco named El Mariní told him that
when the tower of the Cathedral was pulled down, they would find there a great
prophecy of rebellion; and, if this is true, it is certain that the Moriscos knew
about this when they demolished the tower, and perhaps one of them had it [the
prophecy] in his house in order to put it there when he thought it right." According to Mármol, El Mariní died in the first year of the rebellion, and his daughter

gave his papers to Miguel de Luna—another Morisco translator of the parchment and, later, of the lead books.[36]

Mármol's tacit indictment of Luna and Castillo founded a long-standing scholarly convention that points to the two as the probable perpetrators of the forgeries. The evidence behind the charge is strong but entirely circumstantial. By profession, both Luna and Castillo were medical doctors, but both became deeply involved in the affair in their capacity as translators. Aside from his ethnicity and his translations, there is little evidence to convict Castillo, who seems to have died a practicing Catholic in good standing. Luna, by contrast, offers a number of intriguing possibilities. He owned a house at the foot of the Sacromonte, conveniently close to the site of the discoveries, and, according to one modern scholar, he was penanced by the Inquisition.[37] Further suspicion has fallen on Luna because he was the author of a literary fiction called *La verdadera hystoria del rey don Rodrigo* (Granada, 1592). This interesting text purported to be a lost Arabic history of the earliest years of Muslim rule in Spain, composed by one Tarif Abentarique and "translated" by Luna. Modern scholars have noted suspicious similarities between the *plomos* and the *Verdadera hystoria,* which "documents" intermarriage between the Muslim conquerors and native Christian women, the legitimate accession to the Spanish throne by the Muslim kings, and the atmosphere of happy religious tolerance that supposedly prevailed in Muslim Spain.[38] By the time of his death in 1615, Luna had achieved hidalgo status and was married to María de Verastegui, whose Basque name suggests an Old Christian background.[39] One scholar has suggested a possible familial connection between Luna and Castillo, but proof of this relationship has yet to be uncovered.[40] Generally, most critics credit the two Moriscos with the shared authorship of the famous forgeries.

Whether or not Luna and Castillo were indeed the creators of the discoveries in the Torre Turpiana and Sacromonte—and, as I argue in the epilogue, there are reasons to look to additional suspects—the *plomos* reflected the concerns of an increasingly endangered Morisco community. During the decades that followed the Revolt of the Alpujarras, relations between Moriscos and immigrants grew progressively more tense, both in Granada and throughout Spain. In response to the perceived danger of an unrepentant, unassimilated, and possibly treasonous Morisco population, immigrant attitudes grew increasingly hostile and rigid. The rising threat of Morisco banditry and fears of new uprisings led the Crown to order the disarmament of Moriscos in Aragon and Valencia, and the continued growth of the Morisco populations of Valencia and Granada occasioned new directives for forced resettlement in the Castilian interior. Neither strategy met with perfect success, as nobles, landlords, and slave owners resisted royal interference into their local affairs and protected their Morisco clients and property.[41] In the light of the evident failure of Christianization and acculturation, policy makers called for new measures to isolate and neutralize the Morisco threat. Some critics advocated the creation of ghettos; others, more radical and racist, recommended policies that would lead to the eventual extinction of the Morisco community, such as galley service for all Morisco men between the ages of eighteen and forty, or even castration.[42] Somewhat more temperate voices began discussing the possibility of expelling the Moriscos from the Spanish realms. Advocates of the latter policy gained significant support in 1582, when the Council of State, after long debate, endorsed a proposal for expulsion. Fortunately for the Moriscos, however, the more urgent problem of war with the Netherlands, France, and England soon diverted Philip II's attention, and the question of expulsion was laid aside in the interim.

The forging of the finds from the Torre Turpiana and the Sacromonte represents one Morisco response to this increasingly inhospitable political climate. Faced with the possible extinction of the Morisco community, the forgers appear to have hoped to reassert the worth of Morisco identity and culture by cloaking them in Old Christian garb—a strategy that suggests both a familiarity with Castilian Catholic culture and a desperation born of an awareness of the hardening attitudes at court. In 1598 the accession of Philip III (r. 1598–1621) and his favorite, Francisco Gómez de Sandoval y Rojas, Duke of Lerma (1553–1625), and the establishment of peace with France revived the movement toward expulsion of the Moriscos. New and influential voices joined the faction of politicians and prelates advocating expulsion, voices like that of the powerful archbishop of Valencia, Juan de Ribera (1532–1611), a onetime supporter of the Moriscos embittered by his unsuccessful attempts to indoctrinate the Moriscos under his cure. A larger party continued to call for more moderate measures. Leading figures in intellectual and government circles, like Pedro de Valencia and Juan de Idiáquez, wrote memorials against the proposal to expel the Moriscos from the peninsula and advocated polices of conversion and assimilation.[43] By 1608, however, the Duke of Lerma had come to support more drastic expedients, and on April 4, 1609, the Council of State passed a decree expelling the Moriscos of Valencia. Over the next year, the order was extended to the rest of the Spanish kingdoms. By 1614 at least 300,000 persons of Morisco descent had been forced into exile, predominantly in North Africa.[44] Given the extensive expulsions some forty years before, relatively few of these unhappy souls can have come directly from the kingdom of Granada; the data, however, are frustratingly incomplete. The official figure of 2,026 individuals represents the barest of minimums.[45]

Countering the Critics: Pedro de Castro's Campaign for the *Plomos*

Though the *plomos*' many detractors pointed to the suspiciously Morisco characteristics of the documents from the Torre Turpiana and the Sacromonte, their critiques had little immediate impact on the finds' eager acceptance in Granada or their support at court. We have already seen how local critics of the Torre Turpiana parchment like Francisco Aguilar Terrones del Caño and Luis Ortega de Monsalve quickly found themselves silenced. Given the enthusiastic response that greeted both the discoveries in the Torre Turpiana and the finds on the Sacromonte, the prevailing mood in Granada could not have been receptive to public expressions of skepticism. More importantly, the forgers' Islamicizing message never wholly reached the general public—the lead books appeared slowly over the course of some four years, and the process of translation was slowed by the difficulty of the Arabic text and Castro's persistent troubles in finding appropriate translators.[46] Popular awareness of the content of the lead books was also hampered by a papal order issued in January 1596 banning publication on the lead books or their contents.[47] This prohibition, regularly reiterated, forced both defenders and critics alike to observe a cautious circumspection when discussing the finds. Violators, like the unnamed Augustinian friar who in 1599 published the *Prayer and Defense of St. James the Apostle,* one of the texts from the Sacromonte, were liable to find their books recalled and confiscated.[48] Those manuscript translations that did circulate appear to have been confined to scholarly and court circles.[49]

In effect, the difficulties and prohibitions, together with the enthusiastic popular response of Granadinos to the discoveries in the Torre Turpiana and the Sacromonte, helped transform these finds, so redolent of the culture of the despised Moriscos, into icons of Christian immigrant devotion and civic self-consciousness. Their popularity stemmed in part from wider trends at work throughout the early modern Catholic world, as the Counter-Reformation Church reasserted the validity of Catholic extrascriptural tradition and of the cult of the saints and their relics in the face of Protestant critiques. In the century that followed the closing of the Council of Trent in 1563, cities and towns across Catholic Europe enhanced both their spiritual welfare and their earthly prestige by unearthing saintly remains and renovating connections with venerable patron saints, especially paleo-Christian bishops and martyrs whose relics testified to the antiquity of the universal and local Church.[50]

In Rome itself, the rediscovery in 1578 of the "Catacombs of Priscilla," and the bodies of what were assumed to be ancient Christian martyrs bore witness to the Tridentine Church's claims to unbroken continuity with the apostolic age and to the sanctity of the Eternal City itself. Members of the Congregation of the Oratory, founded by the future saint Filippo Neri, an ardent devotee of the ancient martyrs, publicized the catacombs through scholarly production. In erudite works like the monumental *Annales ecclesiastici* (1588–1607) of Cardinal Cesare Baronio (1538–1607) and the posthumous *Roma sotteranea* (1632) of Antonio Bosio (1575–1629), the catacombs and the martyrial remains they held figure as vital proof of the unchanging nature of Catholic belief and practice, "arsenals where one seizes arms to combat against the [Protestant] heretics."[51] The martyrs' symbolic message found additional meanings as their relics began to be dispersed throughout Europe. Over the course of the seventeenth, eighteenth, and well into the nineteenth century, local churches petitioned for and received martyrial remains from the Roman catacombs—a scattering of the sacred that both reinforced the power of the center over the periphery and, as locals integrated catacomb saints into native pantheons, strengthened vernacular devotional forms.[52]

Early modern Spaniards participated enthusiastically in the general passion for paleo-Christian and martyrial relics. Over the course of the sixteenth and seventeenth centuries, communities throughout Spain witnessed repeated *inventios* of ancient martyrial remains. In Córdoba (SS. Asisclo, Victoria, et al., 1575; approved 1582), Arjona (SS. Bonoso and Maximiano, 1628), Abla (SS. Apolo, Isacio, and Crotates, 1629), and Baeza (SS. Justo and Abundio, 1629), miracles and portents heralded the unearthing of the remains of long-lost or unknown martyrs.[53] Other cities renewed their sacred patronage ties through ceremonial translations of holy bodies long ignored or dispersed to other sites during the perilous centuries of Muslim domination. Toledo, for example, celebrated in 1565 the acquisition of the remains of St. Eugenio, its legendary first bishop, and in 1587 the recovery of the relics of St. Leocadia, the city's paleo-Christian virgin martyr. Through the diplomatic intervention of Philip II himself, the monks of the French Abbey of Saint-Denis and the Flemish Abbey of Saint-Ghislain were induced to surrender the relics to Toledo, which, in the presence of the monarch, greeted the return of its founders in Christianity with joyous pomp and ceremony.[54] In 1568 the university town of Alcalá de Henares acclaimed the recovery of the relics of its patron martyrs, SS. Justo and Pastor, and in 1594 Murcia cele-brated the returning remains of its first bishop, St. Fulgencio, and his martyred sister, the virgin St. Florentina.[55] While Philip II's activity as a collector of relics is well known, the efforts of more local enthusiasts like Sancho Dávila y Toledo (1546–1625), bishop of Murcia, or Juan de Ribera, archbishop of Valencia, like-wise tapped into a complex network of domestic and international connections. The result of their efforts, together with those made by figures like the Duke of Lerma and his daughter, the Countess of Lemos, was what one contemporary critic described as an "incredible number" of relics pouring into Spain.[56] Even in communities whose martyrs did not deign to reveal the location of their mortal remains, local leaders encouraged commemoration of long-forgotten or un-known ancient saints.[57]

This outpouring of devotional fervor included an element of rivalry, as cities lodged competing claims to the antiquity of their adherence to Christianity and the prominence of their patron saints. Of the handful of cities that boasted evan-gelization by St. James himself, the most prominent were Santiago de Com-postela, home of the saint's relics, and Zaragoza, site of the miraculous visit to the apostle by the Virgin Mary, who greeted the saint from a perch atop a pillar. With appearance of the *plomos,* Granada was poised to join these cities' exclusive ranks. Likewise, few communities could claim the protection of one of St. James's disciples, the Seven Apostles of Spain. Several of these early evangelists were cu-riously prominent in the years immediately preceding and following the discov-eries on the Sacromonte. Guadix, a town not far from Granada, celebrated the translation of the remains of its patron, St. Torcuato, in 1593, and the receipt of his liturgical office in the following year.[58] In 1595 the city of Ávila transferred the relics of St. Segundo from a parish church to a new chapel in the city's cathedral. The body itself had been discovered some decades earlier, in 1519, in the course of renovations in the saint's small shrine.[59] In 1597 the Andalusian town of Andú-jar feted the arrival of the arm of St. Eufrasio.[60] With the recovery of St. Cecilio's relics and writings, and those of his fellow evangelists Tesifón and Hiscio, all members of the Seven Apostles of Spain were accounted for, and Granada could assert its rightful place among the select group of cities claiming these prestigious spiritual founders.[61] In truth, the discoveries in the Torre Turpiana and the Sacro-monte were not the first relic finds in postconquest Granada. A headless skele-ton wearing a tin pectoral cross that was unearthed in the garden of the Discalced Carmelite Monastery of the Martyrs in 1575 was eventually declared to be that of St. Pedro Pascual de Valencia, bishop of Jaén, executed in Granada in 1300.[62]

However, these discoveries appear to have generated little of the ardor that greeted the relics and writings of Cecilio, a saint more wholly Granada's own.

Devotees of St. Cecilio and his companions found a powerful ally in Pedro Vaca de Castro y Quiñones, Granada's archbishop. Born in 1534, Castro was the youngest son of Cristóbal Vaca de Castro (d. 1571), the famous governor of Peru. Educated in Valladolid and Salamanca, Castro held a doctorate in canon law. At the time of his elevation to the see of Granada, he held the important post of president of Valladolid's Royal Chancery. He also knew Granada well, having previously directed an inspection, or *visita*, of the Royal Chapel, Royal Hospital, and Royal College, as well as having served as president of Granada's Royal Chancery.[63] As archbishop of Granada, Castro could be counted among the most powerful prelates in the country. He was, moreover, a wealthy man, having inherited the family *mayorazgo* after the death of his older brother.[64]

Like his illustrious predecessor, Pedro Guerrero, who led the Spanish faction at the Council of Trent, Castro was one of a number of Spanish bishops who took up in earnest the task of implementing Tridentine reforms at the local level. During his first year as archbishop, he initiated inspections of the cathedral, parish churches, nunneries, and schools.[65] In following years, he celebrated a diocesan synod, reformed Granada's university and colleges, and instituted new regulations governing confession practices and private oratories. Castro's notion of religious reform contained a measure of moral reform as well; consequently, he closed the city's public brothel, forcing its personnel into a home for wayward women.[66] In addition, he forbade clerical attendance at all plays, bullfights, and *juegos de caña*, mock jousts with canes. The archbishop also reformed observance and admission standards in the city's convents and attempted to impose order upon the burgeoning number of competing confraternities by limiting their membership and prohibiting excessive expenditures. As part of his effort to reinforce episcopal authority, he created new standards and controls over monastic preachers and confessors.[67] In 1594 he dispatched to Rome details of all of these activities in an *ad limina* visitation, the diocese's first since these general reports became obligatory in 1585.[68] He also took up the task of rebuilding the rural parish infrastructure that had been destroyed in the conflict with the Moriscos.[69]

While his earliest letters reveal an initially cautious attitude toward the new finds, Castro very quickly became an ardent supporter of the *plomos*.[70] He publicized the finds through his own correspondence with the royal and papal courts and promoted St. Cecilio and the Sacromonte saints both within Granada and beyond by authorizing the press of Juan René Rabut to issue a number of *relaciones*, or news reports, on the discoveries taking place on the hillside.[71] The first of the *relaciones* left the printer's workshop on April 22 or 23, 1595, while the second, illustrated with clumsy woodcuts of the curious texts, began circulating on May 9.[72] At the same time, Castro called on silversmith Alberto Fernández and pressed him into emergency service as an engraver. Fernández created maps of the Sacromonte and illustrations of the plaques, their seals, and the two stones that had contained some of the *plomos*. These and other *relaciones* in succeeding decades advertised the saints of the Sacromonte both at home and abroad; so too did public statements of support by prominent notables.[73] Adherents of the relics and the lead books took care to broadcast the approving opinions issued by Fernando Suárez de Figueroa, bishop of the Canary Islands, and especially the apparent conversion of onetime critic Francisco Aguilar Terrones del Caño.[74]

Castro also lent his patronage to a steady stream of defensive and laudatory texts that circulated both in manuscript and in print. In September 1595, as the controversy over the authenticity of the *plomos* began to heat up, Chancery prosecutor Gregorio López Madera received royal and episcopal permission to print a treatise in defense of the finds.[75] The revised text, reprinted in 1601 and 1602, became one of the most widely known and influential apologies for the Sacromonte finds.[76] Other learned laymen of Granada also took up their pens for the *plomos,* like Juan de Faria, an advocate in the Royal Chancery of Granada, who dedicated to Philip II a short treatise in defense of the Torre Turpiana relics, composed in the form of a dialogue between himself and Morisco translator Miguel de Luna.[77] Other defenders of the *plomos* were clerics, dependents of Archbishop Castro, like Gregorio Morillo, a chaplain at the Sacromonte, or Antonio Covarrubias y Leyva, Pedro de Castro's vicar-general in Seville.[78]

In addition to the difficulties posed by scholarly opponents in Madrid and around Spain, the *plomos* faced persistent challenges from Rome. The Vatican, alarmed by the events in Granada and by the apparently credulous attitude of the archbishop, demanded with growing insistence that the parchment and the lead books be sent to Rome for translation and analysis. Castro frustrated the efforts of successive papal nuncios by cultivating support for the *plomos* at the royal court in Madrid. From the beginning, Castro took care to keep Philip II apprised of events and developments in Granada. The king quickly gave the finds his backing, since, as nuncio Camilo Gaetani informed his superiors in Rome in late 1595, "[the Sacromonte finds are] a pious thing, and they confirm the antiquity of the [Catholic] religion in Spain, and because putting them into doubt undermines the authority of the relics discovered nine years ago [i.e., in 1588]."[79] The position of the Prudent King's successor, Philip III, was somewhat more ambiguous. In 1602 Castro sidestepped what may have been an attempt by the Crown to quiet him with a nomination to the highly prestigious see of Santiago de Compostela.[80] Lerma, the royal favorite, appears to have resolved in 1604 to obey the repeated demands that the lead books be sent to Rome, but nothing came of his decision. Though the critical voices grew louder, the *plomos* continued to enjoy significant backing at court, where Castro lobbied grandees, cardinals, and powerful officials for support. Castro appears to have neutralized the threat posed by the Holy Office, for example, through a network of influence and patronage that extended well into the Suprema, the Inquisition's central governing council, and even to some inquisitors general.[81]

In 1607 the Vatican's persistent orders that Granada relinquish the documents finally prompted Philip III to create a government commission or *junta* to investigate the entire affair and to determine if the *plomos* should be sent to Rome. Summoned to court in early 1609—the very moment that the first edict of Morisco expulsion was promulgated—Castro was honored with three consecutive audiences with the monarch and his favorite, during which he exhibited the original *plomos* and presented his account of the discoveries, illustrated with graphic maps of the locations of the Torre Turpiana and the Sacromonte.[82] The archbishop met with the commission, headed by Inquisitor General Rojas y Sandoval, a close relative of Lerma. In the end, the *junta* sided with the archbishop and opined, the Vatican's wishes notwithstanding, that the *plomos* should remain in Granada and that the monarch should establish a standing committee to monitor the matter.

The Crown's cautious sympathy was, however, not without limits, as Phillip III ignored Archbishop Castro's persistent requests for royal patronage of his newly founded Collegiate Church of the Sacromonte.[83] Castro laid the first stone of this institution, commonly known as the Abbey of the Sacromonte, in February 1609, just before he left for Madrid.[84] Founded in 1607, the Collegiate Church of the Sacromonte was headed by an abbot, Castro's vicar-general Justino Antolínez de Burgos, who governed over twenty canons. The abbey's governing constitutions, which were based on the primitive rule of St. Augustine and the charters of the Society of Jesus and Filippo Neri's Congregation of the Oratory, required the canons to maintain the cult of the martyrs of the Sacromonte and to venture out once or twice a year to isolated areas of the diocese to teach doctrine, to take confessions, and to revive the faith of rural Catholics.[85] Attached to the Abbey of the Sacromonte was a seminary college, the College of St. Dionysius the Areopagite, in which young men studied for the priesthood.[86] Together, the abbey and the college became one of Granada's principal cultural centers.

Pedro de Castro's enthusiastic patronage of the Sacromonte and promotion of the *plomos* were closely linked to his view of their significance for human salvation. The relics and the lead books were, in his estimation, of importance not merely to Granada or to Spain, but to the whole world. He told Pope Paul V in 1611 that "the business of the Sacromonte is one of the greatest things to happen in the world since Adam."[87] Like the (presumably) Morisco forgers, Castro saw the lead books within an eschatological context of a coming world conversion; but the faith to which both Muslims and heretics would return was not the Islamicized Christianity imagined by the *plomos,* but orthodox Catholicism and the institutions of the Roman Catholic Church. The Sacromonte, he informed the *junta* of 1609, represented the fulfillment of the prophecy of Obadiah 20–21, a passage that, according to Castro's interpretation, promised that "there will go forth a transmigration from Jerusalem—that is, St. James and his disciples—they will come to Spain, to the Bosphorus, to the Sacromonte, [and] they will suffer martyrdom there. They will convert Africa and the other cities of all the south to Christ, and it says the order in which the conversion must be done."[88] The result, argued Castro, will be that the leaders of the Church "will convince and condemn the name of Esau—all the Muhammedan sect and the heresies, and all their arts—and all will surrender and will be convinced and will return to the Church. And from there will result and be achieved what Obadiah says, '*et erit domino regnum,*' there will be one flock and one shepherd."[89] Castro also saw his own role in the affair in prophetic terms, identifying himself with the "holy priest" promised by the *plomos*. "*God,*" he reasoned in a 1618 letter to Cardinal Rojas y Sandoval, "*revealed them* to the archbishop [i.e., himself]. It is clear that he was the very one for whom they were preserved, since if they had been held for another person, they would have been revealed by [that person]."[90]

The archbishop threw all of his considerable resources into the discoveries, spending huge sums on the abbey, the relics, and the defense and translation of the lead books—in his last testament, he claimed to have expended some 400,000 ducats on the project.[91] He justified his intransigent refusal to hand over the *plomos* by pointing to the need for new interpreters to decipher the difficult Arabic of the holy texts. In the face of the pointed scholarly criticisms and unflattering rival translations circulating through the court, Castro pronounced the versions by Castillo and Luna to be faulty and launched an ever-wider search for more competent translators. In 1608, for example, he secured the assistance of Bartolomé Aguilar de Anaya, secretary of the Council of War, in seeking out and securing safe conduct for Muslim and Jewish translators from North Africa. Although a royal order in June of that year authorized the entry of two Muslim translators into the Spanish outpost of Melilla, it is not clear whether any such interpreters ever made the trip to Granada.[92] After 1609 the sympathetic *junta* in Madrid extended the search to Spain's viceroys in Sicily and Naples, the ambassador to Venice, and the Duke of Medina Sidonia, who maintained a correspondence with Fez.[93] In 1623 the search was expanded to the Protestant Netherlands, as Castro attempted to recruit the eminent Arabist Thomas van Erpen (1584–1624), professor at the University of Leiden and official interpreter for the independent United Provinces of the northern Netherlands.[94]

Few who labored on the interpretation of the *plomos* created translations that satisfied Castro. For example, Marcos Dobelo, a Syrian translator and professor of Arabic at Rome's La Sapienza University, traveled to Spain in 1610 at the archbishop's behest but soon abandoned his service. Rumor at court held that "the archbishop [Castro] did not allow him to translate according to what he [Dobelo] knew but rather that he wanted him to translate as the archbishop saw fit."[95] Dobelo moved to Madrid, where he established a school of Arabic; his student, Francisco de Gurmendi, became one of the *plomos*' most vocal critics.[96] The Maronite archbishop Juan Bautista Hesronita, a penniless but erudite Dominican friar from Lebanon, opposed the lead books, but agreed to come to Granada and work on their translation for the hefty sum of 200 *escudos* and a per diem wage of forty *reales*. In September 1618 he traveled to Granada and spent several months engaged in the translation of the *plomos*. For a time—and, some alleged, for a price—Hesronita transformed himself into a vocal defender of the lead books, praising their orthodoxy, but by February 1619 he chafed under Castro's controls and set out for Madrid and the court. Relieved of his earnings by highway bandits, the unlucky Maronite attempted to return to Castro's employ but was rebuffed. In Madrid, Paul once again became Saul, and Hesronita rejoined the critical chorus against the discoveries on the Sacromonte.[97]

Despite his victory before the *junta* in 1609 and the cautiously sympathetic attitude of the Crown, Castro's obduracy was the source of concern both in Madrid and in Rome. In 1610, in an effort to separate the archbishop from the *plomos*, Philip III named Castro to the archbishopric of Seville, vacated by the death of Cardinal Fernando Niño de Guevara. Castro appealed to Pope Paul V but was forced to accept the appointment. He succeeded in thwarting the high hopes of the nuncio and other opponents of the *plomos*, however, by claiming the lead books as his own and taking them with him to Seville, where they remained for several years and then were returned to Granada.[98] Though exiled from his beloved Sacromonte, Castro retained his control over the business of the *plomos*, as he continued to search for translators and to defend the precious finds against critics. Castro visited the Sacromonte as frequently as possible—there were at least two extended visits in 1618 and 1620. Aside from his devotion to the Sacromonte saints, the abbey must have seemed a welcome refuge from his constant struggles with the various secular and ecclesiastical corporate bodies of Seville. By the time of his death at the age of eighty-nine on December 20, 1623, Castro had litigated some ninety-seven suits against Seville's university, cathedral chapter, city council, Inquisition, and others.[99]

After Castro's death, the relics and the *plomos* remained in the Sacromonte, protected from papal confiscation by royal patronage of the abbey, which had finally been granted by Philip IV in 1621.[100] As we will see in chapter 5, defense and promotion of the *plomos* fell to the abbey and the city council of Granada, and to Adán Centurión y Córdoba, Marquis of Estepa (1582–1658).[101] After moving to Granada in 1626, this dedicated antiquarian began to investigate the documents from the Torre Turpiana and the Sacromonte. The Marquis soon became one of the *plomos'* most ardent and most public advocates in response to the continuing antagonism of their opponents. He turned his scholarly talents to the task of creating a new translation of the lead books, and in 1632 published at his own expense *Información para la historia del Sacro monte,* a detailed description of the discoveries.

However, the Marquis's efforts met opposition at every turn. An increasingly active Inquisition confiscated his translations in 1631, and no sooner had his book appeared than it was banned for violating the long-standing order prohibiting comment on the *plomos*.[102] Worse, in spite of an apparently successful appearance before the standing *junta* on the Sacromonte, and despite the remonstrations of the city council and the canons of the Abbey of the Sacromonte, in 1631 the king finally acquiesced to the Vatican's demands and ordered that the *plomos* be removed from Granada and brought to Madrid. On March 16, 1632, Mendo de Benavides (d. 1644), president of the Royal Chancery, together with representatives from the archdiocese and the city council and a crowd of onlookers, entered the church of the Abbey of the Sacromonte in order to carry out the royal command. The protesting canons of the Sacromonte refused to hand over their key to the reliquary, but the Chancery officials smashed the locks, removed the lead books, and sent them to Madrid. The human remains and other authorized relics from the Torre Turpiana and Sacromonte remained behind in the church.[103]

That the lead books were installed in the retable of the high altar of the royal Hieronymite monastery in Madrid, displacing an important collection of relics of St. Ursula's 11,000 virgins, testifies to their continuing credibility and support among influential court circles. The Hieronymite prior, Jerónimo de la Cruz, protested the placement and complained that the documents' sanctity was unproven; nevertheless, the *plomos* remained in the retable for the next ten years.[104] In 1641, under continued pressure from the papal nuncio and Inquisitor General Antonio de Sotomayor, Philip IV finally agreed to send the *plomos* to Rome. In September of the following year, after having retrieved the Torre Turpiana parchment from the cathedral chapter of Granada, Bartolomé de Torres and Francisco de Barahona, two Sacromonte canons, set out for Italy with the *plomos* in their care.[105]

If the *plomos'* many critics expected that the confiscation and exportation would mean the documents' eventual disappearance from public discourse, their hopes were indeed fulfilled. Except for the continuing efforts of a handful of intransigent supporters, the controversy over the lead books and the parchment faded from view. By the time of their departure, however, the *plomos* were already firmly embedded in Granadino culture and consciousness. The *plomos* and the paleo-Christian heritage they documented became integral parts of a new communal past, elaborated and articulated during the decades that followed the finds in numerous city histories produced by patriotic local scholars.

CHAPTER THREE

Forging History

Granadino Historiography and the Sacromonte

To antiquity we grant the indulgence of making the origins of cities
more impressive by commingling the human with the divine.

—*Livy*

While the discoveries on the Sacromonte may have raised both eyebrows and
doubts among scholars and critics outside Granada, the local intellectual community responded to the discoveries with enthusiasm. Even as the excavations
continued on the hillside above Granada, patriotic Granadino scholars transformed the human remains and Arabic-inscribed tablets into historical sources
that documented their city's lost Christian past. With the *plomos* as their point of
departure, local historians were able to portray the transformation of Muslim
Granada into a Christian city as less an innovation than a restoration, and its modern population less as immigrants or newcomers than as the legitimate heirs of
an ancient and illustrious Christian city. Although it found expression in various
media, this new vision of Granada took its most coherent form in a collection of
urban histories written by Granadino scholars in the decades following the appearance of the *plomos*. Sponsored and encouraged by the city's secular and ecclesiastical leaders, local literati took the relics and the lead books as the documentary foundation for a new interpretation of Granada's past that emphasized
continuity between the modern and the ancient incarnations of the city and the
constancy of Christian faith.

A Provincial Republic of Letters

The scholars who took up the task of rewriting Granada's history were members of a small but dynamic scholarly community. Neither an intellectual backwater nor a powerhouse of learning, Granada, together with other provincial Spanish cities, harbored an active intellectual life, powered by an energetic group of scholars, poets, and antiquarians. Such scholars were not, in the words of one defender, mere "poetasters or dilettantes," but instead were representatives of an important but still little-known provincial "republic of letters."[1] Modern observers correctly note that the most prominent and ambitious Granadino scholars, among them Luis de Granada (1504–88) and Francisco Suárez (1548–1617), abandoned the city in order to work in more important intellectual centers, like Seville, Salamanca, or Madrid. Other, less famous native and adopted sons, however, stayed at home to pursue a variety of scholarly and literary activities as they made careers for themselves in the Church, the university, and the Royal Chancery.[2] For example, the celebrated Latin poet Juan Latino (1515–73), a slave from North Africa owned by the Duke of Sesa, taught several generations of students in Granada's Ecclesiastical College.[3] The poet and translator Gaspar de Baeza served as a lawyer in the Chancery, where Álvaro Cubillo de Aragón (b. ca. 1600), a poet and prolific playwright, also worked.[4] Praised by the playwright Lope de Vega as "Granada's new Apollo," Juan de Arjona (d. ca. 1600) was both a translator of Publius Papinus Statius's *Thebaidos* and a beneficed priest in the nearby town of Pinos Puente.[5] Pedro Soto de Rojas (1584–1658), a poet best known for *Paraiso cerrado para muchos,* a collection of poems published in 1652, was a canon of the Collegiate Church of El Salvador in the Albaicín.[6]

Reinforcements for this local community of scholars came from a small but steady stream of scholars from other towns and provinces of the peninsula. For example, the Aragonese Juan Clemente (d. 1537), the author of a well-known treatise on Aristotelian theology, joined Granada's cathedral clergy in 1528 as part of the entourage of Archbishop Gaspar de Ávalos.[7] Gregorio Silvestre (1520–69), a noted poet, came to Granada from Portugal in 1541 to fill a position as cathedral organist.[8] These immigrants strengthened the local learned community and promoted its ties to similar groups of scholars in Andalusian cities like Seville and Córdoba, to scholars at the royal court, and to the more distinguished universities of Salamanca and Alcalá de Henares. Granadino scholars who left to pursue their careers elsewhere constituted another bridge to the wider world. Especially important in this regard was Martín Vázquez Siruela (1600–1664), a noted philologist, who began his intellectual career as a tutor to the children of the Marquis of Carpio in Madrid and later became a prebendary in the cathedral of Seville. Vázquez Siruela's letters and manuscripts, scattered in archives in Madrid and Granada, reveal that he maintained regular contact with Granadino scholars.[9] Local scholars eagerly debated and consulted with erudite visitors. When a Jesuit provincial congregation in the 1620s brought to Granada Martín de Roa, a well-known specialist in Andalusian antiquities, the local historian Justino Antolínez de Burgos asked him to pass judgment on some Latin inscriptions recently recovered from a field near the city. Roa's condemnation of the inscriptions as fakes provoked a spirited debate between Antolínez, Vázquez Siruela, and the Sevillano antiquarian Rodrigo Caro.[10] This controversy reveals how Granada's local republic of letters extended beyond the confines of the city itself to a network of scholars active across Andalusia and throughout Spain.

Members of the city's religious houses also participated in local intellectual exchanges as scholars, poets, and orators. The Discalced Mercedarian friar Pedro de San Cecilio, an energetic investigator of Granada's antiquities, pursued his research from the Convent of Our Lady of Bethlehem, while Cipriano de Santa María, a Franciscan tertiary, wrote several theological treatises on Marian themes in his cell in the Monastery of St. Anthony Abbot.[11] Granada's Jesuit college housed a number of well-known scholars, including the theologian Tomás Sánchez (1551–1610), who was famous throughout Europe for his treatise offering sexual advice to married couples.[12]

Patronage, as well as institutional ties, bound Granadino scholars to the larger urban patriciate. Patrons and sponsors, primarily leading members of the city's elite families, were key supporters of this republic of letters. In the first decades of the sixteenth century, the patron par excellence was Iñigo López de Mendoza (1442–1515), Count of Tendilla. From his home in the Alhambra, the count promoted humanist culture in Granada through his patronage of Pedro Mártir de Anglería and Luis de Granada. He also supported scholars like the Flemish classicist Nicolas Cleynaert (1493/4–1542) and the famous humanist Hernán Núñez de Toledo (1470?–1553); both served as tutors to the count's sons.[13] The count's youngest son, the celebrated poet, historian, and diplomat Diego Hurtado de Mendoza (ca. 1503–75), owned one of the city's finest libraries and collections of coins, paintings, and antiquities, which he housed in the Alhambra during his exile from court in the 1570s.[14] Another important early sixteenth-century patron was Alonso de Granada Venegas, patriarch of the powerful noble Morisco family, who hosted an academy frequented by local literary figures, including Juan Latino, Hernando de Acuña, Gregorio Silvestre, and Gaspar de Baeza.[15] In the

1570s and 1580s, Granada Venegas's namesake son continued his father's academy, which was attended by the bookseller Pedro Rodríguez de Ardila, the advocate Juan de Faria, and the poet Luis Barahona de Soto (1548?–1595), among others.[16] In the seventeenth century, the poet Pedro Soto de Rojas held exclusive gatherings in his famous *carmen* in the Albaicín.[17]

An active press helped fuel the local community of scholars. The Nebrijas, a well-known clan of printers who established themselves in the city in the 1530s, hosted meetings of local poets and scholars in the family's home. Granada's first printing press arrived a few years after the Catholic conquest. The German printers Johann Pegnitzer and Meinard Ungut published the first books printed in the city, Francesc Eiximenis's *Vita Christi* and Archbishop Talavera's *Breve y muy provechosa doctrina christiana,* in 1496. By the end of the sixteenth century, Granada boasted a small but active book trade. A wide variety of books and broadsheets emerged from the presses of René Rabut, Sebastian and Hugo de Mena, Baltasar Bolívar, Francisco Sánchez, and others, and they were sold, together with books printed elsewhere, in the stalls, stores, and workshops of booksellers and binders in the aptly named Calle de los Libreros.[18]

Writing Local History in Early Modern Spain

Out of this small and learned group of poets and priests, professors and pressmen originated the histories, sermons, poems, and other texts through which the discourses of Granadino communal identity were developed and articulated. Those erudite civic patriots who turned to the *plomos* in order to write their city's history aimed to create for Granada texts of a type that enjoyed immense popularity in early modern Spain and Europe in general.[19] Rooted in an older tradition of Latin civic panegyrics and vernacular urban chronicles, production of city histories increased during the sixteenth century, eventually peaking during the reign of Philip IV (1621–65). Municipal governments encouraged and sponsored the writing and publication of histories that advanced local, particularist visions of the past centered upon municipal claims to antiquity, nobility, and piety. City histories varied widely in form, including and often combining year-by-year annals of local events, genealogies of noble families, city descriptions (chorographies), treatises on local antiquities, episcopologies, hagiographies, and ecclesiastical histories. Following the conventions of the genre, the authors—primarily local scholars and civic boosters—described in encomiastic terms their city's layout, location, and environs and lauded its modern institutions and leaders. Ancient historical accounts, especially the spurious "Babylonian" histories concocted by Giovanni Nanni (1432?–1502), better known as Annius Viterbensis, supported etymologies of the city's name and origins—usually ascribed in traditional euhemeristic fashion to mythological figures like Hercules or Pharamond, or to biblical characters like Tubal, Noah's grandson and the progenitor of all Spain.[20] Other ancient and classical histories and archaeological remains allowed local historians to affirm their ancient cities' prominence and privileges.

In Spain, as in other parts of Europe, municipal historians placed special weight on their cities' ancient Christian heritage. For Spanish historians, however, this emphasis on Christian antiquity also represented a response to the stigma of centuries of Muslim rule. Eager for any kind of documentary proof attesting to an early embrace of Catholicism, most of these scholars welcomed the appearance, circa 1590, of the so-called "false chronicles" of Flavius Dextrus, Maximus, and Luitprand. These forged annals were the creation of Jerónimo Román de la Higuera (1551–1624), a Jesuit from Toledo, who drew on medieval texts, legends, and his own inventive imagination to provide local scholars throughout the peninsula with names of paleo-Christian bishops, martyrs, and saints.[21] Few municipal historians questioned the reliability of Higuera's chronicles, preferring to mine them for the names and deeds of late antique and Visigothic founders in the faith. Some patriotic scholars sought even deeper Christian roots, claiming evangelization by St. James or by one of the seventy-two disciples sent out by Jesus (Luke 10:1).[22] These details helped municipal historians style their cities as ancient Christian republics, a commonplace of nearly all municipal literature written during this period. In the Christian *civitas,* the earthly city of the faithful that complements the heavenly city, local saints and martyrs represent the virtues of constancy, strength, and valor in defense of the faith, while monasteries and institutions for poor relief exhibit civic charity. As the leader of the Christian republic, the bishop takes a central role in the coordination of the city as a religious center, ensuring and propagating the faith through councils and religious institutions.[23]

Civic historians, especially those writing for Andalusian cities, balanced their emphasis on Christian antiquity with a relative lack of attention to the medieval Muslim era, often either ignoring it completely, or reducing it to participation in the long process of the Christian Reconquest.[24] This last strategy enabled municipal historians to highlight both their city's loyalty and service to the Crown, and the privileges and gifts received in return. The composite image created by these themes combined the well-organized city governed by fair and just rulers of Aristotle's *res publica* with the sacred community founded in faith and piety envisioned in Augustine's *civitas christiana.* These qualities were so fundamental as to constitute the immutable essence of the city: "This community is also presented as if it were a *cuerpo místico,* a mystical body, or as a 'soul': eternal, unchanging, impervious to the vagaries of time. The city is therefore *always* faithful, *always* noble and *always* loyal to its lord."[25]

Prior to the discoveries in the Torre Turpiana and on the Sacromonte, scholars writing such histories for Granada encountered problems unique to the city and to its particular past. While across Europe civic patriots took great pride in the Roman and paleo-Christian heritage of their cities, trumpeting their antiquity in festival decorations, artistic representations, sermons and speeches, and city histories, Granadinos had only a handful of Latin inscriptions to point to as evidence of prominence in antiquity. Because attempts by local scholars and enthusiasts to locate additional remains had revealed little, the few ruins they had took on magnified importance. On one occasion, the city council forcibly confiscated the remains of some Roman statuary discovered under a private residence in the Albaicín and erected the fragments—an inscription and a mutilated head of Furia Sabina Tranquilina, wife of Emperor Marcus Antonius Gordianus (A.D. 225–44)—outside the council's chambers in the Madraza.[26]

Granada's lack of Roman or Visigothic architectural remains exacerbated the difficulty of identifying the city's original name and location. Sixteenth-century scholars agreed that their city was the modern successor to the ancient city known variously as Iliberis, Iliberia, Eliberri, or Iliberri, but they differed as to the precise location of the ancient settlement, the origins of its inhabitants, and the relationship between it and its modern incarnation. Some, like the Flemish scholar Ioannes Vasaeus (Jean Was, ca. 1510–61), citing the tenth-century Córdoban historian Rasis (Aḥmad ibn Muḥammad al-Rāzī, 889–955), held that the ruins of Iliberis were located several leagues to the northeast of the city of Granada, on the slopes of the Sierra Elvira near the town of Pinos Puente.[27] They pointed to Granada's famous Elvira Gate, from which the road to the Sierra Elvira departed, arguing that its name derived from Iliberis. In 1526 the Venetian visitor Andrea Navagiero noted that "there is there [in Granada] an important street, fairly wide and very long, which they call the street of Elvira, a name also given to the gate that is at the end of it. The name Elvira is a corruption of the word Iliberis, since from that place one goes to the ancient city of Iliberis."[28] Over the course of the sixteenth century, local treasure hunters, amateur archaeologists, and tourists visited the supposed site of ancient Iliberis, "digging there, hoping to find treasures, and there they have found very old medals, from the time of the pagans."[29] In 1546 excavations in the Sierra Elvira by the architect Juan de Orea uncovered several Roman statues.[30]

Other scholars, pointing to the testimony of the thirteenth-century Castilian king Alfonso X's *Crónica general,* contended that the ruins of Iliberis were buried under the Alcazaba, the oldest section of Granada's Albaicín district.[31] Confidence in this direct Roman heritage moved Iñigo López de Mendoza, the first captain general of the Alhambra, to style himself "Generalis Granatensis regni capitaneus, ac Illiberitanorum arcius primus praefectus" (Captain General of the Kingdom of Granada and first governor of the fortress of the Illiberians)."[32] Roman inscriptions and coins found in the Alcazaba, such as those uncovered in 1540, lent credence to this view.[33] Confusion among Iliberis, Elvira, and similarly named towns in Catalonia and France further clouded the matter. The difficulty lay in the fact that few ancient authorities made mention of Iliberis, and none were particularly clear about its location.[34] Pliny, for example, listed two towns named Iliberis—one in Andalusia, the other near Narbonne.

The discovery of the *plomos* only complicated the question by describing the resting place of the Sacromonte saints as the "Illipulitan mountain," a reference to the nearby Roman town of Ilipula, also mentioned by Pliny. Where was ancient Iliberis? How was it associated with modern Granada? And if it was indeed under the Albaicín, why did the lead books call the Sacromonte Illipulitan rather than Illiberian? The Torre Turpiana parchment further muddied the nomenclatural waters with its anachronistic description of St. Cecilio as *episcopus Granatensis,* forcing Granada's historians to explain how their legendary prelate could be bishop of both Iliberis and Granada, especially given that no other purportedly ancient documents used the name Granada. Problems like these led some scholars to assert that there was no relationship between ancient Iliberis and modern Granada. Some patriotic Granadinos found particularly distressing assertions like those made by historian Luis del Mármol Carvajal (a Granadino himself) that, far from being an ancient city, Granada was founded by invading Muslims on the site of an older, Jewish settlement.[35] Likewise, just as Granada's ancient pagan past was unclear, the city's early Christian history was hazy and ill-recorded. The medieval legend of the Seven Apostles of Spain told nothing of St. Cecilio's origins or his ministry in Granada. Accounts of the circumstances of his death varied—some calendars and martyrologies classified the Seven Apostles as confessors, while others described them as martyrs—and no one knew the final resting place of the saint's remains.

Despite this confused state of affairs, Granada's new religious leaders endeavored after the fall of the Muslim city to honor their traditional founder in Christianity. In 1492 Archbishop Talavera named the city's newly founded seminary after St. Cecilio and in 1501 established a parish church in his name. However, no further foundations followed, and, during the sixteenth century, the saint's memory languished. Given the lack of information about or relics of the earliest Granadino saints, the Council of Elvira (ca. 306) assumed particular prominence in Granada's ancient Christian history.[36] This earliest of Spanish church councils was a great source of pride for patriotic Granadinos but, like so much of the city's early history, was the subject of controversy and debate, as critics both Catholic and Protestant charged the council with heterodoxy.[37] Granadinos defended the council and their claim to it. Shortly after the discoveries on the Sacromonte, the municipal and ecclesiastical governments of Granada wrote to Philip II, urging him to support efforts for papal approval of a recent book on the Council of Elvira, written by Fernando de Mendoza (1566–1648), a noted scholar of Granadino extraction.[38] However, without clear evidence of the connection between Granada and Iliberis/Iliberia/Eliberri/Elvira, the modern city's claim to the ancient council remained problematic.

The gaps in the historical record and paucity of evidence for Granada's early Christian heritage posed grave difficulties for anyone seeking to write the city's history along Christian lines. More troubling still was the all-too-plentiful evidence of its Muslim Middle Ages. Granada, lamented one patriotic apologist, languished "under the control of barbarians longer than any other city in Spain."[39] On the streets of the city, the sheer ubiquity of the Islamic past left other eras in shadow, and as the last stronghold and symbolic capital of Islam in Iberia, Granada's main role in the national epic of the "Reconquest" was that of the enemy and the vanquished. Worse still, the city had gone without episcopal leadership for several centuries while under Muslim rule. The listing of a continuous succession of bishops was a common feature of the civic history genre, one that conveyed a city's antiquity, its adherence to Christian faith, and often the uninterrupted apostolic succession of its episcopal leadership. Granada's historians frequently cited the Codex Æmilianensis, a tenth-century document preserved in the library of the Escorial that listed the seventy-two bishops of Elvira, beginning with St. Cecilio.[40] The succession was uncertain, however, and for much of the Muslim era there were simply no records or memory of any bishops at all. The episcopal lineages of other prominent cities had similar lacunae—Valencia had few reliable records of bishops after the seventh century, for example, and the episcopal successions of Córdoba and Seville had numerous and notable gaps.[41] Christian leadership in these and other peer cities, however, had been reestablished several centuries earlier in the course of the Christian expansion down the peninsula. By comparison, in 1595 the archdiocese of Granada was scarcely a century old. The city's handful of documented medieval martyrs did little to fill the gap. A shrine in the Albaicín and another hermitage near the Alhambra, established by Ferdinand and Isabella on the site of a number of underground silos in which Christians were imprisoned, commemorated Christians martyred under the Muslim regimes. Although the Hermitage of the Martyrs became a much venerated spot, in general these saints were not prominent on Granada's spiritual landscape.[42]

Given these difficulties, it is hardly surprising that, until the revelations on the Sacromonte, historical writing on Granada consisted almost entirely of summary accounts and narratives of the conquest and fall of the Muslim city in 1492 included in general histories like Lucio Marineo Sículo's *De rebus Hispaniae memorabilibus* (Alcalá de Henares, 1533), Esteban de Garibay y Zamalloa's *Los XL libros d'el compendio historial de las chronicas y universal historia de todos los reynos de España* (Antwerp, 1571), or Pedro de Medina's *Libro de las grandezas y cosas memorables de España* (Seville, 1548), and studies of the Morisco uprising in the Alpujarras, like Diego Hurtado de Mendoza's posthumous *Guerra de Granada* (Lisbon, 1627). The versions of Granadino history contained in these works were often vague or unflattering to local sensibilities. Garibay, for example, contended that the Council of Elvira took place not in Granada but in a town near the Pyrenees.[43] Such texts, however, constituted almost the entire body of literature on the history of Granada until 1595; there exist no known published civic histories, annals, chorographies, or ecclesiastical histories prior to the discovery of the *plomos*. Aside from few encomiastic poems, like Juan de Vilches's (1500–1566) *De urbis Granatae rebus memoralibus,*[44] the only known pre-1595 works on Granadino history include a chronicle of the later Muslim rulers and their battles with the advancing Castilian forces,[45] a falsified genealogy of the noble Morisco Granada Venegas family,[46] and a lost treatise on the lives of Granada's bishops and archbishops.[47] Granada cathedral canon Pedro Guerra de Lorca produced a now-lost "book of the Antiquities . . . of the city of Granada from its first foundation until current times" and *La historia de la vida y martyrio de Sant Çecilio y sus seis compañeros llamados los apóstoles de nr̄a Hespaña,* a short hagiographical treatise on the lives of St. Cecilio and his six companions.[48] Preserved in Spain's National Library and dating from perhaps 1583 or 1584, it is indicative of the interest in Granada's early Christian history that existed prior to the discoveries in the Torre Turpiana and the Sacromonte.[49]

Early Works, 1596–1611

Starved for sources, Granadino historians seized upon the *plomos* as soon as they were uncovered and proceeded to use the books and relics as evidence with which to construct a new version of their city's ancient past. The earliest of these writers, Pedro Guerra de Lorca (d. 1597) and Pedro Velarde de Ribera, began to compose treatises on Granadino history even as the excavations were still taking place on the Sacromonte's scrubby slopes.[50] In their hands, civic history takes the form of *historia sacra*, or sacred history, a category of writing that encompasses and combines a host of genres, including martyrologies, hagiography, and ecclesiastical history.[51] For early modern theorists and commentators of history, sacred history formed a category distinct from civil or secular history. Humanist scholars following ancient models defined the content of history as the actions of men of state and arms, "Peace, War, Counsels, Negotiations, Embassies, Intrigues, and all the different Adventures which are occurent in Human Life."[52] By contrast, *historia sacra*, or, as historian Luis Cabrera de Córdoba termed it, *historia divina*, comprised "sacred [history], which deals with religion and related matters, like holy scripture and positive theology, and . . . ecclesiastical [history, which concerns] canon [law], the decisions of councils and popes, their lives, the lives of the saints, and the government of the Church."[53] Jean Bodin defined sacred history as a separate area of inquiry, the record not of the deeds of men, but of "the strength and power of Almighty God and of the immortal souls, set apart from all else," and as such the proper province not of historians but of theologians.[54] Sacred historians saw divine providence, rather than human action, as the prime causal force behind events. They looked for models in Eusebius and Orosius, rather than Sallust, Livy, or Tacitus, and they often ignored Ciceronian precepts of eloquence. Many humanists therefore shied away from sacred history, especially hagiography, finding it incompatible with their notions of history.[55]

As prominent members of Granada's secular clergy and eyewitnesses to the events surrounding the *plomos*, Granada's earliest historians were well positioned to take up their city's sacred history.[56] Velarde, about whom little is known, describes himself as a native Granadino and a canon in the Collegiate Church of San Salvador; the manuscript *Historia eclesiástica del Monte Santo* is his only known work. Guerra, the son of a high-ranking administrator in the Alhambra, graduated from the University of Granada with a doctorate in theology, and subsequently held benefices in Tendilla (the seat of Granada's powerful Mendoza counts) and in the Alhambra itself. A renowned preacher, he was appointed to a canonry in Granada's cathedral chapter in 1588.[57] While Guerra is best known as the author of *Catecheses mystagogae pro aduenis ex secta Mahometana*, a polemical, anti-Islamic treatise published in Madrid in 1586, his interest in the history and hagiography of Granada predated the appearance of the Torre Turpiana parchment and the Sacromonte tablets.[58] By 1584 he was author of the aforementioned book on Granadino antiquities and *La historia de la vida y martyrio de Sant Çecilio y sus seis compañeros llamados los apóstoles de nrã Hespaña*. Guerra also wrote several treatises in defense of both the Sacromonte and the Torre Turpiana discoveries and was also, according to one source, a "great poet."[59]

Few early modern scholars would have disputed that history, whether human or sacred, was an essential didactic tool. Humanists, following the dictates of Cicero and Quintilian, commonly saw history as a key means of schooling readers in morality and ethical behavior. The values taught by human history, however, differed from those of *historia sacra*, for while human history provided examples of such virtues as justice and prudence, readers of sacred history learned the lessons of faith.[60] For Pedro Guerra de Lorca, the first of Granada's historians, veneration of the saints and their relics is a central lesson of his city's history. By means of the twenty discourses that make up his *Memorias eclesiásticas de la ciudad de Granada*, he says, "what I intend to write and teach is the cult and reverence that one must give to the saints, who were and are the temple of God, and [to] their precious relics, as the faith and Catholic religion teaches us."[61] To this end, Guerra selects the topics that he sees as essential to his purpose; to his dedicatee, Archbishop Castro, he promises to document

some of the other antiquities dealing with the Illiberian Church (which, over many years, I, as one born in this kingdom, have collected), in order to connect its events with the Granadino Church in our own times, since [they are] all one, [and] writing a long catalog of the bishops and archbishops that it has had, together with another [catalog] of the saints, martyrs, and confessors in this kingdom, who have suffered and given true testimony of Christ our Lord and Savior, and have consecrated with their spilled blood not only this Illipulitan mountain, but many places in this kingdom. And after the said catalogs, there is the true understanding of the ancient decrees of the Illiberian Council [Council of Elvira], whose truth and authority the heretics of Magdeburg in our time have tried to obscure and impugn. From all of which the pious reader will have an entire history of the antiquities of our Illiberian and Granadino Church.[62]

Guerra combines inquiry into the ancient origins of Granada with an apology for the relics of the Torre Turpiana and Sacromonte. Using data drawn from a selection of ancient and modern authors, archaeological investigations, interviews conducted with Moriscos, and, of course, the lead books themselves, he examines specific issues and themes related to questions raised by the *plomos*, documents whose authenticity Guerra is eager to support. One discourse, for example, considers the origin and antiquity of the Castilian and Arabic languages; another dis-

cusses the date of the Gospel of St. John.[63] Together with eight discourses on the
lives and deaths of St. Cecilio and his six companions, the Seven Apostles of
Spain,[64] and a discourse on other martyrs and holy figures associated with
Granada (including Christians martyred in the Revolt of the Alpujarras), these
discussions represent the hagiographic heart of Guerra's *Memorias eclesiásticas*.[65]
Guerra's concern for the veneration of Granada's saints, however, is an integral
element of a broader argument for the antiquity (perhaps even primacy) of the
Church in Granada, and the unbroken continuity between past and present.[66] For
ecclesiastical historians both Catholic and Protestant, chronology was a common
rhetorical stratagem for asserting apostolic continuity; it appears here in the form
of discourses on the episcopal succession of Iliberis/Granada and on the Council of Elvira, and on Granadino saints from antiquity to the modern era. The book
concludes with a rehearsal of arguments in favor of the relics and lead books and
exhorts Archbishop Castro to undertake their speedy authentication.

Velarde is likewise concerned with establishing continuity. He writes, he tells
us, with the hope of enlisting the aid of his dedicatee, King Philip III, against the
"murmurers" who impugn Granada's ancient and ecclesiastical history—that is,
St. Cecilio, the *plomos*, and Granada's claim to them and the ancient past they represent.[67] His ecclesiastical history is also a school of proper Catholic belief and
practice, as his apologetics blend historical argument and civic boosterism with
devout and didactic reflections on the cult and veneration of martyrs and on other
Catholic devotions. The introductory pages are a hodgepodge of pious materials
relating primarily to the Sacromonte saints. In addition to the dedicatory epistle,
reader's prologue, and additions to the main text, Velarde includes an illustrated
discussion of miraculous apparitions of crosses in the sky over Italy, the 1600 declaration authenticating the relics, prayers and poems in honor of the Virgin and
the Sacromonte saints (and of the author himself), and the translated text of the
Torre Turpiana parchment. In the first book, "because it is ecclesiastical history,"
Velarde examines Christ's regard for martyrs and the veneration due to the cross,
illustrating his message with concrete examples of the spiritual benefits and
miraculous events that accompanied the processions and other demonstrations
of piety made by Granadinos on the Sacromonte.[68] He continues the lesson in
the second book by combining chapters on the excellent qualities and seminal
role of Spain's Christian martyrs with others on St. Cecilio, the origin and names
of ancient Granada, and the battles fought between the region's various ancient
populations (all, he says, "because it seemed to me useful to verify the name of
the Illipulitan mountains of which the [lead] plaques make mention").[69] In the
third book, Velarde offers solutions to some of the historical conundrums pre-

sented by the Torre Turpiana and Sacromonte finds. He retells the Mozarabic legend of the Seven Apostles and argues for the veneration of relics, both those of the Sacromonte saints as well as those of St. Stephen, found in the Torre Turpiana.[70] The book concludes with an extensive inventory of Christians murdered during the Revolt of the Alpujarras—modern martyrs, he argues, who imitated the example of Granada's paleo-Christian prelates, to whom Granadinos owe gratitude and veneration.[71] Following an index, a different hand has supplemented the text with both a roster of the bishops of Iliberis and Granada (ending with Pedro de Castro) and a list of the famous sons of the city, eminent in poetry, jurisprudence, government, and arms.[72]

Like Guerra's *Memorias eclesiásticas,* Velarde's text is less a comprehensive chronological treatment of Granada's past than a partial, fragmentary sketch of the city's Christian (and pagan) antiquity. Indeed, Guerra, a more experienced and more competent writer, titles his own work not *historia,* or history, but *memorias,* a term that describes not only public acts of remembrance (especially funeral masses) but also individual memoirs, notes or memoranda, as well as chronicles, annals, registers, and other historical records originating in the past. *Memorias,* and their close kin *memoriales,* or memorials, share a fragmentary and disjointed quality; as commentaries on events, annals, or public records, they are, in the words of Francis Bacon, "history unfinished, or the first or rough draughts of history . . . a continuance of the naked events and actions, without the motives or designs, the counsels, the speeches, the occasions and other passages of action."[73] These texts establish some of the basic topoi of Granadino historical writing—the link between Iliberis and Granada; the link between ancient and modern Granada through episcopal succession and through saintly patronage and intervention; the identification of Granada's modern martyrs as the inheritors and imitators of the ancient Sacromonte saints—but they present them with little attention to narrative structure, historical analysis, or even eloquence. There are no reflections on the moral character of Granada's ancient rulers, for example, and no invented speeches.

What holds these "rough drafts" together, however, is their underlying concern for the advancement of the cult of the Sacromonte saints, and, concomitantly, the defense of Granada's claims to an unbroken Christian heritage. Guerra and Velarde are examples of what Simon Ditchfield has called "local Baronios," provincial scholars engaged in parochial offshoots of the confessional controversies that shaped Cardinal Cesare Baronio's *Annales ecclesiastici,* the founding monument of Counter-Reformation *historia sacra.* While their primary focus remains particularist devotion—devotion to their native city and to its newly recovered saints—

their vision is not wholly limited to Granada, or even to Spain. Their emphasis on fostering devotion to the Sacromonte saints and on Granada's claims to apostolic status ties these scholars to contemporary currents of confessional polemic in historical writing. Guerra, for example, undertakes his examination of the Council of Elvira in part to counter the criticisms levied by the Protestant historians known as the Magdeburg Centuriators. The main object of their arguments, however, are the Sacromonte's many critics. The *plomos* are vital to the establishment of an honorable past; their defense, and the promotion of the cult of the Sacromonte saints, are part of these historians' task. Thus, hagiography, martyrology, episcopology, and ecclesiastical history—that is, the many facets and forms of *historia sacra*—are here integral parts of the burgeoning apologetic literature on the Sacromonte, as well as key elements of the developing body of historical writing on Granada.

In the long run, neither Guerra's *Memorias eclesiásticas* nor Velarde's *Historia eclesiástica del Monte Santo* seems to have had much impact in Granada or anywhere else. Neither book ever reached print, nor did it circulate widely in manuscript form—circumstances that suggest that their appeal, and perhaps their intended readership, were limited.[74] The importance of these works lies less in their influence on contemporaries than their demonstration of the ongoing construction of Granadino history upon the foundation of the *plomos*. The historical themes they establish find fuller development in the first "official" account of this developing past, Francisco Bermúdez de Pedraza's *Antigüedad y excelencias de Granada*. Published in Madrid in 1608 but completed by 1602, the *Antigüedad* bears a dedication to the city (i.e., municipal government) of Granada.[75] This dedication and the inclusion of a curious legal disquisition on whether cities may rightfully use public funds to remunerate authors who write about them suggest either that the city council sponsored the writing of the *Antigüedad* or that Bermúdez hoped to convince the council to pay him for his labors after publication. The municipal council considered reprinting the work in 1618.[76]

Born in Granada in 1576, Bermúdez de Pedraza studied liberal arts and law, first at the University of Valladolid and then at that of Granada, where he became an advocate attached to the Chancery.[77] He soon moved to Madrid, and there he published *Antigüedad y excelencias de Granada*, his first book. The following year, 1609, he produced a legal treatise, *Arte legal para estudiar la iurisprudencia*, and *El secretario del rey*, an important study on the office and duties of royal secretaries and scribes.[78] Despite the success of these publications, Bermúdez eventually abandoned his legal career for the Church. He joined the priesthood by 1628 and retired to Granada, where he entered the cathedral chapter, becoming treasurer

in 1637.[79] In Granada, he continued to write, publishing new editions of his previous works, another treatise on the office of the royal secretary, and in 1638 his
Historia eclesiástica, principios y progressos de la ciudad y religión católica de Granada,
which he dedicated to the city's archbishop, Fernando Valdés y Llano.[80] In addition, Bermúdez held a professorship of law at the University of Granada. He published two other works, *Historia eucharística y reformación de los abusos hechos en
presencia de Xpo. nro. señor* (1643) and *Hospital Real de la Corte, de enfermos heridos
en el ánimo de vicios de la Corte* (1644), before his death in Granada in 1655.[81]

Like a more secular version of Guerra's *Memorias eclesiásticas*, Bermúdez's
Antigüedad focuses on Granada's "antiquities"—its ancient foundation, inscriptions, and monuments—as well as its modern institutions and attractions. In the
first of four books, because "it is the common style of serious historians first to
describe the place that they must discuss," Bermúdez describes and celebrates
the location and major monuments and public buildings of Granada, and he com-
mends the citizenry for its accomplishments, morals, valor, and dress. The second book anchors the modern city to its illustrious past. Bermúdez mines both
literary and archaeological sources, including the *plomos,* to establish the age and
prominence of ancient Iliberia and its identity with the modern city of Granada.
His Granada is not only nearly 4,000 years old, founded not by Jews but by the
mythic Phoenician king Hespero and his wife Liberia, but also a free city, confederated with the Roman Empire but never a mere colony. In the Christian era,
it is the first Spanish city to receive the Gospel and is the site of the Council of
Elvira.

The third book, "on the religion of Granada, and its excellent qualities," moves
from the ancient to the medieval era.[82] Bermúdez reduces seven centuries of Islamic rule to two short chapters on the succession of Granada's Muslim rulers
and on the genealogy of the Granada family, a noble Morisco clan descended from
the city's Muslim royalty—even under Islam, Granada is the abode of kings. Following the Catholic conquest, likewise reduced to the final fall of the city, he describes the refoundation of the Granadino Church and its episcopal succession,
its parish churches, monasteries, and convents. As noted by Guerra and Velarde,
religion is the bond that ties ancient and modern Granada; but Bermúdez interprets this link in a curious way, offering a novel solution to the historical problem
posed by the Muslim past. Citing Aquinas's assertion that the perfect republic
must have four attributes—religion, erudition, justice, and strength—Bermúdez
declares that, as far as the first quality is concerned, the city of Granada is astrologically inclined to religiosity and that, while it has not always been Christian, its
constancy and fervor in whatever faith it has held at any given time is itself mer-

itorious: "It is inclined (according to the common opinion of astrologers) to religion, because of which it has since its foundation been very religious, whether in pagan times, or in [the eras] of Moors and Christians."[83] As pagans, Granadinos worshiped many gods, including Apollo, Venus, and Mercury, and after the advent of Christianity, Granada demonstrated its religiosity by serving as host to the Council of Elvira. In the Middle Ages, Granadinos demonstrated their natural religiosity in their persistent adherence to Christianity and, among the Muslims, in their many mosques, their honesty and good morals, and their attraction to Catholicism. The conquest in 1492 elevated the city to new heights of religion. Granada's inhabitants, he notes, frequent the sacraments, care for the poor, and respect the clergy and, during the Revolt of the Alpujarras, they showed their staunch faith by accepting martyrdom rather than convert to Islam.

Bermúdez is unusual among Granadino writers for this unusually tolerant interpretation of medieval Islam, a view that, as we will see in his later works, he abandoned for more mainstream discriminatory attitudes. In the remainder of the third book of the *Antigüedad*, Bermúdez demonstrates the ways in which Granada exhibits the other three characteristics of Aquinas's ideal republic. With respect to erudition, he describes the city's university and colleges and discusses native sons who distinguished themselves both in scholarship and the arts, together with those Granadinos who occupied important governmental and ecclesiastical posts. With respect to Aquinas's third and fourth attributes, justice and strength, Bermúdez describes Granada's ecclesiastical and secular courts and celebrates those Granadinos known for their military exploits. The same star that makes Granadinos religious, he claims, also inclines them to power and independence. These three qualities have always been characteristic of Granada "since the time of the Phoenicians, its first settlers, and since that of the ancient Spaniards." Even as Muslims, Granadinos demonstrated their love of liberty by fighting against the Catholics.[84] These traits, together with other noble attributes bestowed by the benevolent constellation—good health, fame, devotion, and exemption from taxation—are the hallmarks of the city and citizens of Granada.[85]

Finally, in the fourth book Bermúdez offers a passionate defense of the discoveries of the Torre Turpiana and the Sacromonte. This book, probably a later addition (it bears a separate title page, along with a publisher's imprint of 1607), recounts the discoveries and offers solutions to some of the historical problems the finds presented, together with an account of the festivities that accompanied the declaration of authenticity in 1600. Bermúdez culminates with a fervent plea that all Spaniards venerate the Sacromonte and its celebrated saints, maintaining that other cities should acknowledge Granada's superiority, "for being such a great reliquary of bodies of saints, with which you [Granada] exceed the city of Spain [*sic*], richer with these glorious goods."[86]

Like Guerra and Velarde, Bermúdez bridges the centuries by linking Granada to Iliberia and by endowing the modern city with a claim to an ancient past and a continuous existence uninterrupted by changes of fortune or regime. His interpretation rests, however, not primarily upon the evidence of the *plomos* but upon the influence of the stars. The three astrologically induced attributes of liberty, power, and, especially, religiosity are constants that link the ancient to the modern. Just as the positions of the planets at the moment of an individual's birth were thought to determine personality traits during his or her life, so too did the configuration of heavenly bodies govern the character of a city and its inhabitants from its origins through the ages. The qualities of modern Granadinos are identical to those of the inhabitants of ancient Iliberia and are manifest during the Muslim medieval centuries. Bermúdez aims not merely to establish Granada's uninterrupted existence but to prove the constancy of its enduring essence, an essence that transcended changes of religion and regime.[87] Such arguments, grounded not in the antiquity of Granadino Christianity and the institutions of the Church but in the unchanging heavens, make possible a reclamation of both the Islamic past and its physical remains and monuments like the Alhambra, which Bermúdez describes in loving detail. They may also have offered a special attraction to the members of the city council, so ethnically mixed and so often engaged in struggles over power and precedence with Granada's archbishop and cathedral chapter.

As an authorized, or at least welcomed, history of the city, Francisco Bermúdez de Pedraza's *Antigüedad* exercised a profound influence on existing scholarly perceptions of Granada's past. It served as a primary source for Archbishop Pedro González de Mendoza's *Historia del Monte Celia de Nuestra Señora de la Salceda* (Granada, 1616), and for the anonymous *Granada o descripción historial del insigne reino y ciudad ilustrísima de Granada, bellísima entre todas las çiudades* (a now-lost work).[88] Gongorist poet Agustín Collado del Hierro drew heavily on the *Antigüedad* as a guide to the city's marvels and monuments for his poem *Granada,* and playwright Antonio Fajardo Acevedo used it as a source for the description of the city in his play *La Toma de Granada.*[89] The success of the *Antigüedad* may be in part a product of its "official" status; it may also be linked to its publication in Madrid rather than Granada. While the choice of a printer in the capital may have been dictated by the exigencies of the author's legal career, both it and Bermúdez's occasional references to a wider Spanish audience suggest that he hoped to shape the views of Granadinos and non-Granadinos alike.[90]

While they differ in detail, Guerra, Velarde, and Bermúdez reveal the emergent outline of a canonical account of Granadino history—an outline rendered in greater relief by the counterinterpretation of Luis de la Cueva's *Diálogos de las cosas notables de Granada, y lengua española, y algunas cosas curiosas* (1603), the first history of Granada to appear in printed form. Published in Seville in 1603 and dedicated to Cardinal Fernando Niño de Guevara (archbishop of Seville and former president of the Royal Chancery in Granada), these eleven meandering dialogues "of confused erudition" offer an alternative perspective to the emergent official historical narrative.[91] Of the author, little more is known than that he was a cleric, a mathematician, probably a Granadino, and very possibly a Morisco. The first two attributes are testified to by Cueva and his contemporaries; the second two are suggested by his interpretation of Granadino history.[92]

Cueva declares that his primary motive is to prove "that [Granada] has always been the capital city of this province, and that it is the same as Iliberis, the titular city of the cathedral church, much spoken of in the ancient councils."[93] In this and most other aspects of his treatise he differs little from other writers on Granada's past. His format, that of the dialogue, was a style familiar to early modern readers of the urban history genre.[94] In Cueva's text, Cecilio, a native Granadino, guides his curious interlocutor, Cesár, around Granada, pointing out monuments and citing ancient and modern sources, oral traditions, inscriptions and other archaeological evidence to prove the identification of Granada as Iliberis. Other characters include Tesifón, a noble Granadino of Morisco extraction; Rucheli, a geographer on pilgrimage to the Sacromonte; the beneficed priest of the nearby town of Atarfe; some laborers; and a number of gentlemen visiting from Córdoba. Throughout the eleven dialogues, Cueva mounts a patriotic defense of Granada's antiquity, putting into the mouth of the knowledgeable Cecilio arguments for the identification of Granada as the modern descendant of ancient Iliberis.

Where Cueva deviates from the interpretive norm is in his defense of the *plomos* and the Sacromonte. While Granadino historians and Sacromonte apologists usually ignored or downplayed the *plomos'* connections to Morisco culture, Cueva makes these links explicit. The noble Morisco Tesifón, describing the lead books and the parchment, explains that St. Cecilio wrote in Arabic for the benefit of the Arabic-speaking, Christian inhabitants of Granada—the descendants of the Phoenician "Arabs" who conquered ancient Iliberis and called the city Granada, a name the city bore in addition to its original name.[95] Cueva implies that they were the ancestors of the modern Moriscos, noting that the fidelity of the Moriscos to Christianity is of such antiquity that one must note that Granada had Christians a long time after it was conquered by the Moors. The Moriscos of the Alpujarras were held to be the descendants of Christians, and they showed it in their dress, which was collarless smocks with long pleated folds, and they were named Hernando, García, Torcuato, and Turilo. When Boabdil left for Berbery, the people of the Alpujarras said to him, "So, Lord, you go and leave us." He responded, "Christians you were, and Christians you must be."[96]

Cueva's ancient Granada is Iliberis, a Christian city, but a Christian city inhabited by Arabic-speaking Phoenicio-Arabs, the honorable ancestors of the despised Moriscos. Ancient Granada here has a decidedly Morisco appearance to it, its history far closer to the version imagined in the lead books than in any other manuscript or printed account.

While circulation and readership are notoriously difficult to assess, circumstantial evidence suggests that, probably because of his philo-Morisco posture (or perhaps because of his disregard for systematic argumentation or even readability), Cueva's *Diálogos de las cosas notables de Granada* had a limited audience and influence. Aside from a few references in the works of Bermúdez, Cueva is cited neither by Granadino writers nor by writers from outside the city, and his ideas seem to have had no followers. The communal memory he describes is not that of the immigrant majority, but the countermemories of the increasingly threatened Morisco minority, and his text, like the community for which he speaks, appears to have functioned on the margins of the developing narrative of Granadino history, since few Old Christian readers would have cared to see themselves as the modern heirs of ancient Arabs, no matter how venerable their adherence to Christianity.

The more mainstream interpretations such readers preferred found further development in Justino Antolínez de Burgos's *Historia eclesiástica de Granada,* completed in 1611 but published only recently, in 1996. Based in large part on Antolínez's eyewitness experience of the discoveries on the Sacromonte, the *Historia* marks a return to sacred history as the mode for imagining Granada's past. Antolínez's account, which spans from the city's foundation through 1610, places the *plomos* at the center of civic history as the guarantors of a continuity figured not only as a fundamental identity between Granada past and present but also as an enduring constancy in Christian faith and leadership.

Born in 1557 in the northern Castilian city of Valladolid, Justino Antolínez de Burgos belonged to an important patrician family.[97] After studying civil and canon law at the University of Valladolid, in 1585 he became chaplain to Pedro de Castro, then president of the Royal Chancery of that city. In 1587 Antolínez received approval to work as an advocate in the Chancery of Valladolid. Three years later, he followed Castro to Granada, where he occupied a succession of important ecclesiastical and juridical offices and, together with his brother Almerique, served as vicar-general of the archbishopric. When, in 1595, the Sacromonte began to yield up the first of its relics and lead books, the Antolínez brothers took charge of the operation, organizing the excavations and the inquest that preceded the authentication of the relics in 1600. From interviewing those who had witnessed miraculous healings, to supervising laborers as they removed the dirt that had filled the caves, to advocating for the *plomos* at court, Justino Antolínez de Burgos involved himself in every aspect of the Sacromonte affair.

In 1604 Antolínez joined the cathedral chapter of Granada. In 1609, thanks to Castro's support, he was named archdeacon of the cathedral chapter, and in 1610 he became the first abbot of the new Collegiate Church of the Sacromonte. In 1612 Antolínez advanced to the deanship of the cathedral, the most important of the chapter's offices. Subsequently, he divided his time between the cathedral and the Sacromonte until 1627, when he was appointed bishop of Tortosa, in Catalonia, a position that he occupied until his death in 1637.

The *Historia eclesiástica de Granada* is Antolínez's only known historical work. His modern editor rightly calls Antolínez's activity as a historian a "small parenthesis of a few years" in a life dedicated to administrative and pastoral labors.[98] Yet, however parenthetical, Antolínez's desire to write the history of Granada was genuine. He was motivated by his firsthand experience with the *plomos*—the whole affair, he wrote, passed through his own hands[99]—and by what the *plomos* revealed about Granada's ancient Christian past:

> We would have had scanty, confused, and uncertain notice of our glorious pontiff and martyr St. Cecilio, if divine providence had not revealed in our times his relics and a parchment, books, and plaques of lead upon which his memory is preserved. These things, since they were the primary motive I had to write this history, must be in all of it the guiding compass by which we find a port of refuge from difficulties, since one could not ask for nor offer more credible witnesses.[100]

Antolínez's devotion to the saints of the Sacromonte (and to his patron, Archbishop Castro) stands behind his text. The *Historia* is primarily a devotional and apologetic text, designed both as a historical narrative of Granada and as a hagiography devoted to the promotion of the cult of the saints. Dedicated to Castro, the *Historia* comprises three sections. The first part covers the city's history from its foundation through the death of Archbishop Salvatierra in 1588. The second part examines the life of Pedro de Castro, focusing on his tenure in Granada. The third treats the discoveries and authentication of the *plomos*. Of this last section, fully one-third is devoted to answering critics' doubts about and objections to the parchment, lead books, and relics.

Like his predecessors (none of whom he cites), Antolínez structures Granada's history around the continuity between past and present; but in his interpretation, that continuity depends heavily upon the *plomos* and the martyrs they represent. St. Cecilio and his companions, their writings and remains, are not merely historical evidence but are forces at work within history, ensuring constancy in the Christian faith. Antolínez notes in the prologue that "although Spain was lost and governed by Moors for eight hundred years, in general the faith was never lost in these kingdoms; nor was it lacking in Granada, defended, preserved, and augmented by SS. Cecilio, Tesifón, Hiscio, and their disciples from the caverns and ovens [in which the saints were burned alive] of the Sacromonte."[101] As defenders of Christianity, the Sacromonte saints represent the crucial connection between Granada's ancient Christian origins and its modern incarnation. The martyrs themselves are the bridge across the Islamic centuries.

Antolínez begins his narrative with a discussion of the foundation of Granada, its antiquity, and its location, arguing that Granada's ancestor was not Iliberis but Ilipula Laus, a Roman city of Phoenician foundation mentioned by Pliny, which Antolínez locates in the Albaicín. His proofs are both linguistic and archaeological; the latter include Latin inscriptions both genuine and forged, but especially the funerary plaques of SS. Cecilio, Hiscio, and Tesifón. Antolínez also invokes the evidentiary power of the *plomos* to resolve the problem of the city's name. Alluding to certain passages in the lead books, he hints that their eventual publication will finally resolve all questions as to how Ilipula became known as Granada.[102]

Antolínez's circumspection regarding citation of the *plomos* is a response to papal prohibitions against the publication of information about and opinions on the *plomos* and their content—proscriptions that may help account for the *Historia*'s remaining in manuscript long after its completion. Turning to the ministry of St. James in Spain, Antolínez sketches the saint's life as recorded in official sources. He advises the reader of the papal ban, and then inserts, in a conditional voice, forbidden details drawn from the *plomos*—the apostle's visit to Granada and the Sacromonte, the miracle he worked there, the books he hid in the caverns.[103] Some of these prohibited particulars are graphically conveyed in the accompanying collection of engravings completed in the 1610s and 1620s by the master engraver Francisco Heylan for the future publication of the *Historia*.[104] Although it is impossible to know exactly how Antolínez planned to present the

engravings, the close relationship between their iconography and the historiographic program of the written text suggests both that the author collaborated
with Heylan in designing the engravings and that they were meant not merely to
embellish the text but to illustrate and advance its concepts and claims.[105] Antolínez's account of the lives and deaths of St. Cecilio and his companions, for example, suggests that "God willing, it will soon be known . . . if Christ our Re-
deemer gave sight to St. Cecilio and speech to Tesifón, and if, being his disciples,
he handed them over to the apostle St. James."[106]

An accompanying engraving (fig. 3.1) gives graphic form to these barely con-
cealed prohibited particulars. At the center of the picture, a healing light or force
issues from Jesus's mouth to the afflicted boys who kneel before him. Their
names, together with that of their father, Saleh, appear both in Latin script and in
the stylized Arabic of the lead books. Jesus's disciples and the wealthy Saleh's entourage fill the foreground on either side of the central figures—the disciples indicated by their number and their robes, the entourage by its opulence and the
turbans worn by some of its members. In the background, Jesus and the disciples may be seen receiving converts outside the gates of Jerusalem, which lies in
the distance between the hills. At the bottom, an inscription in a cartouche invokes Mark 7:37: "He has done all things well; he makes both the deaf to hear,
and the dumb to speak." While not all are so revealing—some, like that of the
martyrdom of St. Cecilio, simply reiterate in graphic form key events in Antolínez's narrative—the inclusion of such forbidden information may suggest that
Antolínez had hopes that the papal ban might soon be lifted, or that he intended
to circumvent the prohibition by resorting to images rather than words.[107]

From the exemplary deaths of St. Cecilio and his companions, embellished
with edifying speeches and emotional language, Antolínez proceeds chronologically to the Council of Elvira and the succession of Granada's bishops. Based on
a list previously published by the Dominican hagiographer Juan de Marieta, Antolínez's episcopology emphasizes the central role of the Sacromonte martyrs in
ensuring Christian continuity and the uninterrupted transmission of doctrine,
authority, and faith in the Granadino Church from its apostolic foundation to the
modern era.[108] This interpretation receives graphic articulation in an elaborate
engraving entitled "Typus Ecclesiae Garnatensis" (fig. 3.2).[109] In the background
of the engraving lies a landscape studded with eighteen cities, representing the
Iberian Peninsula's most important and apostolic bishoprics. Tracing a route between them is John 1:16, "Of his fullness have we all received." In the foreground,
on a grassy hill representing the Sacromonte and marked with the words "Fundamenta eius in montibus sanctis" (His foundation [is] in the holy mountains;

BENE OMNIA FECIT:ET SVRDOS FECIT
AVDIRE,ET MVTOS LOQVI. *Marci.7.36.37.*

Fig. 3.1. Francisco Heylan, "The Healing of Cecilio and Tesifón." Reproduced
from Justino Antolínez de Burgos, *Historia eclesiástica de Granada,* edited by
Manuel Sotomayor [y Muru] (Granada: Universidad de Granada, 1996).

Psalm 87:1), stands a tower or column, decorated with the likenesses of the bishops and archbishops of Granada in such a way that the prelates' portraits constitute the bricks making up the edifice. A passage from "Urbs beata Hierusalem,"
an anonymous seventh- or eighth-century hymn for the dedication of a church,
rounds the sides and top of the tower; it reads "expoliti lapides suis coaptantur

locis per manum artificis; disponuntur permansuri sacris edificiis" (These polished stones are fitted to their places by the hands of the Builder: they are arranged to remain forever in the sacred edifice).[110] In the base of the tower appear SS. Tesifón, Cecilio, and Hiscio, surrounded by their followers and marked with the motto "Plantaverunt Ecclesiam sanguine sua" (They founded the Church with their blood). Below them, in a grotto marked "Garalnata specus sapientiae" (Granada, cave of wisdom), SS. Cecilio and James stand by a rock under which we see the lead book *Fundamentum ecclesiae*. At the top, above tower's battlements, which are decorated with the "seals of Solomon" found on the *plomos*, sits an armed female figure, crowned with a pomegranate, who represents the Church of Granada. She holds a shield emblazoned with the most elaborate of the Solomonic seals; around her, a thundercloud emits lighting labeled "Boanerges," an epithet of St. James, as four mustachioed winds, representing Heresy, Judaism, Schism, and Paganism, buffet the flame of her torch, which is surrounded by an inscription reading "Indeficiens" (Unfailing). Antolínez's message is clear: the tower or column of the faith in Granada, sustained by the uninterrupted succession of bishops and archbishops, is founded on the Sacromonte martyrs and the holy doctrine of its first prelate and evangelist.

The remainder of the first part of the *Historia* relates the conquest of Granada by Ferdinand and Isabella, and the reestablishment of the Church in the city. Rather than discuss Granada's medieval Muslim regimes, Antolínez substitutes several hagiographical accounts of miracles and martyrdoms endured by Christian captives and missionaries and skips directly ahead to the lives and merits of Ferdinand and Isabella, and to the wars that culminated in the surrender of the city to the Catholic forces. Five lengthy chapters retell in hagiographical mode the life, virtues, and exemplary death of Archbishop Talavera, the first leader of Granada's new ecclesiastical government. Antolínez follows this holy prelate with brief summaries of the lives of the archbishops of Granada, highlighting Archbishop Pedro Guerrero's attendance at the Council of Trent and his reforming activities in Granada.[111] Provoked by Guerrero's reforms, the Morisco revolt in the Alpujarras furnishes Antolínez with a multitude of new martyrs, the modern harvest of the ancient seeds sown by the Sacromonte saints.[112] Both text and engravings dwell at length on their gruesome deaths and inflexible faith, positioning the Alpujarras martyrs as new members of the local sacred pantheon.

Part two treats the life and prelacy of Pedro de Castro. The ten chapters making up the second part are invaluable sources for information about events in Granada in the late sixteenth and early seventeenth centuries, detailing Castro's perpetual conflicts—with the Inquisition, the city council, and the Royal

Fig. 3.2. Francisco Heylan, "Image of the Church of Granada," in Diego Nicolás de Heredia Barnuevo, *Místico ramillete, histórico, chronológyco, panegyrico . . . del . . . illmo. y v. Sr. Don Pedro de Castro Vaca y Quiñones* (Granada, 1741). Reproduced by permission of the Houghton Library, Harvard University.

Chancery—his attempts to reform customs and devotional practices in the city, and his ardent defense of ecclesiastical privilege. As Castro's *fidus Achates,* Antolínez was closely involved in the archbishop's pastoral activities, and his position on Castro's staff and on the cathedral chapter gave him easy access to key documents and letters, some of which appear transcribed in the text.

In the third part of the *Historia,* Antolínez follows the conventions established by earlier Granadino historians and recounts the revelation of the *plomos,* the miracles and investigations that followed, the ceremonies of authentication, and Castro's efforts to defend the *plomos* at court. Although papal prohibitions and editorial concerns force Antolínez to exercise some self-censorship, suppressing some details while revealing others through strategic language and engravings, his privileged position and personal involvement in the affair afford him a depth of detail unmatched by his predecessors. Like Guerra, Velarde, Cueva, and Bermúdez, Antolínez turns history to the cause of polemic, addressing the many objections raised by critics against the *plomos* and the relics. The book concludes with the departure of Pedro de Castro for Seville and the succession of Archbishop Pedro González de Mendoza.

It remains unclear how much support Antolínez's *Historia eclesiástica de Granada* received from the city's authorities. It seems unlikely that the city council would have lent its backing to a work so nakedly ecclesiastical in its sympathies, nor is there evidence of any financial or other encouragements from Archbishop Castro or his successors. Payment both for creating and printing the engravings and for the purchase of 602 reams of paper for the publication of the book came from Antolínez's own funds.[113] These preparations proved to be in vain. Archbishop Castro placed a moratorium on publication of the text in 1616, probably because of the papal ban, and Antolínez's later efforts to publish his work bore no fruit.[114] Despite its failure to reach print, however, Antolínez's *Historia* proved important in the formation of a canonical history of Granada. His history repeats the established themes of the city as *civitas christiana,* figuring Granada as a holy city of saintly martyrs and exemplary prelates, and lending it the luster of antiquity by presenting it as the direct heir of paleo-Christian Iliberis/Ilipula/Granada; but his chronologically comprehensive approach enables him to suggest more persuasively than do his predecessors a continuity between the ancient and the modern *civitas,* in which the centuries are not so much a succession of rulers and regimes but an uninterrupted record of Christian evangelization, episcopal leadership, witness, and faith. Most importantly, Antolínez founds this stability directly upon the *plomos* and the Sacromonte martyrs themselves, placing them at the very center of Granadino history. His approach makes it possible not only to examine ancient history, as in the works of Guerra, Velarde, and Cueva, or to sing the praises of the modern city, as in Bermúdez, but to link the two together and (re)write Granada's forbidden medieval Muslim history according to the needs of its new inhabitants.

Francisco Bermúdez de Pedraza's *Historia eclesiástica de Granada*

Antolínez is too indifferent a writer to develop fully these innovative historiographic possibilities—they are little more than inchoate hints lying beneath the surface of his text. Yet, while it is a challenging and, perhaps, impossible exercise to ascertain with certainty the degree to which any one author influences and shapes the work of another, Antolínez's vision of Granadino history seems to have laid the groundwork for the most influential history of the city written in the seventeenth century—Francisco Bermúdez de Pedraza's *Historia eclesiástica de Granada*, published in Granada in 1638. Though never printed, Antolínez's *Historia* circulated extensively among Granadino scholars.[115] Among those who read it was Bermúdez, who used it as a source for his magnum opus, a massive, erudite survey of Granada's religious history from its ancient origins through 1638. The only early modern history of the city to merit a second printing (Granada, 1652), it remains an indispensable source for historians of early modern Granada.[116]

In a preface, Bermúdez claims that he wrote the *Historia eclesiástica* in emulation of the many city histories published in the three decades that followed the publication of his *Antigüedad*. He characterizes his new history as a corrected reworking of the original, which he describes as "small in body, and even more so in substance."[117] The revision of the *Antigüedad* into the *Historia eclesiástica* also reflects his transition from lay lawyer at court to prominent provincial cleric. Using the *plomos*, Bermúdez both adapts the *Antigüedad*'s image of Granada as an enduring ancient city, immutable in character and continuous in existence, into the familiar framework of civic ecclesiastical history and rewrites the city's history as a narrative in which ancient Christian origins constitute the foundation of Granada's identity. Granada, both ancient and modern, bears the identifying marks of the Christian *civitas:* innumerable saints and martyrs; strong prelates; monasteries, hospitals, and other charitable institutions; and ecclesiastical councils. Rather than destroying or replacing the city's fundamental Christian essence, the centuries of Muslim rule are construed as merely repressing it. The establishment of Catholic and Castilian institutions within the city after 1492 is understood not as a novelty but as a return of Granada to its original state—a restoration of the Christian *civitas* culminating in the revelation of the *plomos* on the Sacromonte. The *plomos* are both testimony of the city's ancient Christian heritage and holy relics, the physical remains of saints. In addition to providing the documentary basis of Bermúdez's vision of his city's past, the *plomos* serve as agents within human history, ensuring a supernatural link between ancient and modern Granada and the constancy of Granada's original Christian character.

In the first chapter of the *Historia eclesiástica,* Bermúdez outlines the book's program and structure. He compares the mystic body of the republic to the human body: just as man is first conceived and then receives life from the soul, so too is the material city "informed by the living spirit of its political government and reformed by the supernatural spirit of the Church and Catholic religion."[118] The human body grows to the peak of health but falls ill and needs medicine to recover. The republic also increases and grows to perfection; sickened with the sins of the age, the city receives the divine medicine of God's mercy and begins to convalesce.[119]

Each of the *Historia eclesiástica*'s four parts represents one stage in the life of the republic. The first two examine the foundation of Granada and its spiritual refoundation with the reception of Christianity. The third treats the infection of Granada's civic body by the disease of Muslim conquest and domination. Through the holy medicine of the Christian Reconquest, Granada "returned triumphant to the grace of her King, to the arms of the Catholic Church her mother, to her original state, and reelevated to greater faith and more heroic virtues."[120] The fourth and last part focuses on Granada's reestablishment as a model Christian city after 1492.

The first section records the city's claims to extraordinary antiquity and honor. Drawing on the *Crónica general* of Alfonso X and the forged histories of Annius of Viterbo and Román de la Higuera, Bermúdez traces the lineage of Queen Liberia, Granada's mythical founder, back through Hercules the Egyptian to Ibero, the son of Tubal. According to this genealogy, Granada is 3,637 years old in 1637, 1,200 years older than Rome itself.[121] Bermúdez insists that Granada's ancient ancestor could only have been Iliberia, which he locates in the Albaicín rather than in the Sierra Elvira, and demonstrates his contention with a series of lengthy and erudite proofs based on local traditions, secondary sources (classical, medieval, and modern), and archaeological evidence. The connection between Iliberia and Granada is crucial, he explains, since by linking the two cities one knows its preachers, prelates, martyrs, and councils, "which are the materials with which the substance of this history is filled."[122] The problematic relationship between the ancient and the modern cities is complicated by the conflicting references in the *plomos* and the paucity of alternative sources. Bermúdez blames the silence in the record on Satan, who, seeing that Iliberia was a holy and apostolic city and "a sacred urn of the ashes of twelve holy martyrs," tried to obscure its memory from history. God, however, preserved the honor of his saints by writing "with pens of steel on tablets of lead and on hard stone, eternal memorials of Iliberia having been in this city."[123] The *plomos* provide Bermúdez the means of bridging the historical gap.

As in the *Antigüedad,* Bermúdez notes that Queen Liberia founded Iliberia/Granada under an auspicious star, endowing the city and its inhabitants, both ancient and modern, with the characteristic traits of independence, power, and religiosity. Liberty-loving Illiberians, he argues, willingly joined in alliance with Rome, remaining a confederated city, rather than a subject colony. Inclined to authority, "this city was a court from the moment they cut its foundation blocks." Attributing to Granada the status of capital of a Carthaginian viceroyalty under Hasdrubal, Bermúdez claims that the city showed its aptitude for governance by preserving its independence during the Roman domination and maintaining its episcopal see under the Visigoths. Since the city's reintegration into Christendom, he argues, royal authority has returned to Granada and is represented by the Chancery.[124] Finally, Granada's status as a restored ancient Christian republic bespeaks its characteristic religiosity.

Having established the continuity between Iliberia and Granada, Bermúdez concludes the first part of the *Historia eclesiástica* with a laudatory description of the ancient city and of modern Granada and its environs. Likening present-day Christian Granada to the two holy cities of Christendom, Rome and Jerusalem, his description of the city's natural features makes special reference to the Sacromonte saints.[125] He claims that the curative properties of a number of local springs and lakes revered by Granada's medieval Muslim inhabitants were due to the power of the martyrs and the enduring memory of the Christian past, and that a certain spring on the banks of the Darro River derives its healing qualities from its proximity to the Sacromonte. Similarly, he notes that a cistern in the Generalife, the site of a minor miracle during the Revolt of the Alpujarras, was holy because it was supposedly built by St. Cecilio: "[The Muslims] said that it flowed by virtue of a saint who was buried in the opposite mountain, without knowing that the Illipulitan mountain was the tomb of St. Cecilio and his companions." Divine providence, comments Bermúdez, preserved the memory of Granada's patron saint even through the Muslim era.[126]

In the second part, Bermúdez turns from the form and foundation of the material body of Granada to the city's conversion to Christianity and the establishment of the Church, a process he compares to the body's animation by the soul. Though they remain uncited, here the *plomos* are his main source. Bermúdez begins his account with the arrival of St. James in Spain, circa A.D. 40. In his view, Granada was St. James's prime destination: it was the first city on the peninsula to receive the Gospel and convert to Christianity, as well as the site of the first mass to be celebrated in Spain:

> Julián adds that St. James was the first to celebrate solemn mass in Spain. . . . It is likely that the first mass that was said in Granada was said by St. James the Apostle, in accordance with the apostolic custom of celebrating [the mass] at great feasts and the consecration of bishops. Having disembarked in Cartagena or Almería, and rested in Granada for a few days, it is believable that the Apostle might have celebrated it there. In the caverns of the mountain where these saints stayed have been found signs of this when they emptied the earth out of them. They found a cross, a brass paten, some lead chrismatories, and a missal of the Apostles' Mass, whose age . . . showed it to be from the time of the Apostles.[127]

The missal in question is one of the *plomos*, the *Ritual of the Mass of St. James*.[128] Bermúdez also employs the *plomos* to challenge Zaragoza's claim to be the site of the first apparition of the Virgin Mary in Spain. Finally, as if visits by St. James and the Virgin were not honor enough for Granada, Bermúdez asserts that SS. Peter, Paul, and John had also stopped in Granada during their travels through the peninsula.[129]

Bermúdez's principal concern in this section is to depict ancient Granada as a Christian republic. As representatives of Granada's early commitment to Catholicism, the martyrs of the Sacromonte establish the city as a bulwark of the faith. They also provide one of the main connections between the ancient city and its modern descendant. Citing St. Isidore of Seville, the Roman Martyrology, the false chronicles, and the most important element, the *plomos* themselves, Bermúdez reinforces Granada's traditional affiliation with St. Cecilio and the legendary Seven Apostles. The *plomos* provide the details of both his life and activities as first bishop of Granada, focusing on his success in converting the city's inhabitants and on his martyrdom with eleven companions upon the Sacromonte.

These martyrs are important for Bermúdez because they represent Granada's constancy in the faith, while their remains, the *plomos,* are the material evidence for the city's deep Christian roots. Using the Sacromonte martyrs as evidence of the city's early embrace of Christianity, Bermúdez compares Granada favorably with Rome, likening the strength of Granada's adherence to the faith to the ties between the Eternal City and Catholicism, forged with the blood of martyrs.[130]

Stressing the eagerness and speed with which the inhabitants of ancient Granada converted to Christianity, Bermúdez explains that Granada's own city council authorized the execution of St. Cecilio, not because it had been ordered to by Rome, but in order to preserve the city's independence and the friendship and confederation with the Romans. Because Granada was by nature and circumstance a free city, "if the Romans wanted to do something, they asked for it in supplication, as a boon, just as one kingdom asks another, and not by a decree where they have no jurisdiction."[131] "Pierced to the heart by the doctrine of their first pastor and leader," Bermúdez writes, the majority of Granadinos converted to Christianity so quickly that by the time of the Council of Elvira, the only pagans left in the city were slaves and lowborn folk.[132] Because of its near-uniform Christianity, he contends, Iliberia/Granada was chosen over all other cities as the site of this important gathering. Like the Sacromonte martyrs, the Council of Elvira supports the image of ancient Granada as a Christian religious center, propagating and reforming the faith under the guidance of conscientious and devout bishops.

A list of these bishops, named in almost unbroken succession from St. Cecilio, and a roster of martyrs from the Apostolic era through the Muslim invasion in the eighth century account for the remainder of the second part of the *Historia eclesiástica*. Bermúdez depicts Granada's early bishops as benevolent prelates, active in reforms, councils, and the fight against heresy. As the spiritual guides of Granada's Christian republic, these bishops are also symbols of the moral state of the whole community. According to Bermúdez, under the influence of the Visigothic kings, Granada's bishops became corrupt and contaminated the faithful.[133] The last of these bishops, Tructemundo, gained his see illegitimately and "opened the door to licentious living," provoking God to chastise the nation by allowing the Muslims to overrun the peninsula. Quoting St. Ambrose, Bermúdez comments that the corruption of Spain's rulers, both secular and ecclesiastical, merited the castigation of the whole nation.

The third part of the *Historia eclesiástica* explores this punishment, the Muslim conquest and occupation. Unlike most early modern Spanish civic historians, Bermúdez draws on sources both medieval and modern to reconstruct the succession of Granada's Muslim rulers and their military exploits.[134] His intention, however, is not to elevate the Muslim past, but to show that Granada remained characteristically the center of authority and the seat of royalty, and to establish a backdrop against which to stage the perseverance of the Christian community. Thus, the changing Islamic regimes, and the struggles and wars among the Muslim kingdoms and with the Christian territories to the north, provide a framework for the tribulations of the Christian city. Bermúdez demonstrates that, for the first four centuries after the Muslim conquest, Christianity in Granada lived on in the Mozarabic population and especially in the local bishops. Devout and competent, Granada's bishops guided their flocks through intermittent persecution and the difficult conditions of life under Muslim rule. The corrupt few, he maintains, were installed by the Muslim regime in an effort to weaken the Christian faithful, who continued to bear witness to their faith by suffering martyrdom in great numbers.

While insisting on the virtue of the remaining Christians, Bermúdez admits that, under the strain of intermittent waves of persecution, the Christian population of Granada gradually declined. Full destruction arrived in the mid-twelfth century with the Almohad regime, which exiled much of the Christian population to Morocco and forbade the election of new bishops. Without episcopal guidance, the remaining Mozarabs gradually converted to Islam. By the time Ferdinand and Isabella recaptured the city in 1492, the indigenous Christian population had disappeared entirely.[135]

But once a Christian city, always a Christian city—this is the way that Bermúdez conceives of his *patria*. Faced with the problematic reality of the abrupt cessation of ecclesiastical leadership and the subsequent extinction of the Mozarabs, Bermúdez shapes his narrative of the succeeding centuries in order to preserve a shred of Christian presence in Granada. Into the progression of consecutive Muslim rulers and regimes, he interjects martyrs and miracles, which reproduce the sacrifice of Granada's first martyrs on the Sacromonte and testify to God's continued concern for his city. The forgeries of the Sacromonte are crucial to Bermúdez's creation of Christian history in the void of the Muslim past. Turning to the *plomos,* he hints that from their tomb in the Sacromonte, the relics of Granada's first bishop and patron saint maintained their protection over the city. In an earlier portion of his text, Bermúdez had asserted the preservative power of the martyrs' remains:

> Granada may tell the cities of Spain that she exceeds them all, not only in fertility of sky and soil, but in being the first who knew the early martyrs, heard their doctrine, and recognized their constancy, and the first in Spain who was ennobled by their blood, and enriched by their relics. These [relics] are those that have maintained her in the Catholic Faith since her first fathers, without ever having lost it to Gentiles or Moors, its light forever preserved among the relics of the Mozarabic Christians, which resulted from the loss of Spain. Among them glowed the sparks of these holy martyrs, buried among the cold ashes of the infidels.[136]

Now, though he does not restate this claim, Bermúdez emphasizes the continuous, silent vigilance of Granada's patron saint, present in the buried *plomos* and in the remainders of his cult. The endurance of the oldest operating church in the city, the Church of St. Cecilio, and the Mozarabic neighborhood surrounding it represents for Bermúdez the survival of Granada's Christianity and serves as a constant reminder of the continuing patronage of St. Cecilio and the *plomos:* "[This neighborhood] has no small defense if its protector is our glorious patron, in whose temple persevered the cult of the true God, despite the infidel Mohammedans, the entire time they possessed this land."[137] As his account turns to the final events of the Reconquest and the successive advances of the Christian forces, the Sacromonte saints suddenly step into human history and actively intervene to aid the city. Drawing on the traditional hagiographical trope of the holy relic as defender and restorer of the Christian community, Bermúdez gives the *plomos* a decisive role:

> It would have been impossible for the Catholic Monarchs to gain Granada by human means . . . but interceding for the victory of our Catholic Monarchs were the holy martyrs St. Cecilio and his companions, their ashes, their bones, their blood shed in the catacombs of the Illipulitan Sacromonte, and for their merits, for the cult and veneration of their relics, forgotten for so many centuries, our Lord easily arranged the submission of so great and powerful a kingdom by means of civil war.

In Bermúdez's interpretation, the miraculous assistance of the *plomos* assured Christian victory; the conquest of the city was completed shortly thereafter.[138]

Immediately after the conquest in 1492, Ferdinand and Isabella began the task of the restitution of the ancient Christian republic. Bermúdez highlights the activities of Isabella in the reconstitution of the city, comparing her to Liberia, Granada's original queenly founder. Previous chapters had described at length Isabella's good government of Castile and prominent role in the Reconquest; in Granada, she becomes the driving force behind the reinstitution of Catholicism, founding monasteries and convents, establishing hospitals and the Inquisition, and expelling the Jews from Spain. According to Bermúdez, because the Church is the immortal soul of the republic, and the bishop is the heart that animates its mystic body, the Catholic Monarchs, as their first act in refounding the Christian republic of Granada, selected Hernando de Talavera to serve as its first archbishop.[139] Bermúdez likens this saintly prelate to his predecessor, St. Cecilio, by stressing his missionary labors among the Morisco inhabitants, his admirable death, and his many posthumous miracles. Talavera's activities and those of his successors make up the fourth and final section of the *Historia eclesiástica,* which treats the reestablishment of the Christian republic of Granada.

Over the course of the next century and a half, Talavera's successors guided the restoration of Granada's Christian republic through propagation of the faith and the establishment of colleges, hospitals, and religious houses. Bermúdez recounts in glowing terms the life and works of each archbishop, highlighting the reforming activities of Granada's more visible prelates like Pedro Guerrero. Granada's civil and ecclesiastical governments, he claims, are models for the rest of Europe.[140] The bloody Revolt of the Alpujarras, which followed Archbishop Guerrero's reforms, provides Bermúdez with a seemingly unlimited supply of fresh Granadino martyrs. For no less than fourteen chapters, he details the gruesome executions of faithful Christians by rampaging Moriscos and compares the massacres to the persecutions of Christians under the Roman Empire.

The unearthing of the *plomos* during the archiepiscopate of Pedro de Castro, yet another exemplary prelate, realizes the full restitution of the ancient Christian republic. Bermúdez reverently relates the tale of their discovery and retells the miraculous healings and prodigious phenomena that demonstrate the authenticity of the relics and the saints' actual power and care for the city. The revelation of the remains of Granada's original martyrs makes manifest Granada's ancient Christian roots and confirms the relationship drawn by Bermúdez between the ancient and modern cities. Their preservation through the centuries, which he regards as miraculous and "against all philosophy," represents for Bermúdez the survival and continuity of Christianity in Granada.[141] As the tangible witnesses of Granada's Christian antiquity, the *plomos* affirm the restoration of the glory of the ancient Christian republic in its modern reincarnation and transform Granada's past into a history of the faith triumphant.

Of the many histories of Granada written in the decades that followed the discovery of the *plomos*, Francisco Bermúdez de Pedraza's *Historia eclesiástica de Granada* offers the most comprehensive solution to the problems posed by the city's history. His broad vision encompasses the entirety of Granada's past, progressing in an orderly fashion from its legendary origins through the Roman, Visigothic, and Muslim centuries and into the modern era. This clear, chronological approach, framed in a corporal analogy of a body conceived, developed, sickened, and restored, lends persuasive power to his arguments for continuity and constancy. By charting the fortunes of Granada as Christian *civitas* through the centuries, Bermúdez demonstrates its immutability and permanence—qualities that invest modern Granada with the legitimacy of antiquity.

Although the *plomos,* the documents upon which Granada's antiquity depended, remained a contested issue in scholarly and courtly circles, Bermúdez's *Historia eclesiástica* eliminates the overtly defensive posture found in earlier writers on Granadino history. Rather than launching arguments against the *plomos'* critics, he assumes the reader's willingness to agree that the lead books and relics are genuine remains and writings of Granada's earliest saints and, as a result, are valid historical evidence. His posture suggests both an audience of convinced locals and a rhetorical strategy by which the *plomos* are covertly integrated into the narrative of Granadino civic history. It may also be a response to the declining fortunes of the *plomos* outside of Granada and the growing hostility with which the Inquisition greeted more openly apologetic works like that of the Marquis of Estepa. Bermúdez's approach to the *plomos* may help account for the success of the *Historia eclesiástica,* which was reprinted in 1652 and soon became an obligatory reference for would-be writers on the history of Granada. For example, his account is a fundamental source for Martín de Angulo y Pulgar's 1649 "Descripción de la ciudad de Granada," as well as for Juan de la Natividad's *Coronada historia . . . de el eximio portento de la Gracia* (Granada, 1697), and Juan de Santibañez's undated manuscript *Historia de la Provincia de Andalucía de la Compañía de Jesús.*[142] Likewise, Francisco Henríquez de Jorquera, an artisan from the nearby town of Alfacar, relies heavily upon Bermúdez's descriptions of Granada and of its past for the historical sections of his 1646 manuscript *Anales de Granada.*[143]

Just as his earlier *Antigüedad* bears indications of backing by the municipal government, Bermúdez's *Historia eclesiástica* carries similar clues of ecclesiastical sponsorship. The inclusion on the title page of the coat of arms of Archbishop Fernando Valdés y Llano, whom Bermúdez describes in his dedicatory letter (addressed to Juan Queipo de Llano, the late archbishop's nephew and bishop-elect of Guadix) as his "Mæcenas," suggests that Bermúdez may have undertaken the project with the prelate's backing, and records held by the cathedral reveal that he received research aid in the form of access to the chapter's founding documents.[144] More generally, the *Historia eclesiástica* reflects and codifies the historical interests, ideology, and identity of Granada's civic elite, of which Bermúdez was a prominent member. As an official historian writing some forty-five years after the first finds on the Sacromonte, he both received and shaped communal memory, codifying what was to be remembered and what to be forgotten by the literate and primarily local audience that bought and read his book.[145] This memory of immemorial and immutable Christian origins, documented by the *plomos* and interpreted by local historians, was not necessarily limited to the literate few. As we will see in chapter 5, rituals and devotions may have helped to disseminate Granada's new history to the wider community, and the enthusiastic response to the discoveries on the Sacromonte, and indeed the *plomos* themselves, may reflect popular traditions about St. Cecilio and Christian Granada that were current prior to 1595. While the sources reveal little of any alternative stories or counterhistories that may have circulated among nonelite Granadinos, the heritage and the identity offered by the official past were at least potentially available to all members of the community—all, that is, but the hapless Moriscos. Except for a handful of families descended from the preconquest ruling elite and the city's important Converso population, the heirs of ancient Iliberis and citizens of Granada's eternal and restored Christian *civitas* were (at least nominally) Old Christians. Although the *plomos* themselves put forward a version of Granadino history that redeemed the Moriscos by transforming the city's patron saint into a converted Arab, the new, official historiography written around them centered on continuity, not conversion. The constitution of Granadino civic identity around an invented Christian heritage pushed the Moriscos outside the community in the narrative of Granadino history and civic tradition.

Local History and *Historia Sacra*

In general, early modern historical writing on cities was heterogeneous, uniting disparate forms and genres in the overarching aim of honoring the *patria chica,* or hometown, which, in an age of nascent nations and national affiliations, still commanded intense loyalty. In Granada, however, the ancient and medieval past was imagined primarily as *historia sacra,* the story of the city's spiritual rather than political past. In part, this was a response to the *plomos,* the documents that undergirded that past. In Granada as in Baronio's Rome, a new sacred archaeology underwrote a new sacred history in which martyrs and martyrdom played a central role. The preference for ecclesiastical histories was also the product of the clerical status, training, and viewpoint of the authors. But the prevalence of *historia sacra* in Granada also speaks to the nature of sacred history itself and the particular demands of Granada's past. Where histories of kingdoms and nations located legitimacy in the sources and succession of political rulers, sacred history emphasized spiritual origins and succession. Few non-Morisco Granadinos would have looked with pride upon their city's long history of political prominence in Muslim Al-Andalus, and its new ruling groups and institutions were too modern, their origins too close to recent memory, to claim the legitimacy of antiquity. Only Catholic Christianity and the Church could claim to have existed in Granada since the age of the Apostles.

For early modern scholars both of sacred and of secular history, the quest for origins was fundamentally a project in ontology. The operative principle of etymology, a traditional humanist tool, deduced the heart of a thing from the origin of its name. For sixteenth- and seventeenth-century historians, as for etymologists and genealogists, "origin defines essence." Origins are not only sempiternal but always present: "Treating many things as we treat only words, in the Renaissance the identifiable (or identified) source of a thing is frequently taken as a principle defining the way it is to be understood and classified. Sources, origins, are then perceived as active guides to how a thing is to be regarded and how it may be expected to perform. The source functions as something perpetually present, though at any specific moment of the continuum it need not be overtly expressed."[146] This understanding of origins, which led defenders of the Catholic Church's unbroken apostolic tradition to search out its earliest roots in the Roman catacombs and Europe's ruling monarchs to trace their familial descent from illustrious biblical and classical founders, likewise moved patriotic Granadinos to recast their city's origins in the mold of an ancient Christian republic. Grounded in the continuity between the ancient and modern cities, and the permanence of the city's Christian faith, this new history uncovered Granada's Christian origins, and thus, despite the external mutations of name, location, appearance, and religion, its unchanging essence. Bermúdez compares these changes in Granada to the aging process: "So powerful are Time's gray hairs that they change a man so that he appears in old age to be a different man than he was in his youth. In such a way do the mystical bodies of cities suffer changes in form and in name."[147] By way of this reasoning, the transformations wrought upon the city and its inhabitants after 1492 would be understood not as a conversion but rather as a restoration and reassertion of its original and unchanged Christian character.

Although the provincial scholars and civic patriots who created Granada's new history seem far removed from the high-flown debates over the proper purpose and style of history that so often occupied their more cosmopolitan contemporaries, they are evidence of the broad acceptance of the new attitudes toward historical sources developed in the humanist "historical revolution" of the fifteenth and sixteenth centuries. For these local scholars, the historian's tools and sources included not only classical histories and medieval annals, but also philology, oral traditions gathered through interviews with elderly Moriscos (a technique used by Guerra de Lorca, Velarde de Rivera, and many others),[148] and inscriptions, ruins, and other archaeological evidence. Like celebrated numismaticist Antonio Agustín (1516–86), they placed greater faith in "medals and tablets and stones than in all that is written by writers."[149] Antiquarians rather than humanists, baroque rather than Renaissance, they generally chose research over readability, and epigraphic and other material evidence over the literary accounts favored by

their early sixteenth-century predecessors.[150] These homegrown Baronios ap-
plied their preferences for inscriptions over eloquence not only to classical antiquity but to the contentious and troublesome matters of ecclesiastical history,
hagiography, and martyrology—that is, to *historia sacra*.[151] In the light of unfa-
vorable assessments by critics on both sides of the confessional divide, by the end
of the sixteenth century writers like Luigi Lippomano and Lorenzo Surio had
brought to bear on hagiography the stringent new standards of evidence, and writing on saints both universal and local expanded dramatically.[152] While not all
practitioners of sacred history chose to meet the new standards for documentation and circumspection, the critical trend continued through the seventeenth
century, with the work of the Bollandists and Maurists, and into the eighteenth
century, reaching an apogee in Spain in Enrique Flórez's *España Sagrada* (first
published in 1747).[153]

For local scholars like Bermúdez and his companions, erudite inquiry into
Granada's antiquity was concomitant with their hagiographical research. Far
from existing outside of or beyond history, hagiography was essential to local historical writing, and to the civic identity it shaped and articulated.[154] Indeed, for
the seventeenth century as for the twelfth, hagiography was history;[155] certainly,
contemporaries often described it that way.[156] Just as local historians dissemi-
nated a particular view of Granadino history, and with it a particular affiliation
with the city, so too did their works advertise and encourage an identification with
and attachment to the city's patron saints. Scholarship may also be a form of worship, and the ecclesiastical histories of Granada can also be read as devotional
texts, meditations on martyrdom and sainthood. Velarde's hymns and long theological excursuses, for example, join author and reader in praise of the Sacromonte saints, and Antolínez's engravings instruct not only in the matter of
Granada's new past but also in its spiritual meaning, inculcating both the cult of
the city and the cult of its saints.

Local devotions and local loyalties do not, however, stand alone, but rather together, in tension and in conjunction with other loci of identity. Hagiographic accounts of ancient martyrdoms in the city and modern martyrdoms in the rural
Alpujarras suggest an identification both with the urban community of Granada
city and with the kingdom of Granada as a whole.[157] These local and regional allegiances overlap with allegiances to Spain—or, as Bermúdez in particular makes
clear, to the Spanish monarchy. His account of Granada's ancient foundation reflects in miniature accounts of Spanish origins found in medieval chronicles and
in the national histories of Ocampo, Garibay, and others, and his emphasis on
Granada's Christian origins is a localized version of their common themes of

Spanish cultural primacy, purity, and essentialism. While his stress on the liberty of ancient Granada may suggest local concerns about encroaching royal authority, it may also reflect a long-standing tendency in Spanish historical writing to emphasize resistance to invaders and outside influences.[158] Indeed, Bermúdez is careful to stress Granada's ties to the Crown: the *Historia eclesiástica* figures Ferdinand and Isabella as "illustrious restorers of this kingdom, fathers of this republic," and the *Antigüedad* features lists of Granadinos who served the Crown in peace and in war.[159] Likewise, the histories figure Granada as not merely a Christian but a Catholic city. Even in the fourth century, Granadinos are orthodox Catholics, and their bishops' constant struggles against the Priscillian and Arian heresies mirror the confessional struggles of the sixteenth and seventeenth centuries.[160]

Throughout Catholic Europe, writers of municipal history fused their parochial concerns with the broader ideological imperatives of Counter-Reformation religious and political policy. The intersections of erudition and ideology in Counter-Reformation historiography are immediately evident in the works of these local scholars, whose careful crafting of an ancient Christian past for their Muslim city is a local variation of Spanish messianic imperialism and Tridentine Catholic evangelism.[161] The engraving created for Antolínez's title page encapsulates this localized imperial ideology (fig. 3.3). At the center of an architectonic retable, flanked by SS. James and Cecilio and framed with the inscription "Mons Sacer Illipulitanus," we see a barren hillside and a map of the caves within it. From the warren of caves, labeled "Gar al-nata" in both Latin and "Solomonic" letters, bursts forth the illuminating light of the Gospel, with the inscription "Hinc orta sedentibus in tenebris" (to them who sat in the region and shadow of death light is sprung up; Matthew 4:16). The rays reach from the caves to the nearby walled city of Ilipula (Granada) and to a cross-crowned globe, whose continents are labeled "Hispania" and "America."[162] The Sacromonte is thus figured as the fount of spiritual enlightenment not just for Granada, but for all Spain and the New World peoples brought by Spain into Christendom.

The insertion of Granada into the national imperial-religious enterprise and the articulation of an avowedly (Old) Christian civic self-consciousness in local historiography were integral elements of the wider program to Christianize Muslim Granada. It was not enough merely to build churches and monasteries or to instruct the Moriscos in the tenets of their new faith; Granada's own history also had to be fitted into the Christian mold. The past, however, could not simply be converted. As was already the case for many Conversos, and soon became so for the unlucky Moriscos, conversion was seldom fully accepted in early modern

Fig. 3.3. Francisco Heylan, title page of Antolínez's *Historia eclesiástica de Granada.*
Reproduced from Justino Antolínez de Burgos, *Historia eclesiástica de Granada,*
edited by Manuel Sotomayor [y Muru] (Granada: Universidad de Granada, 1996).

Spanish society. Origins remained important in the assignation, acquisition, and
preservation of education, offices, honors, and wealth. Thus, what the *linajudo,*
the professional genealogist, did for many elite families with questionable histories, Granada's historians did for their city's problematic past, endowing Granada
with Christian roots of impeccable lineage and an original and unchanging Chris-

tian essence. This new past, taught through their texts, served to rework Granadino communal identity, shoring up fundamental distinctions between members
and nonmembers, and reinforcing communal cohesiveness. In the next chapter,
we will explore how Granadinos instructed themselves and others in this history
and identity through varieties of iconographic and discursive representation in
civic ritual and commemorative ceremonies.

CHAPTER FOUR

Civic Ritual and Civic Identity

At dawn on January 2, 1492, one day after the surrender of Granada to King Ferdinand of Aragon and Queen Isabella of Castile, a large and well-armed party of Castilians entered the Alhambra. At the top of the fortress's most prominent tower, in full view of the defeated Muslim city and the Catholic armies on the plain, officials elevated the cross three times, while ecclesiastics intoned the hymns "Te deum laudamus" and "O cruz ave, spes unica." Standard-bearers then thrice raised the pennants of St. James and of the monarchs, and a herald proclaimed aloud "St. James, St. James, St. James! Castile, Castile, Castile! Granada, Granada, Granada! For the very high, very powerful lords don Ferdinand and doña Isabella, king and queen of Spain, who have won this city of Granada and all its kingdom from the infidel Moors by force of arms, with the aid of God and the glorious Virgin his mother, and the blessed apostle St. James, and with the aid of our very holy father Innocent VIII, and the aid and service of the great prelates, knights, gentlemen, and communities of their kingdoms!" Cannon salvos, trumpet blasts, and bugle calls punctuated the herald's pronouncement and announced the completion of the conquest to the monarchs waiting outside the city.[1]

This ritual act of possession signaled the formal end of the "Reconquest," a centuries-long contest between Muslims and Christians for control of the Iberian Peninsula. News of the victory traveled quickly, spread by word of mouth, letters, and printed accounts.[2] Participants and onlookers across Spain and throughout Christian Europe celebrated the event as a decisive blow against Islam and rejoiced with processions, masses, and plays. The city councillors of Valencia, for example, awarded seventy ducats to the lucky messenger who brought them the tidings and acclaimed the victory with processions and a day of bullfighting in the main plaza.[3] Murcia celebrated the news with mystery plays, while the cathedral chapter and municipal council of Seville marched together in a general procession to the church of St. James.[4] Similar festivities took place in Rome, where papal secretary Carlo Verardi presented *Historia Bætica,* a Latin prose play composed for the occasion.[5] Within a few years of the conquest, Archbishop Talavera had established in both the city and the kingdom of Granada weekly liturgical commemorations of the Christian victory, as well as a daily remembrance at three o'clock, when the cathedral rang a special bell and the faithful gained a plenary indulgence in exchange for three Our Fathers and three Hail Marys.[6] A separate annual feast on January 2 celebrated the dedication of the city to Catholicism.[7]

Like other early modern Europeans, both Protestant and Catholic, Granadinos inscribed their collective memories of the past into a civic ritual cycle.[8] Together with the seasons, the dual liturgical cycles of the Church—Temporale (seasonal and nonseasonal festivities) and Sanctorale (fixed feast days)—ordered the year. Granadinos prayed for the dead on All Souls' Day, sang carols at Christmas, marched in penitential processions for Holy Week, and celebrated the Eucharist and their own Christian community in Corpus Christi, Granada's premier festival.[9] Included in this religious calendar were remembrances of locally significant events, both sacred and profane. Some ceremonies recalled saintly intercession on behalf of the city. In 1588, for instance, the archbishop and cathedral chapter ordered an annual procession to the shrine of SS. Sebastian and Fabian to thank them for their aid in time of plague. The custom was revived in 1614, when both the cathedral chapter and the city council took vows to observe the festivity, raising it to a general procession with the participation of all the city's confraternities, trades, and religious communities.[10] Other ceremonies memorialized important figures in Granada's history, including St. Gregory of Baetica, one of Granada's few identifiable ancient luminaries, and St. Cecilio (the latter especially after the authentication of the relics of the Sacromonte).[11] The Catholic Monarchs received memorial honors three times a year before their tombs in the Royal Chapel. The city council, host of the commemorative ceremonies for Ferdinand and Isabella on May 6 and 7, invited all the city's governing institutions to attend the mass and sermon in the monarchs' memory.

Perhaps the most prominent of the commemorative festivals in the annual civic ceremonial cycle was the yearly celebration of the Toma. The inaugural festival of both the calendar and ceremonial years, the Toma celebrated the origins of modern Granada in the military and religious victory of 1492. As a key component of Granada's "civic liturgy," the Toma annually reenacted those origins and reasserted the meanings and values associated with them.[12] Just as the treatises of civic historians educated literate Granadinos in their city's ancient Christian history, so did this commemorative ceremony instruct local audiences about Granada's more recent past. Together with sermons given as part of the commemoration, the Toma's ritual action constructed, transmitted, and inculcated the shared recollections vital to the constitution of Granadino civic identity. The sermons further linked communal memories of the recent Christian past to the paleo-Christian heritage uncovered on the Sacromonte, tying modern Granadinos to their ancient Christian predecessors. At the same time, however, as Granada's elites appropriated its ceremonies and symbolic objects as weapons in their own internal wars for power and prominence, the Toma represented not only an idealized civic concord and cohesion but also the community's divisions and discords.

The Ceremonies of the Toma

Over the course of the sixteenth century, the annual commemorative celebration of the Toma came to occupy an important place in the city's annual ritual cycle. What began as a liturgical rite dominated by clerics transformed over the course of the decades into a citywide celebration incorporating both civic and ecclesiastical authorities. By 1509 the annual liturgical ceremony on January 2 had expanded to include a solemn procession of Granada's ecclesiastical leadership, joined by the city councillors bearing the city's insignias and the royal standard.[13] A deathbed directive from Ferdinand in 1516 formalized the commemorative ceremony. The king's order stipulated that, in imitation of a similar festival in Seville, the participants should carry his sword. By 1518 the crown and scepter of Isabella had joined the inventory of symbolic objects in the procession.[14]

The immediate result of these innovations was a flurry of lawsuits between various persons and institutions over ownership of the royal relics and the privilege of carrying them in the procession.[15] The inclusion of the sword, banner, and, to a lesser degree, the crown and scepter lent the Toma ceremony an enhanced prestige and prominence, and the ensuing procedural disputes testify to the importance attributed to it by contemporaries. The ceremony became a site upon which rival bodies and local figures jockeying for prominence enacted their struggles. Persistent quarrels and litigation between the cathedral and the Royal Chapel, between the Duke of Sesa and the Marquis of Mondéjar, and among several members of the municipal council frequently interrupted the festivities. The

Royal Chapel, for example, so regularly boycotted the procession that by the mid-eighteenth century, its abstention was written into the Chapel's constitution.[16] Sometimes, as in 1519 and 1520, the warring parties simply canceled the ceremony.[17] While contention over precedence and privileges continued, the intense struggles over the royal objects probably account for their elimination from the ceremony by the end of the sixteenth century.[18]

By the late sixteenth century, the festivities began on January 1, "with many fireworks, fires, and other artillery salvos from the fortress of the Alhambra and the other castles, the ringing of bells, [and] music of kettledrums and trumpets."[19] The following day, the grand procession opened with kettledrums and trumpets, and featured the organized trades with their standards, arranged in an order that began with the armorers and cutlers and ended with the used-clothes dealers.[20] These were followed by "the crosses of all the parish churches, . . . the cross and standard of the cathedral accompanied by four silver candleholders; the curates and beneficed priests, mixed with the clergy of the cathedral; the canons of the Collegiate Church of San Salvador, the chaplains of the Royal Chapel, and the cathedral chapter; and afterward the police wardens, attorneys, scribes, city councilmen, the *corregidor,* and at his right hand the *alférez mayor* of Granada . . . whose lieutenant carries the royal standard." (Originally a military official, the *alférez mayor* was a largely honorific post. Incumbents were charged with carrying the flag or standard of the municipal militia.)[21] The procession departed from the main door of the cathedral and proceeded to Bibarrambla, the city's largest plaza.[22] From there, the procession entered "the street of the *audiencia* of the city [i.e., Zacatín Street], and [into] the Royal Chapel," which it entered through the Gate of the Spice Merchants (also called the Gate of the *Lonja,* the Exchange) while singing the celebratory hymn "Te Deum Laudamus."[23] Once inside, the *alférez mayor* took the royal standard and ceremonially waved or dipped it before the tomb of the Catholic Monarchs. The assembly then proceeded around the tomb and returned to the cathedral, where the standard and the other royal objects were placed on the high altar near the exposed Eucharist.[24] The assembled congregation, joined by the archbishop, heard high mass and a sermon, and received a plenary indulgence.[25] The peal of church bells and the chime of the bell atop of the Alhambra marked the end of the religious ceremony.[26] In the afternoon, crowds watched bullfights and *juegos de caña* and, by the eighteenth century, attended a production of the anonymous historical play called *The Triumph of the Ave Maria.*[27]

The organization and events of Granada's Toma bear close resemblance to the festivities sponsored by other Andalusian towns that celebrated their own conquests. Nearby Málaga observed the anniversary of its conquest in 1487 each August 19 (the feast of St. Louis, bishop of Toulouse), with a mass in the cathedral, a procession in which the *alférez mayor* carried the city's banner, and, occasionally, bullfights and *juegos de caña*.[28] Almería celebrated its conquest in 1490 each December 26 (the feast of St. Stephen) in a festivity known as Día del Pendón (Banner Day).[29] Seville's procession commemorating its own conquest by the sainted king Ferdinand III of Castile in 1248 served as the model for the Granadino celebration. In the Sevillano ceremony, held annually on November 23 (the feast of St. Clement), the city's clergy and municipal officials paraded around the cathedral with Ferdinand III's sword and banner. A sermon and a mass followed the solemn procession.[30]

Outside of Andalusia, some other cities held similar celebrations. Valencia, a city comparable to Granada in its association with medieval Islam and in its large Morisco population, commemorated the 1238 victory of Jaime the Conqueror with an annual procession, mass, and sermon on October 9 (the feast of St. Dionysius the Areopagite). Unlike the Granadinos, Valencians also staged an elaborate and expensive centennial of their conquest, complete with a procession and sermon, ceremonial altars, bullfights, theatrical productions, and other celebratory events.[31] Similar celebrations of locally important events were held in other Catholic cities across early modern Europe. Toulouse, for example, held an annual general procession that commemorated the city's "deliverance" from Protestantism in 1562.[32]

In Granada's Toma, as in these analogous festivals, commemorative ceremony was polyvalent, supporting multiple meanings and interpretations of the ritual actions and the recalled events. At one level, the ceremonies may have been read by contemporaries as a statement on royal authority and Granada's bonds to the Crown. In the early decades of the sixteenth century, the inclusion of the royal standard and of Ferdinand's sword and Isabella's crown and scepter made patent Granada's status as a royal city, reinforcing the ties of loyalty and dependence that helped prevent Granadino participation in the revolts of the Comunidades and Germanías (1520–1522), uprisings against the newly ascended king Charles V that were centered in Castile and Valencia.[33] Although the royal relics no longer figured in the ceremony by the end of the sixteenth century, the standard of the Crown of Castile remained a crucial element of the proceedings. A potent sign of royal authority throughout the Spanish territories, the standard was closely associated with the struggle against Islam and with the sovereign's military might— connotations lent additional potency by the setting of the ritual waving of the banner before the monarchs' sepulchers and the high altar of the Royal Chapel.[34]

Embedded within the chapel's retable, with its life-size images of the dead monarchs, its bas-reliefs depicting key moments in the conquest, and its triumphant Christ crucified, was a near-transparent iconographic program celebrating the union of Castile and Aragon in the persons of Ferdinand and Isabella and the unity of religion within their realms achieved in the conquest of Granada. That the celebration of that conquest took place before the retable and the tombs emphasized Granada's integration into the newly united Crown.[35]

This symbolic statement of loyalty and allegiance to the Crown was paralleled by competing messages of institutional rivalry. Unlike the general procession for Corpus Christi, in which nearly all of Granada's institutions participated, only the most senior of the city's Christian and Castilian authorities—that is, those closest in origin to 1492—took part in the annual Toma festivities. The *corregidor*, the city council, and the diocesan administration (represented by the archbishop and cathedral chapter, the secular clergy, and the parish delegates) all dated their ties to the Crown to the earliest period of postconquest rule (the chaplains of the Royal Chapel, founded some years later, seem to have taken part primarily due to their role as custodians of the royal tombs).[36] The limits placed upon participation were echoed in the procession's short route through a part of the city marked by the buildings housing the same governing bodies featured in the procession itself (fig. 4.1). Relative newcomers like the judges of the Royal Chancery and the Inquisition did not take part in the Toma festivities but celebrated their own ties to the Catholic Monarchs and to the Spanish Crown in their joint observations of the annual memorial services for Ferdinand and for Isabella in the Royal Chapel.[37] Their exclusion from the proceedings underscores the Toma's commemorative aspect—the ritual reenactment of modern Granada's official origins—and its role as a staging ground for elite claims and contests.

Exclusion was not the only mode of elite competition articulated through the Toma. The development of the Toma from a liturgical rite dominated by clerics to a ceremony including the *corregidor* and city councillors and the resulting endemic conflicts between secular and ecclesiastical officials over precedence and etiquette suggest a broader contest over relations of power and status between these two elite groups. The long-standing quarrel between the cathedral chapter and the city council over the latter's right to a cushioned bench, for example, is indicative of this persistent struggle.[38] Similarly, in 1591 conflicts between the city council and Archbishop Pedro de Castro over ecclesiastical immunity to taxation led to a blanket excommunication of the *corregidor* and municipal councillors and to the council's absence from the Toma for some two years.[39] The growing prominence of the lay authorities in the ceremony seems to have coincided with

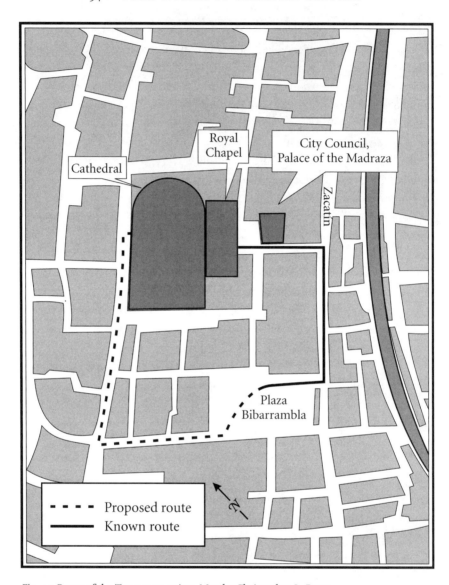

Fig. 4.1. Route of the Toma procession. Map by Christopher L. Brest.

clerical attempts to downgrade the festival's importance.[40] In 1573, for example, Archbishop Pedro Guerrero limited observance of the Toma to within the city of Granada and stipulated that the festivities should end at noon—a command that seems to have been ignored.[41] By the early seventeenth century, moreover, the original liturgical rite celebrating the dedication of the city to Christianity had shifted from January 2 to the first Sunday after January 1, the Feast of the Circumcision. The separation the two festivities may suggest discomfort with the participation of the secular authorities of the city council in the Toma ceremony and an effort to reclaim the clergy's own commemoration of the conquest. The relationship between the two ceremonies remains unclear, however, since in at least one early modern source the instructions for the commemoration of the dedication very plainly describe the Toma ceremony.[42]

For the city councillors, participation in the Toma seems to have offered an opportunity to strengthen publicly their association with the historical origins and source of their institutional legitimacy—the conquest and the Crown. Lacking as it did the validating patina of time, the city council strove to link itself with its royal founders, Ferdinand and Isabella. In 1513, for example, the councillors commissioned an inscription commemorating the monarchs' victory in 1492 to be painted on the ceiling of the council chambers, and by the late sixteenth century, the images of Ferdinand and Isabella had been incorporated into the city's seal (fig. 4.2).[43] The council also strengthened its ties by sponsoring the memorial services for the Catholic Monarchs held each year in the Royal Chapel.[44] Through its ritual reenactment of the foundation moment of modern Granada, the Toma also annually reaffirmed the genealogy of the city council's institutional authority.

While it remains unclear how far exclusion from the Toma ceremonies extended, it seems probable that, as was the case for many such civic rituals, the primary audience for the Toma ceremonies was the same groups that marched in the procession, especially the *corregidor* and the city councillors. The available sources do not reveal whether the general population was permitted to witness the commemorative flag waving before the tombs of the Catholic Monarchs, but it is likely that most would-be onlookers were barred both from the ritual actions in the Royal Chapel and from the mass and sermon that followed in the cathedral.[45] In theory, all Granadinos participated in the ceremonies through the city council, because, as the institutional and legal embodiment of the *res publica,* the republic of Granada, the city council was the city itself and represented all its citizens.[46] In practice, though, less powerful Granadinos likely participated only as onlookers to the procession from the cathedral to the Royal Chapel; as witnesses to royal, municipal, and ecclesiastical power, however, the watching crowds played a role as necessary to that portion of the ceremony as that of the patricians who processed before them.[47] Inside the Royal Chapel, ritual action performed by and for a select elite brought the commemorated events out of the past into a "metaphysical present" and transformed the assembled worthies into witnesses to the rebirth of their city.[48] Outside on the street, participants and on-

Fig. 4.2. Arms of the city of Granada, in *Ordenanzas que los muy ilustres, y muy magníficos señores Granada mandaron guardar, para la buena governación de su república, impressas año de 1552. Que se han buelto a imprimir por mandado de los señores presidente, y oydores de la Real Chancillería de esta ciudad de Granada, año 1670. Añadiendo otras que no están impressas* (Granada, 1672). Reproduced by permission of the Houghton Library, Harvard University.

lookers, rulers and ruled, together ritually reaffirmed the importance of their city's transition to Christian control and its social and political hierarchies, sketching in the process both an idealized, harmonious community and a real city divided by differences of status and power.[49]

"The kingdom of Mohammed has become the kingdom of God"

Other, more explicit commentary on the events of 1492 and the city that commemorated them was an important element of the sermons that were delivered each year to the worthies in the cathedral. Perhaps because it was so predictable—an expected and familiar annual festivity, unlike a royal entry or an emergency rogation—traces of the Toma in Granada's archives are few. However, the sermons were an important part of the Toma, and the handful of extant copies—nine in total and dating from 1611 to 1764—offer a useful and as yet unexplored source for the commemorative celebration.[50] This group of printed sermons, while admittedly small, provides a new perspective on the Toma and its meanings for Granadinos.

It is not surprising that so few of the Toma sermons made the transition from spoken word to printed text (or at least that so few such ephemeral documents have survived). Most individual sermons, or *sueltos* (as opposed to *sermonarios*, sermon collections intended for instruction), recorded the proceedings of an extraordinary occasion—a state funeral, a canonization—rather than an annual event like the Toma.[51] Yet the publication of these sermons suggests some demand for them among the local reading public. It is impossible to estimate the print runs of these pamphlets, nor is it possible to know how closely the printed version resembled a sermon as it was originally delivered. Churchgoers frowned upon preachers who read their sermons aloud or woodenly recited a memorized text, so it was common practice for preachers simply to sketch out their addresses in notes or to memorize them in *loci communes* or bare-bones outline to be elaborated upon in the pulpit. The sermon prepared for publication, therefore, might deviate significantly from the version heard in the church, or it might be very similar.[52]

The sermon, delivered in Castilian before the worthies assembled within the cathedral's sanctuary, was an indispensable part of the Toma festivities.[53] These speeches conform to the type identified by Fray Luis de Granada in his famous treatise on ecclesiastical rhetoric, as the "demonstrative" or epideictic genre. To Fray Luis, such sermons were appropriate for feasts of saints, the Virgin, or Christ, and in this regard differed from the "suasive" or thematic type delivered both in the Ordinary Time—the nonseasonal period of the liturgical cycle—and in the penitential periods of Advent, Lent, and Pentecost.[54] The chief difference between these two types of sermons lay in the fact that the demonstrative sermon sought less to instruct the public than to praise or blame.[55] A preacher planning a panegyric sermon began with the Gospel reading assigned to that day, using it as the *thema* or foundation for a sermon appropriate to the event. This approach could often be difficult, if the day's reading did not lend itself easily to the special circumstance of the celebration, be it a saint's feast, a commemoration, or a thanksgiving. Ideally, the preacher had simultaneously to fulfill the audience's or commissioning patron's expectation of enumeration and praise of the saint's virtues and to deliver a salutary dose of moral doctrine.[56] Most of the sermons examined here tend to subordinate moral doctrine to panegyric.[57]

Preachers writing for Granada's Toma celebration begin with the *thema,* a passage from the day's Gospel reading in Matthew 23, in which Jesus hurls vituperation and threats at Jerusalem, accusing the city of persecuting prophets and warning of coming divine retribution (the destruction of the temple in A.D. 70).[58] At least one orator notes the disparity between the occasion and the assigned text, complaining that "when it was my obligation to describe in careful episodes and studied eloquence for such an excellent and royal city as Granada, the dawn of her heroic beginnings, the triumph of her restoration, the epithets of her honors, the happiness of her glorious deliverance, today the Gospel sings not the beginnings of a city like Jerusalem, but instead laments its end."[59] Here, the preacher identifies the common themes of all the Toma sermons, themes that recall the city histories of Francisco Bermúdez de Pedraza and his fellows: the recollection of Granada's past, both ancient and modern, and the description and praise of the contemporary city. In general, however, the Toma sermons focus on the moment memorialized, the moment of separation from the Muslim past. In the preachers' triumphalist rhetoric, the fall of the city to the forces of Ferdinand and Isabella did not simply end one regime and begin another; rather, it marked the beginning of the restoration, redemption, and consecration of Granada as the city of God on Earth.

Like the Valencian centennial, in which "the history of the holy conquest . . . was the principal affair of the fiesta," commemoration of the conquest of Granada remained the main theme of the sermons' historical content—and indeed, of the entire Toma ceremony.[60] Most preachers recount Granada's ancient or medieval history largely as a means of supporting a central narrative retelling the Catholic victory and the subsequent regeneration of the city. With their focus primarily upon the disjuncture between the Muslim past and the Christian present, treatment of both Granada's recently rediscovered antiquity and its well-known Muslim Middle Ages tends to be brief. Few of the sermons in the collection dwell on Granada's earliest origins; ancient history here consists primarily of the highlights of the Christian past.[61] For example, Fernando de Sosa's 1621 sermon invokes the faithful Christian city of antiquity while berating its medieval Muslim successor:

> Hear me, great city, for I speak to you when the Moorish kings governed you: how is it that you, being so faithful in the happy time of your first glories, when you received the faith seventeen years after the promulgation of the Gospel, through the preaching of your first archbishop, St. Cecilio, and the priest Patricio, his brother and companion and your first archdeacon, are now so unfaithful, a teacher of errors and superstitions? How is it that you, being the seat of doctrine so adorned with wisdom, that they celebrated within your walls the first Church council (after those of the apostles), called the Iliberritan [Council], . . . now you live miserably, blind and deceived, buried in the darkness of ignorance?[62]

Other preachers expressed similar sentiments: Augustinian friar Juan Galvarro's 1611 address compares Granada with the protomartyr St. Stephen, whose octave coincided with the Toma. Like St. Stephen, the first to be martyred for Christ, so was Granada first in the faith—first in Spain to hear the Gospel, host to the first council, site of the first mass in Europe. At the same time, however, he notes that just as St. Stephen forgave his killers, so too did Ferdinand and Isabella forgive "the citizens of this city, who showed themselves to be so contrary and hostile."[63]

The antagonism of preconquest Granadinos toward the representatives of Christianity figures in several of the Toma sermons, coloring treatment of both the ancient and the medieval past. Where some preachers portray ancient Granadinos as devout, in 1720 José Muñoz y Morales invokes the *thema* to lament the martyrdom of the Sacromonte saints at the hands of Granada's ungrateful citizens: "'O Jerusalem, Jerusalem, that killest the prophets and stonest them.' You killed and stoned prophets, my beloved *patria*. This was what you did."[64] Muñoz y Morales' citation in this context points to the importance of the *thema* as a ready-made framework available for the interpretation of the commemorated event. Toma preachers elaborate a symbolic connection between the holy city upbraided by Christ and Granada, both past and present. According to Manuel de la Natividad, a Discalced Trinitarian friar who delivered the sermon in 1701, the martyrdom meted out to prophets confirms a likeness between Jerusalem and Granada: "At one moment, speaking in actuality with Jerusalem, at the other [the Gospel] speaks symbolically with Granada like one who says: 'O Granada, O new

Jerusalem, you have been a theater where St. James my apostle suffered perse-cution, where Cecilio and his companions suffered stones and martyrdom.'"[65] The analogy can also be reversed: in 1762 Francisco de Cardera rejects the like-ness, arguing that "Granada is not ungrateful like Jerusalem."[66] If preconquest Granada was like ancient earthly Jerusalem—or, as the Minim friar Francisco de Paula de la Madriz has it, like Babylon, another famous ancient city whose de-struction was foretold in Scripture—then Granada after the victory of the Catholic Monarchs was like the celestial Jerusalem.[67] The conquest becomes an epoch-making event inaugurating a new era and a new city, a transformation made starker by the contrast with what had gone before.

The Catholic victory marks the pivotal moment at which the old, sinful Granada ends and the new, redeemed Granada begins. The often perfunctory retelling of Granada's ancient and medieval history serves as a blurry backdrop to the principal events of the conquest of the city. Nearly all of the orators recall key episodes in the famous tale: the founding of the Catholic encampment of Santa Fe, the secret negotiations and surrender, and the consecration of the mosques. Their accounts are not necessarily laid out in a clear narrative form, or even in chronological order; most preachers appear to assume their audiences' familiar-ity with the elements of the story. This assumed familiarity reflects the fact that the sermons are lessons not so much in the matter as in the meaning of the past. The preachers offer their audience an exegesis of recent Granadino history, defining the Toma as the moment of metamorphosis, the "happy transforma-tion," from Granada's "wretched beginnings and development" to "its glorious origin."[68] A city, asserts Manuel de la Natividad in 1701, has two foundations: one merely physical and the other spiritual. Only the spiritual foundation, in this view, makes a city of a settlement. "And thus today [Granada] is founded as a city, be-cause today it shook off the yoke of Mohammedan Babylon and returned to the ancient cult of Christ, consecrating to Him new churches and temples."[69]

"The kingdom of Mohammed," exults Fernando de Sosa in 1621, "has become the kingdom of God."[70] The august assembly in the cathedral expected and re-ceived an admiring accolade describing postconquest Granada as a true New Jerusalem. (Re)founded in the Catholic victory, Granada emerges in the Toma ser-mons as God's sanctified city. For Jacinto de la Santíssima Trinidad, a Discalced Augustinian friar who spoke in 1763, the conquest and creation of Christian in-stitutions in the city shows the almighty hand of God actively "ennobling" and "praising" Granada as a "second, new city of Jerusalem."[71] Preachers allegorize Scripture, applying to Granada the traditional attributes and symbols of both the earthly and the heavenly city. Juan Galvarro's 1611 sermon interprets the pomegranates (*granadas* in Castilian) that adorned the robe of the High Priest (i.e., Christ) as an indication of the natural reverence and respect of Granadinos toward things sacred.[72] Manuel de la Natividad praises in rapturous terms not only Granada's earthly attractions of fertility, nobility, wealth, courage, and erudition, but also its divine charms: faith, represented by its primacy in the Church; charity, demonstrated by its many martyrs; and hope, represented by Granadinos' adherence to the doctrine of the Immaculate Conception. These secular merits and theological virtues mark Granada as "the new Jerusalem, and new delight of the world" in the same way that saints, martyrs, and monasteries characterize the Granadino *civitas christiana* in the city histories of Antolínez, Bermúdez, and others.[73]

Perhaps the most comprehensive representation of Granada as a New Jerusalem is that of Luis Tello de Olivares, a secular priest who, in 1640, explicated the description of the celestial city in Revelations 21 as an allegory for the newly restored Granada.[74] The twelve gems that adorn the foundations of the heavenly city are replicated in Granada's own dozen precious stones—that is, the numerous parallels between Granadino and sacred history. The creation of Granada's municipal council imitates the establishment of the Sanhedrin, for example, while, like the luminous celestial city that needs no physical sun or moon for light, postconquest Granada enjoys two metaphorical celestial spheres: a beautiful sun—Ferdinand—and a resplendent moon—Isabella.[75] Such images reiterate the royalist rhetoric of the Toma ceremony, highlighting the special relationship between the victorious monarchs and the grateful city and tracing its roots in local and universal history. God, argues Fernando de Sosa, preserved Granada as a prize for the Catholic Monarchs, who, in fighting for it, joined the ranks of saints and righteous princes who struggled against the oppressors of the Church.[76] Just as David founded his city upon the fortress of Sion, claims Francisco de Paula de la Madriz in 1669, "*Haec est civitas Ferdinandi, & Elisabeth,* say I, gazing at Granada: this is the city of Ferdinand and Isabella."[77]

The Toma and the Torre

The hyperbolic language of the Toma sermons was unique neither to this celebration nor to Granada. In cities throughout early modern Europe, patriotic preachers evoked the glories of the celestial Jerusalem to describe and praise their own communities. Jaime Servera, for example, likened Valencia to a "mystical [House of] Sion," and Jean-Pierre Camus described his native Paris as "the city of perfect beauty, the joy of all the earth, the glory of Jerusalem, the holy Church, the delight of Israel, of Catholics, and the honor of the faithful people."[78] The heavenly Jerusalem provided a traditional and accessible symbolic vocabulary for civic panegyric that echoed and complemented the imagery of Granada as an ancient Christian republic found in the city histories. Unlike Bermúdez and Antolínez, however, the preachers of the Toma concern themselves less with continuity between ancient and modern Granada, and more with the fall of the city as a moment of epochal shift. The representation of Granada as a New Jerusalem bolsters this interpretation by figuring the conquest as a spiritual triumph by martial means.

Although the Toma sermons tend to emphasize the disjuncture between Muslim Granada and Christian Granada, the New Jerusalem, they do not sever all connections between past and present. Like the city histories, the sermons tie the modern city to its newly recovered Christian antiquity, and, as in the city histories, the Sacromonte is the point of overlap between past and present. Basing themselves upon the *thema*'s invective against Jerusalem for executing prophets and missionaries, they link ancient and modern Granada through the blood of martyrs. Granada, argues Francisco de Cardera in 1762, was twice conquered for Christianity: once by St. James and St. Cecilio, and once, using the same sword of faith, by Ferdinand and Isabella. The martyrs of ancient Granada are the celestial protectors of the earthly Jerusalem, the Christian city of Granada; their death, notes Juan Galvarro in 1611, was the price paid for the increase of the faithful: "On this day, at the cost of the blood of so many martyrs, of so many apostles, whose ashes we see today on the Sacromonte of this city, the faithful of this kingdom were won."[79] Despite the modernity of the city's return to Christianity and the relatively recent arrival of many of its citizens, the civic self-consciousness articulated in the Toma is truly ancient and not merely Old Christian. In the light of the discoveries on the Sacromonte, the Toma preachers recall to the collective memory of Granadinos not just the conquest but the whole of their city's Christian heritage and the protection of their newly recovered patron saints.

The saints of the Sacromonte are not the only supernatural advocates interceding in the conquest. The voices of St. Cecilio and his companions, who "at this time were shouting to Heaven from the caverns and caves of the Sacromonte," are joined by that of the protomartyr St. Stephen, whose relic lay hidden in the Torre Turpiana, "and I think because of this," says Fernando de Sosa in 1621, "they achieved victory on the day of his octave."[80] The Church celebrates the feast of St. Stephen, the first recorded Christian martyr (Acts 6–8), on December 26, while his octave falls on January 2, the day of the Toma. The felicitous coincidence between the relics of the Torre Turpiana and the anniversary celebration of the surrender suggests that the forgers of the initial discoveries intended not only to document the existence of St. Cecilio but also to draw attention to Granada's debt of gratitude owed to St. Stephen.

St. Stephen does not seem to have enjoyed much popularity in Granada before the discoveries in 1588. Although he is named as a dedicatee in the papal bull of 1501 that established parishes in Granada, there existed no known church under his advocation.[81] There was, however, a long-standing practice in southern Spain of civic patronage by saints associated with the Christian conquest, as well as a more recent tradition that a church dedicated to the saint had existed in Granada in the early centuries of Christianity.[82] A seventh-century inscription, discovered around 1581 in the course of excavations for the foundation of the church of St. Mary of the Alhambra, records the dedication of a basilica to St. Stephen.[83] The discovery of such a document lent additional credibility to the pious fraud of the Torre Turpiana, committed only a few years later. Equally suggestive is a comment of local historian Pedro Velarde de Rivera, who urges that Granada construct a shrine to St. Stephen, "as there was in its beginnings in this city in the street of the Alcazaba."[84] This remark may indicate a belief among some early modern Granadinos that Granada enjoyed a long-standing, even ancient relationship with the saint—a relationship in need of renewal. A well-known legend credited St. Stephen with the rescue of a Christian nobleman held captive in the Muslim city in the twelfth century, and according to Velarde and his fellow historian Pedro Guerra de Lorca, St. Stephen also interceded on behalf of Granada by preventing the Moriscos of the city from joining the uprising that began on his feast day in 1568. Both urge Granadinos to venerate St. Stephen and honor him as a patron of the city.[85]

The choice of St. Stephen as a relic donor for the forgeries of the Torre Turpiana was evidently strategic and suggests that the forgers sought to advance his cult as well as that of St. Cecilio. The conjunction of the octave, his earthly remains, and an existing festival would have ensured a prominent place for the saint in the hearts and minds of the faithful. Certainly, the significance of the connection between the Torre Turpiana and the Toma was not lost on Granadinos. In 1589, one year after the recovery of the lead box containing the parchment and relics, sculptors Pablo de Rojas, Diego de Aranda, Diego de Navas, and Pedro de Raxis created a new retable for the chapel housing the statue of Granada's tutelary virgin, Our Lady of la Antigua. A gift from Isabella to the cathedral of Granada, the fifteenth-century German statue depicts the Virgin holding the child in her arms and a pomegranate (a *granada*) in her left hand. Popular tradition closely associated this miracle-working image with the Christian conquest: according to legend, fleeing Christians hid the "Visigothic" statue from invading

Moors in a cave between Ávila and Segovia. Discovered centuries later, the statue was venerated in Segovia and adopted by Isabella. The Virgin of la Antigua was "patron of this city, and even of the whole kingdom, since the Catholic Monarchs conquered Granada with her, carrying her in their camp."[86] The new retable coupled the Virgin of la Antigua—an image redolent of the triumph of the original Toma—with the patron saints associated with Granada's newly discovered and documented antiquity: St. Cecilio, St. Stephen, St. John the Evangelist, and St. Gregory of Baetica.[87] The chapter chose to install the relics of St. Stephen and the Virgin in 1601 as part of the Toma ceremony. Later, in 1603, the city council petitioned the cathedral chapter for permission to incorporate the relic of St. Stephen into the Toma festivities for the following year. The chapter apparently rejected the request.[88]

Some preachers find in the overlap between St. Stephen and the Toma a solution to the challenging Gospel reading of the day. Dwelling as it does on destruction and death, the *thema* is a problematic foundation for a sermon that celebrates restoration and victory. We have seen that it provides a convenient framework for interpretation of the historical events of the Toma. The *thema* is also the starting point for the sermons' moral and doctrinal content. Some preachers also use the *thema* and St. Stephen as a starting point for wider considerations of martyrs and martyrdom in general. A full third of Juan Galvarro's address in 1611, for instance, considers the intersections between missionaries and martyrdom, while Fernando de Sosa's 1621 sermon develops an elaborate metaphor of the martyr as a bullfighter in the arena of the world. Historians Manuel Barrios Aguilera and Valeriano Sánchez Ramos have suggested that there existed a "mentality of martyrdom" in Granadino society after 1570—a religious and social cult of martyrdom centered in the Alpujarras among the Old Christian survivors and descendants of victims of Morisco aggression in 1568. Under the initiative of Pedro de Castro and succeeding archbishops, the ecclesiastical establishment in the city of Granada exploited and encouraged these sentiments, linking the modern martyrs with their legendary ancient predecessors as part of the larger ideological program promoting the Christianization and Castilianization of Granada.[89]

It seems likely that this peculiar religious mentality of the Granadino periphery played a role in the metropolis as well and may have been a factor behind the doctrinal lessons and historical interpretations in the Toma sermons. However, the ideological agenda behind the Granadino Church's encouragement of a "mentality of martyrdom" operated within the wider context of an ongoing renaissance in Counter-Reformation Catholicism of devotion to martyrs, both ancient and modern, as examples of heroic triumph in suffering. Seventeenth-century art, literature, and sacred oratory laid out in gory detail the torments of the ancient and modern martyrs, whose heroism and exaltation in the midst of pain elevated the mind to the contemplation of the glory they attained.[90] "Thus," declaims Fernando de Sosa, "the plaza being the world, and the bulls the tyrants, and the body the cape of the soul, what would it be for the body of the holy martyr to come under the power and hands of the impious tyrant, who flogs, tears, and kills it? [It would be] to leave the cape on the horns of the bull [i.e., to escape to Heaven, triumphant]."[91] Granada's Toma preachers find indirect support for their interpretation of the conquest as more a triumph of faith and religion than of might by stressing the paradoxical victory of the Christian martyr over the oppression of tyrants, infidels, and heretics.

Most scholars of baroque festival culture have attended primarily to the extraordinary festival—the royal entry, the canonization, the relic translation—and the annual extravaganza of Corpus Christi, both characterized by lavish display and ephemeral architecture, rather than the more restrained celebrations like the Toma that also ordered local calendars. Like its better-known and more extravagant fellows, the annual commemorative festival could act as a persuasive device, a means of marshaling consensus and consent. Through procession, ritual, and sermons, the Toma ceremony instructed participants and onlookers alike in the claims to political orthodoxy and legitimacy made by some of the city's most powerful governing institutions.[92] The city council and cathedral chapter paraded their royal origins through the streets to the sound of trumpets and fireworks—a characteristic of the early modern festival and a potent reminder of the festival patron's power and wealth—and ensured their continuity with the legitimating past through its reenactment.[93] Until 1588, however, that past was abbreviated, reaching back less than a century to the conquest of the city. With the recovery of the relics and the parchment from the Torre Turpiana, although the ritual elements of the Toma left the original historical narrative of Christian conquest and Castilian institutions fixed and intact, the sermons stretched the boundaries of remembrance—the constitutive narrative of Granadino community and communal identity—to encompass a shadowy but effective antiquity.

Some other local festivities touched tangentially on Granada's past; the ephemeral decorations for Corpus Christi, for example, sometimes included representations of St. Cecilio and his fellow martyrs, St. James, the conquest of Granada, the defeated Muslims, and the victorious Catholic Monarchs, alongside the customary images of scenes from the Old and New Testaments, allegories of divine love, the doctrine of the Real Presence and other mysteries of the Eucharist. The Toma's central concern with history, however, made it unique among the many celebrations included in Granada's civic liturgy.[94] This emphasis on the past, both ancient and modern, lent a particular cast to the civic community of Granada as it was constituted in the festivity. On one level, the procession and ceremonies in the Royal Chapel ritually described the elementary components of temporal, earthly Granadino society—civil and ecclesiastical authorities, governors and governed—rendering visible their legitimacy through the reenactment of their historical origins. On another level, the ceremony and sermons represented that same society as a holy community—a New Jerusalem, a *civitas christiana*—founded upon the triumph of Catholic faith over Muslim infidelity. Like the Corpus Christi procession, which celebrated both the miracle of divine love and unity (manifested in the Eucharist) and that of communal love and unity (manifested in the exaltation of the Host), the Toma publicly reaffirmed Granada's faith and ritually reconstituted the city as a sacred, Christian community through the reenactment of its beginnings.

Membership in this sacred community was both expansive and sharply delimited. While the city council and cathedral chapter maintained pride of place and probably limited access to the ceremonies, the procession from the cathedral to the Royal Chapel was accessible to actors and audience, literate and illiterate alike. At the same time, the Toma rendered manifest the real distinctions of status that existed between Granada's elites and nonelites, and the internal struggles within the ranks of the privileged. In theory, however, the Toma described an inclusive community, "all the people, the small and the great, the low and the high, nobles and plebeians," united in faith and thanksgiving.[95] The origins it celebrated were, at least potentially, the common heritage of all Granadinos—all except the Moriscos, the descendants of the vanquished. Despite baptism and acculturation, most Moriscos remained "domestic enemies," forever excluded from a community unified through the ritually constructed memory of religious and military triumph.[96] Since there are no Morisco commentaries on the Toma, we can only guess at how Granada's Morisco inhabitants experienced the festivity. What contestatory memories of the conquest of Granada they may have had we cannot know.[97]

The sources from which people draw the images and ideas with which they imagine their community, both past and present, can be diverse in the extreme. Speaking of twentieth-century Americans, the historian Carl Becker observed that people patch the past together "from things learned at home and in school, from knowledge gained in business or profession, from newspapers glanced at, from books (yes, even history books) read or heard of, from remembered scraps of newsreels or educational films or *ex-cathedra* utterances of presidents and kings, from fifteen-minute discourses on the history of civilization broadcast by courtesy . . . of Pepsodent, the Bulova Watch Company, or the Shepard Stores in Boston."[98] Much the same can be said for early modern Granadinos, to whom the annual reenactment and oratorical interpretation of Granada's semi-legendary conquest offered an important source for ideas and images with which to imagine their city and themselves.

Though it remained a familiar feature of Granada's festival calendar, by the end of the eighteenth century the Toma had fallen into decline. In the 1880s, as the centerpiece of Granada's celebration of the quatercentenary of its conquest, enthusiasts revived the ceremony as a potent symbol of Spanish imperial might and national unity—an interpretation also preferred by the Franco regime.[99] A new ceremonial, drawn up in 1938, increased the nationalist overtones of the Toma, specifying that with each dip of the banner before the tombs of the Catholic Monarchs, a military band should play the opening bars of the national anthem.[100] Today, several decades after the death of Franco, although the military escort and the national anthem (usually) remain part of the ceremony, there is little consensus among Granadinos about the meaning and value of the Toma. In 1992 and successive years, the local and national press have debated just what the Toma commemorates—national unification, or religious bigotry, genocide, and "ethnic cleansing." Protests and counterprotests have become as traditional a part of the festivities as the procession or the banner waving in the Royal Chapel.[101] Today's openly divisive and contested Toma echoes that of early modern Granada, in which ceremony and sermon both celebrated an idealized civic community founded upon faith and reaffirmed the real differences that divided Granadino society. At the spiritual center of this New Jerusalem lay the Sacromonte; its place in local piety is the topic of the next chapter.

CHAPTER FIVE

The *Plomos* and the Sacromonte in Granadino Piety

Who is so deaf that he has not heard of this city's reputation for religion?

—*Francisco Bermúdez de Pedraza*

On April 3, 1624, the Wednesday of Holy Week, as part of a protracted tour through Andalusia, Philip IV entered the city of Granada to the sound of cheers and artillery accolades. Accompanied by his favorite, the Count-Duke of Olivares, and an extensive entourage of grandees, the monarch took up residence in the Alhambra. On Holy Thursday, in the fortress's famous Comares Hall, Philip performed the ritual lavation of the feet of a dozen selected paupers. The king finally ventured out of the Alhambra on Saturday. Rather than descending into the city below, Philip took the road toward Guadix to make the "station" of the Sacromonte. During his visit, "as devout as it was admirable," the king toured the facilities, venerated the relics of St. Cecilio and his companions, and placed the final seal upon the tomb of Pedro de Castro, who had died in late December of the previous year. The following day, Easter Sunday, representatives of the Abbey of the Sacromonte, the Chancery, the city council, and the archbishop brought the lead books to the Alhambra for private viewing by Philip, Olivares, and the papal nuncio.[1] Over the next few days, the king visited some of Granada's other important religious institutions, including the cathedral, the monasteries of St. Jerome and St. Dominic, the Jesuit college, and the Carthusian monastery outside the city walls. He finally departed the city on Wednesday, April 10, having extracted a substantial subsidy of 20,000 ducats from the city council, as well as other donations from the Abbey of the Sacromonte and other religious houses.[2]

Referring to the travels of England's Elizabeth I, Clifford Geertz has noted how kingly journeys confirm royal dominance: "Royal progresses . . . locate the society's center and affirm its connection with transcendent things by stamping a territory with ritual signs of dominance. When kings journey around the countryside, making appearances, attending fêtes, conferring honors, exchanging gifts, or defying rivals, they mark it, like some wolf or tiger spreading his scent through his territory, as almost physically part of them."[3] Whereas Philip's long Andalusian journey left the imprint of royal power across this part of southern Spain, his tours within the cities hint at another exchange. In each of the cities he visited, Philip pursued a "sacred" itinerary similar to the one he followed in Granada. Much as his father, Philip III, had done when he traveled to Valencia in 1599, "the king worshiped at locales that embodied the spiritual dimensions of regional identity."[4] Philip IV's pilgrimage to the Sacromonte—the very first stop on his tour of local religious institutions—suggests that the monarch may have sought the protection of Granada's patron saints. Like his grandfather Philip II, who filled the Escorial with relics collected from towns and villages throughout the peninsula, the king recognized and affirmed local religious cultures, even as he made them his own. Philip IV's visit confirmed his patronage over the Sacromonte, but also affirmed the importance of the shrine in Granadino religious life and communal identity.

Throughout the early modern period, the Sacromonte stood as but one of several devotional and cultic expressions of communal identity that developed around the *plomos*. The potent presence of the remains of St. Cecilio and his companions and the events that came both before and after their recovery redrew the map of Granada's sacred geography. As a new, local holy site, the geographic center of Granadinos' collective memory of their city's ancient past, the Sacromonte became a principal symbol of the religious aspects of Granadino identity. St. Cecilio too figured as an important symbol of communal self-consciousness, as Granadinos celebrated their invented ancient historical traditions through his cult and through the defense of the *plomos*. These same historical traditions also transformed the universal veneration of the Immaculate Conception of the Virgin Mary into a devotion indigenous to Granada. Together, these devotional discourses reveal some of the intersections between Granadino communal cohesion and identity and the invented past documented by the *plomos*.

"This Mountain with Crosses Crowned"

Prior to the discoveries on the Sacromonte, Granada's sacred geography was predominantly urban, circumscribed by the city's medieval walls and articulated through the network of parishes and religious houses that extended throughout the city. In Sebastián Martínez's rhymed tour of Granada, published in 1550, the parish churches and monasteries serve the visitor to the city as guideposts. Describing the mazelike Morisco district of the Albaicín, for example, he writes:

> You enter by the Mercedarians / and ascend to the Albaicín / where forever are / the Moriscos segregated / very subjected and restrained / [you go] by St. Bartholomew / where I found myself lost / passing by St. Christopher / looking everywhere / you pass by St. Michael / and then to St. Isabel / and if you don't turn around / you go to St. Nicholas / and from there to St. Gregory / which is well known to all.[5]

The parish churches and religious houses hosted many of Granadinos' daily devotions—the masses, baptisms, marriages, funerals, and private prayers that constituted their more quotidian encounters with the sacred. Some of the religious houses possessed miracle-working images that attracted special veneration. Among these, the most famous were the statues of Our Lady of the Rosary and Our Lady of Hope, both in the Dominican Monastery of Santa Cruz la Real.[6] Urban dwellers also worshiped at the various shrines scattered around the city. Some, for example, visited the shrines of St. Sebastian and St. Anthony of Padua, on the banks of the Genil River, or the popular image of Our Lady of Anguish, which was located in the hermitage of St. Ursula and St. Susanna. Others frequented the hermitage of St. Helen, situated on the hill overlooking the Alhambra, or the nearby shrine dedicated to those Christians who had been martyred during the Islamic centuries. These last two hermitages were among the oldest and most venerated Christian shrines in the city.[7]

At the center of this sacred network, in the newest section of the growing city, were the cathedral, begun in 1523, and the adjacent Royal Chapel, completed in 1521. In the early decades of the sixteenth century, most descriptions of the city devoted particular attention to the newly constructed Royal Chapel, which was built to house the tombs of Ferdinand and Isabella. The Venetian traveler Andrea Navagiero, who visited Granada in 1526, recounted in detail the rich decor and cult of the chapel—the marble tombs, the harmonious choir, the precious artwork—pausing only briefly to note the cathedral under construction next door.[8] By the middle of the sixteenth century, however, most descriptions of Granada figured the dome of the still-incomplete cathedral as the spiritual center of the city. In his Latin panegyric to Granada, Juan de Vilches, a cleric from nearby Antequera writing in the 1530s, described the Royal Chapel as merely adjoining the cathedral, already the geographical and spiritual heart of the city.[9] Sebastián Martínez, a native of the Marquisate of Villena, likewise noted both institutions but gave a greater spiritual role to the cathedral:

> What shines most there / are the entombed kings / who are there enclosed / as those who well deserve them / since a city with such growth / with kings and in such a structure / is not to be found in all of Spain. . . . The cathedral church / where Moorish men and women used to walk / there they say the hours / of the divine mystery / since another such archbishop / and who is so enlightening / is not to be found in all of Spain.[10]

In the stylized panoramic views of Joris Hoefnagel, a Flemish artist who visited the city between 1563 and 1565, the Alhambra and the cathedral dominate the skyline. As was common in early modern city views, Hoefnagel stressed the size of the cathedral in relation to the surrounding buildings and, by extension, its dominance over the other churches marking the Granadino landscape.[11] Like Seville's Giralda tower, the cathedral and the Alhambra stand together as iconic markers identifying the city as Granada.[12]

As the institutional heart of the Granadino Church, the cathedral had a greater official role in people's religious lives than the Royal Chapel. Its miracle-working images—Our Lady of la Antigua and a renowned statue of Christ at the Column —attracted the veneration of the faithful, who also attended the daily masses, weekly sermons, annual and extraordinary festivities, and other functions.[13] However, prior to the discoveries in the Torre Turpiana, the cathedral had no relics that could compete with the famous collection of holy bodies housed in the Royal Chapel. This collection originated in a donation from Queen Isabella. By the late sixteenth century, the chapel's sacred treasure rivaled that of the Escorial. Highlights included fragments of the True Cross, thorns from the crown worn by Christ and dried flecks of his blood, and milk and hairs from the Virgin Mary. The treasure also included thousands of lesser relics, as well as the royal remains of Ferdinand of Aragon and Isabella of Castile, their daughter, Juana "the Mad," and her husband, Philip "the Handsome," and the Empress Isabella, wife of Charles V.[14] Together, these saintly and regal bodies marked the Royal Chapel as an important locus of spiritual and secular power within the city and as a potent challenge to the cathedral chapter's dominance. Sebastián Martínez, an elderly priest who testified before the panel of inquiry into the Sacromonte finds, claimed that in the 1560s the cathedral chapter sought to redress the situation and supply it-self with relics. Supposedly, during a visit to Italy as part of Archbishop Pedro Guerrero's delegation to the Council of Trent, the chapter's representative begged Pope Pius IV to give him the body of a saint to take back to Granada. The pope put off the request, telling the petitioner to "go to those mountains of Granada, and take up a handful of dirt and squeeze it, and out will come blood of mar-tyrs."[15] The recovery of the relics of the Torre Turpiana offered the cathedral clergy an opportunity to strengthen the primacy of the cathedral over its rival. By secur-ing for itself the relics recovered from the Torre Turpiana—the arm of St. Stephen, the handkerchief of the Virgin Mary, and the parchment with St. John's new apocalypse—the chapter bolstered the cathedral's sacred aura and attracted the veneration of the faithful. The Marian relic in particular became one of the cathedral's most precious treasures and was regularly exhibited on the feast of the Assumption (August 15) and paraded through the streets in times of national or local distress.[16]

While the Torre Turpiana finds reinforced the cathedral's prominence within the city walls, the discoveries on the Sacromonte effected a reconfiguration of Granada's spiritual geography by establishing a new sacred center outside the ur-ban bounds. For adherents, the holiness of the place and the objects found there were so manifest as to easily sway the most stubborn skeptic: "Seeing the moun-tain, the place, the caverns, the fire, the books and relics," argued an anonymous apologist in 1617, "the mind convinces itself and surrenders to this fact, that it is true. Let them come see it; all will surrender."[17] Those who did come and see it reinforced the sanctity of the terrain. Attentive to the dictum that the *vox populi* is also the *vox Dei,* defenders and devotees often pointed to Granadinos' sponta-neous response to the discoveries as proof of the holiness of the Sacromonte and its relics. The miraculous healings on the hillside also offered strong evidence that the Sacromonte was a site of saintly power. As the "seal and signature of God," miracles testified to the authentic holiness of the relics and of the site where they were discovered.[18]

Marvelous cures and popular devotion were not, however, the only evidence for the sanctity of the Sacromonte. The dossier of the official inquiry into the dis-coveries also includes many depositions about signs seen *before* the relics were revealed. These presages consisted primarily of strange lights seen upon the mountain—some alone, some in procession. Witnesses from all walks of life, from shepherds to tradesmen to Archbishop Castro himself, described mysteri-ous resplendences either at the place where the caves were later uncovered, or moving toward it.[19] Some, like the silk merchant Diego de Angulo, a resident of the parish of St. Mary Magdalene, claimed to have seen strange lights traveling out from the Albaicín toward the uninhabited hillside only a few months before the discoveries. Similarly, the Morisco translator Miguel de Luna reported that some eight months prior to the revelations, while recovering from illness in his house near the hillside, he twice witnessed a great light reflected on the hillside across the valley, opposite the Sacromonte. Neither lightning nor a comet, the light "seemed to flash like an eagle taking flight before a big fire."[20] Others reported resplendences occurring years before the discoveries. Juana de Loaysa, the elderly prioress of the Dominican convent of St. Catherine of Zafra, together with several of her nuns, testified to having seen strange lights on the mountain many times over the previous sixteen years, while Francisco de Molina, a beneficed priest of St. Mary of the Alhambra, claimed to have seen such phenomena repeatedly during the past twenty-five years.[21] The report of such portentous luminous apparitions strengthened the case for the relics' authenticity, establishing the Sacromonte as a place of supernatural power before the discoveries.

Grounded in time, the Sacromonte was also grounded in tradition. The marvelous lights tied the previously unremarkable hill to existing local legends about St. Cecilio and the location of his body. While local tradition held that St. Cecilio's resting place was lost and unknown, his body was thought to lie somewhere near Granada, perhaps near the Roman ruins in the nearby hills known as the Sierra Elvira. One witness, the shoemaker Francisco Gómez, reported that, while visiting the Discalced Carmelite monastery near the Alhambra one night in 1593, he saw across the plain on the distant Sierra Elvira a luminous procession similar to those he had also seen on the Sacromonte. A companion suggested that "it is the body of St. Cecilio, which shows itself around those parts."[22] Other witnesses asserted that St. Cecilio's body had been thought to lie somewhere within the city of Granada. When questioned about the legends surrounding the location of the saint's body, cathedral canon Diego Maldonado replied that the common tradition, which he had learned from his relatives and older residents, was that the body was in Granada, "and this is as clear as the noonday sun."[23] Thus, within Granada's majority immigrant Christian population there does not seem to have existed any tradition linking the saint to the Sacromonte—that is, to the specific place where his relics were found; instead, the connection was made retrospectively through the strange luminescences reported to have been seen there. The hill seems to have been little valued prior to the finds. The board of inquiry asked many witnesses what they knew about the site and whether they knew of caves existing there before the discoveries. Most respondents replied that they knew nothing about the hill, nor had they ever heard of any caves there before 1595.[24] Their descriptions of the Valparaíso, as the area around the Sacromonte was known before the discovery of the relics and the lead books, tended to stress the barrenness of the terrain, unfit even for livestock and producing nothing but wild thyme and other herbs.[25]

Some testimony, however, suggests that for Granada's Morisco minority, the Sacromonte had a long-standing reputation as a sacred site. Juan Trincado de Montoya, a resident of the Albaicín parish of St. John, reported that, before the Morisco uprising of 1568, the site where the caves were later revealed was known for its healing powers. Friends and family would bring to the site articles of clothing that belonged to sick persons and then return them to their owners in the hopes of obtaining a cure.[26] The constable (*alguacil*) Luis de Contreras testified that he had heard from a Morisca folk healer that herbs collected from the same location were particularly potent remedies.[27] Moreover, according to the constable, old Moriscos had told him that there had been a *rábita,* or Muslim hermitage, on the hill, which they called "Ravine of the Christians" and "Hill of the Burned One."[28] Other witnesses before the board of inquiry corroborated and elaborated on these accounts. Salvador de Mendoza, a Morisco, informed the panel that while he had never heard of any caves on the hillside, about fifty years before, his late uncle had told him that the ruins then standing on the mountain were the remains of a *rábita* called "Abenfodail," constructed by a reformed bandit once much feared as a rapist. Further up the slope, his uncle told him, on the site of the holy caves, had been another hermitage called "Rábita del Maxoroch," or "Hermitage of the Burned One," "but they did not tell him why they called it the Hermitage of the Burned, or if the person who had been burned was Moor or Christian, or whether burned for good or ill, nor did he ask."[29] Two other, elderly witnesses, Juan Fernández Megía and Alonso Melgarejo, testified that the Moriscos had called the area where the caves now stood "Andacachene," or "Gully of the Christians."[30] Hieronymo de Escobar, a beneficed priest in the parish of St. Gregory the Great, reported that

> the common people native to the city, the Moriscos, commonly called that hill "Gar Almahroc," which means "burned cave" or "the cave of the burned one," the reason for which he does not know, and that the Morisco laborers and peasants, natives of the kingdom, called it "Raz Alnar," which means "the hill or head of fire" because the peasants said that they often saw fires and resplendences there at night . . . and that the Old Christians conducted no business on this mountain, and there was never livestock on this mountain, nor did [the livestock] rest or sleep there.[31]

Alonso Flores, an elderly Morisco gardener, confirmed that the Morisco taboo against grazing livestock on the Sacromonte was due to the rumor that the mountain contained "*zulaha,* which in our language means saints."[32] None of the witnesses interviewed had ever heard of caves on the Sacromonte, though two witnesses did mention that there had been caves both at the foot of the hill and further up the slope, above the site where the relics and lead books were found. Cristobál de Palacios, a Morisco, testified that the upper caverns had once been home to a Muslim hermit called Hábito.[33]

The testimony collected by the board of inquiry into the authenticity of the relics suggests that the Sacromonte's status as a locus of the sacred had deep roots in Granada's Morisco community. For Moriscos, the Sacromonte was no mere barren hillside—it was charged both with myth and with the memory of a sacred geography quite different from that imagined by their immigrant neighbors. A century after the conquest of the city, and some twenty-five years after the exile of most of the minority population in the wake of the Revolt of the Alpujarras, the remnant of Granada's Moriscos recalled a hermitage or shrine long since vanished and a terrain made sacred by the hidden presence of holy bodies, perhaps Christian, perhaps Muslim—the *zulaha* (ṣulaḥāʾ, saints) mentioned by Alonso Flores.

The witness testimony offers several leads for possible identifications of the name and nature of the remembered sacred site. Witness Salvador de Mendoza's hermitage "Abenfodail" appears in a 1503 list of the *habices*—urban and rural lands dedicated to the upkeep of medieval Granada's mosques and community institutions, later confiscated by the Christian authorities after the Muslim uprising of 1499—as a *rábita* named "Ibn Fodayl." While a list from 1505 locates the *rábita* of Ibn Fodayl within the city walls, in the Axares sector of the Albaicín, the 1503 list of *habices* situates the hermitage "upon the hills of the Darro [River]"—a general description that includes the Sacromonte and its environs.[34] The "Andacachene" described by witnesses Juan Fernández Megía and Alonso Melgarejo offers other possibilities. A similar name appears in the lists of *habices* as "Handachaçena," a piece of confiscated land assigned for the upkeep of the church in Cenes de la Vega, a small town on the Genil River, not far from Granada.[35] While the early sixteenth-century *habices* lists do not specify the exact location of the property, a 1572 inventory of confiscated Morisco properties in Cenes de la Vega alludes to a site called "Handacacenegi," on the left side of the Genil, "at the beginning of the route to Granada"—which is nowhere near the Sacromonte.[36] However, an eyewitness account of the discovery and translation of the *plomos*, written in Arabic in the 1630s by the Morisco scholar Aḥmad ibn

Qāsim ibn al-Ḥajarī, names their discovery site as *Khandaq al-janna,* a name that corresponds to the Sacromonte's original Castilian name of *Valparaíso,* or Valley of Paradise.[37] The name does not seem to have any connection with Christians.

The place-name "Rábita del Maxoroch" or "Gar Almahroc"—that is, Gār al-Mahrūq, Cave of the Burned One—presents greater difficulties. In his account of his visit to Andalusia in 1350, the famous traveler Ibn Baṭṭūṭa describes a visit to Sufi leader Abū ʿAlī ʿUmar, "son of the pious shaikh, the saint Abū ʿAbdallāh Muḥammad, b. al-Mahrūq (the burnt)," in whose lodge or *zāwiya* outside the city he stayed for several days.[38] Could the Gar Almahroc described by the witnesses in 1595 be the Sufi lodge visited by Ibn Baṭṭūṭa?[39] The question is complicated by conflicting references to similarly named or related sites within Muslim Granada. Ibn Baṭṭūṭa also relates a visit to another, different *zāwiya* of a member of the same eminent family. This *zāwiya,* called al-Lidjām, the Bridle, was located "at the top of the suburb of Najd outside Granada and adjoining Mount Sabīka (the Ingot)."[40] Luis Seco de Lucena Paredes has pinpointed the location of a different *rábita* called *rābiṭat al-Wazīr al-Mahrūq,* or the *rábita* of the Vizir al-Mahrūq, within the city in the Najd district, now known as the Realejo.[41] Moreover, Fray José de Sigüenza, a sixteenth-century chronicler of the Hieronymite Order, records the existence of a *rábita* called "the hermitage of the burned one," upon the foundations of which was built Granada's Hieronymite monastery shortly after the conquest of the city. This monastery was located on the other side of the city, outside the city walls.[42] Finally, a *rábita* called "Maharoc" appears in the lists of *habices,* but its location is unspecified.[43]

These multiple and contradictory references suggest that there may have been more than one site in Granada associated with the Mahrūq name. However, it may also be that the appellation is tied not to the Mahrūq clan but to the name's parallel connection to burning and fire. The name "Raz Alnar," or "Rās al-Nār," mountain of fire, appears to be tied to the hillside's long-standing reputation for strange lights and resplendences at night. In the Christian tradition, mysterious lights were common signs that indicated ground sanctified by the blood and bodies of martyrs. Perhaps the best-known Iberian example of such luminous markers involved the supernatural lights that, in 813, revealed the location of the remains of St. James. In early modern Andalusia, witnesses in Córdoba in 1575 saw similar illuminations indicating the locations of the relics of SS. Fausto, Ianuario, and Marcial. In Arjona in the 1630s, dozens of townspeople reported the appearance of strange lights marking the site of the martyrs SS. Bonoso and Maximiano.[44] Granadino historian Pedro Guerra de Lorca reported that he himself had seen the marvelous lights that descended from the sky each May to illuminate the place in ancient Acci (Guadix) where St. Torcuato had suffered martyr-dom.[45]

Muslims too associated supernatural lights with the graves of saints and prophets. Across the Muslim world, saints and prophets both living and dead exercised *baraka*, or spiritual power. After death, the tomb became the center of the saint's continuing power, revealed in portents and miracles. In medieval Muslim hagiography, mysterious illuminations commonly announced the locations of lost and forgotten holy tombs, revealing loci of *baraka*. A bright light shining out of a grave near the town of Beskra, in northeastern Algeria, revealed the site to be the tomb of the prophet Khalid.[46] Late medieval Egyptian guides to the holy tombs in Cairo's famous al-Qarafa graveyard related many stories of holy tombs revealed by strange illuminations. A column of light marked the lost tomb of al-Sayyida al-Sharīfa Maryam, for example, and the tomb of the unknown saint known as "ṣāḥib al-nūr," the "possessor of the light," was indicated by the shaft of light that marked his tomb on Friday nights. Mysterious candles and lamps marked the graves of still other unknown saints.[47] Even some opponents of the cult of saints, like the reforming Hanbalite scholar Ibn Taimiyya (d. 1328), admitted that "the miracles of prophets and saints, such as the descent of lights and angels upon their graves, . . . these things are all true."[48] Similar tales of saintly lights were told in early twentieth-century Morocco. The shrines of Sidi Boqnadel and Sidi al-Mahfi shone at night, as did trees associated with the saints Sidi l-Hosni and Sidi Ahmed Marrui. In Doukkala, *"ignis fatuus* in a desert place is often taken for the sign of an unknown saint having died there; the people make a *mzâra* on the spot and worship the saint under the name of Sîdi l-Grib, 'My lord the Stranger.'"[49]

Across the Muslim world, such holy graves and other sites associated with saints were the focus of *ziyāra*, local pilgrimages or visits by pious individuals. In medieval Granada, too, local people regularly visited the many shrines and hermitages outside the city.[50] During his stay in Granada Ibn Baṭṭūṭa visited one "of renowned sanctity," located on the nearby Sierra Elvira—precisely the place where witnesses reported seeing mysterious lights nearly 250 years later.[51] Their testimony, like that of the other respondents before the panel of inquiry, strongly suggests that, long before the discovery of St. Cecilio's body, the Sacromonte was known to Moriscos as a locus of the sacred, a place infused with saintly *baraka*. The witnesses' depositions suggest that the hillside was remembered as the site of some kind of religious structure, perhaps associated with a Sufi sage whose name is now lost. Could it also have been the site of a holy tomb? Burial practices in medieval al-Andalus generally called for interment either in public cemeteries or on private land in or near the cemeteries, and none of Granada's Muslim cemeteries had been located on the Sacromonte.[52] Although most saintly sepulchers were found in cemeteries, however, it was not unknown for venerated holy men to be buried in or near the *rábitas* associated with them.[53] The land where the discoveries occurred was known to have been under Morisco ownership until the 1570s, when it was confiscated by the Crown.[54] The evidence is too fragmentary to support any definitive identifications; at the very least, the hill's curious Morisco names and its reputation for healing powers and mysterious lights hint at a reputation as a locus of the holy that long predated the discoveries of 1595.

The witnesses' depositions situate the Sacromonte as part of a lost Muslim sacred geography, existing now only in legend and memory. The site's Morisco names and legend probably account for the forgers' decision to present St. Cecilio's martyrdom as one by fire and to confect his relics as the calcified remains of an incinerated body. Just as the fabricators of the lead books and relics sought to preserve Morisco culture by coating it with the veneer of Catholicism, so too did their choice of location both invoke and preserve the traditional holiness of the mountain—at the cost of transforming it from a sacred site meaningful primarily to the Morisco population into the center of an immigrant Christian cult. The division between the two communities is not absolute; the accounts of luminous apparitions and Hieronymo de Escobar's reference to "Old Christian" avoidance of the hill offer tantalizing clues to a possible shared body of popular superstitions attached to the Sacromonte before the discoveries. With the recovery of the relics, however, the character of the site was fundamentally transformed. The saint metamorphosed from a mysterious, hidden, and unnamed absence to a tangible presence, named and known. The hill's wonder-working powers came now not from the *baraka* of a Muslim holy man but instead through the *potentia* of St. Cecilio, made present in and emanating from his physical remains.[55]

These redefinitions effected a reconfiguration of Granada's sacred geography, as the Sacromonte became the extramural complement to the intramural sacred terrain dominated by the cathedral. As the sixteenth century gave way to the seventeenth, the Arabic toponyms and the rapidly vanishing world they recalled were forgotten, and the Castilian nomenclature shifted from Valparaíso to Sacromonte, a name redolent of a new memory of an ancient Christian past. What had been, for the immigrant population, a relatively undifferentiated and amorphous *space* became instead a specific and specifically Christian *place*—a locus of memory and local significance.[56] Once sacred to Muslim Granada, now sacred to Catholic

Granada, the Sacromonte became a key site in the city's symbolic landscape, a literal *lieu de mémoire*.[57]

Perhaps the most striking graphic representation of the Sacromonte as a key element of Granada's new sacred geography and of the iconography of Granadino civic self-consciousness was the series of four maps created in the decade that followed the discoveries upon the hillside. The engraved maps were based on drawings made by the architect Ambrosio de Vico at the behest of Archbishop Castro. The maps were probably directed primarily to local consumers but may also have circulated more broadly. The first three may be those used by Archbishop Castro in a presentation about the Sacromonte that he delivered to Philip III in 1609, while the fourth was intended for inclusion in the abortive *Historia eclesiástica* of Justino Antolínez de Burgos.[58] Together, the four maps offer what Richard Kagan has termed a "communicentric" rather than "chorographic" view of Granada: a view that seeks not to represent the city in precise detail but rather to present an idealized topography, laid out in accordance with the imperatives of Granada's new communal imaginary.[59]

Engraved between 1595 and 1604 by Alberto Fernández, a local silversmith, and published in *Relación breve de las reliquias* (Granada, 1608), the first three maps offer a detailed look at the city together with the holy terrain of the Sacromonte (figs. 5.1–5.3).[60] The first map of the series, "Map of the City of Granada to the Sacromonte de Valparaíso," offers a vista of the city and the Sacromonte oriented by the two pilgrimage routes from the city—one passing next to the gardens bordering the Darro River, the other traversing the hills—to the site of the discoveries, where the subterranean caverns are laid bare for the viewer. Located beyond the walls that enclose the city, yet tied to the urban center by the pilgrimage routes, the newly sacred site is shown to be the target of the devotion of pious Granadinos. While the city itself seems empty, its churches, monasteries, and medieval walls its only landmarks, the paths appear crowded with penitents making their way toward the Sacromonte. The sacred spot is distinguished by its remoteness from the mundane sphere of the city, and by the thick forest of crosses marking its territory and differentiating it from the adjacent barren hills.

The second map, "Description of the Sacromonte de Valparaíso," zooms in on the Sacromonte hill itself, depicting the paths up the mountain and across the hillsides to the crosses and caves. The road from Granada to Guadix in the lower half of the map separates the farms and gardens from the mountain and distinguishes the profane sphere of human activity from the sacred sphere of divine action. In 1633 Franciscan tertiaries transformed this road into a *via sacra*—a ritual route for commemoration of the Passion—further sacralizing the route from the

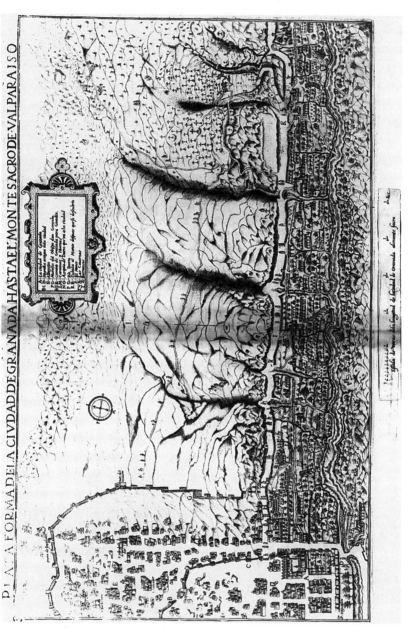

Fig. 5.1. Alberto Fernández, "Map of the City of Granada to the Sacromonte de Valparaíso," in *Relación breve de las reliquias, que se hallaron en la ciudad de Granada en una torre antiquíssima, y en las cavernas del monte Illipulitano de Valparaíso cerca de Granada: sacado del processo, y averigüaciones, que cerca dello se hizieron* (Granada, 1608). Reproduced from Library of Congress, Rare Book and Special Collections Division, BX2315.R4.

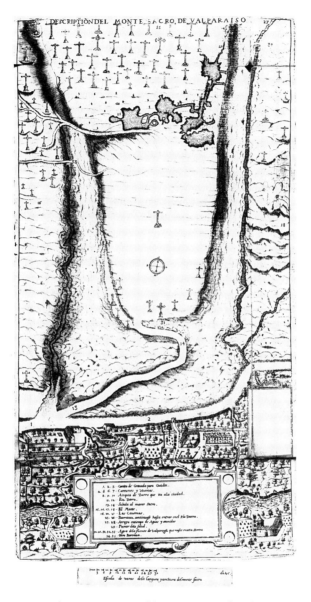

Fig. 5.2. Alberto Fernández, "Description of the Sacromonte de Valparaíso," in *Relación breve de las reliquias, que se hallaron en la ciudad de Granada en una torre antiquíssima, y en las cavernas del monte Illipulitano de Valparaíso cerca de Granada: sacado del processo, y averigüaciones, que cerca dello se hizieron* (Granada, 1608). Reproduced from Library of Congress, Rare Book and Special Collections Division, BX2315.R4.

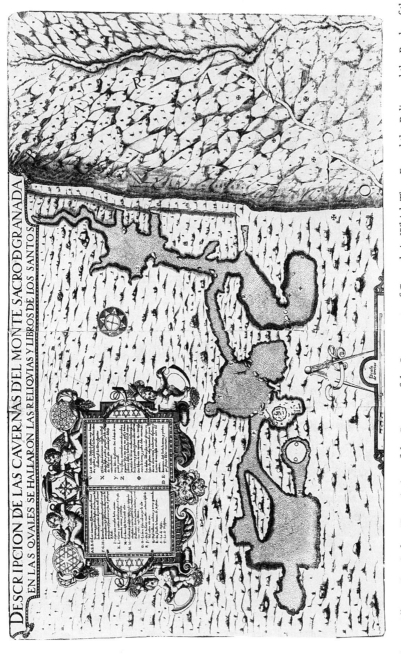

Fig. 5.3. Alberto Fernández, "Description of the Caverns of the Sacromonte of Granada in Which They Found the Relics and the Books of the Saints," in *Relación breve de las reliquias, que se hallaron en la ciudad de Granada en una torre antiquíssima, y en las cavernas del monte Illipulitano de Valparaíso cerca de Granada: sacado del processo, y averigüaciones, que cerca dello se hizieron* (Granada, 1608). Reproduced from Library of Congress, Rare Book and Special Collections Division, BX2315.R4.

city to the Sacromonte.[61] The third map of the series, "Description of the Caverns of the Sacromonte of Granada in Which They Found the Relics and the Books of the Saints," focuses still closer, examining in minute detail the layout of the caves. Letters and a key decorated with the "Solomonic" seals from the lead books mark the original locations of the books and relics.

Together, the three maps document and advance the establishment of the Sacromonte as a religious center for Christian Granada. The Sacromonte described in these cartographic texts is steeped in an ancient Christian past and imbued with a miraculous present. It has become a terrain replete with local meaning: *here* lay the ashes of the city's founder in the faith, *here* the strange and holy texts, *here* the paths beaten by the bare feet of the thousands who came to pray in the caverns. These specifics mark the represented territory as a locally meaningful place and invite the viewer to meditate upon the ancient and the modern pilgrimages by which those meanings and that place were created.[62] The careful depiction of the pilgrimage routes and the crosses marking the hillside recall the processions and festivities and the miracles and illuminations—the practices and experiences that transformed the Sacromonte from a site of Morisco meaning into a place laden with significance for Granada's immigrant Christian population. Places, as Edward Casey has reminded us, are also events—meetings of space and time experienced in the body.[63] These maps recall those experiences, the lived stuff out of which Granadinos created the Sacromonte and, with it, a new communal self-consciousness.

The fourth map, the famous "Plataforma" of the city of Granada, was created in 1613 by engraver Franz Heylan for Antolínez's ecclesiastical history of the city (fig. 5.4). This map, which remained the only full cartographic representation of Granada until the late eighteenth century, depicts the city in minute detail, from the Hospital of St. Lazarus at the northwestern limit to the Hermitage of St. Sebastian and the Gate of the Mills in the southwest, and from the outer walls and the Tower of the Olive above the Albaicín at the northeastern edge to the irrigation canals and gardens that mark the transition from urban to rural terrain in the southeastern part of Granada. Reflecting the didactic and propagandistic aims of his patron, Castro, Vico presents a municipal vista marked by consecrated sites. Walls and rivers break up the urban expanse, but it is Granada's religious institutions—its parish churches, religious houses, hospitals and shrines—that orient and organize the interior space of the city. At the center of the map, and first on the list of identified monuments, is the cathedral—a huge, incomplete building that dwarfs all of the surrounding structures. The city bears the marks of the

Fig. 5.4. Francisco Heylan, "Map of Granada." Drawn by Ambrosio de Vico. Reproduced from Justino Antolínez de Burgos, *Historia eclesiástica de Granada*, edited Manuel Sotomayor [y Muru] (Granada: Universidad de Granada, 1996).

urban changes of the sixteenth century, with new plazas—the scene of religious festivities and *autos da fe*—and new neighborhoods on a nearly regular grid beyond the boundaries of the old city. The streets of the Albaicín, actually narrow and twisting in the manner of medieval Muslim cities, appear unusually straight, as if Castilianized and Christianized through cartographic artifice.[64]

Vico's map describes Granada's urban terrain as a sacred space, the extension and complement of the rural symbolic landscape of the Sacromonte, which lies just beyond the margins of the map, its direction indicated by a small caption. Vico's city is a spiritual landscape, centered on the cathedral and imbued with religious meanings both parochial and universal: parochial in that its landmarks are local, significant primarily to the inhabitants of this landscape, participants in the local religion enacted in the city's shrines and churches; universal in that, like the city history it was originally meant to illustrate, the propagandistic portrayal of Granada as a contemporary *civitas christiana* was intelligible to an audience of both natives and outsiders.[65] Like the first three maps, the Plataforma gives no hint of any contestatory or alternative geographies. While the landscape described in the witness testimony is a palimpsest of different and overlapping memories and meanings, the maps depict a terrain that is univocal and wholly Christian in character. There are no mosques or *rábitas* in the Plataforma or the Sacromonte views. Instead, they depict a Granada in which, a contemporary annalist noted, "the Morisco [street] names have already been abandoned by its Christian settlers, who orient themselves by means of the parishes."[66]

Together, the four maps sketch the contours of the geography of sanctity in Granada as it developed in the wake of the finds on the Sacromonte, as the discovery of the lead books and relics, and the marvelous phenomena that accompanied them, extended the territory of the sacred from the urban into the rural. They both reflect and foster the ongoing reorganization of Granada's sacred landscape from a terrain in which the physical legacy of Islam must have been constantly evident, into one evocative of the uniquely Christian spiritual heritage constituted and made present in the Sacromonte. This shared heritage was a vital element in the constitution of Granadino civic identity—that is, the symbolically constituted sense of belonging to a deep-rooted community. Membership in that community, however, was limited. While the forgers of the lead books chose a site and a saint that might have guaranteed Morisco cultural survival by merging the separate pasts of the two communities, minority and majority, the discursive elaboration of the finds in local culture—in the maps, for example—offered little room for the Morisco community or its history. The alternative sacred terrain recalled by the Morisco witnesses before the panel of inquiry—a terrain marked by the half-remembered *rábitas*, the ambiguous place-names, the curious legends—left few traces in the new sacred geography of Granada.

"His Foundation Is in the Holy Mountains"

Through the seventeenth century, the Sacromonte stood as a primary symbol of the religious dimensions of Granadino identity. Poets both native and non-native celebrated Granada's Sacromonte. In 1598 the influential Córdoban poet Luis de Góngora penned a poem to "this mountain with crosses crowned," and in 1610 Pedro de Antequera y Arteaga (a resident of Granada, though a native of Alcalá de Henares) erected next to the Elvira Gate, Granada's historic main entrance, a verse inscription in Latin that singled out the Sacromonte for special praise among the many Christian and Castilian "trophies" that adorned the city.[67] For visitors to Granada, the Sacromonte became an obligatory stop on the itinerary of important local monuments and institutions. Papal nuncio Camillo Borghese, who toured Spain in 1594 and 1595, left a laconic tourist's guide to the city: "In Granada, see the plain, the Albaicín, the Chancery and its facade. The Alhambra and in it, the hall of Charles V and where the Albencerages were decapitated. The Sacromonte."[68] "It is the pilgrimage of the Granadinos," said Diego de Cuelvis, who visited Granada in 1599. Cuelvis included the Sacromonte as the final item in a list of Granada's "noteworthy holy things," along with the cathedral (which, tellingly, he mistakenly believed to be dedicated to St. Cecilio), the Royal Chapel, and the Sagrario.[69] Both François Bertaut, a French nobleman who toured Spain in 1659, and Grand Duke Cosimo de' Medici, who visited Granada in 1668, made day trips from the city to the Abbey of the Sacromonte and the sacred caves.[70]

For early modern Granadinos, the Sacromonte stood as a symbol of their city's ancient and modern Christian heritage. The mountain was also the earthly home of St. Cecilio, Granada's patron saint. The discoveries in the Torre Turpiana and on the Sacromonte, the ensuing miraculous healings, and the enthusiastic popular response to the finds marked the (re)establishment of ties between Granada and St. Cecilio. In the decades that followed, the city's leaders developed a close relationship with their patron, who, together with the *plomos* and the Sacromonte itself, embodied Granada's spiritual heritage. Through the cult of St. Cecilio and the defense of the *plomos*, Granada's leaders—especially the city councillors—articulated and maintained this close identification between the saint and the city, reflecting and reinforcing Granadino communal identity.

Prior to the recovery of the relics and the *plomos* from the Torre Turpiana and the Sacromonte, St. Cecilio seems to have received scant attention. While evidence is limited, his sixteenth-century cult seems to have consisted primarily of a solemn liturgical commemoration on May 15. Significantly, until the appearance of the *plomos,* Granada's leaders appear to have courted the patronage of another, better-documented ancient prelate, St. Gregory of Baetica.[71] Praised by St. Jerome as the author of several "tracts in a middle style and an elegant composition *On Faith,*" this fourth-century bishop of Iliberia had been an active combatant in the fight against the Arian heresy.[72] Archbishop Hernando de Talavera was reputedly a devotee of St. Gregory, and, according to one Granadino historian, the prelate ordered excavations in the Sierra Elvira in hopes of finding the saint's body.[73] Although the revised breviary of the Granadino Church (1544) accorded greater honors to St. Cecilio, giving him a double major office of confessors while St. Gregory's office was described as merely "solemn," by 1575 St. Gregory's feast had been elevated to a double major as well.[74] Neither saint had an office of his own.[75]

This circumstantial evidence suggests that, throughout much of the sixteenth century, St. Gregory enjoyed significantly more attention than his lesser-known fellow. Indeed, it remains unclear whether St. Cecilio was considered to be Granada's patron saint at all.[76] In the 1580s cathedral canon Pedro Guerra de Lorca complained that, though the Church in Granada honored St. Cecilio with an annual feast day, it offered him neither patronal honors nor daily commemorations. He urged that "this saint be given the dignity due by law of patron and protector of all the kingdom [of Granada], because he is, together with St. Gregory."[77] St. Cecilio had no shrine in the city, and no chapel in the cathedral. Moreover, his parish church seems not to have attracted any particular reverence, and there is no indication of any confraternity dedicated to him. St. Gregory of Baetica, on the other hand, was honored with a hermitage, founded by Ferdinand and Isabella on a site in the Albaicín where two medieval missionaries were thought to have been martyred.[78] The city council, which cared for the shrine and paid its chaplain and sacristan, completed major renovations of the hermitage between 1593 and 1596.[79] By the mid-seventeenth century, the *corregidor* and city councillors attended an annual mass and festivities in honor of the saint, held on April 24.[80]

After the discoveries, this situation changed dramatically. The ingenious forgers endowed St. Cecilio with a body—a concrete object for veneration—and a history. No longer a mere legend, the saint became a palpable presence within the city, not only at the "ancient" parish church under his advocation but, by the mid-eighteenth century, in the heart of the Albaicín in a crumbling medieval building that popular imagination identified as his jail.[81] The saint's power was especially felt on the Sacromonte, where supplicants invoked the saint and his companions in the hope of winning their aid for a miraculous cure. Other Granadinos showed their devotion to the saint in the names they gave their children. Baptismal records from the parishes of St. Cecilio and St. Peter and St. Paul suggest a dramatic surge in babies named Cecilio, peaking in the years immediately following the discovery and the authentication of the relics, and remaining relatively popular in the succeeding decades. In the seventy-five years between 1521 and 1595 (fifty-nine years accounting for gaps for the years 1525–37 and 1561–63), only two Cecilios were baptized in the working-class parish of St. Cecilio. By contrast, during the six-year period of 1595 through 1600, thirteen Cecilios were baptized there (two were abandoned children). This constitutes a sixtyfold increase, from one every thirty years, to two per year. Subsequently, over the course of the seventeenth century, one sees an average of one Cecilio every two years.[82] Similarly, records from the parish of St. Peter and St. Paul, a district populated in the seventeenth century by Granada's "principal people," show no Cecilios between 1556 and 1594, but four between 1595 and 1600.[83] During the seventeenth century, the rate is one Cecilio every five years and, during the first half of the eighteenth, it is one every eight years.[84] Investigations in other parishes around the city will likely reveal similar trends.

The authentication of the relics in 1600 inaugurated a new era in the official cult of St. Cecilio. As part of the solemn mass of declaration and thanksgiving held on Sunday, April 30, the relics were first displayed and identified to the overjoyed public. Then two members of the cathedral chapter brought them to the president and judges of the Royal Chancery, and also to the *corregidor* and members of the city council; in response, the dignitaries stepped forward and knelt to adore the newly authorized holy remains. Several times during the succeeding week, the crowds thronged the cathedral to see the relics. On the following Sunday, Archbishop Castro celebrated a pontifical mass on a richly decorated altar erected over the cave of St. Cecilio—making official the newly Christian character of the Sacromonte—and again showed the relics to the gathered crowds (more than 40,000 people, according to the anonymous chronicler who described the proceedings).[85]

Solemnized through these ceremonies, the renewed relationship between city and saint was pursued by both the ecclesiastical and the civil administrations. For the archbishop and the cathedral chapter, this meant the expansion and development of St. Cecilio's existing cult. During the archiepiscopate of Pedro de Castro, Granada's ecclesiastical officials in the cathedral and the diocesan administration actively promoted the cult of St. Cecilio. Archbishop Castro advocated a close identification between the cathedral, as the heart of the Granadino Church, and the Sacromonte, as the shrine of the city's patron saint. In 1603 Castro proposed to alter the iconographical plan of the cathedral's sanctuary by installing bronze statues of the twelve martyrs of the Sacromonte, together with the Virgin and St. Stephen, in niches in the columns surrounding the altar.[86] He further suggested, according to a report directed to Philip III by royal secretary Francisco González de Heredia in 1609, that "the archbishops [of Granada] call and title themselves [archbishops] of Granada and the Sacromonte."[87] As a reforming archbishop in the Borromean mold, Castro encouraged the association between the two, inasmuch as the connection between St. Cecilio, Granada's ancient bishop and apostle, and the modern Church of Granada enhanced the prestige of the prelate and his clergy, the saint's modern heir and successors.[88]

Granada's city council appears to have had few preexisting ties to the saint and was obliged to create new ones. A conflict between the city council and Archbishop Castro that arose shortly after the authentication ceremony suggests that the city councillors initially may have hesitated to throw their support behind St. Cecilio, preferring to continue their ongoing relationship with St. Gregory of Baetica. Even as the relics and *plomos* were emerging from the caverns of the Sacromonte, the council continued its refurbishment of St. Gregory's hermitage, completed in 1596. After the apotheosis of the relics in 1600, the city council petitioned the archbishop for one of the keys to the reliquary that held the saints' remains, arguing that because the relics had been found within its territory, it had a duty to participate in their care and preservation. Castro adamantly refused, forcing the city to appeal to Philip III for intervention.[89] In a report dated November 20, 1600, written in response to a royal inquiry on the matter, the archbishop contested the council's claim to a right to possess a key. He knew of no other cities that claimed such privilege on these grounds; even in Granada, the city council held no keys to the relics of the Royal Chapel or the cathedral. Nor could the council justify a key on the basis of money or efforts spent on behalf of the relics, he argued, because in the twelve years since the first finds in the Torre Turpiana, and in the five years since the discoveries on the Sacromonte, the city council "has not spent a *maravedí*, nor given even a drop of oil to the saints or to the caverns where they found them, nor in the [ceremonies of] authentication did it do or spend a thing." Archbishop Castro compared Granada's civil government unfavorably with those of Ávila, Guadix, and Andújar (the episcopal seats of three of the original Seven Apostles), claiming that the city council had never even come to say an Ave in the caves, and that it had never visited the caverns during the recent outbreak of plague.[90]

While these accusations must be approached with the archbishop's litigious character and constant concern for ecclesiastical privilege in mind, there may be some merit to Castro's claims. Witness testimony of the excavations on the Sacromonte document the presence of numerous members of the higher clergy and lay officials from the Royal Chancery but not a single representative from the city council. Nor is there any record in the dossier of the panel of inquiry into the discoveries, nor in any other contemporary accounts, of any processions sponsored by the city council. Not until April 26, 1595, did the councillors get around to sending a letter to Philip II to notify him of the discoveries on the Sacromonte.[91] On the other hand, a précis of entries from the now-lost minutes of the meetings of the city council during April 1595 reveals that the *corregidor* and *veinticuatros* sent several emissaries to Archbishop Castro to convey the council's joy and to ask that it be represented in the eventual authentication of the relics. The city council also resolved to petition Philip II for permission to spend 4,000 ducats on festivities in celebration of the finds. Moreover, while it may not have visited the caves during the epidemic of 1600, the city council did promise the saint a silver lamp in gratitude for the lifting of the plague. When the outbreak abated, the councillors vowed to visit the Sacromonte each year on the eve and feast day of St. Cecilio, a festivity now celebrated on February 1, the date of his martyrdom as established by the *plomos,* rather than the traditional festival date of May 15.[92]

The records do not reveal whether the city council fulfilled its vow right away. Celebrations of St. Cecilio's first festival day in 1601 appear to have taken place mainly in the cathedral. On the eve of the feast, the choir of the cathedral sang a motet on the Sacromonte, while torches illuminated the cathedral's bell tower. On the following day, just after lauds, bells, *chirimías* (a kind of woodwind instrument), and fireworks sounded the beginning of the festival. Archbishop Castro celebrated a pontifical mass in which the faithful took Communion and heard a sermon. There was also a caped procession of the cathedral canons and an offering to the saint.[93]

Within a decade, however, the city council had appropriated the annual festival from Granada's ecclesiastical elites. With the departure of Pedro de Castro to Seville, the center of the patronal festivities shifted from the cathedral to the Sacromonte, and with this there was a corresponding transfer of primary control from the archbishop and the cathedral chapter to the city council. In 1611 the city council approached the chapter of the Abbey of the Sacromonte with a proposal to sponsor the celebrations in honor of St. Cecilio.[94] A description of the festival in 1611, probably written by Justino Antolínez de Burgos, notes that the celebration began on the eve of the festival day with torches in the bell tower of the cathedral. The next day, two canons of the Sacromonte met the *corregidor* and city council members at the iron gate of the abbey's church and escorted them inside. The solemn ceremony, also attended by the city's religious, included a high mass (celebrated by Antolínez), music by the Royal Chapel, a sermon by the Jesuit Andrés Rodríguez, and the display of the relics to the faithful.[95] A separate, perhaps rival, ceremony at the cathedral included a caped procession and a sermon by a Franciscan friar.[96]

By the 1620s the archbishop and cathedral chapter seem to have wholly abandoned the feast of St. Cecilio to the city council and the canons of the Abbey of the Sacromonte. In the description of the 1622 celebrations recorded by the eminent linguist Bernardo José de Aldrete, the ceremony was presided over by the elderly Pedro de Castro, now archbishop of Seville, and attended by the *corregidor* and city council, numerous religious, and a good crowd of the faithful.[97] The archbishop of Granada and the cathedral chapter are conspicuous in their absence—though the chapter did lend miters and croziers to the city council for use in the festivities.[98] The festival itself quickly disappears from the minutes of the cathedral chapter's meetings.

The city council's sponsorship of the festival of St. Cecilio on the Sacromonte suggests that, whatever their initial hesitations, the city councillors eventually cultivated a close relationship with the saint. St. Cecilio embodied Granada's Christian traditions, and the veneration of his memory and his remains in the annual feast reflected and reinforced Granadinos' shared Christian heritage. Whereas Archbishop Castro promoted a cult of St. Cecilio that reinforced the prominence and power of the modern archbishop and the clergy, the city council fostered an alternative identification between the saint and itself as representative of the whole city. In lending public support to the cult of St. Cecilio on the Sacromonte, the council allied itself with the symbol and guarantor of Granada's communal continuity.

A curious woodcut stamped on the title page of Francisco Bermúdez de Pedraza's *Antigüedad y excelencias de Granada* illustrates the close ties sought by the city, represented by the municipal council, to its illustrious ancient Christian past (fig. 5.5).[99] Traditionally, Granada's coat of arms celebrated its ties to Ferdinand and Isabella (see fig. 4.2). In it, the king and queen are seated with a pomegranate, a *granada*, at their feet, while castles and lions representing the kingdoms of Castile and León decorate the border around the monarchs. Granada's status as a royal city is symbolized by the crown that sits atop the seal. Pedraza replaced this with one featuring a pomegranate, "the hieroglyph most indicative of its

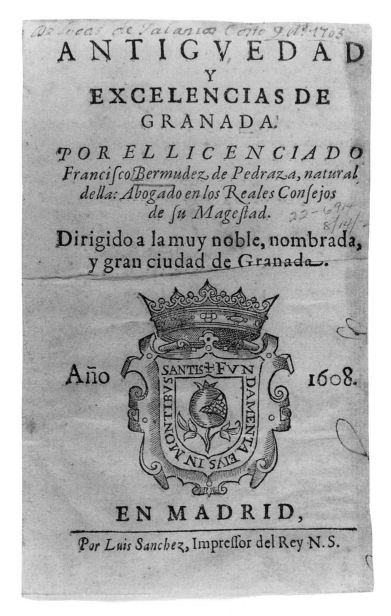

ANTIGVEDAD
Y
EXCELENCIAS DE
GRANADA.

POR EL LICENCIADO
Francisco Bermudez de Pedraza, natural
della: Abogado en los Reales Consejos
de su Magestad.

Dirigido a la muy noble, nombrada,
y gran ciudad de Granada.

Año ~~~~~ 1608.

EN MADRID,

Por Luis Sanchez, Impressor del Rey N.S.

Fig. 5.5. Title page of Francisco Bermúdez de Pedraza, *Antigüedad y excelencias de Granada* (Madrid, 1608). Courtesy of the Bancroft Library, University of California, Berkeley.

[Granada's] attributes and excellencies that the human mind could find."[100] Around the city's namesake fruit is a caption reading "Fundamenta eius in montibus sanctis" (His foundation [is] in the holy mountains). This motto, quoted from Psalm 87:1, presumably refers to the Sacromonte, the founding monument of Granada's religious tradition. Pedraza also provides a lengthy exegesis of the new insignia, which he claims is "the arms and blazon of this city."[101] Did the municipal council, which probably sponsored this book, plan to substitute this new coat of arms for the original? Did Bermúdez, an ardent supporter of the Sacromonte, propose the substitution?[102] Without further documentation, one can only conjecture at the intent behind the woodcut. The illustration does, however, neatly capture the identification among the city, its civil government, and its Christian heritage.

Granada's city council further linked itself to the cult of St. Cecilio and his companions through its dogged defense of the *plomos* in the face of the persistent challenges posed by Madrid and Rome. After Archbishop Castro's transfer to Seville in 1610, his successors in the see of Granada appear to have done little to promote the veneration of St. Cecilio and to have distanced themselves from the ongoing controversy that surrounded the *plomos*. After 1616, for example, rogatory processions that once went to the Sacromonte or to St. Cecilio's parish church were increasingly diverted to other sites and centered upon the Virgin of la Antigua or Our Lady of Anguish.[103] Perhaps in order to diminish the stature of a festivity so prominently under secular control, Granada's ecclesiastical leadership did not elevate the festival of St. Cecilio to the status of an obligatory feast day for city dwellers until 1646.[104] Likewise, after 1610 the cathedral chapter concerned itself decreasingly with the *plomos*. The canons' lack of interest in the affair is most likely closely linked to the division, made shortly after the authentication ceremonies in 1600, between the relics of the Torre Turpiana and those of the Sacromonte. Over the protests of the chapter, Archbishop Castro designated for the cathedral only the earlier finds—the bone of St. Stephen and the Virgin's handkerchief. The ashes and other remains from the caves were housed at the Sacromonte.[105] The cathedral chapter, accordingly, took little part in the protracted defense of the *plomos*. When Archbishop Castro displayed an overly proprietary attitude toward the *plomos* by departing for Seville with them in his luggage, the chapter occupied itself primarily with the return of the parchment from the Torre Turpiana. It later fought with Castro's heirs, the canons of the Sacromonte, for possession of the box that had contained the relics from the Torre Turpiana, and for the investigative dossier that accompanied it.[106] What few efforts it made in defense of the *plomos*, it made exclusively on behalf of the parchment and the other Torre Turpiana finds. Little evidence exists of any letters, financial assistance, or other support for the cause of the *plomos*.[107] Indeed, two petitions submitted by the Collegiate Church of the Sacromonte to the cathedral chapter, dating probably between 1640 and 1642, urged the chapter to involve itself in the affair by writing letters to the inquisitor general and the papal nuncio and by designating commissioners to oversee the case in Rome. I have found no such letters, nor any indication that the requested commissioners were ever appointed.[108]

After the death of Pedro de Castro in 1623, the burden of the defense of the *plomos* fell to the canons of the Sacromonte and to the city council of Granada. The Collegiate Church of the Sacromonte sent several representatives and innumerable letters to the Spanish court, seeking to prevent the removal of the lead books.[109] In 1642 the chapter of the Sacromonte sent canon Bartolomé de Torres to Rome to serve as advocate for the *plomos*. For ten years, Torres lobbied the papal court on behalf of the cause of the *plomos* and returned to Spain only when the chapter's financial resources were totally exhausted. The canons of the Sacromonte spent heavily to support their representative in Rome. By 1652 they had expended more than 10,000 ducats and had gone so deeply into debt that they were forced to seek alms from the faithful both in Spain and in the Latin American colonies in order to support an agent at the Vatican.[110]

The city council of Granada expended both financial and political resources in defense of the *plomos*. Despite their possible reluctance to abandon the patronage of St. Gregory of Baetica, the city councillors early on began a campaign in support of the finds. In 1596 the city council sent council members Juan Fernández de Córdoba and Pedro de Granada Venegas to Madrid to urge that Philip II resist the calls of the papal nuncio for the confiscation of the *plomos*.[111] In 1604, faced with renewed efforts by Rome, the city council enlisted the aid of the Cortes, which petitioned Philip III not to permit the removal of the *plomos* from Spanish soil.[112] The city council also sent Pedro de Granada Venegas and Pedro de Hinojosa Venegas to supplicate the king directly.[113] In the 1640s the councillors joined forces with the canons of the Sacromonte and issued several petitions to the Crown.[114] After the transfer of the *plomos* to Rome, the city council expanded its efforts to direct financial support; in 1662 it granted the Abbey of the Sacromonte 1,500 ducats annually for four years for the upkeep of canon Blas Peinado de Santaella, who left for Rome the same year.[115]

The council's many pleading missives to the Crown reveal the strong local religious traditions behind the city's professed attachment to the *plomos*. "[Granada] holds them in great esteem as books of its saints," wrote the council around 1640, "and because they show that the apostle St. James came and stayed in Granada several times, and that Spain was the first province in heathendom that heard the gospel of Our Lord Jesus Christ."[116] The *plomos* were more than mere historical documents—they were autograph writings of Granada's own saints. Long before the difficulties in their texts became clear, the city council recognized the *plomos* as bearers of saintly *potentia* meant for Granada alone: "This city esteems these holy relics and books . . . ," wrote the city council in 1596, "more than words can express, because it understands that all its goodness, increase, security, and defense consists in having them in it." The *plomos,* miraculously preserved and then revealed by God, were designated especially for Granada by the city's saints.[117]

Several of the sixteen proofs outlined in an unsigned manuscript document (ca. 1630), titled "The reasons why the city of Granada must not permit that they remove from it the books of the Sacromonte," reveal a close identification between the *plomos* and the city of Granada.[118] The books were Granada's patrimony, designated "by special decree" for Granada by the Virgin Mary and St. James. Furthermore, the council and the city residents were in a certain sense the owners of the books: the council by virtue of the key it held, the people by the "right acquired through the interest of devotion awakened by nearness or proximity, which produces almost a sense of ownership in the places where there are relics of saints." Above and beyond the dangers posed by the rigors of travel, the removal of the *plomos* "would cause great grief for this city and kingdom . . . because it justly can have and has confidence that the particular protection of God depends greatly on the presence of this treasure."

The city council's appropriation of the cult of St. Cecilio from clerical control and its protracted defense of the *plomos* suggest that the councillors sought to associate themselves and their recently established secular institution with the prestigious heritage personified in the saint and his remains. In positioning itself as the defender of the city's most ancient Christian antiquity, Granada's municipal council acquired some of the historical continuity it lacked.[119] The city council's careful cultivation of its association with St. Cecilio, together with its struggle with Archbishop Castro over the key to the relics and the cathedral chapter's response to loss of control over the annual festival, is also indicative of the endemic institutional tensions and of the divisive, rather than unifying, characteristics of saints' cults and saintly relics. Saints' cults and the ritual invocation of the city's patron, notes Moshe Sluhovsky, were not always the guarantors of *communitas* that modern scholars have often made them out to be: "They demonstrated the harmonious community but also its rivalries; both an ideal society and a concrete tension-ridden city."[120] As Granada's elite institutions competed among themselves for power and influence, the cult of the patron and its perceived faculty to legitimize authority were valuable propaganda tools.

The sources documenting the festival of St. Cecilio reveal little about average Granadinos' attitudes toward and affiliations with the saint and his cult. The popular response to the discoveries on the Sacromonte, however, and the trends in infant names suggest that, in the early years at least, St. Cecilio and the Sacromonte sparked devotion that transcended social status. According to Archbishop Castro, the crowds that flocked to the hillside to venerate the Sacromonte saints included "not only the masses but also the Chancery and the most dignified [people], and all the religious orders, and [people from] other cities."[121] Witness testimony before the panel of inquiry into the relics includes Granadinos of all social stations, from the mulatta slave Ysabel to Leandro de Palençia, a watchmaker, to Gonzalo de Salazar, an Augustinian friar and bishop of Mérida, Yucatán.[122] While the baptismal registers are less revealing about the status of babies or their parents, they do show the saint to have been popular both in neighborhoods like the parish of St. Peter and St. Paul, inhabited by many of Granada's socially prominent families, and especially in St. Cecilio's eponymous parish in the heart of the Antequerela, a district dominated by silk workers.

St. Cecilio apparently remained a popular figure among Granada's artisanal classes well into the seventeenth century, when some of the city's religious brotherhoods established annual pilgrimages to the Sacromonte. In the 1620s and 1630s, for example, the city's gardeners celebrated a festival on the Sacromonte that included a mock military skirmish; afterward, noted a disapproving Jesuit chronicler, "they divided up into troops of comrades in order to return to their homes, visiting first, as usual, some shrines [taverns?] of their scanty devotion."[123] Other evidence can be found in the events surrounding the unrest that erupted in 1648 in the wake of poor harvests. The rioters, who hailed predominantly from the working-class neighborhood of the Antequerela, forced *corregidor* Francisco Arévalo de Zuazo into hiding and elected a new *corregidor*, Luis de Paz y Medrano. When Arévalo attempted to regain control, the rebel weavers took up the cry of "Long live the king and death to bad government." They forced the parish priest of the Church of St. Cecilio out of the sanctuary and, putting their hands on the altar, swore to defend their cause to the death. Fortunately, the crisis never came to that. After Arévalo slipped out of town disguised as a priest, the city council made peace with the rioters and celebrated the return to calm and civic concord with a mass and a procession in the Church of St. Cecilio.[124] St. Cecilio's parish church thus served as a rallying point for the rebels and as the center for civic reconciliation, but it is difficult to say with any confidence whether the silk workers chose his church because of a particular devotion to the saint, or because they aimed to adopt the rhetoric of Granadino civic culture and secure the protection of the city's patron for their cause, or simply because it was the parish church closest at hand. Such events hint at attitudes and affiliations, but much research remains to be done to chart the full dimensions of popular devotion to St. Cecilio and of the civic self-consciousness of nonelite Granadinos.[125]

Whatever the reasons behind his invocation by the rebel silk weavers, the cult of St. Cecilio and the holy terrain of the Sacromonte continued to be central elements of Granada's unique religious heritage throughout the early modern period. The patron saint—the focus of the particularist devotions and liturgies of a characteristically localized early modern Catholicism—embodied each locality's distinctive history and traditions and, as such, was a key symbol of a community's self-consciousness.[126] In Madrid, Ávila, Cuenca, and many other cities in Spain and throughout Catholic Europe, urban leaders both clerical and lay actively promoted the cults of city saints—especially ancient bishops—even as the Tridentine Church endeavored to regularize the particularist devotions and liturgies of individual localities.[127] In its sponsorship of the civic cult of St. Cecilio and in its defense of the relics and texts, Granada's city council celebrated a communal heritage of Christian antiquity—a communal heritage constituted and made present in the *plomos*—and the communal self-definition it undergirded.

Granada Inmaculada

Deeply rooted in Granada's newly recovered ancient past, the sacred landscape of the Sacromonte and the cult of St. Cecilio tied contemporary devotions to the city's unique past, investing it with local meanings that both informed and reflected Granadino communal identity. A similar domestication was effected on another devotion—that of the Immaculate Conception of the Virgin Mary. Wildly popular throughout seventeenth-century Spain, in Granada the veneration of Mary Immaculate took a peculiarly local twist. Through the historical evidence provided by the *plomos,* Granada came to imagine itself to be the cradle of devotion to the Immaculate Conception. The doctrine became part of the ancient heritage around which Granadinos defined themselves and their city.

Until 1854, when Pope Pius IX defined it as dogma, the doctrine of the Immaculate Conception—the Virgin Mary's exemption from original sin—was a contentious and much-disputed devotion. In Spain, veneration of the Immacu-

late Conception by the Spanish Crown and clergy—especially the Franciscans—
dates from the first decades of the thirteenth century.[128] Ferdinand and Isabella
actively supported the doctrine, and over the course of the fifteenth and sixteenth
centuries, devotion to the Immaculate Conception filtered down from the Crown
to the nobility and eventually to the common people.[129] In order not to provoke
a deeper divide between Catholics and Protestants, both Charles V and Philip II
avoided overt support for the controversial doctrine, but lent their tacit backing
to the defense of the Immaculist writings of Ramón Lull, a thirteenth-century
Franciscan from Palma de Mallorca.

In the second decade of the seventeenth century, a series of conflicts that took
place in Andalusia suddenly elevated the Immaculate Conception to the forefront
of national politics. In 1614 a friar of the Dominican Order—an organization long
opposed to the doctrine—preached in the cathedral of Córdoba a Maculist sermon that offended Álvaro Pizaño de Palacios, a member of the Córdoba cathedral
chapter and a native of Seville.[130] Canon Pizaño de Palacios responded with a sermon defending the Immaculate Conception and was denounced by the Inquisition for violating existing papal bulls prohibiting public debate on the topic. He
was absolved and returned to Seville, where the controversy broke out again the
following year. The doctrine was already a hot issue in Seville. In 1613 a Maculist
sermon by a Dominican friar provoked the ire of Seville's religious authorities,
led by the elderly Pedro de Castro, who had transferred to the see of Seville from
that of Granada in 1610. Upon his return to Seville in 1615, Pizaño de Palacios resumed preaching about the doctrine to eager audiences. The publication of a treatise against the Immaculate Conception during the same year finally lit the fuse
of the explosive issue, and Immaculist fervor, carefully orchestrated by Castro and
his supporters, erupted in the streets of Seville and quickly spread across Andalusia and to cities across Spain. Confraternities and guilds marched through
the city in elaborate processions to demonstrate their veneration for Mary Immaculate.[131] Children swarmed through the streets singing the famous devotional couplets penned by Miguel Cid, a local poet, and set to music by Bernardo
de Toro:

> Let everyone in general
> In a clamorous cry, elect Queen,
> Say that you are conceived
> Without original sin.

Seville's Dominican friars found themselves the objects of much abuse, and
fights often broke out between lay supporters and opponents of the doctrine. A

carpenter who dared to avow openly "the contrary to the pious opinion" was so roughly treated by the devout inmates of the city jail that he had to be put into a separate cell.[132]

By 1616 Philip III had responded to the popular fervor by appointing a committee or *junta* to push for definition of the doctrine of the Immaculate Conception as dogma.[133] Their representative in Rome, Plácido Tosantos, the Benedictine bishop of Cádiz, succeeded in 1617 in convincing Pope Paul V to issue a decretal prohibiting any public defense of the Maculist doctrine of sanctification of the Virgin—the opinion advocated by the Dominican Order. In Seville and across Spain, devotees of the Immaculate Conception responded to the papal order with renewed processions and festivities of jubilation.[134]

Granadinos were far from immune to the sweeping wave of Immaculist sentiment.[135] In 1615 and 1616, Granada's colleges, religious houses, and confraternities held processions and festivities with the approval of Archbishop Pedro González de Mendoza, a Franciscan friar, who blamed the pious ruckus on the "friars of St. Dominic, who began [it] with such indecent and dirty conclusions."[136] One such festival took place in the Franciscan monastery, sponsored by the Immaculist confraternity housed there. The church and cloister were decorated with rich cloths, candles, and altars bearing images and emblems of the Virgin Immaculate. The festivities began with a procession on December 8—the feast of the Immaculate Conception—and featured seven tournaments in which local poets competed for rich prizes.[137] These demonstrations were largely peaceful; by comparison, the festivities held in 1617 in celebration of the new papal edict ended badly, with several Dominican friars wounded.[138] In 1618 the city council, cathedral chapter, and university imitated the example set by Seville and many other cities by publicly swearing to uphold the doctrine of the Immaculate Conception and defend it to the death.[139] Archbishop Felipe de Tarsis (1616–20) presided over the solemn ceremony; among the guests was Pedro de Castro, who had returned to Granada to visit his beloved Sacromonte.[140]

For the citizens of Seville, the Immaculate Conception was integral to a sense of civic and perhaps even national identity. Granadinos too, however, found a special, local meaning in the doctrine, linked to their ancient Christian past.[141] As the indefatigable Pedro de Castro never failed to point out to both king and pope, one of the strongest proofs for the Immaculate Conception was the *plomos* themselves. As putative testimony of the opinions and attitudes of the Apostles, the *plomos* supplied invaluable evidence of the antiquity of the doctrine. One lead book, the *Book of the Fundaments of the Law,* contained the phrase that became the motto of the Collegiate Church of the Sacromonte and of Archbishop Castro himself: "A María no tocó el pecado primero" (Mary was not touched by first sin).[142] Granada and the Sacromonte were thus the cradle of Spanish veneration of the Immaculate Conception of the Virgin Mary, which was, Pedro de Castro informed Pope Paul V, "the general devotion of Spain . . . and it is not a new devotion, but rather very ancient, and was celebrated in the time of St. Ildefonso since St. James the Zebedee preached in Spain."[143]

A remarkable illustration engraved by Bernardo Heylan—a member of the clan of Flemish artists active in Granada—evokes Granadino pride in the city's ancient Immaculist heritage.[144] Published in Alonso de Ferriol y Caycedo's volume commemorating the 1615 celebrations in the Franciscan monastery, and presumably paid for by the powerful confraternity that sponsored the event, the image depicts the crowned Virgin with several common iconographic attributes of the Immaculate Conception (fig. 5.6).[145] The rays of light that surround her recall the Apocalyptic Woman "clothed in the sun," while the rose and lily in each of the upper corners of the composition refer to the Marian litanies' invocation of Mary "sicut lilium inter spinas" (as the lily among thorns; Song of Solomon 4:4). The motto around her head—"Tota pulchra es, amica mea, et macula non est in te" (Thou art all beautiful, my love, and there is no spot in thee; Song of Solomon 4:7)—also derives from the litanies.[146] An inscription in Castilian at the bottom of the engraving reads "Praised be the Most Pure Conception of the Mother of God, conceived without original sin." Below this pious sentiment is reproduced the critical passage from the *plomos,* both in Castilian and in the lead books' curious Arabic, together with an explanatory note that "these Arabic letters are written on the Sacromonte of Granada in the hand of St. Cecilio and St. Tesifón."

The engraving demonstrates the degree to which Granada's local community naturalized the universal doctrine of the Immaculate Conception, making the devotion its own by filtering it through the lens of its own unique religious culture. Similar juxtapositions of St. Cecilio, the *plomos,* and Mary Immaculate occur in other publications related to the Sacromonte and Granadino history. Francisco Heylan's engraved title page of *Relación breve de las reliquias que se hallaron en la ciudad de Granada* (Granada, 1617) shows the Virgin at the top of a retable. St. Cecilio and St. Tesifón are seated beneath her and are writing the lead books, while St. Hiscio and St. James (bearing still more *plomos*) stand on either side of the title (fig. 5.7). Ana Heylan—yet another active member of the Heylan engraving dynasty—engraved the title page to Francisco Bermúdez de Pedraza's *Historia eclesiástica* with Mary emerging from an open pomegranate held up by St. James and St. Cecilio; at either side sit St. Tesifón and St. Hiscio, who pause in their writing to gaze at the Virgin (fig. 5.8).[147] These illustrations represent in visual form

Fig. 5.6. Bernard Heylan, "The Immaculate Conception," in Alonso de Ferriol y Caycedo, *Libro de las fiestas que en honor de la inmaculada Concepción de la Virgen María nuestra señora, celebró su devota y antigua hermandad en san Francisco de Granada* (Granada, 1616). Courtesy of the Biblioteca Nacional de España, Madrid. Photo by the Laboratorio Fotográfico of the Biblioteca Nacional de España, Madrid.

Fig. 5.7. Francisco Heylan, title page of *Relación breve de las reliquias que se hallaron en la ciudad de Granada en una torre antiquíssima, y en las cavernas del Monte Illipulitano de Valparayso cerca de la ciudad: sacado del processo y averigüaciones, que cerca dello se hizieron* (Granada, 1614; Granada, 1617). Courtesy of the Biblioteca Nacional de España, Madrid. Photo by the Laboratorio Fotográfico of the Biblioteca Nacional de España, Madrid.

Fig. 5.8. Ana Heylan, title page of Francisco Bermúdez de Pedraza, *Historia eclesiástica de Granada, principios y progressos de la ciudad y religión católica de Granada* (Granada, 1638). Photo courtesy of the Newberry Library, Chicago.

Granadino self-definition as what one eighteenth-century local patriot called "the ancestral home of the Immaculate Conception."[148]

Though Granadinos participated fully in the Immaculist fervor of the years following 1615, the true crisis of Granadino Marian devotion occurred decades later. On Good Friday, April 6, 1640, someone posted on the doors of the city council a handwritten libel impugning Mary's perpetual virginity. Three days later, the Inquisition declared the author or authors to be heretics and the city councillors put a bounty of 1,000 ducats on their heads. Operating on the assumption that the malefactors were "Hebrews," the city council also began arresting all the city's resident Portuguese. Many in early modern Spain held the Portuguese to be a nation suspect in its faith, a nation of Conversos or crypto-Jews, and Granada's Portuguese inhabitants were detained both as likely culprits and for their own safety.[149] Such precautions were not wholly unfounded, as Granadinos responded to the scandal with violent emotion. Local scholars penned vitriolic responses to the calumnious pasquinade, and over the course of the year, the city's parishes, confraternities, colleges, guilds, religious houses, and other institutions sponsored dozens of festivals and processions to avenge the Virgin's honor.[150] Other Andalusian towns like Écija and Jerez de la Frontera staged similar events to expiate the crime.[151]

Granada's Marian fervor echoed the enthusiastic public response to the discoveries on the Sacromonte some forty-five years earlier, as parades filled the streets by day and by night. Most of the processions ended in an area known as the Campo del Triunfo, or Plain of the Triumph. Here, near the Royal Hospital and the Mercedarian monastery, stood the monument that best expressed the importance of Immaculist devotion in Granadino identity. On September 29, 1621, the city council of Granada voted to erect a memorial dedicated to the triumph of the Immaculate Conception of the Virgin Mary.[152] The original proposal envisioned the erection of the monument upon the Sacromonte, but when planning began some five years later, the site was transferred to an open area near the Royal Hospital, just beyond the Elvira Gate. The city council entrusted the project to architect Francisco de Potes and artist Alonso de Mena. Construction of the Triumph proceeded very slowly. Mena went on strike to protest the council's stingy funding and did not finish the sculpture until 1630.[153]

Though Mena had completed his work, the monument remained incomplete for several more years, due to the intervention of the Inquisition. In late 1630 the local tribunal of the Holy Office got wind of the inscriptions to be included on the monument and promptly ordered a moratorium on construction. The inquisitors alerted the Suprema, the Inquisition's central governing body, which agitated against the Triumph at court.[154] The city of Granada and the Marquis of Estepa countered the Inquisition with pleas before the government committee charged with the affairs of the Sacromonte, and in July 1631 the Holy Office was forced to allow the city council to finish the inscriptions that completed the monument.[155]

Luis de Paracuellos Cabeza de Vaca's *Triunfales celebraciones* (Granada, 1640) includes an illustration of the Triumph engraved by Ana Heylan (fig. 5.9).[156] At the top of the marble monument, which is between fifty and sixty feet tall, stands the crowned Virgin. In her breast, just below her hands, is a reliquary containing a fragment of the True Cross, a gift from Cardinal Baronio to the Jesuits of Granada. Originally, the crown, rays, stellarium, and robes that adorn the Virgin were gilt, as was the carved Corinthian column upon which she stands. Below the column, flanked by four angels who wear banners proclaiming "María sin pecado original" (Mary without Original Sin), is a plinth carved on the south side with the arms of the city of Granada; to the north, St. James the Moorslayer; to the west, St. Cecilio; and to the east, St. Tesifón.[157]

A broad cornice separates the plinth from the base, which consists of a platform adorned with lions' heads, and a pedestal decorated with inscriptions. Ana Heylan's engraving shows a simplified version of the carved text on the southern face of the pedestal, noting only the dedication in 1634; the full inscription, still visible today, commemorates the council's vow of 1618 and the birth of Prince Baltasar Carlos in 1629, as well as the completion date of the monument.[158] The inscriptions on the northern, eastern, and western sides of the pedestal bore the controversial texts that had drawn the opposition of the Inquisition. Each gave an account of the life and acts of the saints depicted above and noted each saint's devotion to the Immaculate Conception, as recorded by the *plomos*. The carving of St. Cecilio even depicts him holding two of the lead books.[159]

The monument to the Triumph of the Immaculate Conception described for Granadinos the religious dimensions of their own civic identity. The city council's project traced modern Granada's devotion to Mary Immaculate backward in time to its intersections with the Sacromonte and the nativity of Christianity, portraying the doctrine as originally and thus uniquely Granadino. Combining ancient history with modern piety, the shrine represented and reinforced the spiritual allegiances and memories that undergirded Granadino communal cohesion. Like the ceremonies and sermons of the Toma, the Triumph reminded Granadinos of their city's past and exalted their claims to a shared faith in an ancient doctrine. It was therefore quite fitting that, in the uproar of 1640, as Granadinos sought to expiate collectively the sin of an individual citizen, the monument to the Immaculate Conception should be the "the target of all the processions."[160]

Fig. 5.9. Ana Heylan, "The Virgin of Triumph of Granada," originally in Luis Paracuellos Cabeza de Vaca, *Triunfales celebraciones, que en aparatos magestuosos consagró religiosa la ciudad de Granada, a honor de la pureza virginal de María Santíssima en sus desagravios, a quien devota las dedica esta ciudad, en todo ilustre, en todo grande* (Granada, 1640). Reproduced from Emilio Orozco Díaz, *El poema "Granada" de Collado del Hierro* (Granada: Patronato de la Alhambra, 1964).

Ironically, the arrest in June of the "heretic" revealed the culprit to be a hermit attached to the same shrine. The city council and the cathedral chapter celebrated his capture with a procession to the Triumph. In an *auto da fe* celebrated later that year, the offender received a penalty of ten years in the galleys—a sentence tantamount to death.[161]

In many respects, the monument to the Triumph of the Immaculate Conception represented most directly the patriotism and piety of Granada's oligarchs, especially the members of the city council.[162] Individual city councilmen paid for the installation and upkeep of the twenty-five lamps that surrounded the monument, and the Virgin of Triumph was adopted as patroness of at least three confraternities, including the Brotherhood of the Maestranza, a group of noblemen dedicated to the cultivation of horsemanship.[163] The Triumph is thus very much an *official* statement of Granadino identity by the city council—an authoritative announcement linking Granada's spiritual heritage and modern religious allegiances.

Even as the monument became the special object of official and elite devotion, however, the spiritual heritage it commemorated and the mass devotions it hosted helped knit together the broad community of believers of all stations. Together, maps, miracles, and monuments, symbolic landscapes and saint's cults, were all aspects of the "civic piety" promoted by Granada's leaders—the "tightly woven, traditional set of public rituals that enhanced community solidarity and maintained the peace."[164] These public religious expressions bonded the community together in shared devotion, and broadcast to native and nonnative alike an image of Granadino orthodoxy and religious ardor. Granadino communal identity coupled an awareness of and pride in the city's spiritual heritage with the confessionalism, or Catholic identity, common to Counter-Reformation Spain. Produced in the upheaval of the Protestant Reformation of the sixteenth century, Catholic confessional identity in areas like Spain and Italy differed somewhat from its German and French counterparts in its lack of strong opposition and, therefore, any overtly polemical component.[165] The violent reaction of Granadinos to a perceived "heretical" act in 1640, however, suggests that Catholic identity in southern Europe could occasionally take on a controversialist dimension like that found in more northerly climes.

Granadinos' articulation of communal and confessional identity through particularized cultic and devotional discourses highlights the continuing importance and power of local religion despite the Church's efforts to inculcate a more universal and uniform Catholic piety. The successful inculcation of confessionalism may, in fact, be due in part to the strength of local devotions and practices. For example, Carlo Borromeo, the prototypical Counter-Reformation prelate, encouraged devotion to the saints and respect for ecclesiastical leadership by reinforcing the traditions of what he called the "Chiesa particolare" of Milan.[166] Similarly, in early modern Germany, the development of Catholic confessionalism occurred not only through centrally directed Tridentine reforms, or the collaboration of the Church and the nascent state in social disciplining, but also through regionally variable traditional religious practices. By the late seventeenth century, strong attachment to local devotions helped create popular confessional identity in Catholic Germany and contributed to the extreme diversity of German Catholicism.[167] In Counter-Reformation Granada, the highly local cults of the saints of the Sacromonte and the Immaculate Conception both produced and reflected a confessionalized communal identity that figured orthodox Catholic piety and the celebration of the city's spiritual past as its most salient characteristics. The overwhelming response to the pasquinade of 1640 suggests that this communal identity was widespread among Granadinos of all stations.[168]

Although the discourses of this local religion were articulated primarily by city elites, the communal feeling they fostered was open to all Granadinos—except, of course, the unhappy Moriscos. Like the ceremonies of the Toma, civic piety had a persuasive dimension, marshaling consensus and shoring up community solidarity by preserving and commemorating the shared past and spiritual allegiances that helped knit together the community. Just as the cult of St. James helped foster nascent national feeling, the Sacromonte and the cults of St. Cecilio and the Immaculate Conception helped nurture a sentiment of communal belonging that was available to elites and nonelites alike.[169] Granadino communal identity was imbedded in an indigenous religious culture that tied the present to the past. The devotional and cultic discourses that developed around the *plomos* connected contemporary Granadino piety with the invented civic past documented by the lead books of the Sacromonte and the parchment of the Torre Turpiana. Like the city histories and the commemorative ceremonies and sermons of the Toma, St. Cecilio, a nativized Immaculate Conception, and the sacred landscape of the Sacromonte recalled and reinforced the shared Christian antiquity central to Granadino communal self-definition.

Epilogue

Every society produces the particular kind of imposture that suits it best.

—*Leonardo Sciascia*

The *plomos* finally reached the Vatican in June 1643. There, a team of six interpreters that included the famous Jesuit polymath Athanasius Kircher (1602–80) undertook a definitive translation, a task that was not completed until 1665.[1] The city of Granada, the Abbey of Sacromonte, and, to a lesser degree, the Spanish Crown, lobbied persistently for a favorable judgment, but their efforts were in vain. The voices of criticism that had dogged the discoveries since 1588 grew increasingly shrill, and it became widely accepted—outside Granada, at least—that the Torre Turpiana parchment and the lead books were indeed forgeries. On March 6, 1682, almost forty years after their arrival in Rome and nearly a century after the first discoveries in the Torre Turpiana, Pope Innocent XI formally condemned the *plomos* as "mere human fictions, fabricated for the ruin of the Catholic faith," heretical texts that smelled suspiciously of Islam.[2] Only the relics from the Torre Turpiana and the Sacromonte—the charred remains of the Sacromonte saints, the bone of St. Stephen, and the handkerchief of the Virgin, all legitimately authorized by Archbishop Castro in 1600—escaped the papal sentence. The Abbey of the Sacromonte, the city of Granada, and the Crown all lodged protests and appeals, but to no avail.[3]

After the publication of the brief in Rome on September 28, the papal nuncio and the Inquisition distributed it to cities across Spain. The sentence was announced in Granada's cathedral on November 24.[4] There are no descriptions of how Granadinos reacted to the unhappy news that day, but the blow cannot have been wholly unexpected, since news of the condemnation had reached Granada several months before the publication of the brief. The canons of the Abbey of the

Sacromonte agitated to have the case reopened, and in June 1682 the university, the cathedral chapter, the archbishop, the city council, and most of Granada's male religious houses petitioned King Charles II to intercede with the Vatican.[5] After the condemnation, both the king and the queen mother sent letters to Rome, but the papal response was emphatically negative.[6]

The *plomos'* supporters did not give up easily. Led by the canons of the Sacromonte, apologists continued to write in defense of their precious texts.[7] The postcondemnation polemic began in 1706 with *Vindicias Cathólicas Granatenses,* a lengthy treatise published in France and attributed to Diego de la Serna Cantoral, a prosecutor in the Chancery of Granada.[8] When possible, supporters at the abbey recruited erudite defenders from outside their own ranks, like the Jesuit Diego de Quadros (1677–1746), a professor of Holy Scripture and Hebrew in the Imperial College of Madrid who examined the affair in 1734.[9] Most eighteenth-century writers on the *plomos,* however, were sons of Granada and canons in the Collegiate Church of the Sacromonte. While Sacromonte canon Vicente Pastor de los Cobos's (1686–1759) *Guerras católicas granatenses* (1735) never reached the press, Diego Nicolás Heredia Barnuevo (1700–1760) published his semi-hagiographic biography of Pedro de Castro in 1741.[10] Luis Francisco de Viana y Bustos (d. 1762), abbot of the Sacromonte and a member of the Royal Academy of History, wrote several works in defense of the *plomos* and Granada's mythic past, including *Disertación eclesiastica crítico-histórica* (Pamplona, 1752) and, with canon José Juan de Laboraria (d. 1765), the unpublished manuscript *Historia authéntica del hecho de los dos descubrimientos de Torre Turpiana y Monte Santo de Granada* (1759).[11]

Abbot Viana's defense of the *plomos* helped set the stage for a new series of discoveries unearthed in Granada in the 1750s. Between 1754 and 1763, Juan de Flores y Oddouz (d. 1789), a prebendary in the cathedral, undertook excavations in the Alcazaba, the oldest quarter of the Albaicín. With the aid of his accomplices—Cristóbal de Medina Conde (1726–98; a.k.a. Cristóbal Conde y Herrera), a canon in the cathedral of Málaga; Juan Velázquez de Echeverría (1729–1808), a member of the Congregation of Clerks Regular Minor; Antonio Fernández de la Cruz, abbot of the Collegiate Church of San Salvador; and others—Flores "discovered" new texts etched on lead tablets and scraps of marble in a strange script similar to that of the funerary plaques found on the Sacromonte. The finds included inscriptions to various Roman emperors and bishops of Iliberis, records from the Council of Elvira, and the genuine remains of the forum of Roman Iliberis. The inscriptions not only defended the evangelization of Granada by St. James and the apostolic origins of the dogma of the Immaculate Conception; they even re-

ferred to the lead books and the treasures of the Torre Turpiana. Unlike the original *plomos,* however, this new collection of ancient remains was quickly revealed
to be a forgery, and the authors were unmasked and punished. Flores and Echeverría received a sentence of eight years' confinement in a monastery, while Medina Conde received a term of four years. The judges also prohibited the three
from ever again writing anything about St. James or the discoveries in the Alcazaba, under pain of banishment from Spanish territory. Most of the recovered objects were destroyed or reburied.[12]

Although these new forgeries and written apologies failed to rehabilitate the
cause of the parchment and the lead books, they do testify to the persistence of
the *plomos* in Granadino culture, and to the continuing desire to invent a Christian past for Granada. Despite the confiscation, condemnation, and permanent
loss of the *plomos,* throughout the eighteenth and well into the nineteenth century Granadinos continued to articulate and to elaborate discourses of identity
around the *plomos* and the imagined communal past.[13] Each year, the ceremonies
and sermon of the Toma retold the tale of ancient spiritual conquest and modern
military reconquest, and each year, the city council renewed the city's bond with
St. Cecilio at his annual festival at the Sacromonte. In the 1780s the cathedral
chapter commissioned a chapel dedicated to St. Cecilio, located in the place of
honor at the center of the ambulatory, directly behind the sanctuary. Decorative
displays for Corpus Christi, Granada's most elaborate annual festivity, often included "hieroglyphs" of St. Cecilio and the Sacromonte as symbols of the city's
spiritual heritage. In 1774, for example, the theme for the decorations was the history of Granada, envisioned as a series of religious victories. In Plaza Bibarrambla, Corinthian columns supported a frieze depicting the most famous incidents
in the Christian conquest of Muslim Granada, while near the Plaza Nueva hung
a painting of the Virgin appearing to St. James and his followers on the Sacromonte. Appended verses elaborated for the literate: "Granada has thus been lib-
erated / From the African yoke that subjected her / And always aided and protected / By Mary, and God in the Sacrament; / A privilege that all Spain enjoys /
Since this Lady in Zaragoza / And on our Granadino Sacromonte / (Leaving her
[Spain] commended to St. James) / In mortal flesh honored our horizon."[14]

Thus, the communal past constituted and made present in the *plomos* remained an important aspect of Granadino communal identity long after their
disappearance and disgrace. That the texts that documented Granada's ancient
heritage were condemned forgeries did not destroy the canonical status of this invented past. As one commentator on the *plomos* and the falsified histories current
in seventeenth-century Spanish historiography has noted, "the problem of the

'false chronicles' is not their falseness but their success."[15] Though the *plomos* themselves disappeared into the bowels of the Vatican, the myth of the Sacromonte remained a vital part of Granadino self-consciousness, especially as articulated by the city's civic and ecclesiastical elites.[16]

Who Forged the *Plomos*?

Forgers' motives are various and often interrelated. It is difficult to separate those who forge for pious reasons from those who forge out of malice or greed. The forgeries of the Torre Turpiana and the Sacromonte were directed at multiple targets; they responded not only to the needs of the beleaguered Morisco minority for cultural survival but also to immigrant Christian Granadinos' desires for an suitably ancient and honorable Christian past. Protective and patriotic forgeries of this sort litter the terrain of European history. Medieval nations, institutions, and individuals regularly reinforced claims to privileges, property, and primacy with faked charters, registers, and other texts—one scholar estimates that two-thirds of all documents issued to ecclesiastics before 1100 are forgeries.[17] The twelfth century in particular seems to have marked a zenith of forgery, as histories like Geoffrey of Monmouth's (d. 1155) *Historia Regum Britanniae* transformed ancient Britons into Trojans and created an enduring fashion for classical and biblical ancestors.[18] The impulse to exalt national and local history through forgery persisted through the Renaissance and Enlightenment. While the late fifteenth-century forger Giovanni Nanni turned his pen to the exaltation of his native Viterbo and of the national traditions of France, Germany, and Spain, for example, the teenaged Curzio Inghirami (1614–55) "discovered" the Etruscscan heritage of his fellow Tuscans.[19] Another talented young forger, Thomas Chatterton (1752–70), enriched the history of his native Bristol with the ballads, genealogies, and antiquarian treatises of the fifteenth-century scholar-poet Thomas Rowley, and James Macpherson's (1736–96) Gaelic songs made an Enlightened poet of the ancient Highland prince Ossian.[20] Like these well-known forgeries, the *plomos* were confected as long-lost documents inscribed in obscure and archaic scripts, their discovery heralded by fanfare both earthly and divine. They are also artfully produced objects that reveal a great deal of historical and archaeological imagination.[21] Unlike some other forgeries, however, the lead books simultaneously produced and appropriated the authority of their purported creator. While the Torre Turpiana prophecy masqueraded as the work of St. John the Evangelist, the lead books aimed not to fit into an established authorial canon but rather to create both canon and author from existing traditions within Granada's Morisco and Old Christian communities.

This shared heritage—Morisco and Old Christian—not only reflects the blended culture of sixteenth-century Granada but also suggests the identities of the architects of the forgeries. Since the sixteenth century, scholars have pointed to two Moriscos, Miguel de Luna and Alonso de Castillo, as the probable creators of the *plomos*. The indictment of Luna and Castillo rests upon their professional activities and upon the close connections between the *plomos* and Morisco culture. Most recently, Mercedes García-Arenal has hypothesized that these forgers worked with the support of one or more of Granada's powerful elite Morisco families, who sought to advance their claims to nobility through the *plomos*.[22] The *plomos*, however, also reflected concerns more directly associated with non-Moriscos. The parchment and lead books lent credence to the city's traditional ties to St. Cecilio and the legendary Seven Apostles of Spain. As we have seen, official devotion to St. Cecilio in sixteenth-century Granada lagged behind that accorded to St. Gregory of Baetica. At the time of the discovery of the lead books, the city council was expanding the cult of St. Gregory through its renovation of the saint's shrine and patronage of his annual festival. The timing of the finds suggests that the authors of the lead books sought to advance the cause of St. Cecilio against that of St. Gregory. Similarly, the creators of the finds in the Torre Turpiana seem to have sought to encourage devotion to St. Stephen. The concern for the veneration of the saints and their bodies—devotions strongly encouraged by the Tridentine Church—and the promotion of a patron saint not controlled by the city's secular elites suggest clerical involvement in the forgeries' creation.[23]

The *plomos* also supported Spain's long-standing claim to have received the Gospel from St. James. Based on a reading of Pedro García de Loaysa Girón's *Collectio conciliorum Hispaniae* (Madrid, 1593), Cardinal Cesare Baronio revised the saint's entry in the Roman Breviary. The new breviary, published in 1602, provoked an uproar in Spain by describing St. James's mission to Iberia as merely a traditional belief of the Spanish Church. Defenders of the legend pointed to the *plomos* as important evidence of the saint's presence in Spain. Mauro Castellá Ferrer, for example, included secondhand accounts of the *plomos* given him by Miguel de Luna and others in his lengthy book on St. James's relationship with Spain throughout the centuries.[24] In creating the lead books, the forgers may have sought to shore up the legend of St. James in Spain and the cult of the saint in Granada, which suggests that they could have been clerics or members of Granada's immigrant Christian community. However, St. James was also popular with some Moriscos, who identified him as one of the followers of Muhammad.[25]

Of the many priests and religious active in Granada in the 1580s and 1590s, one individual emerges as best fitting the profile of a possible co-conspirator. In 1588 Francisco López Tamarid was a respected member of the cathedral clergy, holding the position of prebendary major (*racionero mayor*), as well as that of royal interpreter and interpreter for the Holy Office. A noted expert in Arabic language—his *Compendio de algunos vocablos arábigos* served as an important source for Sebastián de Covarrubias Orozco's *Tesoro de la lengua castellana, o española* (1611)—López Tamarid took an active role in translating the parchment found in the Torre Turpiana.[26] Together with Luna, Castillo, and José Fajardo, a beneficed priest in the parish of St. Cecilio, López Tamarid translated the Arabic portion of the parchment, and sent a copy to royal secretary Mateo Vázquez de Leca.[27]

Was Francisco López Tamarid a Morisco? The catalog of Granada's cathedral archive lists no genealogy to prove his *limpieza de sangre,* or purity from Muslim or Jewish ancestry. Curiously, twenty years earlier, during the Morisco revolt, an identically named beneficed priest in the Alpujarras suffered significant financial losses—real estate, livestock, and movable goods worth the sizable sum of 400 ducats—when his Morisco neighbors took revenge on him for being a traitor to his own people. This Francisco López Tamarid—a priest *and* a Morisco—later became part of the Christian delegation that negotiated with the rebel leader El Habaquí in May 1570.[28] It is highly probable that the two—the scholarly translator from the cathedral and the Morisco priest from the village in the Alpujarras—are one and the same. The Crown rewarded other Morisco priests for their services with important positions in the clerical hierarchy in Granada and elsewhere. Francisco de Torrijos, who also served on the delegation to El Habaquí, outranked the *racionero* López Tamarid as a full canon. Another Morisco on the delegation became a high-ranking member of the chapter of the cathedral of Málaga.[29] As a member of the Granada cathedral clergy, López Tamarid would have had relatively easy access to the site where workers found the lead box containing the parchment and relics. As a Morisco, he would probably have been concerned with the cultural survival of his own endangered ethnic group.[30] As a cleric, he would likely have been concerned with reinforcing devotion to the saints in Granada. On the other hand, in a 1588 letter to Vázquez de Leca, López Tamarid argued that the ancient bishop described in the Torre Turpiana parchment was not the same Cecilio who evangelized Granada but rather a namesake living at least seven centuries later—a suggestion that complicates his candidacy as conspirator for St. Cecilio.[31]

When López Tamarid died is unknown, and there is no evidence that he was associated with the finds on the Sacromonte—a fact that raises the unanswerable question of whether the Torre Turpiana and the Sacromonte forgeries were created by the same person or persons. While the two finds share the same basic concern for Morisco cultural survival, the parchment and relics from Torre Turpiana hint at a second, different agenda. While no one institution seems to have benefited from the finds on the Sacromonte, the 1588 discoveries provided powerful and prestigious relics for the cathedral, on whose terrain they were uncovered. Could a member or members of the cathedral clergy have been involved with the Torre Turpiana forgeries? Without further evidence we can only guess at the truth, but the coincidence of Moriscos and motives in the cathedral is suggestive.

Other factors suggest that the forgers had ties to antiquarian circles. Though highly literate, even (in the case of Castillo) erudite, neither of the Morisco suspects is known to have taken any interest in classical or Christian antiquity. The nature of the forgeries, especially those from the Sacromonte, suggests an author with a passable (though faulty) command of the history of ancient Andalusia and an acquaintance with the small corpus of Latin inscriptions from Granada and its environs, like the seventh-century text recording a church dedicated to St. Stephen or the Roman inscriptions from Iliberis. The forgeries also suggest familiarity with the medieval sources for the legend of St. Cecilio and the Seven Apostles of Spain. Local antiquarians of the sort that fitted this description—the obscure and provincial heirs of the early humanists—could be found all over early modern Europe, busily excavating and interpreting the long lost remains of their cities' antiquity. Occasionally, such scholars were not content to uncover the classical past but created it themselves. Renaissance scholars, so famous for their historicist outlook and critical attitude, sometimes replaced the traditions and myths they debunked with new ones, supported by fabricated textual proofs. The eminent historian Carlo Sigonio (d. 1584) disgraced himself by forging Cicero's *Consolatio,* and even the arch-humanist Erasmus tried to cloak his own religious opinions under the name of St. Cyprian.[32] Early modern Granada had its own humanist forger in the person of cathedral prebendary Juan López Serrano.[33] This well-known local antiquarian provided historian Justino Antolínez de Burgos with important source material, including transcriptions of inscriptions that were later condemned by contemporary scholars as blatant falsifications.[34] López Serrano's name is also linked to a forged inscription that transformed a medieval bridge near Granada into an honorable Roman relic.[35]

Portions of the *plomos* themselves suggest that the forgers may have collaborated with local antiquarians. The Latin and Castilian texts included in the Torre Turpiana parchment, for example, mimic the difficult, crabbed scripts of medieval documents, while the Latin inscriptions etched onto the funerary plaques from the Sacromonte closely resemble the mysterious writings of Spain's pre-Roman inhabitants.[36] While most early modern Spanish antiquarians focused their epigraphic studies on the Iberian Peninsula's Greek and Roman heritage, a few took an interest in the Celtiberian writings that occasionally turned up in fields and excavations.[37] Inscribed on coins, stone, and, importantly, on lead tablets very similar to the Sacromonte plaques, the strange alphabets eluded decipherment—"They [the inscriptions] are all wanderers in their own country," mourned Sevillano scholar Rodrigo Caro.[38] The close resemblance between these ancient writings and the "hispano-betic" letters of the Sacromonte funerary texts suggests that the forgers had connections to the antiquarian circles in which the ancient Celtiberian inscriptions were collected and discussed.[39]

The case indicting Luna and Castillo is circumstantial but deeply grounded in the *plomos*' Morisco origins. Similarly, although the evidence for the involvement of Francisco López Tamarid and other local clerics and antiquarians is admittedly problematic and incomplete, it is rooted in the *plomos*' broader Granadino cultural context. In its focus on the discourses of identity constructed around the *plomos*, one of the underlying aims of this book has been to contextualize them not only within Morisco culture but also within Granada's Christian, immigrant society. The *plomos* and the discourses to which they gave rise were expressions of not just the Morisco community but also of the Granadino community as a whole and of its unique local culture and society.

The *plomos*' embeddedness in Granadino society and culture helps explain the persistent question of how these finds, so patently bogus, so obviously heterodox, could have been accepted as genuine remains of earliest Christianity. The *plomos*, and the discourses to which they gave rise, told Granadinos what they already knew in their hearts—that their city owed nothing to Islam but was instead the direct descendant of a noble and pious ancient Christian republic. The *plomos* were long-lost patents of nobility and certificates of baptism; they were Granada's municipal and communal archive. Like the fabricated genealogies of seventeenth-century forger Alfonso Ceccarelli, the *plomos* documented the past in accordance with the preconceptions, preferences, and perceptions not of outsiders but of local people embedded in local culture.[40]

The close relationship between the *plomos* and their local context is, I think, at the heart of both their successes and their failures. Although the *plomos* failed as efforts to preserve and affirm Morisco ethnic and cultural identity, as the source

for largely Old Christian discourses of communal belonging they were immensely successful. Read through the lens of local needs and local values, the *plomos* became the founding monuments of a Catholic and Castilian Granadino
communal identity. Outside the local context of Granadino society and culture,
however, the *plomos'* Morisco roots became painfully evident. Once pried loose
from their place in local Christian culture and shipped to Madrid, the *plomos* began to succumb to their own internal contradictions. "This," comments Susan
Stewart, "is the vulnerability of forgeries—their incapacity to carry their appropriate contexts with them."[41]

The Sacromonte Today

Despite their confiscation and condemnation, the legacy of the *plomos* persists
in Granadino society. Today, Granadino communal identity is grounded in different symbols. Since its rediscovery in the nineteenth century by romantic writers
like Washington Irving, the Alhambra has become the principal local *lieu de mémoire,* the monument of Granada's once despised Muslim past. The Sacromonte
remains an important symbol of Granada and Granadino civic identity, though
the meanings ascribed to it have changed with time. The Sacromonte is known
now less for its place in an invented Christian antiquity but as a center of Andalusian Gypsy culture. By the beginning of the twentieth century, the area was
home to a large Gypsy population, most of which lived in caves dug into the hills.
Forced evacuations after major floods in the 1960s dramatically reduced the
number of inhabitants in the area, and by the 1980s the vibrant Gypsy culture of
the Sacromonte had degenerated into a collection of tourist-trap bars peddling expensive drinks and tacky flamenco.[42] The Sacromonte underwent some regeneration in the 1990s. The city government extended bus service to the area and
opened a center for Gypsy studies there, but still, few visitors make the journey
along the Camino del Sacromonte, past the Church of the Holy Sepulcher, and
up the hill to the abbey.

Today, those sightseers who do find their way to the Abbey of the Sacromonte
can see not only the cloister, church, and caves, but the *plomos* themselves. After
their censure, the parchment and the lead books were left to molder in some forgotten corner of the Vatican. On June 17, 2000, however, the renewed petitions
of the archiepiscopate of Granada, the Parliament of Andalusia, and the United
Left electoral coalition finally bore fruit, as the future Pope Benedict XVI, Cardinal Joseph Ratzinger, then prefect of the Congregation for the Doctrine of the
Faith (formerly the Congregation of the Roman and Universal Inquisition) trans-

ferred custody of the lead books and the parchment to Antonio Cañizares Llovet, archbishop of Granada. After nearly 360 years, the *plomos* returned to Granada and to the Sacromonte. Today, they are on display in the Abbey of the Sacromonte's small museum.

The *plomos* of the Sacromonte and the mythical Christian heritage they documented remain part of local culture. An online walking guide to the city available in the late 1990s, for example, included a half-day trip focusing on prehistoric, Roman, and Visigothic Granada; its two destinations were the Provincial Archaeological Museum and St. Cecilio's caves on the Sacromonte.[43] Though he is hardly as popular as Our Lady of Anguish, whose image is displayed in almost every bar and restaurant in town, or Leopoldo de Alpandeire, a Capuchin friar venerated by many Granadinos, St. Cecilio remains Granada's patron saint, and city dwellers still make the pilgrimage to the abbey each year on February 1, the date established by the *plomos,* to celebrate with dancing and a traditional meal of cod, green beans, and salted bread.[44] Indeed, after a decline in attendance in the 1970s, St. Cecilio's annual festival day has become increasingly popular.[45] This trend parallels a growing diversity in Granada's religious landscape, as the city has become home to a vibrant and visible Muslim population centered around a recently inaugurated mosque located in the heart of the old Morisco neighborhood of the Albaicín.[46] While most of Granada's approximately 15,000 Muslims are immigrants, at least 1,000 are native Granadinos and former Catholics, some of whom interpret their religious conversion as part of a broader revaluation of Andalusia's Islamic heritage.[47] Like the *plomos,* Islam has returned to Granada; together, they testify to the plurality of pasts and of communal identities available in contemporary Spain.

Notes

ABBREVIATIONS

AASG	Archivo de la Abadía del Sacromonte de Granada
ABFZ	Archivo y Biblioteca de Francisco de Zabálburu, Madrid
ACDF	Archivio della Congregazione per la Dottrina della Fede, Vatican City
ACG	Archivo de la Catedral de Granada
AGI	Archivo General de Indias, Seville
AGS	Archivo General de Simancas
AHN	Archivo Histórico Nacional, Madrid
AMG	Archivo Municipal de Granada
APSC	Archivo de la Parroquia de San Cecilio, Granada
APSPSP	Archivo de la Parroquia de San Pedro y San Pablo, Granada
BBMS	Biblioteca de Bartolomé March Servera, Madrid
BL	British Library, London
BN	Biblioteca Nacional de España, Madrid
BUG	Biblioteca de la Universidad de Granada
RAH	Real Academia de la Historia, Madrid
RBE	Real Biblioteca de El Escorial, San Lorenzo de El Escorial
RBP	Real Biblioteca del Palacio, Madrid
S.O.	Sanctum Officium, ACDF
St. St.	Stanza Storica, ACDF
leg., legs.	legajo, legajos
pt., pts.	parte, partes

INTRODUCTION

1. For an excellent overview of the early modern and modern historiography of the Sacromonte, see the preliminary study included in Royo Campos, *Reliquias martiriales*, xxxix–lxxxii.

2. Ramos López, *El Sacro-Monte de Granada*. Zótico Royo Campos produced a string of short works on themes related to the history of the Sacromonte. As well as the aforementioned *Reliquias martiriales*, the more notable of his opuscules include *El Insigne Colegio-*

Seminario del Sacro-Monte; Albores del Sacro Monte; Abades del Sacromonte; and *Bellezas sacromontanas.*

3. Godoy Alcántara, *Historia crítica de los falsos cronicones.*

4. Fuente, *Historia eclesiástica de España;* Menéndez y Pelayo, *Historia de los heterodoxos españoles.*

5. Alonso, *Los apócrifos;* Caro Baroja, *Las falsificaciones.*

6. Cabanelas Rodríguez, "Cartas del morisco granadino Miguel de Luna"; "Arias Montano y los libros plúmbeos de Granada"; "Un intento de sincretismo islámico-cristiano"; "Intento de supervivencia en el ocaso de una cultura"; and *El morisco granadino Alonso de Castillo.*

7. Hagerty, *Los libros plúmbeos,* 54. Unless otherwise noted, all translations in this book are my own. See also the essays by Hagerty and Cabanelas Rodríguez in *La Abadía del Sacromonte.* On the *plomos* and the *jofor* genre, see López-Baralt, "Crónica de la destrucción de un mundo," 49–58.

8. Kendrick, *St. James in Spain,* 141, and "An Example of the Theodicy-Motive in Antiquarian Thought."

9. Bonet Correa, "Entre la superchería y la fe," 50, 52.

10. Orozco Pardo, *Christianópolis,* 139. See also the comments of López Guzmán, *Tradición y clasicismo,* 39–57.

11. Fuchs, *Mimesis and Empire,* 99–117; Harvey, *Muslims in Spain, 1500 to 1614,* 264–90.

12. Coleman, *Creating Christian Granada,* 188–201; Martínez Medina, "El Sacromonte de Granada y los discursos Inmaculistas postridentistas." For an excellent sampling of current work on the *plomos,* see the 2002 and 2003 issues of the journal *Al-Qanṭara* 23:2 and 24:2.

13. E.g., Ladero Quesada, *La incorporación de Granada;* Cortés Peña and Vincent, *Historia de Granada,* vol. 3.

14. See also Garrido Aranda, *Organización de la iglesia en el reino de Granada;* Gaignard, *Maures et chrétiens à Grenade.*

15. Covarrubias Orozco, *Tesoro,* 672. O'Gorman, *The Invention of America,* 9, comments on this linguistic nexus.

16. Handler, "Is 'Identity' a Useful Cross-Cultural Concept?" 30.

17. Amelang, "Círculos de sociabilidad e identitades urbanas"; Ruiz Ibáñez, *Las dos caras de Jano,* 116–17. Unlike their fellows in Spanish cities and kingdoms outside Castile, early modern Granadino patriots infrequently discussed Granada's *fueros,* the laws and privileges granted and guaranteed by the Crown. Cf. J. Casey, "Patriotism in Early Modern Valencia."

18. Lowenthal, "Fabricating Heritage," 7–11. See also Lowenthal, *The Heritage Crusade,* 119–26.

19. Elliott, "Revolution and Continuity," 105.

20. I borrow this term from Burke, "History as Social Memory," 107.

21. The dossier produced by the panel of inquiry is AASG, C49: *Proceso de las reliquias.* The Archive of the Congregation for the Doctrine of the Faith holds a mid-seventeenth-century copy of this document: ACDF S.O., St. St. R 7 c.

22. Hobsbawm and Ranger, *The Invention of Tradition.*

23. Anderson, *Imagined Communities.* See also Cohen, *The Symbolic Construction of Community.*

24. Nora, *Les lieux de mémoire.* A revised and abridged version has also been published in English: Nora, *Realms of Memory.* See also the comments of Englund, "The Ghost of Nation Past."

25. R. MacKay, *The Limits of Royal Authority,* 3. See Elliott, "A Europe of Composite Monarchies" and "Revolution and Continuity."

26. Sahlins, *Boundaries.* See also Herzog, *Defining Nations.*

27. Thompson, "Castile, Spain and the Monarchy," 156.

28. Christian, *Local Religion.* For Spain, local studies in English include Nalle, *God in La Mancha;* Kamen, *The Phoenix and the Flame;* Bilinkoff, *The Ávila of Saint Teresa;* Coleman, *Creating Christian Granada;* Poska, *Regulating the People.*

29. See esp. Ditchfield, "In Search of Local Knowledge."

30. Holt, "Burgundians into Frenchmen."

31. Bloch, "A Contribution," 56.

PROLOGUE: OLD BONES FOR A NEW CITY

1. For contemporary descriptions, see Centurión y Córdoba, *Información,* fols. 2r–4r; López Madera, *Discursos de la certidumbre,* fols. 37r–40v. A frequently reproduced seventeenth-century engraving by Francisco Heylan depicts the tower with several other local monuments and edifices thought to be of ancient construction. See Moreno Garrido, "El grabado en Granada durante el siglo XVII," 198.

2. In his *De la invención de las reliquias, láminas, y, libros, del Monte Sancto de Granada* (manuscript, 1607; AASG C28 and RAH 9/5843), Gregorio Morillo, a chaplain in the Collegiate Church of the Sacromonte, included lines showing the length of the different dimensions of the box. According to his depiction, the box was 16 cm, 2 mm long; and 12 cm, 6 mm wide. Morillo does not include the box's height.

3. ACDF S.O., St. St. R 7 c(3), fol. 307v.

4. The cathedral chapter recorded the momentous day in ACG, Libros de Actas, vol. 8, fol. 113.

5. Hagerty, *Los libros plúmbeos del Sacromonte,* 25.

6. The full text of the prophecy is reprinted in ibid., 22–23.

7. Kagan, *Lucrecia's Dreams.*

8. AASG, leg. 5, fols. 15–16: letter to royal almoner Pedro García de Loaysa Girón, Granada, April 20, 1588. On Salvatierra, see López Rodríguez, *Los arzobispos de Granada,* 84–101.

9. Letters: AASG, leg. 5, fols. 17–20. On Philip II's relic collection, see Andrés, "Historia y descripción del Camarín de reliquias de El Escorial"; Lazure, "Monarchie et identité spirituelle." On Arias Montano's involvement in the discoveries, see Cabanelas Rodríguez, "Arias Montano."

10. Centurión y Córdoba, *Información,* fols. 11r–12v.

11. Among the local worthies assembled to consider the 1588 finds was the future saint

Juan de la Cruz, then prior of Granada's Discalced Carmelite monastery. Hagerty, "Los libros plúmbeos," 31. Ximénez, *Descripción*, 276, listed the piece from the handkerchief among the most important Marian relics in the royal collection. One eighteenth-century writer reported that the relic sent to the Escorial miraculously healed king Philip II of pain in his head, eyes, and right hand incurred in an accident. See Heredia Barnuevo, *Místico ramillete*, 100. According to Diego de Escolano, archbishop of Granada from 1668 to 1672, the other half of the handkerchief was preserved in a Discalced Carmelite convent in Puebla, Mexico. Escolano, who had been bishop of Segovia before his move to Granada, claimed that this half of the relic had been in the possession of St. Hieroteo, who brought it to Spain when he came to evangelize Segovia, from whence it made its way to the colonies. Escolano, *Chronicon Sancti Hierothei*, 703.

12. ACG, Libros de Actas, vol. 8, fol. 151. Terrones's treatise against the relics is included in AASG, leg. 4, pt. 1, fols. 31–36. Terrones became a celebrated preacher at the royal court in Madrid and was later appointed bishop of the sees of Tuy and León. On his critique of the finds from the Old Tower, see also Terrones del Cano, *Obras completas*, 407–49.

13. Heredia Barnuevo, *Místico ramillete*, 12. On Marmól's assessment of the relics from the minaret, see Cabanelas Rodríguez, *El morisco granadino*, 250–56.

14. On the translator, Isidro García, S.J. (1566–1604), a teacher of rhetoric at Granada's Jesuit college, see *Historia del Colegio de San Pablo, Granada 1554–1765*, 41.

15. Bermúdez de Pedraza, *Historia eclesiástica*, fol. 268.

16. AASG, C49, fols. 271–77, 327–32, 415–30. See also Coleman, *Creating Christian Granada*, 199.

17. AASG, C49, fol. 13r.

18. AASG, C49, fols. 280–88.

19. AASG, C49, fols. 280–81.

20. AASG, leg. 5, fol. 186r; Alonso, *Los apócrifos*, 98.

21. Centurión y Córdoba, *Información*, fols. 81r, 85r.

22. López Madera, *Discurso de la certidumbre*, fol. 5. Only a handful of the crosses remain on the Sacromonte: one from the town of Iznalloz; one erected by the soldiers of the Alhambra (1595); one by the porters (*ganapanes*) of the Plaza Bibarrambla and Plaza Nueva (1602); and one from the Brotherhood of the Nativity of the Mother of God (1604). On the crosses, see Gallego y Burín, *Granada*, 360–62.

23. Gila Medina, "La Cruz de Guadix en el Sacromonte granadino"; Hagerty, "Los libros plúmbeos," 23.

24. Alonso, *Los apócrifos*, 79; Centurión y Córdoba, *Información*, fol. 86v.

25. AASG, C49, fols. 215–21.

26. AASG, C49, fols. 69–99, 102–14.

27. On the social background of the miracle recipients, see Coleman, *Creating Christian Granada*, 199.

28. AASG, C49, fols. 20r, 25r.

29. Antolínez de Burgos, *Historia*, 525–28; Centurión y Córdoba, *Información*, fols. 90r–95r.

30. On Luna and Castillo, see Cabanelas Rodríguez, "Cartas del morisco granadino Miguel de Luna" and *El morisco granadino Alonso de Castillo*.

31. Canon Guerrero was the nephew and namesake of Pedro Guerrero (1501–76), arch-bishop of Granada and leader of the Spanish faction at the Council of Trent. For the sentence on the relics, see *Sentencia con que se autorizaron las reliquias; Sentencia con que se calificaron las reliquias de doze mártyres; Nos Don Pedro de Castro.*

32. RAH 9/3662, n. 134: *Relación de lo que ha passado en la qualificación de las reliquias que se hallaron en la ciudad Granada 1600,* unpaginated. See also Orozco Pardo, "Una fiesta alegórica en Plaza Bibarrambla."

ONE: GRANADA IN THE SIXTEENTH CENTURY

1. For a discussion of Granada's population at the turn of the fifteenth century, see Cortés Peña and Vincent, *Historia de Granada,* 47–48. Bernard Vincent has suggested elsewhere that Granada's population in 1492 may have numbered around 100,000. Vincent, "Economía y sociedad en el reino de Granada en el siglo XVI," 163.

2. Travelers often commented with displeasure on the narrowness of Granada's streets; e.g., Hillgarth, *The Mirror of Spain,* 52 n. 168.

3. Münzer, *Viaje por España y Portugal,* 89–141. For an early visual representation of Granada by a foreign visitor, see Angulo Iñiguez, "La ciudad de Granada vista por un pintor flamenco de hacia 1500." See also Vincent, "La vision du royaume de Grenade."

4. Seco de Lucena Paredes, *La Granada nazarí del siglo XV.*

5. Münzer, *Viaje por España y Portugal,* 91.

6. Navagiero, *Il viaggio,* fol. 18v.

7. Lalaing, "Relation du premier voyage," 206.

8. Gallego y Burín, *Granada,* 126, 284, 344, 346, 384–85, 387.

9. Garrido Atienza, *Las capitulaciones para la entrega de Granada,* 273.

10. Garrad, "The Original Memorial," 215–16; Fernández de Madrid, *Vida de Fray Fernando de Talavera,* 53–54.

11. On converts from Islam before 1499, see Pérez Boyero, "Los mudéjares granadinos."

12. On Christian attitudes toward Islamic architecture, see Marías, *El largo siglo XVI,* 181–97.

13. On Granada's Jewish community, see Lacave, "Las juderías del reino de Granada"; Gonzalo Maeso, *Garnata al-Yahud.* On the debates over the size of the Jewish population in Granada in 1492, see Spivakovsky, "The Jewish Presence in Granada."

14. Münzer, *Viaje por España y Portugal,* 101.

15. On the building of the cathedral, see Rosenthal, *The Cathedral of Granada.* On the decline of the mosque-cathedral in the early modern period, see Suberbiola Martínez, "El ocaso de las mezquitas-catedrales del reino de Granada."

16. Nieto Alcaide, "El mito de la arquitectura árabe"; Rosenthal, *The Palace of Charles V in Granada.* On Charles V's sojourn in Granada, see Vilar Sánchez, *1526.*

17. For a useful summary of urban reforms in sixteenth-century Granada, see Cortés Peña and Vincent, *Historia de Granada,* 24–43; Viñes Millet, *Historia urbana de Granada;* Vincent, "De la Granada mudéjar a la Granada europea."

18. On population changes before 1500, see Ladero Quesada, "La repoblación"; Galán

Sánchez, "Los vencidos," 537–42. On immigration after 1500, see Coleman, *Creating Christian Granada*, 19–31.

19. Ruiz Martín, "Movimientos demográficos," 143–52.

20. Cortés Peña and Vincent, *Historia de Granada*, 56–57; Ladero Quesada, "La repoblación," 493. Peinado Santaella includes a useful table outlining immigrant origins in "La sociedad repobladora," 506.

21. López de Coca Castañer, "El trabajo de mudéjares y moriscos," 123–26.

22. Coleman, *Creating Christian Granada*, 27–28.

23. López Muñoz, *Las cofradías de la Parroquia de Santa María Magdalena*, 47; Cortés Peña and Vincent, *Historia de Granada*, 98, 133–34.

24. Cortés Peña and Vincent, *Historia de Granada*, 95–104.

25. Medina, *Libro de las grandezas y cosas memorables de España*, 191.

26. Cortés Peña and Vincent, *Historia de Granada*, 142.

27. López de Coca Castañer, "El trabajo de mudéjares y moriscos," 126–28.

28. Henríquez de Jorquera, *Anales*, 1:82. On the Alcaicería building, see Gallego y Burín, *Granada*, 226–29, and López Guzmán, *Tradición y clasicismo*, 74–79.

29. Garzón Pareja, *La industria sedera en España;* Garrad, "La industria sedera"; Cortés Peña and Vincent, *Historia de Granada*, 135–41. For an overview of industry in Granada, see Garzón Pareja, "Industria de Granada (1492–1900)"; Castillo and Díaz López, "Las actividades económicas."

30. The discussion that follows owes a great deal to Coleman, *Creating Christian Granada*.

31. Kagan, *Lawsuits and Litigants*.

32. Gan Giménez, "La ciudad de Granada en el siglo XVI," 13–14, and *La Real Chancillería de Granada;* Kagan, *Lawsuits and Litigants*, 169–70; Ruiz Rodríguez, *La Real Chancillería*. On the Chancery building, see Gallego y Burín, *Granada*, 329–34.

33. See López Nevot, *La organización institucional;* Ruiz Povedano, "Las ciudades y el poder municipal."

34. Galán Sánchez, *Los mudéjares*, 143–50.

35. López Guzmán, *Tradición y clasicismo*, 73, 517–19; Gallego y Burín, *Granada*, 230–32.

36. BN, MS 5989, fol. 92, cited in Calero Palacios, *La enseñanza*, 31.

37. Over the course of the century, the number of positions on the council rose rapidly, from twenty-six councilmen in 1556, to forty-four in 1584. López Nevot, *La organización institucional*, 113–16. See also the list of new *veinticuatrías* in Garzón Pareja, *Historia de Granada*, 1:203–4.

38. Cortés Peña and Vincent, *Historia de Granada*, 173–74. On the Mendozas in Granada, see Nader, *The Mendoza Family*.

39. Suberbiola Martínez, *Real Patronato de Granada;* Cortés Peña, "A propósito de la Iglesia y la conquista del Reino de Granada." For an overview of the founding of the Church in Granada, see Marín López, "La Iglesia y el encuadramiento religioso."

40. Marín López, *El Cabildo de la Catedral*. See also Gan Giménez, "Los prebendados."

41. Castillo Pintado, "El servicio de Millones." These figures for 1591 are supported by the numbers given in Archbishop Pedro de Castro's 1596 *ad limina* visitation, which esti-

mates the number of religious to be around 1,200 (600 male, 600 female), and the number of secular priests to be about 220. Vincent, "De la Granada mudéjar a la Granada europea," 313. For an overview of the Granadino Church in the sixteenth century, see Martínez Medina, "La Iglesia."

42. For a recent survey of the Inquisition in early modern Granada, see Pérez de Colosia, "La Inquisición."

43. Kagan, *Students and Society*, 198.

44. On education in late sixteenth-century Granada, see Calero Palacios, *La enseñanza*, and Calero Palacios, Arias de Saavedra, and Viñes Millet, *Historia de la Universidad de Granada;* Henares Cuéllar and López Guzmán, *Universidad y ciudad*. On the *colegios* of Granada, see López Rodríguez, *El Colegio Real de Santa Cruz;* Martín Hernández, *Un seminario español pretridentino*.

45. Ruiz Rodríguez, *La Real Chancillería*, 19.

46. Gan Giménez, "En torno al Corpus granadino."

47. López Nevot, *La organización institucional*, 354–55.

48. Cepeda Adán, "Los últimos Mendozas granadinos del siglo XVI."

49. AMG, "Personal," leg. 930, pieza 78; ACG, Libros de Actas, vol. 9, fols. 334v–336r; Antolínez de Burgos, *Historia*, 445–51.

50. López Nevot, *La organización institucional*, 215–17.

51. Cortés Peña and Vincent, *Historia de Granada*, 182.

52. ACG, Libros de Varios Asuntos, vol. 2, fols. 367–92.

53. Cortés Peña and Vincent, *Historia de Granada*, 190. See also Ruiz Povedano, "Las ciudades y el poder municipal."

54. Soria Mesa, *La venta de señoríos*, 58, 129; Vilar, "Formes et tendances de l'opposition sous Olivares," 273; Lera García, "Venta de oficios en la Inquisición de Granada." López Madera became a leading defender of the relic finds in Granada. Born in Madrid, López Madera was the son of Gregorio López Madera, physician to Charles V and Philip II. After receiving his doctorate in law from the University of Valencia, López Madera taught in Alcalá de Henares. He entered royal service, serving as a judge in the Casa de Contratación in Seville, then as prosecutor in Granada, and then as a prosecutor for the Council of Finance in Madrid. In 1604 he was named to the ranks of the *Alcaldes de Casa y Corte*, a prominent body whose main duty was the policing of the capital. He served as *corregidor* of Toledo, and in 1619 Philip III elevated him to the Council of Castile. A member of the Order of St. James since 1631, López Madera retired from the council in 1641 and died in Madrid in 1649. See Pérez Pastor, *Bibliografía madrileña*, 278–80, 417–18; Ballesteros Robles, *Diccionario biográfico matritense*, 385; Fayard, *Los miembros del Consejo de Castilla*, 76; Martínez Torres and García Ballesteros, "Gregorio López Madera (1562–1649)."

55. Moreno Olmedo, *Heráldica y genealogía granadinas*, 168; Obra Sierra, *Mercaderes italianos en Granada*.

56. On the geographical and social backgrounds of the city councillors, see Coleman, *Creating Christian Granada*, 40–42, 77–81, 185–86; López Nevot, *La organización institucional*, 132–50.

57. Soria Mesa, "Nobles advenedizos."

58. Bennassar, *Valladolid en el Siglo de Oro*, 375–79; Phillips, *Ciudad Real*, 106–8.

59. García Pedraza, "La asimilación del morisco don Gonzalo Fernández el Zegrí"; Moreno Olmedo, *Heráldica y genealogía granadinas*, 43–44, 88–91, 104–6; Soria Mesa, "De la conquista a la asimilación" and "La asimilación de la élite morisca en la Granada cristiana." For a good survey of the origins of Granada's urban oligarchs, see Ruiz Povedano, "Las élites de poder."

60. López Nevot, *La organización institucional*, 147–48.

61. Peinado Santaella and Soria Mesa, "Crianza real y clientelismo nobilario." On Conversos in Granada, see Coleman, *Creating Christian Granada*, 25–26, 79–80, 88; Martz, "Toledanos and the Kingdom of Granada, 1492–1560s"; Ruiz Povedano, "Las ciudades y el poder municipal," 643–45; Soria Mesa, "Los judeoconversos granadinos en el siglo XVI."

62. Cited in López de Coca Castañer, "Judíos, judeoconversos y reconciliados."

63. *Actas de las Cortes de Castilla*, 197.

64. See Soria Mesa, *La venta de señoríos*, especially the appended tables of estates and purchasers.

65. Domínguez Ortiz, "El Estado de los Austrias," 131.

66. Navagiero, *Il viaggio*, fol. 26r–v. This characterization held true more nearly a century and a half later. Cosimo de' Medici, who visited Granada in 1668, remarked that "Del resto la Città è poplare essendovi la nobilità scarsissima, e nuova." Sánchez Rivero and Mariutti de Sánchez Rivero, *Viaje de Cosme de Médicis*, 210.

67. Pérez Boyero, "Los señoríos y el mundo rural," 585.

68. López Nevot, *La organización institucional*, 127–28.

69. Castillo Fernández, "Las estructuras sociales"; Marín López, *El Cabildo de la Catedral*, 287.

70. Coleman, *Creating Christian Granada*, 88; Marín López, *El Cabildo de la Catedral*, 149–55; Gan Giménez, "Los prebendados," 149–52.

71. See Ruiz Povedano, "Las élites de poder," 390–92.

72. For an overview of new approaches, see Castillo Fernández, "La asimilación de los moriscos granadinos."

73. Garrad, "The Original Memorial," 211.

74. Tapia Garrido, "La costa de los piratas," 97; Borja de Medina, "La Compañía de Jesús," esp. 30.

75. García Pedraza, *Actitudes ante la muerte*, 643–754.

76. Soria Mesa, "La asimilación de la élite morisca," 652; Galán Sánchez, *Los mudéjares*, 249–92, 385–99. On intermarriage, see Coleman, *Creating Christian Granada*, 51–52.

77. Domínguez Ortiz and Vincent, *Historia de los moriscos*, 17–26.

78. Coleman, *Creating Christian Granada*, 60–63; Ruiz Martín, "Movimientos demográficos."

79. Lalaing, "Relation du premier voyage," 208.

80. Coleman, *Creating Christian Granada*, 63.

81. Caro Baroja, *Los moriscos*, 136–40.

82. Coleman, *Creating Christian Granada*, 67. See Perceval, *Todos son uno*.

83. Domínguez Ortiz and Vincent, *Historia de los moriscos*, 31.

84. Ibid., 132–33.

85. Hess, "The Moriscos"; Gaignard, *Maures et chrétiens à Grenade*, 38–39, 47.

86. After the conversion of Granada's *mudéjar* population, the *farda* was extended to Granada's growing Old Christian population; in practice, however, tax exemptions made most immigrants immune to payment. Galán Sánchez, "Los vencidos," 550; J. Castillo Fernández and Muñoz Buendía, "La hacienda," 110–23.

87. Technically, the Inquisition had operated in Granada since 1499, through the tribunal of Córdoba, but it had not been very active. García Fuentes, *La Inquisición en Granada en el siglo XVI*, xvii.

88. López Rodríguez, "El colegio de los niños moriscos de Granada"; Álvarez Rodríguez, "La Casa de Doctrina del Albaicín"; Borja de Medina, "La Compañía de Jesús"; Griffin, "Un muro invisible"; Garrido Aranda, "Papel de la Iglesia de Granada en la asimilación de la sociedad morisca"; Edwards, "Christian Mission in the Kingdom of Granada, 1492–1568."

89. Domínguez Ortiz and Vincent, *Historia de los moriscos*, 28–33; Garrad, "La industria sedera."

90. López Martín, "El concilio provincial de Granada de 1565"; Marín Ocete, "El Concilio provincial de Granada en 1565."

91. See Hitos, *Mártires de la Alpujarra*.

92. Vincent, "Economía y sociedad en el reino de Granada en el siglo XVI," 191–203, and "La expulsión de los moriscos del Reino de Granada." On Moriscos in Granada after 1570, see Vincent, "Los moriscos que permanecieron."

93. Martín Casares, *La esclavitud en la Granada del siglo XVI*. See also Obra Sierra, "Protocolos Notariales."

94. Cortés Peña and Vincent, *Historia de Granada*, 55–56; Ruiz Martín, "Movimientos demográficos," 140–41. See also Vincent, "La población de las Alpujarras en el siglo XVI."

95. AGS, Cámara de Castilla, leg. 2172, quoted in Cortés Peña and Vincent, *Historia de Granada*, 142. See also García Gámez, "La seda del Reino de Granada."

96. Vincent, "El Albaicín," 157–59.

97. Barrios Aguilera, *Moriscos*, 13; Ruiz Martín, "Movimientos demográficos," 152. On immigration to Granada after 1570, see also Barrios Aguilera and Birriel Salcedo, *La repoblación del reino de Granada*.

98. See also Vincent, "La repoblación del reino de Granada (1570–1580)."

99. León, *Grandeza y miseria en Andalucía*, 104.

100. See Vincent, "Economía y sociedad en el reino de Granada en el siglo XVI," in *Historia de Andalucía*, 215–17; "Las epidemias en Andalucía durante el siglo XVI"; "La peste atlántica de 1596–1602"; and "Les pestes dans le royaume de Grenade aux XVIe et XVIIe siècles." On continued famine and demographic decline, see Gil Bracero, "Crisis y fluctuaciones agrícolas." See also Pérez Moreda, "The Plague in Castile at the End of the Sixteenth Century and Its Consequences."

101. Quoted in Cortés Peña and Vincent, *Historia de Granada*, 59–61.

102. AASG, leg. 5, fols. 1–3.

103. Góngora y Argote, *Obras poéticas de D. Luis de Góngora*, 92. Cf. Hillgarth, *The Mirror of Spain*, 103, 110–11.

104. Cortés Peña and Vincent, *Historia de Granada*, 61–65. See also Barrios Aguilera, "El Albaicín de Granada."

105. Bosque Maurel, *Geografía urbana de Granada*, 241–45.

106. Cortés Peña and Vincent, *Historia de Granada*, 142–44. See also García Gámez, "La seda del Reino de Granada."

107. Jouvin, "El viaje de España y Portugal," 822, 824.

108. Kamen, *Spain, 1469–1714*, 171. See Pike, *Aristocrats and Traders*, 1–20.

TWO: CONTROVERSY AND PROPAGANDA

1. Counts of the books vary from author to author. The titles include *On the Fundaments of the Faith; On the Essence of God; Ritual of the Mass of St. James the Apostle; Book of the Preaching of St. James the Apostle; Book of the Famous Acts of Our Lord Jesus and of the Virgin Mary, His Mother; On the Reward of Believers in the "Certainty of the Gospel"; Prayer and Defense of St. James the Apostle, Son of Xameh Zebedee, against All Kinds of Adversities; Lament of Peter, Apostle and Vicar, after the Denial of Our Lord Jesus; History of the Certainty of the Holy Gospel; On the Great Mysteries That St. James the Apostle Saw on the Sacromonte; Book of the Enigmas and Mysteries That the Virgin St. Mary Saw, by the Grace of God, on the Night of Her Colloquy; Book of Sentences on the Faith, Transmitted by St. Mary, Virgin Immaculate, to St. James the Apostle; History of the Seal of Solomon, Son of David, Prophet of God, According to St. Mary; On the Comprehensible [Aspects] of Divine Power, Clemency, and Justice over All Creatures; On the Nature of Angels and on Their Power; Account of the House of Peace and of the House of Vengeance and Torments; On the Famous Deeds of the Apostle St. James and on His Miracles; Second Part of the Comprehensible [Aspects] of Divine Power, Clemency, and Justice over All Creatures; Second Part of the Famous Deeds of the Apostle St. James; Certainty of the Gospel.* Several others were never found (or never written), including *Second Part of the Fundaments of the Faith*, and *Death of the Virgin*.

2. On the Seven Apostles, see García Villada, *Historia eclesiástica de España*, 147–68; Sotomayor y Muro, "La Iglesia en la España romana"; and Vives, "Tradición y leyenda en la hagiografía hispánica."

3. The texts of the lead books have never been translated into English. A Spanish translation by Adán Centurión y Córdoba, Marquis of Estepa, is available in Hagerty, *Los libros plúmbeos*. Note, however, that the Marquis was an ardent devotee of the Sacromonte saints, and his translation should be read with this in mind. See Hagerty, "La traducción interesada."

4. A lead book with this title was recovered from the Sacromonte, but no one has succeeded in translating it. For this reason it is also often called the *Libro mudo*, or the *Mute Book*.

5. Hagerty, *Los libros plúmbeos*, 125–26.

6. Ibid., 129.

7. Ibid., 130.

8. Ibid., *Los libros plúmbeos*, 134. Francisco Javier Martínez Medina suggests that this and similar descriptions were read as referring to Philip II, while Hagerty argues that the authors of the lead books most probably had in mind Ottoman sultan Selim II. Martínez Medina, "Los libros plúmbeos del Sacromonte de Granada," 633; Hagerty, *Los libros plúmbeos*, 131.

9. Hagerty, *Los libros plúmbeos,* 68–69.

10. Ibid., 96.

11. Ibid., 83–84.

12. Ibid., 113, 69. Cf. Matthew 3:17, Mark 1:11, Luke 3:22. See also Hagerty, *Los libros plúmbeos,* 69.

13. Cardaillac, *Moriscos y cristianos,* 235–78; Epalza, *Jésus otage,* 129–226; Anawati, "ʿĪsā."

14. Hagerty, *Los libros plúmbeos,* 157. See also Christodouleas and Matar, "The Mary of the Sacromonte."

15. Wensinck, "Maryam." On Christian theology in the *plomos,* see Martínez Medina, "El Sacromonte de Granada, un intento de reinculturación," 361–63, and "Los hallazgos del Sacromonte."

16. Hagerty, *Los libros plúmbeos,* 79–80, 84–89, 213.

17. Vespertino Rodríguez, *Leyendas aljamiadas,* 42–49. Solomon's ties to the Iberian Peninsula extend beyond his ring; his jewel-encrusted table was supposedly found in Toledo in the eighth century by the invading North African forces. See Rubiera Mata, "La mesa de Salomon."

18. See, for example, the condemnation issued in 1526 by Pedro Manuel, bishop of León, against illicit healers who used the seal of Solomon in healing cures, in García y García, *Synodicon Hispanum,* 361. Among both Old Christians and Conversos, the seal was frequently connected with *Clavicula Salomonis,* a popular medieval magical text. See Caro Baroja, *Vidas mágicas e Inquisición,* 1:135–51.

19. Labarta, "Supersticiones moriscas"; Cardaillac-Hermosilla, *La magie en Espagne,* 58–60.

20. Hagerty, *Los libros plúmbeos,* 304.

21. Cardaillac-Hermosilla, "Le héros, maître du pouvoir magique: Salomon," 153.

22. Cited in Coleman, *Creating Christian Granada,* 193 (his translation).

23. Labarta, "Supersticiones moriscas," 169, 185; Hagerty, *Los libros plúmbeos,* 73. See also the detailed comments of Harvey, *Muslims in Spain,* 385.

24. Surtz, "Morisco Women, Written Texts, and the Valencia Inquisition"; Cardaillac-Hermosilla, *La magie en Espagne,* 60–62.

25. Soria Mesa, "Una version genealógica"; Terrones del Cano, *Obras completas,* 441.

26. Luis F. Bernabé Pons has argued that the *plomos* should be considered in tandem with the Gospel of Barnabas, a sixteenth-century apocryphal account of the life of Jesus retold in Arabic from a Muslim viewpoint. See Bernabé Pons, *El Evangelio de San Bernabé; El texto morisco del Evangelio de San Bernabé;* and "La conspiración granadina de los libros plúmbeos."

27. Cardaillac, "Le prophetisme, signe de l'identité morisque." According to López-Morillas, *The Qurʾān in Sixteenth-Century Spain,* 17, the Morisco taste for the *jofor*—the preferred reading of an endangered and oppressed minority—parallels a similar fondness for the Quranic Apocalypse.

28. Antonio de Covarrubias, a high-ranking canon in the cathedral of Toledo and member of the Council of Castile, was a noted specialist in canon law and Greek philology. See Alonso, *Los apócrifos,* 73; and Aldea Vaquero, Marín Martínez, and Vives Gatell, *Diccionario de historia eclesiástica,* 1:638.

29. AASG, leg. 5, fols. 69, 88; Kendrick, *St. James in Spain*, 207. On Mariana's reply to Castro's hopeful inquiry, see Cirot, *Mariana, historien*, 50–51, 416–17.

30. Cabanelas Rodríguez, "Arias Montano y los libros plúmbeos de Granada"; Domenichini, "Quattro inediti di Benito Arias Montano sulla questione sacromontana (1596/1598)."

31. J. L. Villanueva, *Viaje literario*, 3:169–70, quoted in Alonso, *Los apócrifos*, 76–77.

32. Alonso, *Los apócrifos*, 209–10.

33. BN, MS 2316; also in AASG, C40. On Valencia's treatise on the *plomos*, see Magnier, "The Dating of Pedro de Valencia's *Sobre el pergamino y láminas de Granada*." On Valencia, see Gómez Canseco, *El humanismo después de 1600: Pedro de Valencia*. See also Valencia's comments on the *plomos* in BN, MS 7187 and BN, MS 12964.

34. ACDF, S.O., St. St. R 6 a, fol. 106.

35. Though he began as a translator of the *plomos*, Las Casas soon became their ardent critic and a personal enemy of Archbishop Pedro de Castro. Francisco de Gurmendi learned Arabic in Madrid at the school of Marcos Dobelo, a Syrian who worked for a time as a translator of the *plomos*. Gurmendi eventually achieved enough facility with the language to publish *Doctrina phísica y moral de príncipes* (Madrid, 1615), a translation of an Arabic text. On Las Casas, see Alonso, *Los apócrifos*, 148–55, 160–78; Borja de Medina, "La Compañía de Jesús," 4–9. On Las Casas's critique of the *plomos*, see Benítez Sánchez-Blanco, "De Pablo a Saulo." See also Morocho Gayo, "Pedro de Valencia." On Gurmendi, see Alonso, *Los apócrifos*, 209–10.

36. The texts of Mármol's letters to Archbishop Castro are reprinted in Cabanelas Rodríguez, *El morisco granadino Alonso de Castillo*, 250–56.

37. Hagerty, *Los libros plúmbeos*, 41, has suggested that translator Alonso de Castillo and treasure hunter "fulano de Castillo" may have shared a family connection. More suggestive, however, is the fact that the discoverers brought their first find, the plaque of St. Mesitón, to the nobleman Alonso Venegas de Alarcón, a prominent member of the Granada Venegas family, one of Granada's powerful families of Morisco extraction. Although he could not fully decipher the document, he rewarded the discoverers with 200 ducats, declaring that the tablet "was not the treasure they sought, but instead another, much greater one, because it was the body of a saint." Were the treasure hunters also Moriscos, clients or dependents of the wealthy Granada Venegas clan? Curiously, according to his own testimony before the panel of inquiry, Miguel de Luna happened to drop by Venegas's home just as the nobleman was examining the newly discovered inscription. AASG, C49, fol. 8r–v.

38. Godoy Alcántara, *Historia crítica*, 97–101; Márquez Villanueva, "La voluntad de leyenda de Miguel de Luna"; Luna, *La verdadera hystoria*.

39. AASG, leg. 5, fols. 737–38; Cabanelas Rodríguez, "Cartas del morisco granadino Miguel de Luna."

40. Cabanelas Rodríguez, *El morisco granadino Alonso de Castillo*, 293; Godoy Alcántara, *Historia crítica*, 104.

41. Cortés Peña and Vincent, *Historia de Granada*, 65–69.

42. Ibid., 69–72.

43. Among those urging more clement policies was Granada's Pedro de Castro, who vociferously protested the expulsion order in a letter to the king dated January 24, 1610. See Domínguez Ortiz and Vincent, *Historia de los moriscos*, 281–82.

44. Ibid., 159–200.

45. Lapeyre, *Géographie de l'Espagne morisque*, 205. The Crown granted exemptions from the expulsions of the 1570s and 1609–14 to many prominent Morisco families. See Lera García, "Survie de l'Islam dans la ville de Grenade au début du dix-huitième siècle." There are tantalizing hints of Islamicizing Morisco veneration for the *plomos* after the expulsions. In 1619 the Inquisition of Granada condemned to perpetual prison a certain Alonso de Luna, son of "doctor Luna," for espousing a messianic form of Islam centered on the lead books of the Sacromonte. Could he be a son of interpreter and probable forger Miguel de Luna? See Vincent, "Et quelques voix de plus."

46. Coleman, *Creating Christian Granada*, 195. The last of the lead books surfaced in Madrid in late 1606. An anonymous Granadino had found it and hidden it in the hopes of economic gain. Years later, finding himself gravely ill, he returned it to royal secretary Alonso Núñez de Valdivia y Mendoza, from whom it eventually passed into the hands of Archbishop Castro. AASG, leg. 5, fols. 379–446.

47. On the papal prohibition, see Alonso, *Los apócrifos*, 94, 122.

48. AASG, leg. 5, fols. 262–66. Some publications, however, seem to have escaped the censors; see, e.g., *Oración compuesta por el Glorioso Apóstol Santiago*. Local preachers who were privy to the lead books' contents may have sometimes dropped hints in their public sermons, such as the reference to an archangel guarding the Sacromonte in Cueva, *Diálogos*, fol. Eiii; Hagerty, *Los libros plúmbeos*, 129.

49. E.g., Alonso, *Los apócrifos*, 162, 166.

50. Sallmann, *Naples et ses saints*, 79.

51. These are the words of Bosio's seventeenth-century editor, Giovanni Severano. Bosio, *Roma sotteranea*, 25*. See also Ditchfield, "Text before Trowel." On Baronio and the catacombs, see Cignitti, "Cesare Baronio cultore dei martiri."

52. On the transfer of relics from the catacombs to other areas of Europe, see Bouza Álvarez, *Religiosidad contrarreformista*; Johnson, "Holy Fabrications"; Ditchfield, "Martyrs on the Move."

53. Córdoba: Roa, *Flos sanctorum*. Arjona: *Relación y memorial sacado de las ynformaciones*; Aldrete, *Fainomena sive coruscantia lumina*. Abla: Suárez, *Historia del obispado de Guadix y Baza*, 279–83. Baeza: Rus Puerta, *Historia eclesiástica*, fols. 224v–233r. Compare these finds to the spectacular *inventiones* of martyrial relics in the Sardinian cities of Sassari and Cagliari in 1614. See Manca, *Relación de la invención de los cuerpos de los santos martires*; Esquivel, *Relación de la invención de los cuerpos santos*.

54. Depluvrez, "Le retours de Saint Eugène et Sainte Léocadie."

55. Alcalá: Morales, *La vida, el martyrio, la invención, las grandezas*. Murcia: García Pérez, "Mentalidades, reliquias y arte en Murcia, ss. XVI–XVII."

56. Cirot, *Mariana, historien*, 417. Dávila, a son of the Marquis of Velada, was known as the "relics bishop." His famous collection, praised in verse by the poet Luis de Góngora y Argote, is described in Dávila y Toledo, *De la veneración que se debe a los cuerpos de los san-*

tos. On Bishop Dávila, see Candel Crespo, *Un obispo postridentino*. On Ribera's relic collection, see Ehlers, "Negotiating Reform," 203–9. On relic collecting by Lerma and others, see Bouza Álvarez, *Religiosidad contrarreformista*, 166–69.

57. E.g., [Quintanadueñas], *Gloriosos martyres*.

58. Suárez, *Historia del obispado de Guadix y Baza*.

59. See Ciança, *Historia de la vida, invención, milagros, y translación de S. Segundo*; Cátedra, *Un santo para una ciudad*.

60. Terrones de Robres, *Vida*.

61. The relics of St. Indalecio, evangelist of Almería, were held at the Asturian Monastery of San Juan de la Peña. Pasqual y Orbaneja, *Vida de San Indalecio*, part 3; Briz Martínez, *Historia de la fundación, y antigüedades de San Juan de la Peña*, 565–601.

62. Bermúdez de Pedraza, *Historia eclesiástica*, fol. 118r.

63. The main source for details on the life of Pedro de Castro remains Heredia Barnuevo's semi-hagiographic biography, *Místico ramillete*. See also the biographical sketches in Alonso, *Los apócrifos*, 37–49; Henares Cuéllar and Hagerty, "La significación de la fundación en la cultura granadina de transición al siglo XVII"; Aldea Vaquero, Marín Martínez, and Vives Gatell, *Diccionario de historia eclesiástica*, 4:2683; and López Rodríguez, *Los arzobispos de Granada*, 102–13.

64. See Viforcos Marinas and Paniagua Pérez, *El leonés don Cristóbal Vaca de Castro*, 118–22, 129–37.

65. Heredía Barnuevo, *Místico ramillete*, 12. On the *visita* of 1594, see Marín López, *El Cabildo de la Catedral*, 311–20.

66. Antolínez de Burgos, *Historia*, 385–96; Herrera Puga, "La mala vida en tiempos de los Austrias"; Cortés Peña and Vincent, *Historia de Granada*, 163. On Castro's relations with the university, see López Rodríguez, "Don Pedro de Castro y la Universidad de Granada."

67. Heredía Barnuevo, *Místico ramillete*, 13–14; Antolínez de Burgos, *Historia*, 430–31, 441; Szmolka Clares, "Cofradías y control eclesiástico en la Granada barroca"; A. D. Wright, *Catholicism and Spanish Society*, esp. 144–45. Castro's concern with these issues continued throughout his twenty years as archbishop of Granada; many of these concerns are included on a 1609 list of problems to be resolved by canon Juan de Matute Torrecilla, the archbishop's representative in Rome: AASG, leg. 1, pt. 2, fols. 147–76.

68. Marín López, "Un memorial de 1594"; Alonso, *Los apócrifos*, 45–49.

69. Gómez-Moreno Calera, *La arquitectura religiosa granadina*, 267ff.

70. On Castro's shift from caution to enthusiastic support, see Coleman, *Creating Christian Granada*, 198–99.

71. Juan René Rabut was a second generation printer, son of René Rabut, a French immigrant who arrived in Granada in the 1540s and worked with the Nebrijas. On René Rabut and his printing dynasty in Granada and Málaga, see Peregrín Pardo and Viñes Millet, *La imprenta en Granada*, and López-Huertas Pérez, *Bibliografía*, 1:160–64, 204.

72. The first *relación* is included with a letter from Archbishop Castro to Philip II, dated April 23, 1595: AGS, Patronato Eclesiástico, leg. 44 (1595). For the second, see BN, MS 6437, n. 2; BN R-24033, n. 3. The *relación* of May 9 is reprinted in Moreno Garrido, "El grabado en Granada a fines del siglo XVI."

73. *Memoria de las grandes marauillas; Relación cierta y verdadera de la invención de las reliquias y libros; Relación breve de las reliquias* (1608); *Relación breve de las reliquias* (1614; 1617); *De los libros, y sanctos martyres.* On the maps, see chapter 5.

74. For Terrones's 1597 statement in support of the *plomos,* see AASG, leg. 4, pt. 1, fols. 1114–17; BN, MS 6437, fols. 38–39; Aguilar de Terrones, *Dictamen de Don Fernando Suárez de Figueroa.* Alonso, *Los apócrifos,* 87, contends that another early critic, Luis del Mármol Carvajal, also revised his opinions after the new discoveries on the Sacromonte. I can find no evidence of this change of heart; moreover, had Mármol altered his views, advocates of the *plomos* would surely have advertised the "conversion" of such an influential adversary.

75. AASG, leg. 5, fols. 96–98; AASG, C24: Gregorio López Madera, *Discurso sobre las laminas, reliquias y libros que se an descubierto en la ciudad de Granada este año de 1595* (Granada, 1595).

76. López Madera, *Discursos,* and *Historia y discursos de la certidumbre.* Alonso, *Los apócrifos,* 78–91, examines these and other early publications on the *plomos.*

77. RBE d.iv.21: Juan de Faria, *Dialogismo y lacónico discurso: en defensa de las reliquias de San Cecilio, que se hallaron en la iglesia maior, de la ciudad de Granada;* also AASG leg. 4, pt. 1, fols. 436–41. These are but a handful of the treatises written by supporters of the Sacromonte. See, e.g., BN, MS 1603, fols. 144r–95r: Juan Herreros de Almansa, *Invención del Sacro Monte de Granada. Con las vidas de los sanctos que en el fueron martiriçados* (manuscript, 1624); Centurión y Córdoba, *Información;* AASG, C22: Pedro de Jesús María, *Discurso apologético en defensa de los libros del Sacro Monte Yllipulitano de la ziudad de Granada* (manuscript, 1642).

78. BN, MS 5732, fols. 27–39; BN, MS 9227, fols. 197–216: Antonio Covarrubias y Leiva, *Discursos del Dr. Antonio Covarrubias y Leyva escritos en defensa de las reliquias descubiertas en la torre turpiana, y en los cavernas de Monte Valparaíso de Granada.* Also AASG, C18: Antonio Covarrubias y Leiva, *Discursos y escritos en defensa de las reliquias descubiertas en la Torre Turpiana y en las cavernas del Monte Balparaíso de Granada* (manuscript, copy dated 1756). This Antonio Covarrubias y Leiva should not be confused with the famous Hellenist of the same name. On Morillo, see the prologue.

79. Alonso, *Los apócrifos,* 102.

80. Ibid., 166–67.

81. Ibid., 151–52.

82. Heredia Barnuevo, *Místico ramillete,* 133.

83. Papers relating to the 1607 and 1609 *juntas,* and to the permanent *junta* on the Sacromonte, are contained in AHN, Consejos, leg. 17088². This legajo also includes Castro's petitions for royal patronage.

84. On the building of the abbey, see Gómez-Moreno Calera, *La arquitectura religiosa granadina,* 250–65, and *El arquitecto granadino,* 42–49; see also Hagerty, "Los libros plúmbeos," 28–30.

85. For the constitutions of the Collegiate Church of the Sacromonte, see Vaca de Castro y Quiñones, *Gnomon seu gubernandi norma Abbati.*

86. For the college's governing constitutions, see Vaca de Castro y Quiñones, *Constituciones de el . . . Colegio de Theólogos del Señor San Dionysio Areopagita.* See also Royo Campos, *El Insigne Colegio-Seminario.*

87. Quoted in Alonso, *Los apócrifos*, 204.

88. Obadiah 20–21: " . . . et transmigratio Jerusalem, quæ in Bosphor est, possidebit civitates Austri. Et ascendent salvatores in montem Sion judicares montem Esau: et erit Domino regnum." AASG, leg. 5, fol. 532v.

89. AASG, leg. 5, fol. 532v (emphasis in the original).

90. AASG, leg. 5, fol. 845 (emphasis in the original).

91. The document is reprinted in López Rodríguez, *Los arzobispos de Granada*, 107–13. See also García Valverde, "La donación del Arzobispo Don Pedro de Castro al Sacromonte"; and Ollero Pina, "La carrera, los libros y la obsesión del Arzobispo D. Pedro de Castro y Quiñones (1534–1623)."

92. AASG, leg. 5, fols. 456–70.

93. AASG, leg. 5, fol. 620; AHN, Consejos, leg. 17088[2], August 12, 1618. On the search for translators, see Alonso, *Los apócrifos*.

94. J. Martínez Ruiz, "Cartas de Thomas van Erpen (Thomas Erpenius) en un Archivo de Granada (1623–1624)."

95. AHN, Consejos, leg. 17088[2].

96. Alonso, *Los apócrifos*, 202–3. On Dobelo, see Levi Della Vida, *Ricerche sulla formazione*, 280–87.

97. Alonso, *Los apócrifos*, 217–33. Hesronita was but one of at least nineteen individuals involved in the translation of the lead books, many of whom came into conflict with Castro. See Ecker, "Arab Stones"; Rodríguez Mediano and García-Arenal, "Diego de Urrea y algún traductor más." On the accusations that Castro bribed Hesronita, see Harvey and Wiegers, "The Translation from Arabic of the Sacromonte Tablets and the Archbishop of Granada." For an interesting eyewitness account by a translator, see Ibn al-Ḥajarī, *Kitāb Nāṣir al-dīn ʿalā ʾl-qawm al-kāfirīn. The Supporter of Religion against the Infidels.* See also Wiegers, "The 'Old' or 'Turpiana' Tower in Granada."

98. Alonso, *Los apócrifos*, 194–202.

99. Sánchez Moguel, "El Arzobispo Vaca de Castro y el Abad Gordillo."

100. See the decree in AGS, Patronato Real, leg. 39, no. 86.

101. Aguilar y Cano, *El Marqués del Aula*; Alonso, *Los apócrifos*, 263–68.

102. Kendrick, *St. James in Spain*, 108–15. The order recalling the Marquis's book is included in AHN, Consejos, leg. 17088[2].

103. BN, MS 6437, fols. 68–81. The parchment from the Torre Turpiana was not included in the shipment.

104. AASG, leg. 5, fols. 1133–38, contains an account of the translation and installation of the *plomos* in Madrid. On the Hieronymite's complaints, see Cruz, *Sacrarum virginum vindicatio*. The Sacromonte quickly responded with a lengthy treatise by canon Francisco de Barahona y Miranda: *Memorial del Dr. Dn. Francisco Barahona y Miranda.*

105. According to Heredia Barnuevo, *Místico ramillete*, 146, Bartolomé de Torres was a native of Vegel, in the bishopric of Cádiz. Francisco de Barahona y Miranda, a Granadino, served as Pedro de Castro's Madrid agent for the *plomos* in 1617; see his letter to Castro listing the *plomos'* enemies in BN, MS 5953, fol. 205. Both Torres and Barahona were among the first appointees to canonries in the abbey. It is possible that some of the lead books escaped the transfer to Rome. Cabanelas Rodríguez, *El morisco granadino Alonso de Castillo,*

263, claimed to have personally examined a leaf from one of the books, by permission of its anonymous owner. See also Harvey, *Muslims in Spain*, 383.

THREE: FORGING HISTORY

Portions of this chapter revise material first published in Harris, "Forging History."
Epigraph: Livy, *The Rise of Rome*, 3.

1. Martín Angulo y Pulgar, *Epístolas satisfactorias* (Granada, 1635), fol. 54, quoted in Gallego Morell, "Algunas notas."

2. Cortés Peña and Vincent, *Historia de Granada*, 197–98. Luis de Granada, a Dominican, moved to Valladolid, returning to his native city only between 1534 and 1537. The Jesuit theologian Francisco Suárez pursued his academic career in Salamanca, Rome, and Coimbra.

3. Marín Ocete, *El negro Juan Latino*.

4. Marín Ocete, *Gregorio Silvestre*, 46; Cortés Peña and Vincent, *Historia de Granada*, 198.

5. See Menéndez y Pelayo, *Biblioteca de traductores españoles*, 190–200.

6. On Soto de Rojas, see Gallego Morell, *Pedro Soto de Rojas*. Among his poems is "Himeneo de San Cecilio, y la Santa Iglesia de Granada," published in Pedro Soto de Rojas, *Desengaño de amor en rimas* (Madrid, 1623), fols. 166r–72r.

7. Gan Giménez, "Los prebendados," 185.

8. Marín Ocete, *Gregorio Silvestre*.

9. Though an important figure in Granadino and Sevillano intellectual circles, Vázquez Siruela remains mysteriously ignored by historians, perhaps because he never succeeded in finishing or publishing any of his many manuscripts. He is best known for his correspondence with his more famous friend, the bibliographer Nicolás Antonio. On Vázquez Siruela, see Gallego Morell, "Algunas notas"; Medina Conde, *El fingido Dextro*, 38–56. On his correspondence with Nicolás Antonio, see Jammes and Gorsse, "Nicolás Antonio et le combat pour la verité."

10. BBMS, Varios escritos de Martín Vázquez de Siruela, MS, fols. 4v–9r. On Roa, see Martín Pradas and Carrasco Gómez, "Datos biográficos inéditos sobre el Padre Martín de Roa"; Ordóñez Agulla, "El P. Martín de Roa y la historia antigua de Écija"; Ramírez Arellano, *Ensayo de un catálogo biográfico*, 543–49. On Caro, see Gómez Canseco, *Rodrigo Caro*.

11. Regrettably, I have been unable to locate Pedro de San Cecilio's *Cronología pontificia, Iliberitana o Cronología de los obispos de Granada* (Granada, 1667). Best known as a historian of his order, Fray Pedro also wrote several works on Granadino saints, including the now lost manuscript *Memorial de los santos de Granada*, mentioned by Bermúdez de Pedraza. See San Cecilio, *Annales del orden de Descalzos*, and *Vida y martyrio de D. Fr. Pedro de Valencia*. BN, MS 3893 includes an interesting note from Fray Pedro to Vázquez Siruela. On the works of Cipriano de Santa María, see López-Huertas Pérez, *Bibliografía*, 2:603–10.

12. On Tomás Sánchez, see Sommervogel, *Bibliothèque*, 530–38; Backer and Backer, *Bibliothèque*, 686.

13. Marín Ocete, *Gregorio Silvestre*, 28–29. On Mendoza's patronage of humanists, see Szmolka Clares, "Iñigo López de Mendoza y el humanismo granadino."

14. Spivakovsky, *Son of the Alhambra*, 380–81.

15. González Vázquez, "El humanismo clásico en la Granada del primer Renacimiento," 19. On Hernando de Acuña, see Rodríguez Marín, *Luis Barahona de Soto*, 37.

16. Rodríguez Marín, *Luis Barahona de Soto*, 170–73. Rodríguez de Ardila was the author of the pamphlet *Las honras que celebró la famosa y gran ciudad de Granada*.

17. Francisco Trillo y Figueroa relates an amusing joke involving a forged inscription, played at Soto's academy on the gullible Vázquez Siruela. See Trillo y Figueroa, *Apologético historial sobre la antigüedad de Granada*, 184–85.

18. Several recent publications have greatly expanded the available literature on printing and the book trade in early modern Granada. See Peregrín Pardo and Viñes Millet, *La imprenta en Granada;* López-Huertas Pérez, *Bibliografía;* Osorio Pérez, Moreno Trujillo, and Obra Sierra, *Trastiendas de la cultura*. See also García Oro and Portela Silva, *Felipe II y los libreros*, 18, 57–63. According to Gallego Morell, *Cinco impresores*, 78–79, Bolívar may have been at the center of a writers' circle that met in his shop.

19. On Spain, see Kagan, "Clio and the Crown"; Quesada, *La idea de ciudad*. For Andalusian city histories, see Guinea Díaz, "Antigüedad e historia local en el siglo XVIII andaluz"; Domínguez Ortiz, "La historiografía local andaluza." On France, see Dolan, "L'identité urbaine et les histoires locales"; Ehmke, "The Writing of Town and Provincial History in Sixteenth-Century France." For Britain, see Mendyk, *Speculum Britanniae*.

20. On Hercules and Tubal in Spanish city histories, see Redondo, "Légendes généalogiques et parentes fictives"; Lida de Malkiel, "Túbal, primer poblador de España"; Tate, "Mythology in Spanish Historiography." See also Estévez Sola, "Aproximación a los orígenes míticos de Hispania" and "Algo más sobre los orígenes míticos de Hispania." For an example of classical mythology in city genealogy, see Lleó Cañal, *Nueva Roma*, 153–63. The bibliography on Annius of Viterbo and his critics is extensive. See, among others, Grafton, "Traditions of Invention"; Stephens, *Giants in Those Days*, 98–138.

21. On the "false chronicles," see Godoy Alcántara, *Historia crítica;* Caro Baroja, *Las falsificaciones;* Hitchcock, "The *Falsos Chronicones* and the Mozarabs." On another of Higuera's hagiographic forgeries, see Martínez de la Escalera, "Jerónimo de la Higuera S.J." Higuera wrote several times to Archbishop Castro about the *plomos*, composed a treatise in their defense, and later confected new chronicles that defended the Sacromonte discoveries. To his credit, Castro did not encourage the Jesuit's gestures and ignored his requests for money. Kendrick, *St. James in Spain*, 118–19; Medina Conde, *El fingido Dextro*, 8–25 and appendix.

22. By the mid-sixteenth century, for example, local historians in Evora, Portugal, had transformed St. Mancio, a martyr of the late sixth or early seventh century, into a contemporary of Jesus and the first bishop of the city. Fernández Catón, *San Mancio*. On the legend of St. James in the sixteenth and seventeenth centuries, see Kendrick, *St. James in Spain*, and Rey Castelao, *La historiografía del Voto de Santiago*.

23. Quesada, *La idea de ciudad*, 41–57.

24. Domínguez Ortiz, "La historiografía local andaluza"; Gascó, "Historiadores, falsarios y estudiosos de las antigüedades andaluzas," 11.

25. Kagan, "Clio and the Crown," 90. On *civitas* as community, see Kagan, "*Urbs* and *Civitas* in Sixteenth- and Seventeenth-Century Spain."

26. Bermúdez de Pedraza, *Antigüedad*, fols. 34v–35v; Velázquez Echevarría, *Paseos por*

Granada y sus contornos, 2:164–65. The column remained in situ well into the nineteenth century. Hidalgo Morales, *Iliberia, o Granada,* 282–83.

27. Joannes Vasaeus, *Chronicon rerum memorabilium Hispaniae,* vol. 1 (Salamanca, 1552), in Luque Moreno, *Granada en el siglo XVI,* 283–84; Al-Razi, *Crónica del moro Rasis,* 23–26.

28. Navagiero, *Il viaggio,* fol. 21v.

29. Mármol Carvajal, *Historia del rebelión,* 35. For a description of the site in 1526, see Navagiero, *Il viaggio,* fols. 29v–30r.

30. Mentioned in BN, MS 1499: Guerra de Lorca, *La historia de la vida.*

31. Alfonso X appears to regard Iliberis and Granada as one and the same entity; his list of bishoprics subject to Toledo includes "Libira que es Granada." Alfonso X, *Primera crónica general de España,* 196.

32. Nader, "'The Greek Commander' Hernán Núñez de Toledo," 470.

33. The discoveries of 1540 are mentioned in Cueva, *Diálogos,* fol. Aiiiiv. For some later discoveries, see Vergara Gavira, *Verdadera declaración de las monedas antiguas.* See also Roldán Hervás, *Historia de Granada,* 222–24.

34. The literature on Iliberis and Granada is extensive. On nineteenth- and early twentieth-century views, see the introductory essay to Eguílaz y Yanguas, *Del lugar donde fue Iliberis.* For more recent perspectives, see Viñes Millet, *Historia urbana de Granada,* 1–9; Roldán Hervas, *Granada romana,* 221–37; Roca Roumens, Moreno Onorato, and Licano Preste, *El Albaicín y los orígenes de la ciudad de Granada.* Modern archaeological investigations have established Iliberis's location as within the confines of the Albaicín.

35. Mármol Carvajal, *Historia del rebelión,* 34–36, based on the description by Rasis. See also the account by Hurtado de Mendoza, *Guerra de Granada,* 97–98.

36. See Orlandis and Ramos-Lissón, *Historia de los concilios,* 25–63.

37. Polman, *L'élément historique dans la controverse religieuse du XVIe siècle,* 103, 134, 414–15; García Villada, *Historia eclesiástica,* 307–9.

38. F. de Mendoza, *De confirmando Concilio Illiberitano* (reprinted in Mansi, *Sacrorum conciliorum nova et amplissima collectio,* cols. 397–406), and *La defensa y aprovación del Concilio Illiberritano.* See AGS, Patronato Eclesiástico, leg. 44; see also letters from the Crown to various persons at the papal court: AGS, Estado, Roma, leg. 1855. On Mendoza, see Nicolás Antonio, *Biblioteca hispania nova,* 1:380–81. On Mendoza's interventions in the *plomos* affair, see Alonso, *Los apócrifos,* 50, 66–69, 85–87.

39. Cueva, *Diálogos,* fol. Biir. See Wulff Alonso, *Las esencias patrias,* 41–42.

40. Antolín, "El códice emilianense de la biblioteca de El Escorial."

41. On Valencia: Olmos y Canalda, *Los prelados valentinos.* On Córdoba: Gómez Bravo, *Catálogo de los obispos de Córdoba,* 105.

42. On the shrine in the Albaicín, see chapter 5. The shrine by the Alhambra was established by Ferdinand and Isabella. Originally controlled by the Royal Chapel, in 1573 it came under the control of the Discalced Carmelite friars, who founded on the site a monastery, called "of the Martyrs," dedicated to SS. Cosme and Damian. See Gallego y Burín, *Granada,* 160; Henríquez de Jorquera, *Anales,* 1:240. According to tradition, among the medieval Christians executed on the site was St. Pedro Pascual de Valencia, bishop of Jaén. See Ximena Jurado, *Catálogo de los obispos de las iglesias catedrales,* 314–18; Gallego y

Burín, *Granada,* 127; B. Taylor, *Structures of Reform,* 406–11; Riera i Sans, "La invenció literària de sant Pere Pasqual." In 1610, in front of the parish church of St. Mary of the Alhambra, Archbishop Pedro de Castro raised a commemorative column to two Franciscan missionaries executed in 1397.

43. Garibay y Zamalloa, *Los XL libros del compendio historial,* 1:226 (1628 edition).

44. Luque Moreno, "Granada en la poesía de Juan de Vilches" and *Granada en el siglo XVI.*

45. RAH 9/5947, fols. 67–86: "Historia de la Casa Real de Granada." Juan de Mata Carriazo suggests that this manuscript, which appears to date from the middle of the sixteenth century, may be a source or even a draft of Garibay y Zamalloa. Carriazo, "La 'Historia de la Casa Real de Granada.'"

46. Soria Mesa, "Una version genealógica."

47. Mentioned in Bermúdez de Pedraza, *Historia eclesiástica,* fol. 80r. The author, a Juan Nuñez, probably composed this lost episcopology in the 1580s.

48. BN, MS 1499. On the lost book on Granada's antiquities, see fol. 260v.

49. Gabriel Pasqual y Orbaneja refers to a 1584 treatise by Guerra de Lorca on "the lives of the seven disciples of St. James, and the martyrdoms they suffered." Internal evidence in BN, MS 1499: Guerra de Lorca, *La historia de la vida* suggests a date between 1581 and 1588. See Pasqual y Orbaneja, *Vida de San Indalecio,* 26.

50. Guerra's manuscript is signed but undated. Internal references to discoveries happening on the Sacromonte suggest that he began the work in mid-1595 and completed it sometime before his death in 1597, making it the earliest of the post-Sacromonte histories of Granada. See AASG, C48: Pedro Guerra de Lorca, *Memorias eclesiásticas de la ciudad de Granada,* fols. 182r, 269v, 281v. BN, MS 1583: Pedro Velarde de Rivera, *Historia eclesiástica del Monte Santo, ciudad, y reino de Granada,* fol. 72v, tells us that he began writing on July 22, 1595. He probably completed the manuscript some time after 1600, since it includes a dedication to Philip III, the text of the decree authenticating the relics, and a number of additions made after 1600.

51. On early modern *historia sacra,* see Ditchfield, *Liturgy.*

52. Rapin, *Instructions for History,* 19.

53. Cabrera de Córdoba, *De historia, para entenderla y escribirla,* 34.

54. Bodin, *Method,* 15–17.

55. See the comments of Ditchfield, "Ideologia religiosa ed erudizione nell'agiografia dell'età moderna"; Cochrane, *Historians and Historiography in the Italian Renaissance,* 416–20, 445–78.

56. Guerra claimed to have cured his sister's servant girl of a debilitating affliction by application of a cloth that had been touched to the relic of the Virgin found in the Torre Turpiana. AASG, C49, fols. 164–75. In 1594 he carried the original parchment and a letter from the Granada cathedral chapter to Arias Montano in Seville. Alonso, *Los apócrifos,* 53–54.

57. On Guerra, see Antonio, *Biblioteca hispana nova,* 2:199; Gan Giménez, "Los prebendados," 191.

58. Guerra de Lorca, *Catecheses mystagogae pro aduenis ex secta Mahometana.*

59. According to ACG, Libros de Actas, vol. 9, fol. 30r, he presented one of these apolo-

getic treatises for the inspection of the cathedral chapter in April 1593. See also AASG, leg. 4, pt. 1, fols. 188–209, and AASG, C52: Luis Francisco Viana and Joseph Juan de Laboraria, *Historia authéntica del hecho de los dos descubrimientos de Torre Turpiana y Monte Santo de Granada desde el año de 1588 hasta el presente de 1756,* fol. 54r. On Guerra as poet, see García, *Relaciones topográficas de España,* 77.

60. Bodin, *Method,* 15. Cf. Degory Wheare, *Relectiones hyemales,* 355–60.

61. AASG, C48: Guerra de Lorca, *Memorias eclesiásticas,* fol. 172r.

62. Ibid., fol. 169v.

63. An anonymous redactor has crossed out both the discourse on the prophecy and a preceding section on the texts of the Torre Turpiana and Sacromonte discoveries, probably to enforce conformity with papal prohibitions against writing about the content of the *plomos.* See Alonso, *Los apócrifos,* 94.

64. A brief comparison between Guerra's *Memorias eclesiásticas* and his earlier *Historia de la vida y martyrio de Sant Çecilio y sus seis compañeros* reveals the degree of influence on Guerra's rendition of the lives of the Seven Apostles. In the latter, he had argued that the Seven could not possibly be disciples of St. James, as they were described in the breviaries of the Order of St. James and in Ávila's office of St. Segundo, and he bemoaned the fact that "[St. Cecilio's] mode of martyrdom is not written, nor that of the rest, his companions" (BN, MS 1499: Guerra de Lorca, *La historia de la vida,* fol. 261v). In *Memorias eclesiásticas,* the saints are disciples of St. James, and their martyrdom is gruesome and fiery.

65. Guerra cites as his source for the martyrs of the Alpujarras depositions taken in 1568 and 1569 by Lázaro de Velasco, apostolic notary, from refugees fleeing the area. Archbishop Pedro Guerrero later sent the depositions to Rome and to Philip II in order to forward the beatification and canonization of the martyrs. AASG, C48: Guerra de Lorca, *Memorias eclesiásticas,* fols. 342v, 357r. Later archbishops, including Pedro de Castro and Diego de Escolano (1668–72) investigated the martyrs with an eye toward their sainthood. See Escolano, *Memorial a la Reyna N.S. cerca de las muertes;* Hitos, *Mártires de la Alpujarra;* Barrios Aguilera and Sánchez Ramos, *Martirios y mentalidad martirial en las Alpujarras.*

66. See AASG, C48: Guerra de Lorca, *Memorias eclesiásticas,* fol. 307r–v. On Guerra's episcopal list, see Antolínez de Burgos, *Historia,* xlviii–xlix.

67. BN, MS 1583: Velarde de Rivera, *Historia eclesiástica del Monte Santo,* fol. 12v.

68. Ibid., fol. 29v.

69. Ibid., fol. 30r. Based in part on the testimony of the Torre Turpiana parchment, he argues that ancient Granada had three names—Iliberis, Ilipula Magna, and Granada— which could be used separately or simultaneously.

70. Velarde's treatment of the ministries and martyrdoms of the Seven Apostles suggests that he enjoyed far less access to the *plomos* and their contents than did Guerra. For example, his account, which relies on traditional medieval liturgical texts and, perhaps, garbled hearsay about the new finds, describes SS. Cecilio and Tesifón as "Hebrews," rather than Arabs. BN, MS 1583: Velarde de Rivera, *Historia eclesiástica del Monte Santo,* fol. 163r.

71. Ibid., fol. 288r.

72. Velarde's account of the martyrs of the Alpujarras and one of the appended lists is included in Foulché-Delbosc, "Documents relatifs à la Guerre de Grenade."

73. Bacon, *The Advancement of Learning and New Atlantis,* 71–72.

74. Guerra and his *Memorias* appear among the names of illustrious local writers appended to Velarde and are mentioned in Rodríguez Escabias, *Discurso*, fol. 6v, while Velarde appears in a list of local writers included in Bermúdez de Pedraza, *Antigüedad y excelencias de Granada*.

75. The approval for printing and royal license are dated 1602, while the *tasa* (valuation) dates from 1608. For a general discussion of this book, see Calatrava, "Encomium urbis."

76. AASG, leg. 7, pt. 2, fol. 23r.

77. Voigt, *Juan de Valdés*, 123–24; Viñes Millet, *Figuras granadinas*, 126–29; Bermúdez de Pedraza, *Historia eclesiástica*, fol. 173r. According to Garzón Pareja, *Historia de Granada*, 160, there is a portrait of Bermúdez in Granada's Hieronymite monastery.

78. Bermúdez de Pedraza, *Arte legal para estudiar la iurisprudencia* and *El secretario del rey*. See also his pamphlet on the preeminence of royal secretaries: *Por los secretarios de V. Magestad*.

79. Henríquez de Jorquera, *Anales*, 2:701, 782. In a letter to Pedro de Castro, dated January 3, 1618, Bermúdez speaks of having received minor orders from the hands of the archbishop and a desire to "retire to rest and work in things closer to the service of God." At the time of his appointment to the cathedral chapter, Bermúdez was still not fully ordained and was working as a lawyer and *fiscal* of the *real donativo*. In his later publications, he bitterly recalls his experience at court. AASG, leg. 7, pt. 2, fol. 23; AGS, Patronato Eclesiástico, leg. 112.

80. Bermúdez de Pedraza, *Panegyrico legal* and *Historia eclesiástica*.

81. Bermúdez de Pedraza, *Historia eucharística* and *El Hospital Real de la Corte*. Voigt, *Juan de Valdés*, asserts that Bermúdez served as rector of the University of Granada several times, but offers no evidence for this claim.

82. Bermúdez de Pedraza, *Antigüedad*, fol. 66r.

83. Ibid., fol. 100r. See St. Thomas Aquinas, *On Kingship, to the King of Cyprus*. On celestial influence over community characteristics, see Glacken, *Traces on the Rhodian Shore*.

84. Bermúdez de Pedraza, *Antigüedad*, fols. 141v–142r.

85. Traditionally, three main factors were thought to influence the character of cities and their inhabitants: climate (latitude), province, and the astrological configuration at the time of foundation. See North, *Horoscopes and History*, 164; Boll, *Sternglaube und Sterndeutung*, 106–7, 113.

86. Bermúdez de Pedraza, *Antigüedad*, fol. 187v.

87. Cf. Hardin, "Conceiving Cities."

88. This text, now known primarily from the notes of the nineteenth-century bibliophile Bartolomé José Gallardo, included lists of illustrious Granadinos based closely on those found in Bermúdez. A fragment of the *Descripción historial*—a list of eminent sculptors from Granada—is preserved in London's British Library: BL, Egerton 586 (14). See Gallardo, *Ensayo de una biblioteca española*, 865–74; Garrido Atienza, *Antiguallas granadinas*, 150.

89. Orozco Díaz, *El poema "Granada" de Collado del Hierro*, 174–87.

90. E.g., Bermúdez de Pedraza, *Antigüedad*, fol. 150r.

91. Viñanza, *Biblioteca histórica de la filología castellana*, 19.

92. Bermúdez de Pedraza, *Historia eclesiástica,* fol. 8v.

93. Cueva, *Diálogos,* "Luys de la Cueva al Letor."

94. On the urban dialogue genre, see Amelang, "Imágenes de la cultura urbana en la España moderna."

95. Cueva, *Diálogos,* fols. Giiv, Fiir–Fiiv.

96. Ibid., fol. Giiiiv. On Cueva's defense of the Moriscos, see Caro Baroja, *Los moriscos del Reino de Granada,* 208–10.

97. This and the following biographical information is drawn from Manuel Sotomayor y Muro's introduction to Antolínez de Burgos, *Historia,* xi–xxvii. One of Antolínez's brothers, Agustín, became archbishop of Santiago de Compostela.

98. Ibid., xxix.

99. Ibid., 23. While several versions of Antolinez's *Historia* exist, my discussion follows the fourth and final redaction, the version approved for publication in 1611 and published in 1996.

100. Ibid., 91. See also Sotomayor y Muro's introduction, xxix–xxx.

101. Antolínez de Burgos, *Historia,* 19. See also ibid., 23, 97.

102. The lead book in question is the *On the Famous Deeds of the Apostle St. James and on His Miracles.* In one passage, St. James points to the caves of the Sacromonte, calling them "Garnata," and tells his disciples that the city below will one day take its name from the caves. See Sotomayor y Muro's note to Antolínez de Burgos, *Historia,* 39.

103. Noted by Sotomayor y Muro, in Antolínez de Burgos, *Historia,* 43, 92.

104. See Moreno Garrido, "El grabado en Granada durante el siglo XVII," 82–97.

105. Antolínez de Burgos, *Historia,* xxxviii–xxxix, xli.

106. Ibid., 43.

107. While there exist no concrete indications that the author intended this illustration to accompany this particular text, this is the link established by Manuel Sotomayor y Muro, Antolínez's most recent editor. In general, I agree with Sotomayor y Muro's decisions tying individual images with particular textual loci. However, the inclusion of engravings *not* created for this text presents the potential for confusion or misapprehension by the reader.

108. Marieta, *Catálogo de los obispos y arçobispos de Granada.*

109. The engraving reproduced here is included, along with several others created for Antolínez's *Historia eclesiástica,* in Heredia Barnuevo's *Místico ramillete* (1741).

110. Translation by J. M. Neale, in Britt, *The Hymns of the Breviary and Missal,* 349–50.

111. See Marín Ocete, *El arzobispo don Pedro Guerrero;* Coleman, *Creating Christian Granada,* 145–76.

112. Antolínez de Burgos, *Historia,* 261.

113. Ibid., xl–xliv.

114. Ibid., xl. By 1622, however, Castro lamented the lack of a published history that would promote and defend the Sacromonte, and he proposed to take advantage of Antolínez's unpublished manuscript, since "much of it is history, and therefore true." AASG, leg. 5, fol. 1004r.

115. On the continued importance of manuscripts in an age of print, see Bouza, *Corre manuscrito.*

116. In addition to Antolínez, Bermúdez cites another, lost history of Granada, a "his-

tory . . . of its foundation, loss, and restoration" by a Calderón de Velasco, advocate in the Chancery of Granada. Bermúdez de Pedraza, *Historia eclesiástica,* 80v.

117. Ibid., preface; see also fol. 75v.

118. Ibid., fol. 1r.

119. On the ubiquity of this analogy and corresponding medical metaphors in Spanish political writing, see Elliott, "Self-Perception and Decline in Early Seventeenth-Century Spain," 249.

120. Bermúdez de Pedraza, *Historia eclesiástica,* fol. iv.

121. Ibid., fol. 3r.

122. Ibid., fol. 28r.

123. Ibid., fol. 9r.

124. Ibid., fols. 5r–v, 16v–17v.

125. Ibid., fols. 29r, 30r, 31r; also fol. 52r.

126. Ibid., fol. 38r–v; also fols. 29r, 34v.

127. Ibid., fol. 45. The source to which Bermúdez refers is one of Román de la Higuera's forged histories of early Spain. See Godoy Alcántara, *Historia crítica,* 199–220. The brass paten wound up as part of the extensive relic collection of Sancho Dávila y Toledo. According to Royo Campos, *Albores del Sacro Monte,* 46, the paten is now in Ávila, in the chapel of the Marquises of Velada.

128. This document represented a tacit challenge to the Mozarabic rite, which was closely associated with Toledo, the seat of the primate of Spain. Defenders of the primacy of Toledo and royal historians like Ambrosio de Morales cited a passage in a tenth-century document (itself an eleventh-century forgery) housed in the library of the Escorial, which claimed that the mass of the Apostles was brought to Spain by followers of St. James. This Apostolic mass, they argued, was the Mozarabic mass itself. Granadinos, pointing to the lead book *Ritual of the Mass of St. James the Apostle,* argued for the greater antiquity, and thus the primacy of their own recently created local tradition. See, e.g., Antolínez de Burgos, *Historia,* 593. On the tradition of the Apostolic Mozarabic mass, see García Villada, *Historia eclesiástica,* 151–57.

129. Bermúdez de Pedraza, *Historia eclesiástica,* fols. 47–48. On SS. Peter and Paul in Spain, see García Villada, *Historia eclesiástica,* 127–45, and Vega, "La venida de san Pablo a España y los Varones Apostólicos."

130. Bermúdez de Pedraza, *Historia eclesiástica,* fol. 52.

131. Ibid., fol. 51v. Bermúdez suggests that sympathetic city council members aided St. Cecilio in temporarily evading arrest.

132. Ibid., fols. 49v, 56v.

133. Ibid., fol. 95r.

134. Bermúdez's main source for the earliest years of Muslim rule is Luna's *La verdadera hystoria.* Other sources include Florián de Ocampo's *Corónica general de España,* Rodrigo Ximénez de Rada's *Crónica de España,* the *Primera crónica general* of Alfonso X, the *Crónica general* of Alfonso XI, and Juan de Mariana's *Historia de rebus hispaniae.*

135. Bermúdez de Pedraza, *Historia eclesiástica,* fol. 110.

136. Ibid., fol. 52.

137. Ibid., fol. 96.

138. Ibid., fol. 153. Sallmann, *Naples et ses saints,* 336, suggests that the hagiographic commonplace of the saint's body as city defender dates perhaps from the fifth century. For a tenth-century example, see Sot, "La topographie religieuse et la référence aux origines de l'église de Reims au Xe siècle."

139. Bermúdez de Pedraza, *Historia eclesiástica,* fol 173.

140. Ibid., fol. 1.

141. Ibid., fol. 269v.

142. Villa-Real y Valdivia, *Hernán Pérez del Pulgar,* 322–33; J. de la Natividad, *Coronada historia;* BUG Caja B48, B49, B50: Juan de Santibañez, *Historia de la Provincia de Andalucía de la Compañía de Jesús* (manuscript, n.d.). See also RAH 9/138: Juan Francisco Córdoba y Peralta, *Historia de Granada y del Alpujarra* (manuscript, ca. 1755); Velázquez Echevarría, *Paseos por Granada;* Álvarez, *Excelencias de Granada.*

143. This fascinating text, first published in 1934 and reissued in 1987, consists of three books. The first offers a town-by-town description of the kingdom and city of Granada, while the second narrates the conquest by the Catholic Monarchs. The third and most notable book relates important events in the city and its surroundings for the years 1588, 1590, and 1603 to 1646. Bermúdez is Jorquera's most frequently cited source, especially in chapters 39–43 of book 1, which treat Granada's saints, episcopal succession, and medieval Muslim rulers. These chapters can only be read in the original manuscript, which is held by the Institución Colombina in Seville, since the editors of both the 1934 and the 1987 editions chose to excise them because of Jorquera's close reliance on Bermúdez.

144. ACG, Libros de Actas, vol. 13, fol. 73r.

145. Connerton, *How Societies Remember,* 14–16. See also Orest Ranum's observations on national identity and history in the early modern period: *National Consciousness, History, and Political Culture in Early-Modern Europe,* 11. On readership and circulation of city histories in early modern Spain, see Kagan, "Clio and the Crown," 96–99.

146. Rothstein, "Etymology, Genealogy, and the Immutability of Origins." On etymology in Spanish historiography, see Rubio Lapaz, *Pablo de Céspedes y su círculo,* 78–79.

147. Bermúdez de Pedraza, *Historia eclesiástica,* fol. 3v.

148. Many early modern Spanish historians accepted oral traditions, such as ballads, as legitimate documentary evidence. See Sieber, "The Frontier Ballad and Spanish Golden Age Historiography."

149. Quoted in Beltrán Fortes, "Entre la erudición y el coleccionismo: anticuarios andaluces de los siglos XVI al XVIII," 111. The classic study on early modern antiquarians and historical method is Momigliano, "Ancient History and the Antiquarian."

150. See Cochrane, "The Transition from Renaissance to Baroque."

151. Roberto Bizzocchi finds similar connections between early modern antiquarians and genealogists. See Bizzocchi, *Genealogie incredibili.*

152. Boesch Gajano, "La raccolta di vite di santi di Luigi Lippomano"; Martinelli, "Cultura umanistica, polemica antiprotestante, erudizione sacra nell 'De probatis Sanctorum historiis' di Lorenzo Surio."

153. See, for example, the precepts for writing hagiography laid out by Claude Fleury, ecclesiastical historian and confessor to Louis XV, quoted in Gaquère, *La vie et les oeuvres de Claude Fleury (1640–1723),* 364–65.

154. See Ditchfield, *Liturgy*, 137–39, 273–327.

155. Lifschitz, "Beyond Positivism and Genre."

156. E.g., Sigüenza, *Historia de la Orden de San Jerónimo*, 343.

157. There is little evidence to suggest a sense of affiliation with Andalusia, a territory that, until the nineteenth century, was seen as a separate entity from the kingdom of Granada. See Domínguez Ortiz, "La identidad de Andalucía," 18.

158. Wulff Alonso, *Las esencias patrias*, 13–63.

159. Bermúdez de Pedraza, *Historia eclesiástica*, fol. 211v.

160. Bermúdez alone is willing to speculate that some bishops listed in his episcopology may have been Arians. Ibid., fols. 68r–69r.

161. See Rubio Lapaz, *Pablo de Céspedes y su círculo*, esp. 69–102.

162. An earlier version of this frontispiece identified the city as Iliberia, rather than Ilipula, a redaction that suggests that as Antolínez's interpretation of Granadino history evolved, it came to rely ever more heavily on the testimony of the lead books. See Antolínez, *Historia*, xlvi.

FOUR: CIVIC RITUAL AND CIVIC IDENTITY

Portions of this chapter revise material first published in Harris, "Ceremonias y sermones."

1. As reported in the anonymous *La tres celebrable, digne de memoire, et victorieuse prinse de la cité de Granade* (dated January 4, 1492), reprinted in Hamel, "Un incunable français relatif à la prise de Grenade." For an interesting discussion of how sixteenth- and seventeenth-century historians muddled and changed the events of the surrender, see Pescador del Hoyo, "Cómo fue de verdad la toma de Granada, a la luz de un documento inédito." The cross raised above the Alhambra was later donated to the cathedral of Toledo by its owner, Cardinal Pedro González de Mendoza. López Gómez, *La procesión del "Corpus Christi" de Toledo*, 73–74.

2. Some early accounts are included in Garrido Atienza, *Las capitulaciones para la entrega de Granada*, 313–21.

3. Carreres Zacarés, *Ensayo de una bibliografía de libros de fiestas*, 177–79.

4. Rubio García, *La procesión de Corpus en el siglo XV en Murcia*, 83, 182–87; Carriazo, "Alegrías que hizo Sevilla por la toma de Granada."

5. Carrasco Urgoiti, *El moro de Granada*, 94.

6. For example, every Wednesday the canons of the cathedral of Almería, one of the archbishopric of Granada's three suffragan sees, said a mass in honor of the "exaltación de nuestra santa Fe en la rendición de Granada." López Andrés, *Real patronato eclesiástico y estado moderno*, 182.

7. On the daily plenary indulgence, Bermúdez de Pedraza, *Historia eclesiástica*, fol. 192r; Velázquez Echeverría, *Paseos por Granada*, 1:1. On the *festum deditionis urbis*, see *Breuiarium de camera secundum consuetudinem sancte romane ecclesie*; *Manuale sacramentorum secundum consuetudinem sanctae ecclesiae*.

8. For an overview of civic ritual in early modern Spain, see Mateos Royo, "All the Town Is a Stage."

9. On Granada's Corpus Christi festival, see Garrido Atienza, *Antiguallas granadinas*. See also Gan Giménez, "En torno al Corpus granadino," and Cuesta García de Leonardo, *Fiesta y arquitectura efímera*.

10. St. Sebastian was the dedicatee of one of the first parishes established in Granada (later under the advocation of St. Isabel). A prestigious confraternity devoted to St. Sebastian (and St. Fabian) was well established by the 1520s. The annual procession to St. Sebastian's shrine on the banks of the Genil River was originally a function of this confraternity, with the reluctant participation of the cathedral chapter. Coleman, *Creating Christian Granada*, 107–8; Henríquez de Jorquera, *Anales*, 2:521–22, 591. Cf. Trexler, *Public Life in Renaissance Florence*, 76–77.

11. Sacromonte saints Hiscio and Tesifón also received commemoration, at least during the tenure of Pedro de Castro. See ACG, Libros de Actas, vol. 9, fols. 264 bis r–266r; ACG, Libros de Actas, vol. 10, fol. 83r; Castilla, *Sermón de S. Hiscio obispo y mártyr*; Perea, *Sermón en común de mártyres*.

12. On "civic liturgy," see Muir, *Civic Ritual in Renaissance Venice*, 74–78.

13. Brisset, "Otros procesos conmemorativos centenarios," 138.

14. Garrido Atienza, *Las fiestas de la Toma*, 15–17, 20–22.

15. On the contests over Ferdinand's sword, see Camp, "A Divided Republic," 58–61.

16. Garrido Atienza, *Las fiestas de la Toma*, 28–34.

17. Marín López, *El Cabildo de la Catedral*, 84.

18. Garrido Atienza, *Las fiestas de la Toma*, 29. See also the historical notes included in *Las Fiestas de la Toma*.

19. Henríquez de Jorquera, *Anales*, 2:521.

20. The marching order of the trades was the same as that observed in the Corpus Christi procession. See *Ordenanzas*, 247. I have been unable to ascertain when the trades joined the procession.

21. Bermúdez de Pedraza, *Antigüedad*, fol. 77v. On the development of the *alférez mayor*'s ceremonial role within the city council, see López Nevot, *La organización institucional*, 312–16.

22. It is unclear which door was the "main door" for the cathedral in the sixteenth and seventeenth centuries. Construction began in the 1520s, and between 1561 and 1620 the only roofed areas fit for religious ceremonies were the rotunda of the sanctuary and the ambulatory that went around it. The closest completed door was the Portal of Pardon, which opens from the main transept onto the Calle de la Cárcel, named for the city jail, which faced the cathedral. Diego de Siloe finished the first stage of this richly decorated entrance in the 1530s. Eighteenth-century processions in thanksgiving for successful royal births customarily departed from this door, traveling down the Calle de la Cárcel, through the fishmarket, to Bibarrambla, Zacatín, Pilar del Toro in Plaza Nueva, and returning via Calle de la Cárcel to the same entrance. The cathedral's facade and three principal doors were not in place until the end of the seventeenth century. The eighteenth-century itinerary for the Toma, however, calls for the procession to enter the street at the Plaza of the Colleges, which lay directly in front of the facade and its doors. Rosenthal, *The Cathedral of Granada*, 23; Cuesta García de Leonardo, *Fiesta y arquitectura efímera*, 30, 32; Morales Hondonero Castillo y Salazar, *Ceremonias que esta ciudad de Granada ha de observar*, 6–7.

23. *Erección de la Yglesia Metropolitana de Granada*, 43r. While this text describes the procession as that of the Dedication of the City and lists its date as the first Sunday after the Feast of the Circumcision, the event described is clearly the Toma. See Garrido Atienza, *Las fiestas de la Toma*, 22–23, for the procession's itinerary in 1519.

24. Presumably, by the end of the sixteenth century, at least, the procession did not return to the cathedral by the same route but passed through the door that linked the Royal Chapel to the adjacent cathedral. See Gallego y Burín, *Granada*, 272.

25. ACG, leg. 12, pieza 1; Bermúdez de Pedraza, *Antigüedad*, fol. 77v.

26. *Descripción de la solemne y sumptuosa fiesta*, fol. 199v. In 1555, the municipal council paid the bell ringer fourteen ducats for his labors during the festival. Jiménez Vela, *Inventario de los libros*, 225. On the role of the Alhambra in the festivities, see Viñes Millet, *La Alhambra de Granada*, 206.

27. Henríquez de Jorquera, *Anales*, 2:521; *El triunfo del Ave María*. This play celebrated a famous incident in the conquest of Granada, when the knight Hernando del Pulgar infiltrated the besieged Muslim city and posted a placard in praise of the Virgin Mary on the doors of the main mosque. On this play and others like it, see Carrasco Urgoiti, *El moro de Granada*, 83–90.

28. On Málaga's festival of St. Louis, see Villena Jurado, *Málaga en los albores del siglo XVII*, 146–48; Reder Gadow, "¿Conmemoración política o religiosa?" For the episcopal order declaring the annual commemoration, see Roa, *Málaga*, fols. 49r–50r.

29. Brisset, "Rituales de conquista," 116; López Andrés, *Real patronato eclesiástico y estado moderno*, 183.

30. Artacho y Pérez-Blázquez, *Manuscrito sevillano*, 106. Until 1576 the presiding cleric who said the mass carried the sword. By royal order, the protocol was changed and the sword entrusted to the *asistente* (i.e., Seville's *corregidor*). Ortiz de Zúñiga, *Anales eclesiásticos y seculares*, 3:277–78; 4:76–78, 83–84.

31. Narbona Vizcaíno, "El Nueve de Octubre." Granadinos seem not to have celebrated centennials of the Toma with any more extravagance or ceremony than usual. Garrido Atienza, *Las fiestas de la Toma*, 38.

32. Schneider, *The Ceremonial City*, 118–20.

33. Vincent, "La *toma* de Granada," 45. While Granada, like the rest of Andalusia, remained largely untouched by the unrest in Castile, there were some simultaneous Morisco uprisings in nearby Cazorla, Huéscar, and Baza, which may have been connected to or inspired by the revolts in Valencia. Garzón Pareja, *Historia de Granada*, 1:447–57.

34. The royal standard played a particularly important role in ceremonies surrounding the accession of new kings. See Ruíz, "Unsacred Monarchy"; A. MacKay, "Ritual and Propaganda in Fifteenth-Century Castile." On the royal standard in the Americas, see Valenzuela Márquez, *Las liturgias del poder*, 322–30.

35. Martínez Medina, *Cultura religiosa en la Granada renacentista y barroca*, 163–75.

36. In the late sixteenth century, the Royal Chapel participated in only three general processions each year: Corpus Christi, St. Mark, and the Toma. *Traslado de las constituciones de la Capilla Real de Granada*, 13.

37. ACG, Libros de Actas, vol. 11, fols. 351v–352r. After her death in 1504, Granada's city councilmen honored Isabella on December 27, the feast of St. John the Apostle and

the day of the queen's burial. They later moved the annual ceremony to December 18, the feast of Our Lady of the O and the anniversary of the arrival of the body of the queen in Granada. During the mid-sixteenth century, the council transferred the ceremony a second time to November 25, the anniversary of Isabella's death. By the mid-seventeenth century, the city council alone attended this annual service and the companion ceremony in honor of Ferdinand on January 23, both staged in the cathedral (though at the expense of the Royal Chapel). The Chancery and the Inquisition held separate observances in the Royal Chapel on the same dates; only for the ceremonies honoring both monarchs in May did all three sit down together. The royal chaplains' persistent refusal to attend the honors in the cathedral helped fuel the endemic conflict between the Royal Chapel and the cathedral chapter. See *Ordenanzas*, 12v; Morales Hondonero Castillo y Salazar, *Ceremonias que esta ciudad de Granada ha de observar*, 10–11, 27; *Ordenanças*, 142–43; Marín López, *El Cabildo de la Catedral*, 99, 103.

38. Antolínez de Burgos, *Historia*, 445–51.

39. Garrido Atienza, *Las fiestas de la Toma*, 34–38.

40. Heinz Schilling argues that by 1650, in cities throughout Catholic Europe, processions and the sacred and civic history they often recalled were no longer strictly clerical affairs but "urban events" shared by clergy and laity alike. Schilling, "Urban Architecture and Ritual in Confessional Europe," 19.

41. See *Constituciones Synodales del arçobispado de Granada*, fol. 38v.

42. BN, MS 6265: *Las buenas y loables costumbres y cerimonias que se guardan en la sancta yglesia de Granada y en el choro della*, fol. 12v. The text of the office for the *festum deditionis urbis* is included in BN, MS 13059.

43. Gallego y Burín, *Granada*, 231.

44. Like the sixteenth-century Toma ceremony, the annual memorials to the Catholic monarchs employed the sword, crown, and scepter as potent royal relics. During the mass, the objects were placed either on an altar between the two graves or upon the statues above the tombs. Henríquez de Jorquera, *Anales*, 1:71.

45. Bonet Correa, *Fiesta, poder y arquitectura*, 11. Similar exclusion was observed in Toulouse. Schneider, *The Ceremonial City*, 171.

46. Wood, "Voting the *millones* in Segovia," 50–53. Linguistically, the *ciudad*, the city, is the citizens, the city council (and its representative at the Cortes), and the physical structure of the urban environment. See Covarrubias Orozco, *Tesoro*, 320.

47. Schneider, *The Ceremonial City*, 138.

48. Connerton, *How Societies Remember*, 42ff., 70. See also Middleton and Edwards, Introduction to *Collective Remembering*, 7; Frijda, "Commemorating."

49. Sluhovsky, *Patroness of Paris*, 67–69.

50. Galvarro y Armenta, *Sermón*; Sosa, *Sermón*; Tello de Olivares, *Ciudad symbólica*; Madriz, *Sermón*; M. de la Natividad, *Encantos*; Muñoz y Morales, *La nombrada y gran ciudad*; Cardera, *Granada reconocida*; Santíssima Trinidad, *Granada rendida*. Outside this small collection held by the rare books section of the library of the University of Granada, I have located one anonymous, manuscript sermon, dated 1584, within a larger collection of assorted sermons preached in various churches around Granada during the second half of the sixteenth century. The text makes no mention of the day's proceedings and deals with

the sin of hypocrisy, which, claims the author, is the cause for the drought, plague, and other ills then punishing Granadinos. See BN, MS 8318, 70r–73v.

51. H. Smith, *Preaching in the Spanish Golden Age*, 29–30.

52. Ibid., 31–32. It seems likely that the erudite apparatus of references found in the margins of these printed sermons (especially in the later ones) was added or at least enlarged upon printing.

53. Sermons given in cathedrals or collegiate churches were delivered within the confines of the enclosed choir. When both the chapter and the laity were present, the canons would abandon their stalls and sit on benches in the choir, facing the preacher. In Granada, between the cathedral's consecration in 1561 and the completion of the choir in 1620, the choir was located in the sanctuary, or *capilla mayor*. H. Smith, *Preaching in the Spanish Golden Age*, 14; Rosenthal, *The Cathedral of Granada*, 23. Selection of the preacher to deliver the year's sermon fell to the cathedral chapter, which chose the speaker from among the city's numerous secular and religious clergy.

54. Granada, *Obras del V.P.M. Fray Luis de Granada*, 561–64.

55. For a useful discussion of the Renaissance revival of classical epideictic in ecclesiastical rhetoric, see O'Malley, *Praise and Blame in Renaissance Rome*, esp. chap. 2.

56. Herrero Salgado, *La oratoria sagrada en los siglos XVI y XVII*, 323–25.

57. This tendency is true of sermons commemorating similar events in other cities. Cf. for Almería: Gabriel Pasqual y Orbaneja, "Oración laudatoria a tan catholicíssimos príncipes, con las circunstancias de esta conquista" (1682), in Pasqual y Orbaneja, *Vida de San Indalecio*, 106. For Valencia: Blai Arbuixec, *Sermó de la s. conquista;* Estevan Bru, "Sermón en la solemne fiesta, que hizo la mui ilustre ciudad de Valencia, por cumplirse el quinto siglo de su gloriosa conquista" (1740), in Orti y Mayor, *Fiestas centenarias*, 261–306. For Seville: Cano de Montoro, *Conquista de Sevilla*.

58. "O Jerusalem, Jerusalem, that killest the prophets and stonest them which are sent to thee, how often would I have gathered thy children together, even as a hen gathereth her chickens under her wings, and ye would not! Behold, your house is left unto you desolate. For I say unto you, Ye shall not see me henceforth, till ye shall say, Blessed is he that cometh in the name of the Lord" (Matthew 23:37–39).

59. Tello de Olivares, *Ciudad symbólica*, fol. 1r.

60. Orti y Mayor, *Fiestas centenarias*.

61. Only Tello de Olivares (1640) and Muñoz y Morales (1720) devote any significant attention to pre-Christian Granada. Local antiquarian Gabriel Rodríguez Escabias was provoked to indignation by a Toma sermon in 1644, in which the orator asserted that ancient Granada had existed in a different location than its modern descendant. Rodríguez Escabias, *Discurso*, fols. 1r–2r.

62. Sosa, *Sermón*, fol. 16v. Sosa enjoyed a prosperous career in the cathedrals of Almería and Granada. He was appointed precentor of the Granada cathedral chapter in 1646 and served as dean of the school of theology of the University of Granada. See Gan Giménez, "Los prebendados," 207; López-Huertas Pérez, *Bibliografía*, 925–30.

63. Galvarro y Armenta, *Sermón*. A native of Seville, Galvarro taught theology at the University of Granada. Antonio, *Biblioteca hispana nova*, 1:697.

64. Muñoz y Morales, *La nombrada y gran ciudad*, 9.

65. M. de la Natividad, *Encantos*, 2–4.

66. Cardera, *Granada reconocida*, 5, 32.

67. Madriz, *Sermón*, fol. 4r–v.

68. Muñoz y Morales, *La nombrada y gran ciudad*, 16.

69. M. de la Natividad, *Encantos*, 6.

70. Sosa, *Sermón*, fol. 23r.

71. Santíssima Trinidad, *Granada rendida*.

72. Galvarro y Armenta, *Sermón*. He refers to Exodus 28:31–34.

73. M. de la Natividad, *Encantos*, esp. 33.

74. A native Granadino, Tello de Olivares rose through the cathedral chapter of Granada. He was appointed to the see of Mondoñedo in 1669, but in 1671 he died of injuries sustained in a fall. For many years he held the *prima* chair of Holy Scripture in the University of Granada. See Gan Giménez, "Los prebendados," 208; López Rodríguez, "Cátedras de Teología," 258; López-Huertas Pérez, *Bibliografía*, 938–41.

75. Tello de Olivares, *Ciudad symbólica*, fols. 9v–10v.

76. Sosa, *Sermón*, fols. 11r–15v.

77. Madriz, *Sermón*, fol. 9r.

78. Jaime Servera, *Oración panegyrica en la solemnísima fiesta que la santa metropolitana iglesia de Valencia hizo día 4 de Noviembre de 1714 a sus ínclitos mártires San Juan de Perusa y San Pedro de Saxoferrato* (Valencia, 1714), quoted in Sebastián, *Contrarreforma y barroco*, 140; Jean-Pierre Camus, quoted in Worcester, *Seventeenth-Century Cultural Discourse*, 206.

79. Galvarro y Armenta, *Sermón*.

80. Sosa, *Sermón*, fol. 17r.

81. Henríquez de Jorquera, *Anales*, 1:227–28, notes that the parish of St. Ildefonso had secondary dedications to two other saints—St. Catherine and St. Stephen.

82. Rodríguez Becerra, "La toma de Zahara," 154–55.

83. E.g., Bermúdez de Pedraza, *Historia Eclesiástica*, fol. 75r–v, who argues that the basilica must have been erected in the Alhambra (an assumption shared by later scholars, and criticized by Gómez-Moreno y Martínez, "Monumentos romanos y visigóticos de Granada," 89–92). For the text of the inscription, see Vives, *Inscripciones cristianas*, 100–101. The inscription is currently in Granada's Museo Nacional de Arte Hispanomusulmán.

84. BN, MS 1583: Velarde de Rivera, *Historia del Monte Santo*, fol. 219v.

85. Bermúdez de Pedraza, *Historia eclesiástica*, fols. 113v–114v; AASG, C48: Guerra de Lorca, *Memorias eclesiásticas*, fols. 239r–245v; BN, MS 1583: Velarde de Rivera, *Historia del Monte Santo*, fols. 217v–220r.

86. Henríquez de Jorquera, *Anales*, 1:65–66; Bermúdez de Pedraza, *Historia eclesiástica*, fol. 234r–v; Rosenthal, *The Cathedral of Granada*, 117. The Virgin of la Antigua remained popular well into the seventeenth century but was gradually supplanted by Our Lady of Anguish (Nuestra Señora de las Angustias), a virgin better suited to baroque tastes and Counter-Reformation piety. See Moreno Garrido, "La iconografía de la Virgen de la Antigua en el grabado granadino del siglo XVII"; López Muñoz, "Contrarreforma y cofradías en Granada," 332–34, 1227–29.

87. Sánchez-Mesa Martín, *Técnica de la escultura policromada granadina*, 102–4. The presence of the Evangelist corresponds to the new prophecy of St. John included in the lead

box from the Torre Turpiana. Henríquez de Jorquera, *Anales,* 1:66, identifies this figure not as St. John the Evangelist but as St. Tesifón. The retable was replaced in 1718 with a baroque arrangement juxtaposing the Virgin of la Antigua with St. Cecilio and St. Gregory of Baetica. Gallego y Burín, *Granada,* 269. The cathedral clergy encouraged the association between the Toma and the Torre by displaying the Virgin of la Antigua with the handkerchief relic from the Torre Turpiana on solemn occasions, for example, the ceremonies of amends made to the Virgin in 1640 after an anonymous "heretic" left a placard impugning her purity on the doors of the city council's chambers. See Paracuellos Cabeza de Vaca, *Triunfales celebraciones;* Henríquez de Jorquera, *Anales,* 2:856. For more on these events, see chapter 5.

88. Heredía Barneuvo, *Místico ramillete,* 99; ACG, Libros de Actas, vol. 9, fol. 336v.

89. Barrios Aguilera and Sánchez Ramos, "La herencia martirial" and *Martirios y mentalidad martirial en las Alpujarras.* See also Barrios Aguilera, "El fin de la Granada islámica: una propuesta," and "Un ensayo de revisión historiográfica de los mártires de las Alpujarras de 1568 (seguido de un apéndice documental, selección de las *Actas de Ugíjar*)," in Hitos, *Mártires de la Alpujarra,* vii–lxv.

90. Studies of martyrdom in Counter-Reformation Catholic ideology and devotion have generally focused on its role in art and iconography. The most comprehensive of these is still Mâle, *L'art religieux,* 109–49. See also Knipping, *Iconography of the Counter Reformation in the Netherlands,* 1:128–38; Herz, "Imitators of Christ." On attitudes toward martyrdom among both Catholics and Protestants in early modern England, France, and the Netherlands, see Gregory, *Salvation at Stake.* For a discussion of similar attitudes in twentieth-century Andalusian piety, see Mitchell, *Passional Culture.*

91. Sosa, *Sermón,* fol. 8v.

92. Sermons, notes John Elliott, played an important and as yet underexamined role in maintaining the political status quo. See Elliott, "Power and Propaganda in the Spain of Philip IV," 151.

93. On fireworks, see Maravall, *Culture of the Baroque,* 246–47.

94. The festivity's core concern with history becomes exceptionally clear when Toma sermons are compared with those given during other, related ceremonies, such as the annual honors for the Catholic Monarchs. See Ramos Gavilán, *Oración panegyrica;* Castillo, *Oración fúnebre panegyrica.* On Corpus Christi, see Garrido Atienza, *Antiguallas granadinas,* esp. 46–48, 56; Cuesta García de Leonardo, *Fiesta y arquitectura efímera,* esp. 109.

95. Sosa, *Sermón,* fol. 23r.

96. Galvarro y Armenta, *Sermón.*

97. An effort to suppress Almería's Banner Day festival in 1546 offers a hint at Morisco reactions to such festivities. Supporters of the motion noted that the commemoration "caused such pain to the Moriscos that on that day they would remain enclosed in their houses, spilling out weeping." Quoted in Grima Cervantes, "Anotaciones cronológicas para la historia de Almería," 313.

98. Quoted in Lowenthal, *The Heritage Crusade,* 105.

99. González Martínez, "La fiesta de la toma de Granada en tiempos liberales."

100. AMG, leg. 2403, 3–4. Curiously, the annual *fiesta* of St. Cecilio, which was revived

in the 1980s after falling into decline, also includes the opening bars of the national anthem, which is played during the elevations of the Host and the Chalice.

101. Similar debate has erupted in Almería and other cities with ceremonies commemorating Christian conquest.

Portions of this chapter revise material first published in Harris, "The Sacromonte and the Geography of the Sacred in Early Modern Granada."

Epigraph: Bermúdez de Pedraza, *Antigüedad*, fol. 110r.

1. AASG, leg. 5, fols. 1022r–1025r.

2. Henríquez de Jorquera, *Anales*, 1, 660–61; Herrera y Sotomayor, *Jornada;* Juan de Cabrera, *Entrada de su Magestad en la ciudad de Granada* (Seville, 1624), summarized in Alenda y Mira, *Relaciones de solemnidades y fiestas públicas de España*, 242–43; Heredia Barnuevo, *Místico ramillete*, 221; Elliott, *The Count-Duke of Olivares*, 158.

3. Geertz, "Centers, Kings, and Charisma," 125.

4. E. Wright, *Pilgrimage to Patronage*, 54.

5. Martínez, *Las partidas de la gran ciudad de Granada*. See Orozco Pardo, *Christianópolis*, 64–70, 155–59.

6. Henríquez de Jorquera, *Anales*, 1:232. On the image of Our Lady of Hope, see Gallego y Burín, *Granada*, 173.

7. Henríquez de Jorquera, *Anales*, 1:262–74.; Gallego y Burín, *Granada*, 154, 158, 191, 194. The hermitage of St. Helen was an obligatory stop for sixteenth-century visitors to Granada, who customarily scribbled their names and their home countries upon its crumbling walls. According to Henríquez de Jorquera, the hermitage of St. Helen suffered after the Morisco revolt of 1568. It lost its confraternity to the nearby Discalced Carmelite Monastery of the Martyrs, and was reduced to the care of a single hermit. Antoine Jouvin, a French traveler who visited Granada in the 1660s, noted that the shrine contained a number of relics. See Braun, *Civitates orbis terrarum;* Jouvin, "El viaje de España y Portugal," 823. On the shrine on the Alhambra, see chapter 3.

8. Navagiero, *Il viaggio*, fols. 23r–24r.

9. Juan de Vilches, *De urbis Granatae rebus memoralibus*, in Luque Moreno, *Granada en el siglo XVI*, 93–100, 260.

10. This passage comes from a *villancico* appended to his longer verse description of Granada. Martínez, *Las partidas*.

11. Gil Sanjuán and Sánchez López, "Iconografía y visión histórico-literaria de Granada a mediados del quinientos," 101. See also Gil Sanjuán and Pérez de Colosía Rodríguez, *Imágenes del poder*. The drawings of Anton van den Wyngaerde, who visited Granada in 1567, were idealized views but still truer to life than those of Hoefnagel, who was more concerned with creating dramatic local landscapes that captured the general spirit of a place rather than its topographical details. On Wyngaerde, see Kagan, *Spanish Cities of the Golden Age*. On Hoefnagel, see Nuti, "The Mapped Views by Georg Hoefnagel."

12. See Marcos Martín, "Percepciones materiales e imaginario urbano en la España

moderna." On representations of Seville, see *Iconografía de Sevilla, 1400–1650; Iconografía de Sevilla, 1650–1790.*

13. According to Henríquez de Jorquera, *Anales,* 1:66, the statue of Christ at the Column was previously in a chapel in the Sagrario, where it gained a reputation for working miracles. In 1588, after carrying the image in a rogation procession for the success of the Armada, the cathedral chapter appropriated the statue and moved it to the cathedral.

14. See the undated list in AGS, Patronato Eclesiástico, Memoriales y expedientes, leg. 104. See also the list compiled during a *visita* in 1590: AGS, Patronato Eclesiástico, Visitas, leg. 282, fol. 341; and Santacruz Molina, *Copia de las reliquias.*

15. AASG, leg. 4, pt. 1, fol. 1132r.

16. Heredia Barnuevo, *Místico ramillete,* 99. The cathedral chapter also exhibited the relic of St. Stephen each year on his feast day, December 26. See also ACG, Libros de Actas, vol. 9, fols. 274v, 283r (1601); ACG, Libros de Actas, vol. 10, fol. 98r (1611). For an example of the display of the relic of the Virgin during an emergency procession, see Paracuellos Cabeza de Vaca, *Triunfales celebraciones;* Henríquez de Jorquera, *Anales,* 2:856.

17. BN, MS 6637, fol. 200r. In 1597 an early critic, Francisco Terrones del Caño, retracted his objections and issued a statement in favor of the *plomos.* He claimed to have been convinced in part by an inspection of the mountain and the caves. On publications advertising Terrones's statement in support of the *plomos,* see chapter 2.

18. Antolínez de Burgos, *Historia,* 643. See also López Madera, *Discursos,* 12v.

19. Castro claimed that on several occasions during his tenure as president of the Chancery, he had seen processions of lights upon the mountain. Centurión y Córdoba, *Información,* fol. 57v.

20. AASG, C49, fols. 28v–29r, 31r.

21. AASG, C49, fols. 30r, 58v–62v.

22. AASG, C49, fol. 35v. Interestingly, other witnesses reported seeing similar lights on the Sierra Elvira on March 18, 1596—a full year after the recovery of the relics of St. Cecilio from the Sacromonte. AASG, leg. 3, pt. 1, fols. 207–30.

23. AASG, C49, fols. 178r–179r. Also questioned on this topic were canons Francisco de Torrijos and Pedro Guerra de Lorca. Canon Maldonado mentions a hermitage dedicated to St. Cecilio, but I cannot verify or locate this shrine.

24. E.g., AASG, C49, fols. 16r, 27r, 33v, 36r, 38r–46v, 48v, 50r, 52r, 57v, 58v, 59v, 246–57.

25. E.g., AASG, C49, fols. 42v–43v.

26. AASG, C49, fol. 46v. Similar cures were sought at a spring at the foot of the hill, known to Granada's Moriscos and non-Moriscos alike for its healing powers. Bermúdez de Pedraza, *Antigüedad,* fol. 13v.

27. Popular witchcraft beliefs could transform the healing powers of the Sacromonte into death-dealing poison. In her 1635 trial before the Granada Inquisition, Barbula de Bertondo was accused of creating a venomous concoction of mercury, vinegar, holy water, and dirt from the Sacromonte for a customer who wished to be rid of his wife. Fernández García, "Hechicería e Inquisición en el reino de Granada en el siglo XVII."

28. AASG, C49, fol. 50r.

29. AASG, C49, fols. 36r–37r.

30. AASG, C49, fols. 39v, 41r.

31. AASG, C49, fol. 38r.

32. AASG, C49, fol. 16r.

33. AASG, C49, fols. 46v, 48v, 50r. According to one scholar, Archbishop Hernando de Talavera visited a Muslim hermit who lived in a cave on the outskirts of the city shortly after assuming the see of Granada. See Fernández, *Fray Hernando de Talavera,* 221.

34. Quoted in Hernández Benito, "Toponimia y sociedad." See also Seco de Lucena Paredes, "De toponimia granadina.," 84. Respondent Salvador de Mendoza's tale about the repentance of Ibn Fodail may reflect hagiographic accounts of the bandit saint al-Fuḍail ibn ʿIyāḍ, who died in 803 in Mecca. See Shaʿrānī, *Vite e detti di santi musulmani,* 115–17.

35. Villanueva Rico, *Habices de las mezquitas,* 228.

36. Quoted in Santiago Simón, "Algunos datos sobre la posesión," 159. Santiago Simón suggests that this place-name may be derived from the Arabic *Khandaq al-sinhājī,* a place-name marking the ravine as the property of the Berber tribe of the same name.

37. Ibn al-Ḥajarī, *Kitāb Nāṣir al-dīn,* 66.

38. Ibn Baṭṭūṭa, *The Travels of Ibn Baṭṭūṭa,* 943. See Lévi-Provençal, "Le voyage d'Ibn Baṭṭūṭa dans le royaume de Grenade (1350)." The Maḥrūq clan was well-known in Granada. One member, Muḥammad b. Aḥmad b. Muḥammad b. al-Maḥrūq (d. 1328), became vizir to the kingdom's Nasrid rulers. Harvey, *Islamic Spain, 1250–1500,* 185–87.

39. According to Torres Balbas, "Rábitas hispanomusulmanas," 481, late medieval and early modern Arabic speakers in Iberia tended to treat the terminology of *rābiṭa* and *zāwiya* as interchangable.

40. Ibn Baṭṭūṭa, *The Travels of Ibn Baṭṭūṭa,* 944. Ibn Baṭṭūṭa visited Abū ʾl-Ḥasan ʿAlī b. Aḥmad b. al-Maḥrūq, nephew to Abū ʿAlī ʿUmar. According to the fourteenth-century Granadino historian Ibn al-Khaṭīb, the nephew was the author of a now lost mystical treatise, *Nukat al-Nājī.* Viguera Molíns, "La religión y el derecho," 172.

41. Seco de Lucena Paredes, "De toponimia granadina" and *La Granada nazarí del siglo XV,* 160–61.

42. Torres Balbas, "Rábitas hispanomusulmanas," 481–82. Following Sigüenza, Bermúdez de Pedraza noted that the *rábita* "had been burned three times by Christians and as many times rebuilt by the hermit. But the last time, when the [Catholic] Monarchs were in Santa Fe, [both] he and the hermitage were burned. The hermitage was on the site where now is located the hospital of St. John of God." Bermúdez de Pedraza, *Historia eclesiástica,* fol. 174v.

43. Hernández Benito, "Toponimia y sociedad."

44. On Córdoba, see Roa, *Flos sanctorum,* fol. 164v. On Arjona, *Relación y memorial sacado de las ynformaciones;* Rus Puerta, *Historia eclesiástica,* fols. 145v–147v.

45. Guerra also says that similar lights had been seen at the site of ancient Urci (Almería), where St. Indalecio was martyred, and near the town of Illora, where, he conjectures, martyrs must have died during the persecution of the early Church. In his testimony before the panel of inquiry, canon Francisco de Torrijos reported that such phenomena had been seen by Moriscos in Berja, the see of St. Tesifón. BN, MS 1499: Guerra

de Lorca, *La historia de la vida,* fols. 265r–267r; AASG, C49, fols. 177r–v, 338. See also the brief and scandalized comments of Tapia Garrido, *Historia general de Almería y su provincia,* 244.

46. Goldziher, "Veneration of Saints in Islam," 321.

47. C. Taylor, *In the Vicinity of the Righteous,* 55.

48. Memon, *Ibn Taimīya's Struggle against Popular Religion,* 294.

49. Westermarck, *Ritual and Belief in Morocco,* 161–62. Equivalent beliefs are found in hagiographical accounts of Jewish saints from Morocco. See Ben-Ami, *Culte des saints,* 29–30.

50. Ibn al-Khaṭīb, *Correspondencia diplomatica,* 17.

51. Ibn Baṭṭūṭa, *The Travels of Ibn Baṭṭūṭa,* 943; AASG, C49, fol. 35v; leg. 3, pt. 1, fols. 207–30.

52. Fierro, "El espacio de los muertos." The panel of inquiry was very concerned about the possibility that the Sacromonte had been the site of Muslim burials. Witnesses were asked whether they knew of any graves on the site. While most answered no, one respondent offered other possibilities. Hieronymo de Escobar (cited earlier) testified that during the uprising of 1568 rebel Moriscos had unearthed their dead from the parish cemeteries and reburied them on the mountain. This witness later retracted his testimony. AASG, C49, fols. 39r–v, 542r. See also García Pedraza, *Actitudes ante la muerte,* 2:636, 1007.

53. E.g., Caro Baroja, *Los moriscos del Reino de Granada,* 130.

54. ABFZ, carpeta 161, pieza 129.

55. Aigle and Mayeur-Jaouen, "Miracle et *karāma,*" 24–27; Brown, *The Cult of the Saints.* For an example, see Bermúdez de Pedraza, *Historia eclesiástica,* fols. 29r, 34r, 38r–v.

56. See, among others, Tuan, *Space and Place;* Norton, *Explorations in the Understanding of Landscape,* 119–22.

57. Nora, "Between Memory and History"; *Les lieux de mémoire;* and *Realms of Memory.*

58. Heredia Barnuevo, *Místico ramillete,* 133.

59. Kagan, "*Urbs* and *Civitas,*" 76–77, and *Urban Images of the Hispanic World.*

60. *Relación breve de las reliquias* (1608). On Fernández, see Moreno Garrido, "El grabado en Granada durante el siglo XVII," 52–55.

61. Henríquez de Jorquera, *Anales,* 1:255, 267–68; 2:735–36. On Granada's *via sacra* to the Sacromonte, see Vander Hammen y León, *Via sacra;* Gullién Marcos and Villaranca Jiménez, "El Sacro Monte granadino." On other devotional routes in Granada, see López Muñoz, "Contrarreforma y cofradías en Granada," 880–93.

62. On maps as guides to prayer, see Melion, "*Ad ductum itineris et dispositionem mansionum ostendendam.*" I am grateful to Professor Melion for bringing this aspect of early modern cartography to my attention.

63. E. Casey, "How to Get from Space to Place."

64. My discussion here is informed by Orozco Pardo, *Christianópolis.* The labyrinthine character of the Albaicín is not the only information suppressed in the map. Also missing or unlabeled is the Madraza, the seat of Granada's city council. On the Plataforma, see Moreno Garrido, Gómez-Moreno Calera, and López Guzmán, "La Plataforma de Ambrosio de Vico"; Gómez-Moreno Calera, *El arquitecto granadino,* 144–58.

65. Cf. Hills, "Mapping the Early Modern City."

66. Henríquez de Jorquera, *Anales,* 1:32–33. See Harley, "Maps, Knowledge, and Power."

67. "Al Monte Santo de Granada," in Góngora y Argote, *Obras poéticas,* 194; Antequera y Arteaga, *Excelencias de Granada, expressadas en un epigramma.* This text is reproduced in Orozco Pardo, *Christianópolis,* 159–66. See also the anonymous "Romance de Granada" (ca. 1600), included in Orozco Díaz, *Granada en la poesía barroca.* The Sacromonte figures in both the poetic and prose descriptions of Granada by Rojas Villandrando, *El viaje entretenido,* 186–92. On the Sacromonte in Granadino poetry, see also Orozco Díaz, *El poema "Granada."* Regrettably, I have not been able to locate Rodrigo Fernández de Ribera, *Canción al Santo Monte de Granada* (Granada, 1617).

68. Luque Moreno, *Granada en el siglo XVI,* 362.

69. Ibid., 344–45.

70. Bertaut, "Diario del viaje de España," 2:589–91; Sánchez Rivero and Mariutti de Sánchez Rivero, *Viaje de Cosme de Médicis,* 203–6.

71. The rivalry for patron status between St. Gregory of Baetica and St. Cecilio (and, in the late seventeenth century, St. John of God) merits further investigation. To date, the only treatment of this topic is Martínez Medina, *San Cecilio y San Gregorio.* On the multiplication of city patrons in the early modern period, see Sallmann, "Il santo patron cittadino nell '600 nel Regno di Napoli e in Sicilia."

72. Jerome, *On Illustrious Men,* 139; Sotomayor y Muro, "Iglesia en la España romana," 218–32.

73. AASG, C48: Guerra de Lorca, *Memorias eclesiásticas,* fol. 168v.

74. According to Antolínez de Burgos, *Historia,* 102, St. Gregory of Baetica's feast was celebrated with a double office. On April 23, 1596, the cathedral chapter voted to celebrate St. Gregory's feast "with great solemnity" but did not specify the rank. ACG, Libros de Actas, vol. 9, fol. 134r.

75. Conde y Herrera, *Sepulcro duplicado del proto-mártyr thaumatúrgico,* 3, claims that the 1544 breviary gave St. Cecilio a double common office. I have been unable to consult the 1544 breviary, but the calendar of the annual cycle of divine offices is included in *Manuale sacramentorum.* See also *Breuiarium de camera secundum consuetudinem sancte romane ecclesie; Officia quae in ecclesia Granatensis.* The readings for the second nocturn of the feast of St. Cecilio were very general and were based on Petrus de Natalibus's account of the Seven Apostles of Spain. See Natalibus, *Catalogus sanctorum,* fol. 89r: "De sanctis torquato et sociis eiis." Godoy Alcántara, *Historia crítica,* 79, notes that, in the years immediately preceding the Sacromonte discoveries, Guadix and Ávila, cities claiming the patronage of two of the Seven Apostles (Torcuato and Segundo, respectively), had obtained offices for their saints. When Archbishop Martin Carrillo y Aldrete (1642–53) officially declared the patronal feast day in 1646, St. Cecilio had not yet obtained his own office. Records of the cathedral chapter show that in 1638, St. Cecilio received the common office of martyrs on his feast day, and the office of a single martyr on his octave, a practice that was protested by the cathedral master of ceremonies (ACG, Libros de Actas, vol. 13, fol. 181r). In 1703 Granada received papal approval for an office of St. Cecilio (double, first class, with octave). Both the festival declaration of 1646 and the 1702 office may be found in AMG, Festejos, leg. 1930. See also Cuesta García de Leonardo, *Fiesta y arquitectura efímera,* 173–74. In 1729

the office of St. Cecilio was extended to all of Spain. See the 1729 letter of Archbishop Francisco Perea y Porres (1720–33) to the cathedral chapter, ACG, leg. 29, no. 1.

76. According to Royo Campos, *Albores del Sacro Monte*, 112, St. Gregory was Granada's patron saint for the first century after the Christian conquest, until he was replaced by popular acclaim by St. Cecilio. See also Martínez Medina, *San Cecilio y San Gregorio*, 51–53.

77. BN, MS 1499: Guerra de Lorca, *La historia de la vida*, fol. 262r.

78. Pedro Guerra de Lorca claims that the hermitage was founded by Archbishop Talavera. He also cites witness testimony taken in 1573 documenting an oral tradition attributed to the Moriscos, which held that two Christian virgins named Juana and María received martyrdom on the site where the hermitage now stands. AASG, C48: Guerra de Lorca, *Memorias eclesiásticas*, fols. 168v, 339r. See also the comments of Martínez de Buendía, *Noticia breve*, 15.

79. Gallego y Burín, *Granada*, 391.

80. Henríquez de Jorquera, *Anales*, 1:263; AMG, Festejos, leg. 896, pieza 5: "Antecedentes sobre la función de San Gregorio," 1654. I have been unable to ascertain when the city council began sponsoring the annual festivities for St. Gregory, but it seems likely that the completed renovations and the attendance are related. The first mention of the festivities in the council's minutes is in 1614 (AMG, Actas Capitulares, vol. 8, fols. 11v–16v); however, the records for 1566–1603 and 1604–13 are lost. In 1604 the city councilmen resolved that masses would be said in the hermitage on Sundays and feast days, rewarding the officiants with three *reales* for each mass (AMG, Actas Capitulares, vol. 7, fols. 136r–139r).

81. According to an inscription inside the shrine, the shrine was created in 1752 by Francisco de Cascaxares del Castillo Blancas y Pastor, president of the Royal Chancery. See Ramos López, *Breve reseña*. For a similar process of reidentification of local topography in the light of a Sacromonte saint, see Sánchez Ramos, "El culto a San Tesifón en Berja (Almería)."

82. In the parish of St. Cecilio, baptisms during the seventeenth century break down as follows: 1601–10: 9; 1611–20: 3; 1621–30: 2; 1631–40: 8; 1641–50: 4; 1651–60: 4; 1661–70: 4; 1671–80: 2; 1681–90: 6; 1691–1700: 4. I have not included in this data set any female children baptized as Cecilia, since they could also represent devotion to St. Cecilia, patron saint of music. Only one child received the name of another of the Sacromonte saints—an abandoned boy, baptized Tesifón in 1634. APSC: Joseph Francisco de Torres, *Abecedario general de los ocho primeros libros bautismos de esta yglesia parroquial de señor san Cecilio mártir, y primero obispo de esta ciudad de Granada* (manuscript, 1769).

83. Henríquez de Jorquera, *Anales*, 1:218.

84. In the parish of St. Peter and St. Paul, seventeenth- and eighteenth-century baptisms with the name of Cecilio break down as follows: 1601–10: 2; 1611–20: 3; 1621–30: 2; 1631–40: none; 1641–50: none; 1651–60: 3; 1661–70: 3; 1671–80: 4; 1681–90: 1; 1691–1700: 1; 1701–10: 1; 1711–20: 4; 1721–30: 1. Between 1731 and 1756, no children received the names Cecilio. Baptisms with the name of Tesifón occurred in 1598, 1636, 1645, 1664, and 1668. In 1677 an infant was baptized Cecilio Tesifón (I have included this child in the list of Cecilios). APSPSP, Libros de Bautismos, vols. 1–6, 1556–1756. Such fashions in naming were common after the discovery of a new patron saint. The names Julián and Juliana

became popular in Cuenca after the body of that saint was found to be incorrupt during a translation in 1516, and in the 1570s many parents in Andújar named their newborns in honor of St. Eufrasio, whose previously unknown status as patron had recently been revealed through the scholarly efforts of a native son. Nalle, "A Saint for All Seasons"; Terrones de Robres, *Vida*, fol. 227v.

85. RAH 9/3662, n. 134.

86. ACG, Libros de Actas, vol. 9, fol. 314v.

87. AHN, Consejos, leg. 17088[2].

88. Cf. Jiménez Monterserín, *Vere pater pauperum*, 282.

89. AGS, Patronato Eclesiástico, leg. 55.

90. AASG, leg. 5, fols. 280r–281v; also AGS, Patronato Eclesiástico, leg. 55 (dated September 24, 1600). Later that year, the king ruled that the city must receive a key. However, it appears that Castro may have continued to refuse the council's request: a November 1616 letter from the city council to Castro, then in Seville, includes a petition for a key so that "[on] the day when this city [council] goes to the Sacromonte they can show [the relics] and the devotion of the people will grow." By the following year, however, the chapter of the Abbey of the Sacromonte recommended to Castro that the city be given a key, along with the president of the Chancery (in the name of the king), the archbishop of Granada, and the Sacromonte chapter itself. By 1624 the city council possessed its key. Heredia Barnuevo, *Místico ramillete*, 95–97; AASG, leg. 5, fols. 768, 774–78, 1065–67.

91. ABFZ, carpeta 161, pieza 104. The apologetic councillors claimed that it "has not been carelessness, but rather much care not to tire Your Majesty with a duplicated account, knowing how the archbishop has done it with such punctuality."

92. AASG, leg. 5, fol. 250r; Heredia Barnuevo, *Místico ramillete*, 97–98.

93. ACG, Libros de Actas, vol. 9, fols. 263r–264v. In 1602 Jorge de Texerina, dean of the cathedral chapter, funded the cathedral's annual feast of St. Cecilio with an annuity of 6,000 *maravedís*. ACG, Libros de Actas, vol. 9, fol. 309r–v.

94. AASG, Libros de Actas, vol. 1, fol. 28v.

95. AASG, leg. 7, pt. 1, fols. 847–48. The city council apparently left the festivities on the Sacromonte "with little pleasure," angry at the author of this document for having refused to allow dances before the sacrament as were done during Corpus. The city claimed that Pedro de Castro had previously given permission for the dances, but the author rejected the dances as scandalous because the dancers were women and actors.

96. Few of the sermons given on St. Cecilio's day reached print. See Navas, *Oración panegyrica;* Conde y Herrera, *Sepulcro duplicado*. There are several in Barcia y Zambrana, *Despertador christiano santoral* and *Despertador christiano de sermones doctrinales*. I have been unable to locate Diego Luis del Castillo, *Oración evangélica al glorioso mártyr señor S. Cecilio, primer obispo de Granada, y patrón principal de su arçobispado* (Granada, 1704).

97. J. Martínez Ruiz, "Cartas inéditas de Bernardo J. de Aldrete (1608–1626)," 505. Bernardo José de Aldrete (1560–1641), a canon in the cathedral of Córdoba, was one of the most famous scholars of his day. With his first book, *Del origen y principio de la lengua castellana o romance que oi se usa en España* (Rome, 1606), Aldrete incurred the displeasure of Archbishop Castro, who objected to Aldrete's assertion that Castilian derived from Latin, as this thesis cast into doubt the authenticity of the Torre Turpiana parchment. By 1614 Al-

drete had passed into the camp of Sacromonte supporters, and into the pay of Castro, to whom he dedicated his *Varias antigüedades de España, África, y otras provincias* (Antwerp, 1614). This book's remarkable frontispiece includes depictions of St. James and St. Cecilio holding some of the lead books.

98. ACG, Libros de Actas, vol. 11, fol. 224r.

99. On this text, see chapter 3.

100. Bermúdez de Pedraza, *Antigüedad,* fol. 60r.

101. Ibid.

102. The illustration appears again at the end of the first and third parts of Bermúdez's *Historia eclesiástica.* The same device, its elements recreated out of separate woodcuts, reappears in Conde y Herrera, *Sepulcro duplicado.*

103. ACG, Libros de Actas, vol. 9, fols. 368r, 372v; vol. 10, fols. 25v, 226r, 236v, 293v; Henríquez de Jorquera, *Anales,* 2:523, 529, 536, 537, 539, 596, 619, 697, 751, 809, 851, 857, 909, 927.

104. AMG, Festejos, leg. 1930. Archbishop Martín Carrillo y Aldrete (1642–53) appears to have identified closely with his ancient predecessor. He took possession of the see of Granada on January 2, 1642, the day of the Toma, and formally entered the city on February 1, the feast of St. Cecilio. In 1643 he gave 10,000 *maravedís* for three annual masses in the cathedral: one on the day of St. Cecilio, one on the day of St. Martin, and one on the day of his own death. Henríquez de Jorquera, *Anales,* 2:904; ACG, Libro de Actas, vol. 14, fol. 50v.

105. ACG, Libros de Actas, vol. 9, fols. 198v–199v, 201r, 246r; ACG, Libros de Actas, vol. 10, fol. 73r–v.

106. ACG, Libros de Actas, vol. 10, fol. 161r; vol. 12, fol. 62v; ACG, leg. 1, doc. 99.

107. For example, on August 13, 1630, the chapter resolved to write to Miguel Santos de San Pedro, Granada's archbishop-elect, about several matters, including the relics of the Torre Turpiana. On February 13, 1632, the city council asked the chapter to "come to the defense [so] that they do not take away the books of the Sacromonte." Rather than sending letters protesting the confiscation, the canons agreed to say a prayer to the Holy Spirit for the resolution of the affair. ACG, Libros de Actas, vol. 12, fols. 105r, 172v.

108. ACG, leg. 25, piezas 9 and 13. A letter dated July 10, 1640, from Blas de Tineo, a high-ranking member of the chapter, includes a notice that the *consejo de cámara* (an inner council within the Council of Castile) has been occupied with the *plomos* affair, such that "with these and other concerns, they have not seen our request," phrasing that suggests that the cathedral was not involved in the effort for the *plomos.* ACG, leg. 29, pieza 1.

109. See, e.g., *Señor. El Patronato del Sacro monte de Granada.*

110. By 1659 the canons were running a substantial deficit, outspending their budget each year by a sum equal to approximately a third of the abbey's annual income (AGS, Patronato Eclesiástico, Memoriales y Expedientes, leg. 231, n. 19, fol. 4v). After a pastoral visitation by Archbishop Diego de Escolano in 1672, the canons were ordered not to divert any more money from the abbey's regular funds to finance their efforts in Rome, but instead to depend on charitable giving (ACG, leg. 327, doc. 1). BN R-24033 includes several printed appeals for donations, while the 1661 royal order on the abbey's charitable solicitations in the Indies is preserved in Agi, indiferente, 430, libro 40, fols. 304v–305v. See also *Aviéndose*

descubierto cerca de la Ciudad de Granada; La Grande necessidad con que se halla el Doctor don Blasio de Santaella.

111. Centurión y Córdoba, *Información*, fols. 103v–105v. According to Bermúdez de Pedraza, *Antigüedad*, fol. 131r, the poetic works of Pedro de Granada Venegas included a number of poems to the Sacromonte.

112. *Actas de las Cortes de Castilla*, 33:274, 311. See Egido, "Religiosidad 'popular' y Cortes tradicionales de Castilla," 109.

113. AMG, Actas Capitulares, vol. 7, fols. 110v–114r; AGS, Patronato Eclesiástico, leg. 63.

114. Printed petitions dated 1640, 1641. AHN, Consejos, leg. 17088²; BN, MS 6437, fols. 85–89.

115. AMG, Propios, leg. 1915, piezas 1662 and 1674, as well as AASG, leg. 5, fol. 1268.

116. AHN, Consejos, leg. 17088²; BN, MS 6437, fols. 85v–86r.

117. Centurión y Córdoba, *Información*, fol. 104r.

118. AMG, leg. 1863, pieza 1705: "Los motivos por que la ciudad de Granada no debe permitir que se saquen della los libros del Sacro Monte." Though anonymous, the handwriting on the document appears to be that of Martín Vázquez Siruela, canon of the Sacromonte. If he is indeed the author, the document is also indicative of the close ties between the abbey and the city council and suggests that the canons sought to aid, encourage, and influence the council members in their efforts.

119. See Webb, *Patrons and Defenders*, 135; Vauchez, "Patronage des saints et religion civique dans l'Italie communale à la fin du Moyen Age."

120. Sluhovsky, *Patroness of Paris*, 67. Cf. Orozco Pardo, *Christianópolis*, 106.

121. AASG, leg. 5, fol. 186.

122. AASG, C49, fols. 13v, 27r, 766r–767v.

123. *Historia del Colegio de San Pablo*, 121.

124. BN, MS 11017, published in Garzón Pareja, "Revueltas urbanas de Granada en el siglo XVII." See also *Memorial histórico español*, 161–63, 184–88; Domínguez Ortiz, *Alteraciones andaluzas*, 55–68.

125. For some observations on civic identity beyond elite groups, see Barry, "Bristol Pride," 39.

126. Cf. Sánchez Ferro, "La ciudad en procesión."

127. See Ditchfield, *Liturgy*, and Sallmann, *Naples et ses saints*, 79. On the saints of Madrid, see Bilinkoff, "A Saint for a City"; Río Barredo, *Madrid*, 93–118. On Ávila: Cátedra, "L'invention d'un saint" and *Un santo para una ciudad*. On Cuenca: Nalle, "A Saint for All Seasons."

128. My account follows Stratton, *The Immaculate Conception*, and Cortés Peña, "Andalucía y la Inmaculada Concepción en el siglo XVII."

129. Stratton, *The Immaculate Conception*, 36–37.

130. Renowned for his eloquent oratory, Pizaño de Palacios started life as an abandoned infant taken in by the Church. See Pacheco, *Libro de descripción de verdaderos retratos*, 233–38.

131. An eyewitness description by Fray Pedro de San Cecilio is recopied in Ortiz de Zuñiga, *Anales eclesiásticas y seculares*, 236–38.

132. *Memorial sumario de algunas relaciones*, fol. 2v. On the Immaculate Conception in

Seville, see Serrano y Ortega, *Glorias sevillanas;* Ortega, *La tradición concepcionista en Sevilla;* Ros, *La Inmaculada y Sevilla.*

133. See Meseguer Fernández, "La Real Junta de la Inmaculada Concepción (1616–1817/20)"; Frías, "Felipe III y la Inmaculada Concepción."

134. On one festival in Seville, see Domínguez Guzmán, "Una curiosa fiesta universitaria en Sevilla en 1617."

135. See the very general discussions of Gan Giménez, "Religiosidad granadina del siglo XVII"; and Cortes Peña, "La religiosidad popular."

136. Quoted in Recío, "La Inmaculada en la predicación franciscano-española," 123.

137. Ferriol y Caycedo, *Libro de las fiestas.* On this text, see Escalera Pérez, *La imagen de la sociedad barroca andaluza,* 383–86. See also Terrones, *Sermón predicado;* Soriano, *Sermón predicado.*

138. Pou y Martí, "Embajadas de Felipe III a Roma pidiendo la definición de la Inmaculada Concepción," 409. For a sermon given as part of the 1617 festivities, see Miguel Avellán, *Declamación.*

139. Henríquez de Jorquera, *Anales,* 2:622, 624. According to López Muñoz, "Contrarreforma y cofradías en Granada," 1363, oaths in defense of the Immaculate Conception became a common practice of Granada's confraternities, including the non-Marian ones.

140. Castro remained popular with Granadinos because of the grain and money he regularly sent for the relief of the famine-stricken poor of the city. See *Recibimiento i fiesta.*

141. Cf. Johnson, "Holy Fabrications."

142. Despite the prohibitions against publicizing the content of the *plomos,* at least two theologians—Gonzalo Sánchez Lucero and Álvaro Pizaño de Palacios—used this passage and others as evidence in favor of the doctrine of the Immaculate Conception. Both scholars were closely associated with Pedro de Castro. In 1596 Archbishop Castro nominated Sánchez Lucero, a Sevillano, to one of the canonries of the Collegiate Church of San Salvador, in the Albaicín. Sánchez Lucero won appointment to the cathedral chapter as *canónigo magistral* in 1597. AGS, Patronato Eclesiástico, leg. 47; Gan Giménez, "Los prebendados," 206; Pacheco, *Libro de descripción de verdaderos retratos,* 227–231; Antonio, *Biblioteca hispana nova,* 1:560; Sánchez Lucero, *Dos discursos theológicos.* Álvaro Pizaño de Palacios—the same individual who caused a commotion with his sermon in Córdoba in 1614—was a client and friend of Archbishop Castro, to whom he dedicated his *Segundo discurso.* On the intersections between the Sacromonte and the scholarly debate on the Immaculate Conception, see Martínez Medina, "El Sacromonte de Granada y los discursos Inmaculistas postridentinos."

143. Letter dated February 21, 1617, BN, MS 4011, fol. 85r. See also the letter from Pedro de Castro to Philip III, dated July 28, 1615, BN, MS 4011, fols. 59–60.

144. On Bernardo Heylan, see Moreno Garrido, "El grabado en Granada durante el siglo XVII," 58–59.

145. According to López Muñoz, "Contrarreforma y cofradías en Granada," 1521–22, the confraternity of the Immaculate Conception in the Franciscan monastery was one of the most powerful and wealthy religious brotherhoods in the city.

146. Stratton, *The Immaculate Conception,* 40–42.

147. On both of these engravings, see Moreno Garrido, *La iconografía de la Inmaculada*. On Ana Heylan, see Moreno Garrido, "El grabado en Granada durante el siglo XVII," 59.

148. Velázquez Echevarría, *Paseos por Granada*, 2:142.

149. Henríquez de Jorquera, *Anales*, 2:846–47.

150. For publications, see BN, MS 6948, fols. 325–39: Francisco Guillén de Águila, *Jueves Santo en la noche deste año de 1640 puso un sedisioso en las casas del Cabildo . . . libello infame*; Parrilla de Torres, *María desagraviada*. For descriptions of the festivities, see Henríquez de Jorquera, *Anales*, 2:846–75; and Paracuellos Cabeza de Vaca, *Triunfales celebraciones*. On the latter text, see Escalera Pérez, *La imagen de la sociedad barroca andaluza*, 389–97. See also *Relación de la grandiosa fiesta*; Rodríguez Escabias, *Exortación al herege*. Rodríguez Escabias authored *Discurso apologético por la verdad* and several devotional works.

151. See Jiménez de Santiago, *Desagravios a la virginidad en el parto de María Santíssima*; Colindres, *Triumpho de Christo*. During the same year, Málaga also hosted festivities in honor of the Immaculate Conception, which may be related to the events in Granada. See Fernández Basurte, "El concejo y las fiestas de la Inmaculada en Málaga. 1640."

152. AASG, leg. 5, fol. 964.

153. Gallego y Burín, *Granada*, 317.

154. AHN, Inquisición, Consejo de la Suprema Inquisición, Libros del Consejo, Libros registros de cartas a tribunales, Libro 614, fol. 254r, notes receipt on December 3, 1630, of a letter from the tribunal of Granada about the inscriptions.

155. AHN, Consejos, leg. 17088[2]: *junta* meetings on April 16, May 23, and July 12, 1631. See also AHN, Inquisición, Consejo de la Suprema Inquisición, Libros del Consejo, Libros registros de cartas a tribunales, Libro 614, fol. 267v.

156. This engraving is known only from a reproduction in Orozco Díaz, *El poema "Granada" de Collado del Hierro*. See Moreno Garrido, "El grabado en Granada durante el siglo XVII," 136.

157. The figures of St. Cecilio and St. Tesifón contain reliquaries, but it is unclear whether relics of the saints were ever installed in the monument.

158. Gallego y Burín, *Granada*, 317, 327, n. 49; Kendrick, *St. James in Spain*, 106–9.

159. The full texts of the inscriptions are included in [Serna Cantoral], *Relación breve de las reliquias que se hallaron en la ciudad de Granada*, 1:143–45. Only the city council's inscription remains today. The Holy Office ordered the removal of the other three in 1777.

160. Henríquez de Jorquera, *Anales*, 2:849.

161. Ibid., 2:879. See also Marín de Rodezno, *Decisio Granatensis*; Pulido Serrano, "La fe desatada en devoción."

162. Some rival elite groups preferred to show their loyalty to the Virgin Immaculate at other sites around the city; the judges of the Royal Chancery, for example, gave thanks for the arrest of the hermit at the Discalced Trinitarian Monastery of Our Lady of Grace. Henríquez de Jorquera, *Anales*, 2:862.

163. López Muñoz, "Contrarreforma y cofradías en Granada," 1365, includes one founded in 1646; see also E. Martínez Ruiz, "Fundación y constituciones de la Hermandad del Santo Rosario de Nuestra Señora del Triunfo de Granada en 1698." An illustration of the Virgin of Triumph appears in *Reglas y estatutos*. This image, an engraving by Miguel de Gamarra, an artist of modest talents who specialized in depictions of devotional images

popular in Granada, dates from the second half of the seventeenth century. See Moreno Garrido, "El grabado en Granada durante el siglo XVII," 66, 145–46, 216. On the Maestranza, see Arias de Saavedra, *La Real Maestranza de Caballería de Granada en el siglo XVIII*.

164. Kamen, *The Phoenix and the Flame*, 171.

165. Nalle, "Catholicism in Comparative Perspective." I am very grateful to Professor Nalle for her kindness in providing me with a copy of this paper.

166. Marocchi, "L'immagine della Chiesa in Carlo Borromeo."

167. Forster, "With and Without Confessionalization."

168. On confessionalism, confessionalization, and communal identity in another Catholic context, see Di Simplicio, "Confessionalizzazione e identità collettiva."

169. See Fros, "Culte des saints et sentiment national"; Schreiner, "*Maria Patrona. La Sainte Vierge.*"

EPILOGUE

Epigraph: Sciascia, *The Council of Egypt*, 144. This novel revolves around a forgery perpetrated in late eighteenth-century Sicily. Like the *plomos*, Giuseppe Vella's fabricated Arabic codex provided documentation for an obscure and contested era of the island's history. I am grateful to James Amelang for bringing this interesting book to my attention.

1. For details on developments in Rome, see Alonso, *Los apócrifos*, 311–402. Materials relating to the Vatican translations are collected in ACDF, S.O., St. St., I 3 i, R 6 a–c, R 7 a–i.

2. Hagerty, "Los libros plúmbeos," 27.

3. AGS, Estado, legs. 3068 and 3069; AHN, Consejos, leg. 17088[2].

4. Alonso, *Los apócrifos*, 397. Copies of the brief can be found in AHN, Consejos, leg. 17088[2], and AGS, Estado, leg. 3066.

5. The letters are collected in AHN, Consejos, leg. 17088[2]. See also *Señor. El Abad.* The Sacromonte also issued a print defense of the relics, whose credibility was endangered by the negative judgment placed on the lead books and the parchment. See *Relación de la grande autoridad y certeza de las reliquias del Sacro Monte.*

6. Papers related to the Crown's efforts on behalf of the *plomos* through 1683 are included in AGS, legs. 3068 and 3069.

7. Barrios Aguilera, "Granada en escorzo." See also Barrios Aguilera's preface to Heredia Barnuevo, *Místico ramillete*, xlvii–lxxi.

8. [Serna Cantoral], *Relación breve de las reliquias que se hallaron en la ciudad de Granada.* The title page of this text reprints the engraved title page of the 1617 publication of the same name (fig. 5.7). It is usually referred to as *Vindicias Cathólicas Granatenses*, however, because this title appears in the second volume and at the top of all the pages. On the author, see Fayard, *Los miembros del Consejo de Castilla*, 62, 79, 211.

9. RAH, 9/2301, n. 174.

10. RAH 9/2265–67: Vicente Pastor de los Cobos, *Guerras católicas granatenses* (manuscript in 3 vols., 1735); also at AASG, along with several other works on the *plomos*. Heredia Barnuevo, *Místico ramillete.*

11. AASG, C50: *Disertación eclesiástica crítico-histórica en que el cathólico reyno de*

Granada vindica la religiosa piedad de su constante culto, a las sagradas antiquíssimas lypsanas, que se hallaron al fin del siglo XVI en la Torre Turpiana, y en el Sacro Monte; advirtiendo el modo único decoroso de leer la bulla de la Santidad de Inocencio XI (Pamplona, 1752). This book was published under the pseudonym "Cecilio Santos Urbina y Desfusa." AASG, C51: Viana and Laboraria, *Historia authéntica*. Viana and Laboraria wrote this history at the orders of Fernando VI. For papers related to their commission, see AHN, Consejos, leg. 170881.

12. See Sotomayor y Muro, *Cultura y picaresca*; Álvarez Barrientos, "Historia y religiosidad popular en las falsificaciones granadinas del siglo XVIII"; Álvarez Barrientos and Mora Rodríguez, "El final de una tradición" and "Las falsificaciones granadinas del siglo XVIII."

13. The account of ecclesiastical historian Enrique Florez (1701–73) of his visit to the Abbey of the Sacromonte in 1770 offers eloquent testimony to the continued affection of Granadinos for the *plomos* and relics. See Méndez, *Noticias sobre la vida, escritos y viajes,* 300–301.

14. Lecorp, *La espada del Señor,* 32. See also Dalda y Pérez, *El Monte Santo eucharístico;* Cuesta García de Leonardo, *Fiesta y arquitectura efímera.*

15. Córdoba, "Las leyendas en la historiografía del Siglo de Oro," 238. See also Eco, "The Force of Falsity."

16. González Alcantud, "El mito fallido sacromontano y su perdurabilidad local a la luz del mozarabismo maurófobo de F. J. Simonet."

17. Constable, "Forgery and Plagiarism in the Middle Ages," 11.

18. Grafton, *Forgers and Critics,* 23.

19. Rowland, *The Scarith of Scornello.*

20. The literature on Chatterton and Macpherson is extensive. See, among others, Haywood, *The Making of History.*

21. Grafton, *Forgers and Critics.*

22. García-Arenal, "El entorno de los plomos."

23. Gómez de Liaño, *Los juegos del Sacromonte,* 201, suggests that the clergy of Granada were "in some way the *co-author,* or even the principle *author*" (emphasis in the original). Cf. Barrios Aguilera, *Los falsos cronicones contra la historia,* 115–17.

24. Castellá Ferrer, *Historia del apóstol de Iesus Christo Sanctiago Zebedeo,* esp. fols. 174ff.

25. Cardaillac, *Moriscos y cristianos,* 42–43. On the controversy over St. James and the Roman Breviary, see Kendrick, *St. James in Spain;* Rey Castelao, *La historiografía del Voto de Santiago;* González Novalín, "Baronio y la cuestión jacobea."

26. The *Compendio* is reprinted in Mayáns y Siscár, *Orígenes de la lengua española,* vol. 2. On López Tamarid's work as an interpreter for the Inquisition, see Ron de la Bastida, "Manuscritos árabes en la Inquisición granadina (1582)"; Cruz Sotomayor, "Una mirada a Francisco López Tamarid."

27. AASG, leg. 5, fols. 34–37 (June 25, 1588); BN, MS 1583. See also the letter to Vázquez de Leca from Fajardo, who seeks a new, more lucrative benefice. AASG, leg. 5, fols. 28–33 (June 27, 1588).

28. AGS, Cámara de Castilla, leg. 2188. This source is discussed in Domínguez Ortiz and Vincent, *Historia de los moriscos,* 150–51, and in Vincent, "50.000 moriscos almerienses." López Tamarid served as vicar of the Alpujarreño town of Vera, and held benefices

in Sorbas and Antas. See López Martín, *La Iglesia en Almería y sus obispos*, 260; Tapia Garrido, *Historia general de Almería y su provincia*, 234. On his activities during the Revolt of the Alpujarras, see Gil Albarracín, "Francisco López Tamarid, clérigo, guerrero y humanista, y la Almería de su tiempo."

29. Castillo Fernández, "El sacerdote morisco Francisco de Torrijos."

30. However, notarial records from Almería and Vera show that during the Revolt of the Alpujarras, López Tamarid did not hesitate to benefit from the misfortune of captured and defeated Moriscos. Between 1569 and 1571 he bought at least three Morisco slaves, including one from Antas, where he held a benefice. See Cabrillana, *Almería morisca*, and *Documentos notariales referentes a los moriscos (1569–1571)*.

31. AASG, leg. 5, fols. 34–37.

32. Grafton, *Forgers and Critics*. Some scholars were themselves deceived by enterprising artists who created "classical" coins and cameos for the expanding collectors' market. See Jones with Craddock and Barker, *Fake? The Art of Deception*, 136–39.

33. López Serrano received his appointment in the cathedral in May 1595. Previously, he had been serving in a parish in the Albaicín. From the moment of their appearance, he took considerable interest in the *plomos*. His letters reveal him to have been investigating related esoteric topics, like the mystical meanings of King Solomon's ring—a problem possibly inspired by one of the Sacromonte texts, *History of the Seal of Solomon*, and the starred insignia that marked all of the lead books. RAH 9/3662, n. 142, includes a short, anonymous treatise against the relics from the Torre Turpiana together with three letters from López Serrano to Francisco de Medina, secretary to Archbishop Rodrigo de Castro of Seville (no relation to Archbishop Pedro de Castro), dating between May 7, 1595, and September 2, 1597. The archive of the Collegiate Church of the Sacromonte holds numerous works by López Serrano, including notes on the visit of St. James to Spain, the foundation of Granada, the succession of the city's bishops, and a signed treatise on one of the lead books, the *Liber Fundamentum Ecclesiae*. AASG, C48, fol. 378 (dated March 3, 1602); leg. 4, pt. 2; leg. 2, fol. 219.

34. BBMS, Varios escritos de Martín Vázquez de Siruela, MS, fols. 4v–9r; RBP, II/158, fols. 29r–30v.

35. Scholarly opinion is divided on whether the bridge, located in the town of Pinos Puente, was constructed in the ninth century or later. Some have suggested that it is Visigothic in origin. Peinado Santaella, *De Ilurco a Pinos Puente*, 109. For the false inscription, see Ernst Hübner, *Corpus inscriptionum latinarum*, 2:21.

36. For a discussion of the paleographic aspects of the parchment, see van Koningsveld and Wiegers, "The Parchment of the 'Torre Turpiana.'"

37. Alvar Ezquerra, "El descubrimiento de la presencia fenicia en Andalucía," 156. On early modern studies of ancient Andalusia, see Wulff Alonso, "Andalucía antigua en la historiografía española (XVI–XIX)"; Álvarez Martí-Aguilar, *La antigüedad en la historiografía española del s. XVIII*, 75–102.

38. Caro, *Poesía castellana y latina*, 235. I am grateful to Professor Joaquin Pascual Barea for providing me with this reference.

39. Hagerty, *Los libros plúmbeos*, 34. A cache of ancient inscriptions discovered in Cazlona in 1618, for example, was the subject of a learned treatise by the Marquis of Estepa.

See Aguilar y Cano, *El Marqués del Aula*, 26–28; Delgado, *Nuevo método de clasificación de las medallas autónomas de España*, 149–59.

40. Bizzocchi, "La culture généalogique dans l'Italie du seizième siècle." See also Lowenthal, "Fabricating Heritage."

41. Stewart, *Crimes of Writing*, 55.

42. Fernández-Nieto et al., *El Sacromonte*.

43. "Rutas por Granada," Guía de Granada, http://www.moebius.es/ii/granada/rutas1 .htm#pie, accessed September 15, 1999.

44. On Fray Leopoldo's cult in contemporary Granada, see Slater, *City Steeple, City Streets*.

45. "Aquellas romerías de San Cecilio."

46. The establishment of the new mosque, which was dedicated on July 10, 2003, has not been without controversy. In the months following its dedication, anti-Muslim graffiti invoking Granada's long history of Christianity appeared on walls around the Albaicín. See R. Mendoza, "Vecinos del Albaicín rechazan una pintada aparecida ayer contra la nueva mezquita"; V. F., "Vecinos del Albaicín critican la proliferación de pintadas xenófobas."

47. Riding, "Pride in Spain's Islamic Roots Is Blooming Again"; C. Smith, "Where the Moors Held Sway, Allah Is Praised Again."

Bibliography

MANUSCRIPT SOURCES

Archivio della Congregazione per la Dottrina della Fede, Vatican City
    Sanctum Officium
    Stanza Storica, I 3 i, R 6 a–c, R 7 a–i
Archivo de la Abadía del Sacromonte de Granada
    legs. 1, pt. 2; 2; 3, pt. 1; 4, pts. 1–2; 5; 7, pts. 1–2
    Libros de Actas: vol. 1
    Manuscritos: C18, C22, C24, C28, C40, C48, C49, C50, C51, C52
Archivo de la Catedral de Granada
    legs. 1, 12, 25, 29, 225, 327
    Libros de Actas: vols. 8–14
    Libros de Varios Asuntos: vol. 2
Archivo General de Indias, Seville
    Indiferente, 430, L. 40
Archivo General de Simancas
    Cámara de Castilla: leg. 2188
    Estado
        Negociación de Roma: legs. 1855, 3066, 3068, 3069
    Patronato Eclesiástico: legs. 44, 47, 55, 63, 102, 112
        Memoriales y expedientes: legs. 104, 231
        Visitas: leg. 282
    Patronato Real: leg. 39, no. 86
Archivo Historico Nacional, Madrid
    Consejos: leg. 17088[2]
    Inquisición
        Libros del Consejo, Libros registros de cartas a tribunales, Libro 614
Archivo Municipal de Granada
    Actas Capitulares: vols. 7–8
    Festejos: legs. 896, 1930
    legs. 1863, 2403
    Personal: leg. 930
    Propios: leg. 1915

Archivo Parroquial de San Cecilio, Granada
  Joseph Francisco de Torres, *Abecedario general de los ocho primeros libros bautismos de esta yglesia parroquial de señor san Cecilio mártir, y primero obispo de esta ciudad de Granada* (manuscript, 1769)
Archivo Parroquial de San Pedro y San Pablo, Granada
  Libros de bautismos, 1–6.
Archivo y Biblioteca de Francisco de Zabálburu, Madrid
  Carpeta 161, piezas 104, 129
Biblioteca de Bartolomé March Servera, Madrid
  Varios escritos de Martín Vázquez de Siruela
Biblioteca de la Universidad de Granada
  Caja B48–50
Biblioteca Nacional de España, Madrid
  Manuscritos: 1499, 1583, 1603, 2316, 3893, 4011, 5732, 5953, 6265, 6437, 6637, 6948, 7187, 8318, 9227, 12964, 13059
British Library, London
  Egerton 586 (14)
Real Academia de la Historia, Madrid
  Colección Biblioteca de Cortes: 9/2301, 9/2265–67
  Colección Jesuitas (Tomos): 9/3662 (vol. 89)
  Colección Luis de Salazar y Castro: 9/138
  Manuscritos: 9/5843, 9/5947
Real Biblioteca de El Escorial, San Lorenzo de El Escorial
  d.iv.21
Real Biblioteca del Palacio, Madrid
  II/158

PRINTED SOURCES

Actas de las Cortes de Castilla, publicadas por acuerdo del Congreso de los diputados a propuesta de su Comisión de gobierno interior. Madrid: Imprenta Nacional, 1862–1919.
Aguilar de Terrones, Francisco. *Dictamen de Don Fernando Suárez de Figueroa . . . sobre unos libros sagrados hallados en el Monte de Valparaíso . . . y de Don Francisco Aguilar de Terrones acerca de unos huesos y cenizas . . . en dicho monte.* Granada, 1597.
Aguilar y Cano, Antonio. *El Marqués del Aula.* Seville: Imp. de E. Rasco, 1897.
Aigle, Denise, and Catherine Mayeur-Jaouen. "Miracle et *karāma*. Une approche comparatiste." In *Miracle et Karāma*, edited by Denise Aigle, 13–35. Turnhout: Brepols, 2000.
Aldea Vaquero, Quintín, Tomás Marín Martínez, and José Vives Gatell, eds. *Diccionario de historia eclesiástica.* 4 vols. Madrid: CSIC, 1972–75.
Aldrete, Bernardo José de. *Del origen y principio de la lengua castellana o romance que oi se usa en España.* Rome, 1606.
———. *Fainomena sive coruscantia lumina, triumphalisque crucis, signa sanctorum martyrum Albensium Urgauonensium Bonosi et Maximiani et alíorum . . .* Córdoba, 1631.

————. *Varias antigüedades de España, África, y otras provincias.* Antwerp, 1614.

Alenda y Mira, Jenaro. *Relaciones de solemnidades y fiestas públicas de España.* Madrid: Sucesores de Rivadeneyra, 1903.

Alfonso X. *Primera crónica general de España que mandó componer Alfonso el Sabio y se continuaba bajo Sancho IV en 1289.* Edited by Ramón Menéndez Pidal. Madrid: Editorial Gredos, 1955.

Alonso, Carlos. *Los apócrifos del Sacromonte (Granada).* Valladolid: Editorial Estudio Agustiniano, 1979.

Al-Razi, Ahmad b. Muhammad. *Crónica del moro Rasis: versión del Ajbar muluk al-Andalus de Ahmad ibn Muhammad ibn Musà al-Razi, romanzada para el Rey don Dionís de Portugal hacia 1300 por Mahamad, Alarife y Gil Pérez.* Edited by Diego Catalan and María Soledad de Andrés. Madrid: Editorial Gredos, 1975.

Alvar Ezquerra, Jaime. "El descubrimiento de la presencia fenicia en Andalucía." In *La antigüedad como argumento. Historiografía de arqueología e historia antigua en Andalucía,* edited by José Beltrán Fortes and Fernando Gascó, 153–69. Seville: Junta de Andalucía, 1993.

Álvarez, Tomás Antonio. *Excelencias de Granada.* Edited by Cristina Viñes Millet. Granada: Universidad de Granada, 1999.

Álvarez Barrientos, Joaquín. "Historia y religiosidad popular en las falsificaciones granadinas del siglo XVIII." In *La religiosidad popular,* vol. 1, *Antropología e historia,* edited by Carlos Álvarez Santaló, María Jesús Buxó i Rey, and Salvador Rodríguez Becerra, 348–56. Barcelona: Editorial Anthropos; Seville: Fundación Machado, 1989.

Álvarez Barrientos, Joaquín, and Gloria Mora Rodríguez. "Las falsificaciones granadinas del siglo XVIII. Nacionalismo y arqueología." *Al-Qanṭara* 24, no. 2 (2003): 533–46.

————. "El final de una tradición. Las falsificaciones granadinas del siglo XVIII." *Revista de dialectología y tradiciones populares* 40 (1985): 163–89.

Álvarez Martí-Aguilar, Manuel. *La antigüedad en la historiografía española del s. XVIII: el Marqués de Valdeflores.* Málaga: Universidad de Málaga, 1996.

Álvarez Rodríguez, J. Rosaura. "La Casa de Doctrina del Albaicín. Labor apostólica de la Compañía de Jesús con los moriscos." *Cuadernos de la Alhambra* 19–20 (1983–84): 233–47.

Amelang, James. "Círculos de sociabilidad e identidades urbanas: un caso barcelonés." *Torre de los Lujanes: Boletín de la Real Sociedad Económica Matritense de Amigos del País* 2002: 15–24.

————. "Imágenes de la cultura urbana en la España moderna." In *Imágenes de la diversidad. El mundo urbano en la Corona de Castilla (s. XVI–XVIII),* edited by José Ignacio Fortea Pérez, 87–101. Santander: Universidad de Cantabria, 1997.

Anawati, G. C. "ʿĪsā." *Encyclopaedia of Islam.* CD-ROM ed. Leiden: Brill, 1999.

Anderson, Benedict. *Imagined Communities: Reflections on the Origin and Spread of Nationalism.* Rev. ed. London: Verso, 1991.

Andrés, Gregorio de. "Historia y descripción del Camarín de reliquias de El Escorial." *Anales del Instituto de Estudios Madrileños* 7 (1971): 53–60.

Andújar Castillo, Francisco, and Julián Pablo Díaz López, "Las actividades económicas." In *Historia del reino de Granada,* vol. 2, *La época morisca y la repoblación,* edited by Manuel Barrios Aguilera, 59–100. Granada: Universidad de Granada, Legado Andalusí, 2000.

Angulo Iñiguez, Diego. "La ciudad de Granada vista por un pintor flamenco de hacia 1500." *Al-Andalus* 5 (1940): 468–72.

Antequera y Arteaga, Pedro de. *Excelencias de Granada, expressadas en un epigramma.* Granada, 1610.

Antolín, G. "El códice emilianense de la biblioteca de El Escorial." *Ciudad de Dios* 72 (1907): 184–95, 366–78, 542–51, 628–41; 73 (1907): 108–20, 279–91, 455–67; 74 (1907): 135–48, 215–27, 382–93, 565–77, 644–49.

Antolínez de Burgos, Justino. *Historia eclesiástica de Granada.* Edited by Manuel Sotomayor [y Muru]. Granada: Universidad de Granada, 1996.

Antonio, Nicolás. *Biblioteca hispana nova; sive, Hispanorum scriptorum qui ab anno MD. ad MDCLXXXIV. floruere notitia.* 2 vols. Madrid, 1783–88.

"Aquellas romerías de San Cecilio." *El Ideal,* February 6, 2000.

Aquinas, St. Thomas. *On Kingship, to the King of Cyprus.* Translated by Gerald B. Phelan. Edited by I. Th. Eschmann. Toronto: Pontifical Institute of Mediaeval Studies, 1982.

Arias de Saavedra, Inmaculada. *La Real Maestranza de Caballería de Granada en el siglo XVIII.* Granada: Universidad de Granada, 1988.

Artacho y Pérez-Blázquez, Fernando de. *Manuscrito Sevillano.* Seville: Guadalquivir, 1997.

Avellán, Miguel. *Declamación que hizo . . . en las fiestas de la Inmaculada Concepción de nuestra Señora, que se celebraron en san Francisco de Granada . . .* Granada, 1617.

Aviéndose descubierto cerca de la ciudad de Granada, el año de 1595. en el monte que llamavan de Valparaiso . . . las Cavernas, y Hornos en que vivieron, y padecieron martirio los santos, Cecilio . . . , Hiscio . . . , Tesifón . . . y otros ocho santos . . . D. Pedro de Castro y Quiñones, arçobispo que era entonces de Granada, y después de Sevilla, a sus expensas prosiguió el descubrimiento . . . Granada, 1655.

Backer, Augustin, and Alois Backer. *Bibliothèque des écrivains de la Compagnie de Jésus, première série.* 7 vols. Liege, 1853–61.

Bacon, Francis. *The Advancement of Learning and New Atlantis.* Edited by Arthur Johnston. Oxford: Clarendon Press, 1974.

Ballesteros Robles, Luis. *Diccionario biográfico matritense.* Madrid: Imprenta Municipal, 1912.

Barahona y Miranda, Francisco de. *Memorial del Dr. Dn. Francisco Barahona y Miranda, canónigo del Sacro monte y rector de la imperial Universidad de Granada en nombre de su insigne iglesia colegial, acerca de la pretensión del prior del convento real de Madrid de la orden de San Gerónimo.* N.p., n.d.

Barcia y Zambrana, Joseph de. *Despertador christiano de sermones doctrinales sobre particulares assumptos . . . tomo tercero.* Madrid, 1719.

———. *Despertador christiano santoral, de varios sermones de santos, de aniversarios de ánimas, y honras, en orden a excitar en los fieles la devoción de los santos, y la imitación de sus virtudes.* Madrid, 1725.

Barrios Aguilera, Manuel. "El Albaicín de Granada sin moriscos. Memoriales para su restauración." *Chronica Nova* 23 (1996): 439–63.

———. *Los falsos cronicones contra la historia (o Granada, corona martirial).* Granada: Universidad de Granada, 2004.

———. "El fin de la Granada islámica: una propuesta." *XX Siglos* 3 (1992): 70–84.

———. "Granada en escorzo. Luis Francisco de Viana y la historiografía del Sacromonte." *Demófilo. Revista de cultura tradicional de Andalucía* 35 (2000): 45–80.

———. *Moriscos y repoblación en las postrimerías de la Granada islámica.* Granada: Diputación Provincial de Granada, 1993.

Barrios Aguilera, Manuel, and Margarita M. Birriel Salcedo. *La repoblación del reino de Granada después de la expulsión de los moriscos. Fuentes y bibliografía para su estudio. Estado de la cuestión.* Granada: Universidad de Granada, 1986.

Barrios Aguilera, Manuel, and Valeriano Sánchez Ramos. "La herencia martirial. La formación de la sociedad repobladora en el reino de Granada tras la guerra de las Alpujarras." *Hispania* 198 (1998): 129–56.

———. *Martirios y mentalidad martirial en las Alpujarras. De la rebelión morisca a las Actas de Ugíjar.* Granada: Universidad de Granada, 2001.

Barry, Jonathan. "Bristol Pride: Civic Identity in Bristol c. 1640–1775." In *The Making of Modern Bristol,* edited by Madge Dresser and Philip Ollerenshaw, 25–47. Tiverton: Redcliffe Press, 1996.

Beltrán Fortes, José. "Entre la erudición y el coleccionismo: anticuarios andaluces de los siglos XVI al XVIII." In *La antigüedad como argumento. Historiografía de arqueología e historia antigua en Andalucía,* edited by José Beltrán Fortes and Fernando Gascó, 105–24. Seville: Junta de Andalucía, 1993.

Ben-Ami, Issachar. *Culte des saints et pèlerinages judéo-musulmans au Maroc.* Paris: Maisonneuve & Larose, 1990.

Benítez Sánchez-Blanco, Rafael. "De Pablo a Saulo: traducción crítica y denuncia de los libros plúmbeos por el P. Ignacio de las Casas, S.J." *Al-Qanṭara* 23, no. 2 (2002): 403–36.

Bennassar, Bartolomé. *Valladolid en el Siglo de Oro. Una ciudad de Castilla y su entorno agrario en el siglo XVI.* 2d ed. Valladolid: Ayuntamiento de Valladolid, 1989.

Bermúdez de Pedraza, Francisco. *Antigüedad y excelencias de Granada.* Madrid, 1608. Reprint. Granada: Delegación de Granada del Colegio Oficial de Arquitectos de Andalucía Oriental, 1981.

———. *Arte legal para estudiar la iurisprudencia. Con la paratitla, y exposición a los títulos de los quatro libros de Instituciones de Justiniano.* Salamanca, 1612; Madrid, 1633; Lisbon, 1737.

———. *Historia eclesiástica, principios, y progressos de la ciudad, y religión católica de Granada.* Granada, 1638. Reprint. Granada: Editorial don Quijote, 1989.

———. *Historia eucharística y reformación de los abusos hechos en presencia de Xpo, nro. señor.* Granada, 1643; Cádiz, 1694.

———. *El Hospital Real de la Corte, de enfermos heridos en el ánimo de vicios de Corte: su origen, malicia, preservación y medicina curativa de ellos.* Granada, 1644; Madrid, 1645.

———. *Panegyrico legal, preeminencias de los secretarios del rey, deducidas de ambos derechos, y precedencia de Luys Ortiz de Matienzo, Antonio Carnero, y don Yñigo de Aguirre, sus secretarios.* Granada, 1635.

———. *Por los secretarios de V. Magestad, el Licenciado Vermúdez de Pedraza, Abogado de sus Consejos.* N.p., n.d.

———. *El secretario del rey* . Madrid, 1609; Madrid, 1620; Granada, 1637; Naples, 1696.

Bernabé Pons, Luis F. "La conspiración granadina de los libros plúmbeos." In *La política y los moriscos en la época de los Austria: actas del encuentro: Sevilla la Nueva, Palacio de Baena, 3, 4 y 5 diciembre 1998,* edited by Rodolfo Gil Grimau, 77–90. Madrid: Ediciones Especiales, Fundación del Sur, 1999.

———. *El Evangelio de San Bernabé: un evangelio islámico español.* Alicante: Universidad de Alicante, 1995.

———. *El texto morisco del Evangelio de San Bernabé.* Granada: Universidad de Granada, Instituto de Cultura Juan Gil-Albert, 1998.

Bertaut, François. "Diario del viaje de España." In *Viajes de extranjeros por España y Portugal,* vol. 2, edited by J. García Mercadal, 549–687. Madrid: Aguilar, 1952.

Bilinkoff, Jodi. *The Ávila of Saint Teresa: Religious Reform in a Sixteenth-Century City.* Ithaca: Cornell University Press, 1989.

———. "A Saint for a City: Mariana de Jesús and Madrid, 1565–1624." *Archiv für Reformationsgeschichte* 88 (1997): 322–37.

Bizzocchi, Roberto. "La culture généalogique dans l'Italie du seizième siècle." *Annales ESC* 4 (1991): 789–805.

———. *Genealogie incredibili. Scritti di storia nell'Europa moderna.* Bologna: Il Mulino, 1995.

Blai Arbuixec, Gaspar. *Sermó de la s. conquista de la molt insigne, noble, leal, e coronada ciutat de Valencia.* Valencia, 1666. Reprint. Valencia: Librerías "París-Valencia," 1985.

Bloch, Marc. "A Contribution towards a Comparative History of European Societies." In *Land and Work in Medieval Europe: Selected Papers,* 44–81. Translated by J. E. Anderson. Berkeley: University of California Press, 1967.

Bodin, Jean. *Method for the Easy Comprehension of History.* Translated by Beatrice Reynolds. New York: Octagon Books, 1966.

Boesch Gajano, Sofia. "La raccolta di vite di santi di Luigi Lippomano. Storia, struttura, finalità di una costruzione agiografica." In *Raccolte di vite di santi dal XIII al XVIII secolo. Strutture, messaggi, fruizioni,* edited by Sofia Boesch Gajano, 110–30. Fasano di Brindisi: Schena, 1990.

Boll, Franz. *Sternglaube und Sterndeutung; die Geschichte und das Wesen der Astrologie.* Leipzig and Berlin: B. G. Teubner, 1926.

Bonet Correa, Antonio. "Entre la superchería y la fe: el Sacromonte de Granada." *Historia 16* 16 (1981): 43–54.

———. *Fiesta, poder y arquitectura. Aproximaciones al Barroco español.* Madrid: Ediciones Akal, 1990.

Borja de Medina, Francisco de. "La Compañía de Jesús y la minoría morisca (1545–1614)." *Archivum Historicum Societatis Iesu* 57 (1988): 3–136.

Bosio, Antonio. *Roma sotteranea.* Edited by Giovanni Severano. Rome, 1632. Reprint. Edited by Vincenzo Fiocchi Nicolai. Rome: Edizioni Quasar, 1998.

Bosque Maurel, Joaquín. *Geografía urbana de Granada.* Zaragoza: Consejo Superior de Investigaciones, 1962. Reprint. Granada: Universidad de Granada, 1988.

Botero, Giovanni. *Razón destado, con tres libros de la grandeza de las ciudades.* Translated by Antonio de Herrera. Burgos, 1603.

Bouza, Fernando. *Corre manuscrito. Una historia cultural del Siglo de Oro.* Madrid: Marcial Pons, 2001.

Bouza Álvarez, José Luis. *Religiosidad contrarreformista y cultura simbólica del Barroco.* Madrid: Consejo Superior de Investigaciones Científicas, 1990.

Braun, Georg. *Civitates orbis terrarum, 1572–1618.* [By] Braun & Hogenberg. Edited by R. A. Skelton. Amsterdam: Theatrum Orbis Terrarum, 1965.

Breuiarium de camera secundum consuetudinem sancte romane ecclesie Cum historijs nouarum festiuitatum ecclesie granatensis. Granada, 1506.

Brisset, Demetrio E. "Otros procesos conmemorativos centenarios: la toma de Granada." *Revista de dialectología y tradiciones populares* 50 (1995): 131–54.

———. "Rituales de conquista: un estudio comparativo." *Demófilo: Revista de cultura tradicional de Andalucía* 18 (1996): 111–24.

Britt, Matthew, ed. *The Hymns of the Breviary and Missal.* New York: Benziger Brothers, 1922.

Briz Martínez, Juan. *Historia de la fundación, y antigüedades de San Juan de la Peña y de los reyes de Sobrarve, Aragón, y Navarra . . .* Zaragoza, 1620.

Brown, Peter. *The Cult of the Saints: Its Rise and Function in Latin Christianity.* Chicago: University of Chicago Press, 1981.

Burke, Peter. "History as Social Memory." In *Memory: History, Culture and the Mind,* edited by Thomas Butler, 97–113. Oxford: Basil Blackwell, 1989.

Cabanelas Rodríguez, Darío. "Arias Montano y los libros plúmbeos de Granada." *Miscelánea de estudios árabes y hebraicos* 18–19 (1969–70): 7–41.

———. "Cartas del morisco granadino Miguel de Luna." *Miscelánea de estudios árabes y hebraicos* 14–15 (1965–66): 31–47.

———. "Intento de supervivencia en el ocaso de una cultura: los libros plúmbeos de Granada." *Nueva revista de filología hispánica* 30, no. 2 (1981): 334–58.

———. *El morisco granadino Alonso de Castillo.* 2d ed. Granada: Patronato de la Alhambra, 1991.

———. "El Sacromonte punto de confluencia doctrinal entre Islam y la Cristiandad." In *La Abadía del Sacromonte. Exposición artístico-documental. Estudios sobre su significación y orígenes,* 34–40. Granada: Universidad de Granada, 1974.

———. "Un intento de sincretismo islámico-cristiano: los libros plúmbeos de Granada." *Segundo Congreso Internacional de Estudios sobre las Culturas del Mediterráneo occidental,* 131–42. Barcelona: Universidad de Barcelona, 1978.

Cabrera de Córdoba, Luis. *De historia, para entenderla y escribirla.* Madrid, 1611. Reprint. Edited by Santiago Montero Díaz. Madrid: Instituto de Estudios Políticos, 1948.

Cabrillana, Nicolás. *Almería morisca.* 2d ed. Granada: Universidad de Granada, 1989.

———. *Documentos notariales referentes a los moriscos (1569–1571).* Granada: Universidad de Granada, 1978.

Calatrava, Juan. "Encomium urbis: La *Antigüedad y excelencias de Granada* (1608) de Francisco Bermúdez de Pedraza." In *Iglesia y sociedad en el Reino de Granada (ss. XVI–XVIII),* edited by Antonio Luis Córtes Peña, Miguel Luis López-Guadalupe Muñoz, and Antonio Lara Ramos, 467–85. Granada: Universidad de Granada, Diputación de Granada, 2003.

Calero Palacios, María del Carmen. *La enseñanza y educación en Granada bajo los reyes Austrias.* Granada: Diputación Provincial de Granada, 1978.

Calero Palacios, María del Carmen, Inmaculada Arias de Saavedra, and Cristina Viñes Millet. *Historia de la Universidad de Granada*. Granada: Universidad de Granada, 1997.

Cámera Muñoz, Alicia. *Arquitectura y sociedad en el Siglo de Oro. Idea, traza y edificio*.
Madrid: Ediciones El Arquero, 1990.

Camp, C. Kathryn. "A Divided Republic: Moriscos and Old Christians in Sixteenth Century
Granada." Ph.D. diss., University of Michigan, 2001.

Candel Crespo, Francisco. *Un obispo postridentino: Don Sancho Dávila y Toledo (1546–1625)*.
Ávila: Diputación Provincial de Ávila, Instituto "Gran Duque de Alba," 1965.

Cano de Montoro, Fernando. *Conquista de Sevilla por el santo rey Don Fernando Tercero de
León, y de Castilla*. Seville, 1631.

Cardaillac, Louis. *Moriscos y cristianos: un enfrentamiento polémico (1492–1640)*. Translated
by Mercedes García-Arenal. Madrid: Ediciones F.C.E.; Mexico City: Fondo de Cultura
Económica, 1979.

———. "Le prophetisme, signe de l'identité morisque." In *Actes du II Symposium International du C.I.E.M. sur Religion, identité et sources documentaires sur les Morisques Andalous*,
edited by Abdeljelil Temini, 1:138–46. Tunis: Institut Supérieur de Documentation, 1984.

Cardaillac-Hermosilla, Yvette. "Le héros, maître du pouvoir magique: Salomon." In *Mélanges Louis Cardaillac*, vol. 1, edited by Abdeljelil Temini, 145–59. Zaghouan: Fondation Temimi pour la Recherche Scientifique et l'Information, 1995.

———. *La magie en Espagne: morisques et vieux chrétiens au XVIe et XVIIe siècles*. Zaghouan:
Fondation Temimi pour la Recherche Scientifique et l'Information, 1996.

Cardera, Francisco Tomás María de. *Granada reconocida a los favores de Dios, le repite su
agradecimiento, viéndose conquistada segunda vez con las mismas armas, que la primera*.
Granada, 1762.

Caro, Rodrigo. *Poesía castellana y latina e inscripciones originales*. Translated and edited by
Joaquín Pascual Barea. Seville: Diputuación de Sevilla, 2000.

Caro Baroja, Julio. *Las falsificaciones de la historia (en relación con la de España)*. Barcelona:
Seix Barral, 1992.

———. *Los moriscos del Reino de Granada: ensayo de historia social*. 5th ed. Madrid: Ediciones
Istmo, 2000.

———. *Vidas mágicas e Inquisición*. 2 vols. Madrid: Taurus, 1967.

Carrasco Urgoiti, María Soledad. *El moro de Granada en la literatura (del siglo XV al XX)*.
Madrid: Revista de Occidente, 1956.

Carreres Zacarés, Salvador. *Ensayo de una bibliografía de libros de fiestas celebradas en Valencia y su antiguo reino*. Vol. 2. Valencia: Imprenta Hijo de F. Vives Mora, 1925.

Carriazo, Juan de Mata. "Alegrías que hizo Sevilla por la toma de Granada." In *Homenaje
al Profesor Carriazo*, vol. 1, *En la frontera de Granada*, 537–50. Seville: Universidad de
Sevilla, 1971.

———. "La 'Historia de la Casa Real de Granada'. Anónimo castellano de mediados del
siglo XVI." In *Homenaje al Profesor Carriazo*, vol. 1, *En la frontera de Granada*, 143–92.
Sevilla: Universidad de Sevilla, 1971.

Case, Thomas E. "Cide Hamete Benengeli y los *Libros plúmbeos*." *Cervantes: Bulletin of the
Cervantes Society of America* 22:2 (2002): 9–24.

Casey, Edward S. "How to Get from Space to Place in a Fairly Short Stretch of Time: Phenomenological Prolegomena." In *Senses of Place*, edited by Steven Feld and Keith H. Basso, 13–52. Santa Fe, N.M.: School of American Research Press, 1996.

Casey, James. "Patriotism in Early Modern Valencia." In *Spain, Europe and the Atlantic World: Essays in Honour of John H. Elliott*, edited by Richard L. Kagan and Geoffrey Parker, 188–210. Cambridge: Cambridge University Press, 1995.

Castellá Ferrer, Mauro. *Historia del apóstol de Iesus Christo Sanctiago Zebedeo patrón y capitán general de las Españas*. Madrid, 1610.

Castilla, Gabriel de. *Sermón de S. Hiscio obispo y martyr, uno de los que murieron gloriosamente en este Sancto Monte de Granada*. Granada, 1605.

Castillo, Diego del. *Oración fúnebre panegyrica, en las honras, y annuales memorias, que celebró la nobilíssima ciudad de Granada, a las magestades cathólicas de los invictíssimos reyes D. Fernando, y D. Ysabel, sus libertadores, en su Real Capilla, día siete de Mayo de 1668*. Granada, 1668.

Castillo Fernández, Javier. "La asimilación de los moriscos granadinos: un modelo de análisis." In *Disidencias y exilios en la España moderna. Actas de la IV Reunión de la Asociación Española de Historia Moderna*, vol. 2, edited by Antonio Mestre Sanchís and Enrique Giménez López, 347–61. Alicante: Caja de Ahorros del Mediterráneo, Universidad de Alicante, 1997.

———. "Las estructuras sociales." In *Historia del reino de Granada*, vol. 2, *La época morisca y la repoblación*, edited by Manuel Barrios Aguilera, 179–230. Granada: Universidad de Granada, Legado Andalusí, 2000.

———. "El sacerdote morisco Francisco de Torrijos: un testigo de excepción en la rebelión de las Alpujarras." *Chronica Nova* 23 (1996): 465–92.

Castillo Fernández, Javier, and Antonio Muñoz Buendía. "La hacienda." In *Historia del reino de Granada*, vol. 2, *La época morisca y la repoblación*, edited by Manuel Barrios Aguilera, 101–78. Granada: Universidad de Granada, Legado Andalusí, 2000.

Castillo Pintado, Álvaro. "El servicio de Millones y la población del reino de Granada en 1591." *Saitabi* 11 (1961): 69–91.

Cátedra, María. "L'invention d'un saint. Symbolisme et pouvoir en Castille." *Terrain* 24 (1995): 15–32.

———. *Un santo para una ciudad: ensayo de antropología urbana*. Barcelona: Editorial Ariel, 1997.

Centurión y Córdoba, Adán. *Información para la historia del Sacro monte llamado de Valparaíso y antigüamente illipulitano, junto a Granada*. Granada, 1632.

Cepeda Adán, José. "Los últimos Mendozas granadinos del siglo XVI." In *Miscelánea de estudios dedicados al Profesor Antonio Marín Ocete*, 1:183–204. Granada: Universidad de Granada, 1974.

Cervantes Saavedra, Miguel de. *Don Quixote: The Ormsby Translation, Revised Backgrounds and Sources, Criticism*. Edited by Joseph R. Jones and Kenneth Douglas. New York: W. W. Norton, 1981.

Christian, William A. *Local Religion in Sixteenth-Century Spain*. Princeton, N.J.: Princeton University Press, 1981.

Christodouleas, Tina P., and Nabil Matar. "The Mary of the Sacromonte." *Muslim World* 95, no. 2 (2005): 199–215.

Ciança, Antonio de. *Historia de la vida, invención, milagros, y translación de S. Segundo, primero obispo de Ávila*. Madrid, 1595. Reprint. Ávila: Diputación Provincial de Ávila, Caja de Ahorros de Ávila, 1993.

Cignitti, Benedetto. "Cesare Baronio cultore dei martiri." In *A Cesare Baronio. Scritti vari*, edited by Filippo Caraffa, 299–306. Sora: Vescovo di Sora, 1963.

Cirot, Georges. *Mariana, historien*. Bordeaux: Feret, 1905.

Cochrane, Eric. *Historians and Historiography in the Italian Renaissance*. Chicago: University of Chicago Press, 1981.

———. "The Transition from Renaissance to Baroque: The Case of Italian Historiography." *History and Theory* 19 (1980): 21–38.

Cohen, Anthony P. *The Symbolic Construction of Community*. London: Tavistock, 1985.

Coleman, David. *Creating Christian Granada: Society and Religious Culture in an Old-World Frontier City, 1492–1600*. Ithaca: Cornell University Press, 2003.

Colindres, Pedro de. *Triumpho de Christo, y María, consagrado a los desagravios de los ultrajes, que contra su ley, original, y virginal pureza publicó horrendamente sacrilegio el cartel, que se fixó en Granada. Predicado en la última fiesta de las nueve, que dedicó el Real Convento de la Seráphica Religión en . . . Xerez de la Frontera*. Ecija, 1641.

Conde y Herrera, Christóbal. *Sepulcro duplicado del proto-martyr thaumatúrgico; primero obispo y único patrono de Granada, Señor San Cecilio*. Granada, 1758.

Connerton, Paul. *How Societies Remember*. Cambridge: Cambridge University Press, 1989.

Constable, Giles. "Forgery and Plagiarism in the Middle Ages." *Archiv für Diplomatik, Schriftsgeschichte, Siegel-und Wappenkunde* 29 (1983): 1–41.

Constituciones Synodales del arçobispado de Granada hechas por . . . Pedro Guerrero Arçobispo de la Sancta Yglesia de Granada en el sancto synodo que su Señoría Reverendíssima celebró a quatorze días del mes de octubre del año M.D. LXXII. Granada, 1573.

Córdoba, Pedro. "Las leyendas en la historiografía del Siglo de Oro: el caso de los 'falsos cronicones.'" *Criticón* 30 (1985): 235–53.

Cortés Peña, Antonio Luis. "A propósito de la Iglesia y la conquista del Reino de Granada." In *Iglesia y cultura en la Andalucía moderna. Tendencias de la investigación, estado de las cuestiones*, 135–58. Granada: Proyecto Sur, 1995.

———. "Andalucía y la Inmaculada Concepción en el siglo XVII." In *Religión y política durante el antiguo régimen*, 103–48. Granada: Universidad de Granada, 2001.

———. "La religiosidad popular. La Inmaculada. El Sacromonte." In *Reino de Granada. V Centenario. II: Hacia la Modernidad*, 113–20. Granada: Ideal, 1991.

Cortés Peña, Antonio Luis, and Bernard Vincent. *Historia de Granada*, vol. 3, *La época moderna, siglos XVI, XVII y XVIII*. Granada: Editorial Don Quijote, 1983.

Covarrubias Orozco, Sebastián de. *Tesoro de la lengua castellana, o española*. Madrid, 1611. Edited by Felipe C. R. Maldonado, revised by Manuel Camarero. Madrid: Editorial Castalia, 1995.

Cruz, Jerónimo de la. *Sacrarum virginum vindicatio*. N.p., n.d.

Cruz Sotomayor, Beatriz. "Una mirada a Francisco López Tamarid, traductor y primer editor del pergamino de la Torre Turpiana." In *Hommage à l'École d'Oviedo de Études Aljamiado (dédié au Fondateur Álvaro Galmés de Fuentes)*, edited by Abdeljelil Temimi, 191–

210. Zaghouan: Fondation Temimi pour la Recherche Scientifique et l'Information, 2003.

Cuesta García de Leonardo, María José. *Fiesta y arquitectura efímera en la Granada del siglo XVIII*. Granada: Universidad de Granada, 1995.

Cueva, Luis de la. *Diálogos de las cosas notables de Granada, y lengua española, y algunas cosas curiosas*. Seville, 1603. Reprint. Edited by José Mondéjar. Granada: Universidad de Granada, 1993.

Dalda y Pérez, Alfonso. *El Monte Santo eucharístico. Idea alegórica con que se adornó la Plaza Vivarrambla, y acostumbrada estación, que sirvió a la procession solemnísima de el más augusto de los mysterios este año de 1751, en que la muy noble ciudad de Granada desahogó sus bien nacidos afectos en la executoriada pompa de tan solemnes cultos*. Granada, 1751.

Dávila y Toledo, Sancho. *De la veneración que se debe a los cuerpos de los santos y sus reliquias*. Madrid, 1611.

De los libros, y sanctos martyres, que se hallaron en el Monte Sacro Illipulitano cerca de la ciudad de Granada, y en la Torre Turpiana. N.p., n.d.

Delgado, Antonio. *Nuevo método de clasificación de las medallas autónomas de España*. Vol. 1. Seville: A. Izquierdo y García, 1871. Reprint. Madrid: Juan R. Cayón, 1975.

Depluvrez, Jean-Marc. "Le retours de Saint Eugène et Sainte Léocadie a Tolède en 1565 et 1587 (analyse de deux translations)." In *Les signes de Dieu aux XVIe et XVIIe siècles*, edited by Geneviève Demerson and Bernard Dompnier, 113–32. Clermont-Ferrand: Faculté des Lettres et Sciences humaines de l'Université Blaise Pascal, 1993.

Descripción de la solemne y sumptuosa fiesta, aparato, y ceremonias, que el tribunal del Santo Oficio desta ciudad de Granada hizo en la celebración de la beatificación del glorioso, y invicto mártir Pedro de Arbués. Granada, 1664.

Di Simplicio, Oscar. "Confessionalizzazione e identità collettiva: Il caso italiano: Siena 1575–1800." *Archiv für Reformationsgeschichte* 88 (1997): 380–411.

Ditchfield, Simon. "Ideologia religiosa ed erudizione nell'agiografia dell'età moderna." In *Santità, culti, agiografia. Temi e prospettive*, edited by Sofia Boesch Gajano, 79–90. Rome: Viella, 1997.

———. "'In Search of Local Knowledge': Rewriting Early Modern Italian Religious History." *Cristianesimo nella storia* 19 (1998): 255–96.

———. *Liturgy, Sanctity and History in Tridentine Italy: Pietro Maria Campi and the Preservation of the Particular*. Cambridge: Cambridge University Press, 1995.

———. "Martyrs on the Move: Relics as Vindicators of Local Diversity in the Tridentine Church," *Studies in Church History* 30 (1993): 283–94.

———. "Text before Trowel: Antonio Bosio's *Roma sotteranea* Revisited." *Studies in Church History* 33 (1997): 343–60.

Dolan, Claire. "L'identité urbaine et les histoires locales publiées du XVIe au XVIIIe siècle en France." *Canadian Journal of History* 27 (1992): 278–98.

Domenichini, Daniele. "Quattro inediti di Benito Arias Montano sulla questione sacromontana (1596/1598)." *Anales de la literatura española* 5 (1986–87): 51–66.

Domínguez Guzmán, Aurora. "Una curiosa fiesta universitaria en Sevilla en 1617: la celebrada por el Colegio Mayor de Santa María de Jesús en honor de la Inmaculada." *Archivo Hispalense* 73 (1990): 31–44.

Domínguez Ortiz, Antonio. *Alteraciones andaluzas*. Madrid: Nárcea, 1973.

———. "El Estado de los Austrias y los municipios andaluces en el siglo XVII." In *Les élites locales et l'état dans l'Espagne moderne du XVIe au XIXe siècle*, edited by Martine Lambert-Gorges, 129–42. Paris: CNRS Éditions, 1993.

———. "La historiografía local andaluza en el siglo XVII." In *Los extranjeros en la vida española durante el siglo XVII y otros artículos*, edited by León Carlos Álvarez Santaló, 449–65. Seville: Diputación Provincial de Sevilla, 1996.

———. "La identidad de Andalucía." *Anuario de historia moderna y contemporánea* 4 (1977): 17–25.

Domínguez Ortiz, Antonio, and Bernard Vincent. *Historia de los moriscos. Vida y tragedia de una minoría*. Madrid: Editorial Revista de Occidente, 1978.

Ecker, Heather. "'Arab Stones': Rodrigo Caro's Translations of Arabic Inscriptions in Seville (1634), Revisited." *Al-Qanṭara* 23, no. 2 (2002): 347–402.

Eco, Umberto. "The Force of Falsity." In *Serendipities: Language and Lunacy*, 1–21. Translated by William Weaver. New York: Columbia University Press, 1998.

Edwards, John. "Christian Mission in the Kingdom of Granada, 1492–1568." *Renaissance and Modern Studies* 31 (1987): 20–33.

Egido, Teófanes. "Religiosidad 'popular' y Cortes tradicionales de Castilla." In *La religiosidad popular*, vol. 2, *Antropología e historia*, edited by Carlos Álvarez Santaló, María Jesús Buxó i Rey, and Salvador Rodríguez Becerra, 96–110. Barcelona: Editorial Anthropos, and Seville: Fundación Machado, 1989.

Eguílaz y Yanguas, Leopoldo. *Del lugar donde fue Iliberis*. Madrid: Imprenta de los Sres. Lezcano, 1881. Reprint. Edited by Manuel Espinar Moreno. Granada: Universidad de Granada, 1987.

Ehlers, Benjamin. "Negotiating Reform: Archbishop Juan de Ribera (1532–1611) and the Colegio de Corpus Christi, Valencia." *Archiv für Reformationsgeschichte* 95 (2004): 185–209.

Ehmke, Edwin G. "The Writing of Town and Provincial History in Sixteenth-Century France: Developing a Myth of Local Identity." Ph.D. diss., University of Southern California, 1979.

Elliott, J. H. *The Count-Duke of Olivares: The Statesman in an Age of Decline*. New Haven: Yale University Press, 1986.

———. "A Europe of Composite Monarchies." *Past and Present* 137 (1992): 48–71.

———. "Power and Propaganda in the Spain of Philip IV." In *Rites of Power: Symbolism, Ritual, and Politics since the Middle Ages*, edited by Sean Wilentz, 145–73. Philadelphia: University of Pennsylvania Press, 1985.

———. "Revolution and Continuity in Early Modern Europe." In *Spain and Its World, 1500–1700: Selected Essays*, 92–113. New Haven: Yale University Press, 1989.

———. "Self-Perception and Decline in Early Seventeenth-Century Spain." In *Spain and Its World, 1500–1700*, 241–61. New Haven: Yale University Press, 1989.

Englund, Steven. "The Ghost of Nation Past." *Journal of Modern History* 64 (1992): 299–320.

Epalza, Mikel de. *Jésus otage. Juifs, chrétiens et musulmans en Espagne (VIe–XVIIe s.)*. Paris: Cerf, 1987.

Erección de la Yglesia Metropolitana de Granada, dignidades y prebendas de ella, y de todas las demás yglesias colegiales, y parroquiales de su arçobispado, abadías, beneficios, y sacristías del. Hecha en virtud de bulas de la Santidad de Inocencio Octavo. Granada, 1677.

Escalera Pérez, Reyes. *La imagen de la sociedad barroca andaluza. Estudio simbólico de las decoraciones efímeras en la fiesta altoandaluza, siglos XVII y XVIII.* Málaga: Universidad de Málaga, Junta de Andalucía, 1994.

Escolano y Ledesma, Diego. *Chronicon Sancti Hierothei, posteae Secoviensis ecclesiae episcopi.* Madrid, 1667.

———. *Memorial a la Reyna N.S. cerca de las muertes que en odio de la fe y religión Christiana dieron los moriscos revelados a los christianos viejos (y algunos nuevos) residentes en las Alpuxarras deste reyno de Granada, en el levantimento del año 1568.* Granada, 1671.

Espinosa, Pedro. *Flores de poetas ilustres de España.* 2d ed. Edited by Juan Quirós de los Ríos and Francisco Rodríguez Marín. Seville: Imp. de E. Rasco, 1896.

Esquivel, Francisco de. *Relación de la invención de los cuerpos santos, que en los años 1614 1516 y 1616 fueron hallados en varias yglesias de la ciudad de Caller y su arçobispado.* Naples, 1617.

Estévez Sola, Juan Antonio. "Algo más sobre los orígenes míticos de Hispania." *Habis* 24 (1993): 207–18.

———. "Aproximación a los orígenes míticos de Hispania." *Habis* 21 (1990): 139–52.

Farrer, J. A. *Literary Forgeries.* London: Longmans, Green, 1907.

Fayard, Janine. *Los miembros del Consejo de Castilla (1621–1746).* Translated by Rufina Rodríguez Sanz. Madrid: Siglo XXI, 1982.

Fernández, Fidel. *Fray Hernando de Talavera. Confesor de los Reyes Católicos y primer arzobispo de Granada.* Madrid: Biblioteca Nueva, 1942.

Fernández Basurte, Federico. "El concejo y las fiestas de la Inmaculada en Málaga. 1640." *Espacio, tiempo y forma,* serie IV, Historia Moderna, 7 (1994): 195–210.

Fernández Catón, José María. *San Mancio. Culto, leyenda y reliquias. Ensayo de crítica hagiográfica.* León: Centro de Estudios e Investigación San Isidoro (CSIC-CECEL), 1983.

Fernández de Madrid, Alonso. *Vida de Fray Fernando de Talavera. Primer arzobispo de Granada.* Edited by Félix G. Olmedo. Madrid: Editorial "Razón y Fe," 1931. Reprint. Edited by Francisco Javier Martínez Medina. Granada: Universidad de Granada, 1992.

Fernández García, María de los Ángeles. "Hechicería e Inquisición en el reino de Granada en el siglo XVII." *Chronica Nova* 15 (1986–87): 149–72.

Fernández-Nieto, Fidel, Concepción García Caro, Juan Peña Fernández, and Salvador Sánchez Sánchez. *El Sacromonte: la muerte de un barrio.* Granada, 1981.

Ferriol y Caycedo, Alonso de. *Libro de las fiestas que en honor de la inmaculada Concepción de la Virgen María nuestra señora, celebró su devota y antigua hermandad en san Francisco de Granada.* Granada, 1616.

Fierro, Maribel. "El espacio de los muertos: fetuas andalusíes sobre tumbas y cementerios." In *L'urbanisme dans l'Occident musulman au Moyen Âge. Aspects juridiques,* edited by Patrice Cressier, Maribel Fierro, and Jean-Pierre Van Staëvel, 153–89. Madrid: CSIC, Casa de Velázquez, 2000.

La Fiesta de la Toma. Nota histórica y ceremonial que ha de observar el excelentíssimo ayuntamiento de Granada en los actos conmemorativos de la reconquista de esta ciudad los días 1 y 2 de enero. 2d ed. Granada, 1955.

Forster, Marc R. "With and Without Confessionalization: Varieties of Early Modern German Catholicism." *Journal of Early Modern History* 1, no. 4 (1997): 315–43.

Foulché-Delbosc, Raimundo. "Documents relatifs à la Guerre de Grenade." *Revue Hispanique* 31 (1914): 486–523.

Frías, Lesmes. "Felipe III y la Inmaculada Concepción." *Razón y Fe* 10 (1904): 21–33, 145–56, 293–308; 11 (1904): 180–98; 12 (1905): 322–36; 13 (1905): 62–75.

Frijda, Nico H. "Commemorating." In *Collective Memory of Political Events: Social Psychological Perspectives*, edited by James W. Pennebaker, Dario Paez, and Bernard Rimé, 103–27. Matwah, N.J.: Lawrence Erlbaum Associates, 1997.

Fros, Henry. "Culte des saints et sentiment national. Quelques aspects du problème." *Analecta Bollandia* 100 (1982): 729–35.

Fuchs, Barbara. *Mimesis and Empire: The New World, Islam, and European Identities*. Cambridge: Cambridge University Press, 2001.

Fuente, Vicente de la. *Historia eclesiástica de España*. 2d ed. Vol. 5. Madrid: Compañía de Impresores y Libreros del Reino, 1874.

Gaignard, Catherine. *Maures et chrétiens à Grenada, 1492–1570*. Paris: Editions L'Harmattan, 1997.

Galán Sánchez, Ángel. *Los mudéjares del Reino de Granada*. Granada: Universidad de Granada, 1991.

———. "Los vencidos, exilio, integración y resistencia." In *Historia del reino de Granada*, vol. 1, *De los orígenes a la época mudéjar (hasta 1502)*, edited by Rafael G. Peinado Santaella, 525–65. Granada: Universidad de Granada, Legado Andalusí, 2000.

Gallardo, Bartolomé José. *Ensayo de una biblioteca española de libros raros y curiosos*. Vol. 1. Madrid, 1862.

Gallego Morell, Antonio. "Algunas notas sobre Don Martín Vázquez Siruela." In *Estudios dedicados a Menéndez Pidal*, 4:404–24. Madrid: CSIC, 1962.

———. *Cinco impresores granadinos*. Granada: Universidad de Granada, 1970.

———. *Pedro Soto de Rojas*. Granada: Universidad de Granada, 1948.

Gallego y Burín, Antonio. *Granada. Guía artística e histórica de la ciudad*. Edited by Francisco Javier Gallego Roca. Granada: Editorial Comares, 1996

Galvarro y Armenta, Juan. *Sermón on la octava del protomartyr San Estevan, en la qual se celebra la conquista de la muy ilustre ciudad de Granada*. Granada, 1611.

Gan Giménez, Pedro. "La ciudad de Granada en el siglo XVI. Cuestiones político-administrativas." In *La Granada de Fray Luis. IV Centenario, 1588–1988*, 1–14. Granada: Centro de Estudios Históricos de Granada y su Reino, 1988.

———. "En torno al Corpus granadino del siglo XVII." *Chronica Nova* 17 (1989): 91–130.

———. "Los prebendados de la iglesia granadina. Una bio-biliografía." *Revista del Centro de Estudios Históricos de Granada y su Reino* 4 (1990): 139–212.

———. *La Real Chancillería de Granada (1505–1834)*. Granada: Centro de Estudios Históricos de Granada y su Reino, 1988.

———. "Religiosidad granadina del siglo XVII: la Iglesia y la sociedad." In *El barroco en Granada*, 5:127–33. Córdoba, 1987.

Gaquère, François. *La vie et les oeuvres de Claude Fleury (1640–1723)*. Paris: J. de Gigord, 1925.

García, Juan Catalina, ed. *Relaciones topográficas de España. Relaciones de pueblos que pertenecen hoy a la provincia de Guadalajara*, vol. 3, in *Memorial histórico español: colección de documentos, opúsculos y antigüedades que publica la Real Academia de la Historia*. Vol. 43. Madrid: La Academia, 1905.

García Fuentes, José María. *La Inquisición en Granada en el siglo XVI: fuentes para su estudio*. Granada: Departamento de Historia de la Universidad de Granada, 1981.

García Gámez, Félix. "La seda del Reino de Granada durante el segundo proceso repoblador (1570–1630)." *Chronica Nova* 25 (1998): 249–73.

García Oro, José, and María José Portela Silva, eds. *Felipe II y los libreros. Actas de las visitas a las librerías del Reino de Castilla en 1572*. Madrid: Editorial Cisneros, 1997.

García Pedraza, Amalia. *Actitudes ante la muerte en la Granada del siglo XVI. Los moriscos que quisieron salvarse*. 2 vols. Granada: Universidad de Granada, 2001.

———. "La asimilación del morisco don Gonzalo Fernández el Zegrí: edición y análisis de su testamento." *Al-Qanṭara* 16 (1995): 41–58.

García Pérez, Francisco José. "Mentalidades, reliquias y arte en Murcia, ss. XVI–XVII." In *Mentalidades e ideología en el antiguo régimen. II Reunión Científica. Asociación Española de Historia Moderna, 1992*, vol. 2, edited by Leon Carlos Álvarez Santaló and Carmen María Cremades Griñán, 237–45. Murcia: Universidad de Murcia, 1993.

García Valverde, María Luisa. "La donación del Arzobispo Don Pedro de Castro al Sacromonte: el inventario de sus bienes." *Cuadernos de Arte de la Universidad de Granada* 27 (1996): 283–95.

García Villada, Zacarías. *Historia eclesiástica de España*, vol. 1, *El cristianismo durante la dominación romana*. Madrid: Compañía Ibero-Americana de Publicaciones, 1929.

García y García, Antonio, ed. *Synodicon Hispanum*. Vol. 3. Madrid: Biblioteca de Autores Cristianos, 1984.

García-Arenal, Mercedes. "El entorno de los plomos: historiografía y linaje." *Al-Qanṭara* 24, no. 2 (2003): 295–326.

Garibay y Zamalloa, Esteban de. *Los XL libros d'el compendio historial de las chronicas y universal historia de todos los reynos de España*. 4 vols. Barcelona, 1628. Reprint. Lejona: Editorial Gerardo Uña, 1988.

Garrad, Keith. "La industria sedera granadina en el siglo XVI y su conexión con el levantamiento de las Alpujarras (1568–1571)." *Miscelánea de estudios árabes y hebraicos* 5 (1956): 73–104.

———. "The Original Memorial of Don Francisco Núñez Muley." *Atlante* 2 (1954): 199–226.

Garrido Aranda, Antonio. *Organización de la iglesia en el reino de Granada, y su proyección en Indias*. Seville: Escuela de Estudios Hispano-Americanos, 1979.

———. "Papel de la Iglesia de Granada en la asimilación de la sociedad morisca." *Anuario de historia moderna y contemporánea* 2–3 (1975): 69–103.

Garrido Atienza, Miguel. *Antiguallas granadinas. Las Fiestas del Corpus*. Granada: Imprenta de D. José López Guevara, 1889. Reprint. Edited by José Antonio González Alcantud. Granada: Universidad de Granada, 1990.

———. *Las capitulaciones para la entrega de Granada*. Granada: Tip. Lit. Paulino Ventura

Travaset, 1910. Reprint. Edited by José Enrique López de Coca Castañer. Granada: Universidad de Granada, 1992.

———. *Las fiestas de la Toma.* Granada: Imprenta de D. Francisco de los Reyes, 1891. Reprint. Edited by José Antonio González Alcantud. Granada: Universidad de Granada, 1998.

Garzón Pareja, Manuel. *Historia de Granada.* 2 vols. Granada: Diputación Provincial de Granada, 1980.

———. "Industria de Granada (1492–1900)." *Actas del I Congreso de Historia de Andalucía. Andalucía Contemporánea (Siglos XIX y XX),* 2:67–82. Córdoba: Monte de Piedad y Caja de Ahorros de Córdoba, 1979.

———. *La industria sedera en España. El arte de la seda de Granada.* Granada: Real Chancillería de Granada, 1972.

———. "Revueltas urbanas de Granada en el siglo XVII." In *Actas II Coloquios de Andalucía "Andalucía Moderna,"* 2:75–80. Córdoba: Publicaciones del Monte de Piedad y Caja de Ahorros de Córdoba, 1983.

Gascó, Fernando. "Historiadores, falsarios y estudiosos de las antigüedades andaluzas." In *La antigüedad como argumento. Historiografía de arqueología e historia antigua en Andalucía,* edited by José Beltrán Fortes and Fernando Gascó, 7–28. Seville: Junta de Andalucía, 1993.

Geertz, Clifford. "Centers, Kings, and Charisma: Reflections on the Symbolics of Power." In *Local Knowledge: Further Essays in Interpretive Anthropology,* 121–46. New York: Basic Books, 1983.

Gil Albarracín, Antonio. "Francisco López Tamarid, clérigo, guerrero y humanista, y la Almería de su tiempo." *Roel. Cuadernos de civilización de la cuenca de Almanzora* 11 (1990–91): 33–47.

Gil Bracero, Rafael. "Crisis y fluctuaciones agrícolas en la segunda mitad del siglo XVII en Granada." *Anuario de historia contemporánea* 10 (1983): 5–29.

Gil Sanjuán, Joaquín, and María Isabel Pérez de Colosía Rodríguez. *Imágenes del poder. Mapas y paisajes urbanos del Reino de Granada en el Trinity College de Dublín.* Málaga: Junta de Andalucía, Universidad de Málaga, 1997.

Gil Sanjuán, Joaquín, and Juan Antonio Sánchez López. "Iconografía y visión histórico-literaria de Granada a mediados del quinientos." *Chronica Nova* 23 (1996): 73–133.

Gila Medina, Lázaro. "La Cruz de Guadix en el Sacromonte granadino." *Boletín del Instituto de Estudios "Pedro Suárez"* 5 (1992): 51–55.

Glacken, Clarence J. *Traces on the Rhodian Shore: Nature and Culture in Western Thought from Ancient Times to the End of the Eighteenth Century.* Berkeley: University of California Press, 1973.

Godoy Alcántara, José. *Historia crítica de los falsos cronicones.* Madrid: Real Academia de la Historia, 1868. Reprint. Edited by Ofelia Rey Castelao. Granada: Universidad de Granada, 1999.

Goldziher, Ignác. "Veneration of Saints in Islam." In *Muslim Studies,* vol. 2, edited by S. M. Stern, 255–341. London: Allen & Unwin, 1971.

Gómez Bravo, Juan. *Catálogo de los obispos de Córdoba, y breve noticia histórica de su iglesia catedral, y obispado.* Córdoba, 1778.

Gómez Canseco, Luis. *El humanismo después de 1600: Pedro de Valencia.* Seville: Universidad de Sevilla, 1993.

———. *Rodrigo Caro: un humanista en la Sevilla del seiscientos.* Seville: Diputación Provincial de Sevilla, 1986.

Gómez de Liaño, Ignacio. *Los juegos del Sacromonte.* Madrid: Editora Nacional, 1975. Reprint. Granada: Universidad de Granada, 2005.

Gómez-Moreno Calera, José Manuel. *El arquitecto granadino Ambrosio de Vico.* Granada: Universidad de Granada, 1992.

———. *La arquitectura religiosa granadina en la crisis del Renacimiento (1560–1650). Diócesis de Granada y Guadix-Baza.* Granada: Universidad de Granada, 1989.

Gómez-Moreno y Martínez, Manuel. "Monumentos romanos y visigóticos de Granada." *Boletín del Centro Artístico de Granada* 5, no. 84 (1890): 89–96.

Góngora y Argote, Luis de. *Obras poéticas de D. Luis de Góngora.* Vol. 1. New York: Hispanic Society of America, 1921.

González Alcantud, José Antonio. "El mito fallido sacromontano y su perdurabilidad local a la luz del mozarabismo maurófobo de F. J. Simonet." *Al-Qanṭara* 24, no. 2 (2003): 547–74.

González Martínez, José. "La fiesta de la toma de Granada en tiempos liberales." In *Las tomas: antropología histórica de la ocupación territorial del reino de Granada,* edited by José Antonio González Alcantud and Manuel Barrios Aguilera, 643–59. Granada: Diputación Provincial de Granada, 2000.

González Novalín, José Luis. "Baronio y la cuestión jacobea. Manipulaciones en el sepulcro compostelano en tiempo del Cardenal." In *Baronio e l'arte: atti del convegno internazionale di studi, Sora, 10–13 ottobre 1984,* edited by Romeo De Maio, 173–88. Sora, Italy: Centro di studi sorani "Vincenzo Patriarca," 1985.

González Vázquez, José. "El humanismo clásico en la Granada del primer Renacimiento." In *El Reino de Granada y el Nuevo Mundo. V Congreso Internacional de Historia de América,* 2:11–27. Granada: Diputación Provincial de Granada, 1994.

Gonzalo Maeso, David. *Garnāta al-Yahūd. Granada en la historia del judaismo español.* Granada: University of Granada, 1963. Reprint. Edited by María Encarnación Varela. Granada: Universidad de Granada, 1990.

Grafton, Anthony. *Forgers and Critics: Creativity and Duplicity in Western Scholarship.* Princeton, N.J.: Princeton University Press, 1990.

———. "Traditions of Invention and Inventions of Tradition in Renaissance Italy: Annius of Viterbo." In *Defenders of the Text: the Traditions of Scholarship in an Age of Science, 1450–1800,* 76–103. Cambridge: Harvard University Press, 1991.

Granada, Luis de. *Obras del V.P.M. Fray Luis de Granada,* vol. 3, *Los seis libros de la retórica eclesiástica, o de la manera de predicar.* Biblioteca de Autores Españoles, vol. 11. Madrid, 1856.

La grande necessidad con que se halla el Doctor don Blasio de Santaella, que a cinco años que está en Roma, solicitando la calificación de los libros, que Dios descubrió en este S. Monte de Granada, y el no poder esta iglesia continuar el socorrerle, por estar gravada su hazienda con grandes censos, que se han tomado para este efecto. Nos a obligado a valernos de la piedad de los fieles, para que con sus limosnas sean partícipes en obra tan heroyca . . . N.p., n.d.

Gregory, Brad S. *Salvation at Stake: Christian Martyrdom in Early Modern Europe.* Cambridge: Harvard University Press, 1999.

Griffin, Nigel. "'Un muro invisible': Moriscos and Cristianos Viejos in Granada." In *Mediaeval and Renaissance Studies on Spain and Portugal in Honour of P. E. Russell,* edited by F. W. Hodcroft, D. G. Pattison, R. D. F. Pring-Mill, and R. W. Truman, 133–54. Oxford: Society for the Study of Medieval Languages and Literatures, 1981.

Grima Cervantes, Juan. "Anotaciones cronológicas para la historia de Almería." In *Almería y el reino de Granada en los inicios de la modernidad (s. XV–XVI). Compendio de estudios,* 303–19. Almería: Arráez Editores, 1994.

Guerra de Lorca, Pedro. *Catecheses mystagogae pro aduenis ex secta Mahometana. Ad Parochos, & Potestates.* Madrid, 1586.

Guinea Díaz, Patricio. "Antigüedad e historia local en el siglo XVIII andaluz." *Florentia Iliberritana* 2 (1991): 241–58.

Gullién Marcos, Esperanza, and María del Mar Villaranca Jiménez. "El Sacro Monte granadino. Un itinerario ritual en la España del XVII." In *Los caminos y el arte: actas, VI Congreso Español de Historia del Arte, CEHA, Santiago de Compostela, 16–20 de junio de 1986,* 3:183–91. Santiago de Compostela: Universidade de Santiago de Compostela, 1989.

Gurmendi, Francisco de. *Doctrina phísica y moral de príncipes.* Madrid, 1615.

Hagerty, Miguel José. *Los libros plúmbeos del Sacromonte.* Madrid: Editora Nacional, 1980. Reprint. Granada: Editorial Comares, 1998.

———. "Los libros plúmbeos y la fundación de la Insigne Iglesia Colegial del Sacromonte." In *La Abadía del Sacromonte. Exposición artístico-documental. Estudios sobre su significación y origines,* 18–33. Granada: Universidad de Granada, 1974.

———. "La traducción interesada: el caso del marqués de Estepa y los libros plúmbeos." In *Homenaje al Prof. Jacinto Bosch Vilá,* 2:1179–86. Granada: Universidad de Granada, 1991.

Hamel, Georges. "Un incunable français relatif à la prise de Grenade." *Revue Hispanique* 36 (1916): 159–69.

Handler, Richard. "Is 'Identity' a Useful Cross-Cultural Concept?" In *Commemorations: The Politics of National Identity,* edited by John R. Gillis, 27–40. Princeton, N.J.: Princeton University Press, 1994.

Hardin, William. "Conceiving Cities: Thomas Heywood's *Londini Speculum* (1637) and the Making of Civic Identity." *Comitatus: A Journal of Medieval and Renaissance Studies* 28, no. 2 (1997): 17–35.

Harley, J. B. "Maps, Knowledge, and Power." In *The Iconography of Landscape: Essays on the Symbolic Representation, Design and Use of Past Environments,* edited by Denis Cosgrove and Stephen Daniels, 277–312. Cambridge: Cambridge University Press, 1988.

Harris, A. Katie. "Ceremonias y sermones: la fiesta de la Toma y la identidad cívica en la Granada moderna." In *Actas del III Congreso de Historia de Andalucía. Córdoba, 2001,* vol. 3, *Andalucía moderna,* 137–47. Córdoba: Publicaciones Obra Social y Cultural Cajasur, 2003.

———. "Forging History: The *Plomos* of Granada in Francisco Bermúdez de Pedraza's *Historia eclesiástica.*" *Sixteenth Century Journal* 30, no. 4 (1999): 945–66.

———. "The Sacromonte and the Geography of the Sacred in Early Modern Granada." *Al-Qanṭara* 23, no. 2 (2002): 517–43.

Harvey, L. P. *Islamic Spain, 1250–1500.* Chicago: University of Chicago Press, 1990.

———. *Muslims in Spain, 1500 to 1614.* Chicago: University of Chicago Press, 2005.

Harvey, L. P., and G. A. Wiegers. "The Translation from Arabic of the Sacromonte Tablets and the Archbishop of Granada: An Illuminating Correspondence." *Qurṭuba* 1 (1996): 59–78.

Haywood, Ian. *The Making of History: A Study of the Literary Forgeries of James Macpherson and Thomas Chatterton in Relation to Eighteenth-Century Ideas of History and Fiction.* Rutherford: Fairleigh Dickinson University Press, 1986.

Henares Cuéllar, Ignacio, and Miguel José Hagerty. "La significación de la fundación en la cultura granadina de transición al siglo XVII." In *La Abadía del Sacromonte. Exposición artísticodocumental. Estudios sobre su significación y origines,* 41–46. Granada: Universidad de Granada, 1974.

Henares Cuéllar, Ignacio, and Rafael López Guzmán, eds. *Universidad y ciudad. La Universidad en la historia y la cultura de Granada.* 2d. Granada: Universidad de Granada, 1997.

Henríquez de Jorquera, Francisco. *Anales de Granada. Descripción del reino y ciudad de Granada. Crónica de la Reconquista (1482–1492). Sucesos de los años 1588 a 1646.* 2 vols. Edited by Antonio Marín Ocete. Granada: Facultad de Letras, 1934. Reprint. Edited by Pedro Gan Giménez. Granada: Universidad de Granada, 1987.

Heredia Barnuevo, Diego Nicolás de. *Místico ramillete, histórico, chronológyco, panegyrico . . . del . . . illmo. y v. Sr. Don Pedro de Castro Vaca y Quiñones.* Granada, 1741, 1863. Reprint. Edited by Manuel Barrios Aguilera. Granada: Universidad de Granada, 1998.

Hernández Benito, Pedro. "Toponimia y sociedad: la ciudad de Granada a fines de la Edad Media." *Cuadernos de la Alhambra* 28 (1992): 253–70.

Herrera Puga, Pedro. "La mala vida en tiempos de los Austrias." *Anuario de historia moderna y contemporánea* 1 (1974): 5–32.

Herrera y Sotomayor, Jacinto de. *Jornada que su magestad hizo a la Andaluzía.* Madrid, 1624.

Herrero Salgado, Félix. *La oratoria sagrada española en los siglos XVI y XVII.* Madrid: Fundación Universitaria Española, 1996.

Herz, Alexandra. "Imitators of Christ: The Martyr-Cycles of Late Sixteenth Century Rome Seen in Context." *Storia dell'arte* 62 (1988): 53–70.

Herzog, Tamar. *Defining Nations: Immigrants and Citizens in Early Modern Spain and Spanish America.* New Haven: Yale University Press, 2003.

Hess, Andrew C. "The Moriscos: An Ottoman Fifth Column in Sixteenth-Century Spain." *American Historical Review* 74 (1968): 1–25.

Hidalgo Morales, José. *Iliberia, o Granada: memoria histórico-crítica, topográfica, cronológica, política, literaria y eclesiástica de sus antigüedades, desde su fundación hasta nuestros días.* 2d ed. Granada: J. M. Zamora, 1848.

Hillgarth, J. N. *The Mirror of Spain, 1500–1700: The Formation of a Myth.* Ann Arbor: University of Michigan Press, 2000.

Hills, Helen. "Mapping the Early Modern City." *Urban History* 23 (1996): 145–70.

Historia del Colegio de San Pablo, Granada 1554–1765. Transcribed by Joaquín de Béthencourt. Edited by Estanislao Olivares. Granada: Facultad de Teología, 1991.

Hitchcock, Richard. "The *Falsos Chronicones* and the Mozarabs." *Journal of the Institute of Romance Studies* 3 (1994–95): 87–96.

Hitos, Francisco A. *Mártires de la Alpujarra en la rebelión de los moriscos (1568)*. Madrid: Apostolado de la Prensa, 1935. Reprint. Edited by Manuel Barrios Aguilera. Granada: Universidad de Granada, 1993.

Hobsbawm, Eric, and Terence Ranger, eds. *The Invention of Tradition*. Cambridge: Cambridge University Press, 1983.

Holt, Mack P. "Burgundians into Frenchmen: Catholic Identity in Sixteenth-Century Burgundy." In *Changing Identities in Early Modern France*, edited by Michael Wolfe, 345–70. Durham: Duke University Press, 1997.

Hübner, Ernst. *Corpus inscriptionum latinarum. Consilio et auctoritate Academiae litterarum regiae Borussicae editum*. 16 vols. Berlin, 1863–.

Hurtado de Mendoza, Diego. *Guerra de Granada*. Lisbon, 1627. Reprint. Edited by Bernardo Blanco-González. Madrid: Editorial Castalia, 1970.

Ibn Baṭṭūṭa. *The Travels of Ibn Baṭṭūṭa, A.D. 1325–1354*. Vol. 4. Edited by C. Defrémery and B. R. Sanguinetti. Translated by H. A. R. Gibb and C. F. Beckingham. London: Hakluyt Society, 1994.

Ibn al-Ḥajarī, Aḥmad ibn Qāsim. *Kitāb Nāṣir al-dīn ʿalā ʾl-qawm al-kāfirīn. The Supporter of Religion against the Infidels: Historical Study, Critical Edition and Annotated Translation*. Edited and translated by P. S. van Konigsveld, Q. al-Samarrai, and G. A. Wiegers. Madrid: Agencia Española de Cooperación Internacional, 1997.

Ibn al-Khaṭīb. *Correspondencia diplomática entre Granada y Fez (siglo XIV): extractos de la "Raihana alcuttab" (mss. de la Biblioteca del Escorial)*. Translated and edited by M. Gaspar Remiro. Granada: Impr. de el Defensor, 1916.

Iconografía de Sevilla. Vols. 2–3. Madrid: Ediciones El Viso, 1988–89.

Jammes, Robert, and Odette Gorsse. "Nicolás Antonio et le combat pour la verité (31 lettres de Nicolás Antonio à Vázquez Siruela)." In *Hommage des hispanistes français à Noël Salomon*, 411–30. Barcelona: Laia, 1979.

Jerome. *On Illustrious Men*. Translated by Thomas P. Halton. Washington, D.C.: Catholic University of America, 1999.

Jiménez de Santiago, Francisco. *Desagravios a la virginidad en el parto de María Santíssima . . . opuestos a los carteles, y libelos que el hebreo puso en Granada . . . celebrados en el religiosíssimo convento de frailes menores de S. Francisco de los Capuchinos . . . en el insigne ternario, que celebró en esta ciudad domingo 17 de junio*. Ecija, 1640.

Jiménez Monteserín, Miguel. *Vere pater pauperum. El culto de San Julián en Cuenca*. Cuenca: Diputación Provincial de Cuenca, 1999.

Jiménez Vela, Rosario. *Inventario de los libros de cabildo del Archivo Municipal de Granada 1518–1566*. Granada: Universidad de Granada, 1987.

Johnson, Trevor. "Holy Fabrications: The Catacomb Saints and the Counter-Reformation in Bavaria." *Journal of Ecclesiastical History* 47 (1996): 274–97.

Jones, Mark, with Paul Craddock and Nicolas Barker, eds. *Fake? The Art of Deception*. Berkeley: University of California Press, 1990.

Jouvin, A. "El viaje de España y Portugal." In *Viajes de extranjeros por España y Portugal*, vol. 2, translated and edited by J. García Mercadal, 747–841. Madrid: Aguilar, 1952.

Kagan, Richard L. "Clio and the Crown: Writing History in Habsburg Spain." In *Spain, Europe and the Atlantic World,* edited by Richard L. Kagan and Geoffrey Parker, 73–99. Cambridge: Cambridge University Press, 1995.

———. *Lawsuits and Litigants in Castile, 1500–1700.* Chapel Hill, N.C.: University of North Carolina Press, 1981.

———. *Lucrecia's Dreams: Politics and Prophecy in Sixteenth-Century Spain.* Berkeley: University of California Press, 1990.

———. *Students and Society in Early Modern Spain.* Baltimore: Johns Hopkins University Press, 1974.

———. *Urban Images of the Hispanic World, 1493–1793.* New Haven: Yale University Press, 2000.

———. "*Urbs* and *Civitas* in Sixteenth-and Seventeenth-Century Spain." In *Envisioning the City: Six Studies in Urban Cartography,* edited by David Buissaret, 73–108. Chicago: University of Chicago, 1998.

———, ed. *Spanish Cities of the Golden Age: The Views of Anton van den Wyngaerde.* Berkeley: University of California Press, 1989.

Kamen, Henry. *The Phoenix and the Flame: Catalonia and the Counter Reformation.* New Haven: Yale University Press, 1993.

———. *Spain, 1469–1714: A Society of Conflict.* 2d ed. New York: Longman, 1991.

Kendrick, T. D. "An Example of the Theodicy-Motive in Antiquarian Thought." In *Fritz Saxl, 1890–1948: A Volume of Memorial Essays from His Friends in England,* edited by D. J. Gordon, 309–25. London: Thomas Nelson and Sons, 1957.

———. *St. James in Spain.* London: Methuen, 1960.

Knipping, John B. *Iconography of the Counter Reformation in the Netherlands: Heaven on Earth.* 2 vols. Nieuwkoop: B. de Graaf, 1974.

Labarta, Ana. "Supersticiones moriscas." *Awrāq* 5–6 (1982–83): 161–90.

Lacave, José Luis. "Las juderías del reino de Granada." *Chronica Nova* 20 (1992): 243–52.

Ladero Quesada, Miguel Ángel. "La repoblación del reino de Granada anterior al año 1500." *Hispania* 28 (1968): 489–563.

———, ed. *La incorporación de Granada a la Corona de Castilla: actas del Symposium Conmemorativo del Quinto Centenario, Granada 2 al 5 de diciembre de 1991.* Granada: Diputación Provincial de Granada, 1993.

Lalaing, Antoine de. "Relation du premier voyage de Philippe le Beau en Espagne, en 1501." In *Collection des voyages des souverains des Pays-Bas,* vol. 1, edited by M. Gachard, 121–385. Brussels: F. Hayez, 1876.

Lapeyre, Henri. *Géographie de l'Espagne morisque.* Paris: S.E.V.P.E.N., 1959.

Lazure, Guy. "Monarchie et identité spirituelle dans la collection de reliques de Philippe II à la Escorial." In *Corps saints et lieux sacrés dans l'espace de l'Europe moderne,* edited by Philippe Boutry and Pierre-Antoine Fabre. Paris: EHESS, forthcoming.

Lecorp, Antonio José. *La espada del Señor, y de Fernando en la conquista de Granada por los Reyes Cathólicos Don Fernando, y Doña Isabel, lograda a impulsos de su zelo por la extensión, y exaltación de la fe, y en premio de la devoción y culto al SSmo. Sacramento. Pensamiento con que se adornó la estación para la procession, y solemnidad del día del Señor en la ciudad de Granada, en 2. de junio de 1774 . . .* Granada, 1775.

León, Pedro de. *Grandeza y miseria en Andalucía. Testimonio de una encrucijada histórica (1578–1616).* Edited by Pedro Herrera Puga. Granada: Facultad de Teología, 1981.

Lera García, Rafael de. "Survie de l'Islam dans la ville de Grenade au début du dix-huitième siècle." *Revue d'histoire maghrébine* 13, nos. 43–44 (1986): 59–82.

———. "Venta de oficios en la Inquisición de Granada." *Hispania* 48, no. 170 (1988): 909–62.

Levi Della Vida, Giorgio. *Ricerche sulla formazione del più antico fondo dei monoscritti orientali della Biblioteca Vaticana.* Vatican City: Biblioteca Apostolica Vaticana, 1939.

Lévi-Provençal, E. "Le voyage d'Ibn Baṭṭūṭa dans le royaume de Grenade (1350)." In *Mélanges offerts à William Marçais par l'Institut d'études islamiques de l'Université de Paris,* 205–24. Paris: G.-P. Maisonneuve, 1950.

Lida de Malkiel, María Rosa. "Túbal, primer poblador de España." *Ábaco* 3 (1970): 9–48.

Lifschitz, Felice. "Beyond Positivism and Genre: 'Hagiographical' Texts as Historical Narrative." *Viator* 25 (1994): 95–113.

Livy. *The Rise of Rome: Books One to Five.* Translated by T. J. Luce. New York: Oxford University Press, 1998.

Lleó Cañal, Vicente. *Nueva Roma: mitología y humanismo en el Renacimiento sevillano.* Seville: Diputación Provincial de Sevilla, 1979.

López Andrés, Jesús María. *Real patronato eclesiástico y estado moderno. La Iglesia de Almería en época de los Reyes Católicos.* Almería: Instituto de Estudios Almerienses, 1995.

López de Coca Castañer, José Enrique. "Judíos, judeoconversos y reconciliados en el reino de Granada a raíz de su conquista." *Gibralfaro* 29 (1978): 7–22.

———. "El trabajo de mudéjares y moriscos en el reino de Granada." In *VI Simposio Internacional de Mudejarismo: Teruel, 16–18 de septiembre de 1993: Actas,* 97–136. Zaragoza: Centro de Estudios Mudéjares, Instituto de Estudios Turolenses, 1995.

López Gómez, Juan Estanislao. *La procesión del "Corpus Christi" de Toledo.* Toledo: Diputación Provincial de Toledo, 1993.

López Guzmán, Rafael. *Tradición y clasicismo en la Granada del XVI. Arquitectura civil y urbanismo.* Granada: Diputación Provincial de Granada, 1987.

López Madera, Gregorio. *Discursos de la certidumbre de las reliquias descubiertas en Granada desde el año de 1588 hasta el de 1598.* Granada, 1601.

———. *Historia y discursos de la certidumbre de las reliquias, laminas y prophecía descubiertas en el Monte Santo, y Yglesia de Granada, desde el año mil y quinientos y ochenta y ocho, hasta el de mil y quinientos y noventa y ocho.* Granada, 1602.

López Martín, Juan. "El concilio provincial de Granada de 1565 y sus provisiones sobre los moriscos del reino de Granada." *Anthológica Annua* 36 (1989): 509–41.

———. *La Iglesia en Almería y sus obispos.* Vol. 1. Almería: Instituto de Estudios Almerienses, Caja Rural de Almería, Unicaja, 1999.

López Muñoz, Miguel Luis. *Las cofradías de la Parroquia de Santa María Magdalena de Granada en los siglos XVII y XVIII.* Granada: Universidad de Granada, 1992.

———. "Contrarreforma y cofradías en Granada. Aproximación a la historia de las cofradías y hermandades de la ciudad de Granada durante los siglos XVII y XVIII." Ph.D. diss., Universidad de Granada, 1992.

López Nevot, José Antonio. *La organización institucional del municipio de Granada durante el siglo XVI (1492–1598)*. Granada: Universidad de Granada, 1994.

López Rodríguez, Miguel A. *Los arzobispos de Granada. Retratos y semblanzas*. Granada: Arzobispado de Granada, 1993.

———. "Cátedras de Teología, Cánones y Sagrada Escritura de la Antigua Universidad de Granada, anejas a prebendas eclesiásticas (1526–1776)." *Archivo teológico granadino* 50 (1987): 185–320.

———. "El colegio de los niños moriscos de Granada." *Miscelánea de estudios árabes y hebraicos* 25 (1976): 32–68.

———. *El Colegio Real de Santa Cruz de la Fe de Granada*. Salamanca: Universidad de Salamanca, 1979.

———. "Don Pedro de Castro y la Universidad de Granada." *Boletín de la Universidad de Granada* 33, nos. 109–10 (1974–75): 5–28.

López-Baralt, Luce. "Crónica de la destrucción de un mundo: la literatura aljamiado-morisca." *Bulletin hispanique* 82 (1980): 16–58.

López-Huertas Pérez, María José. *Bibliografía de impresos granadinos de los siglos XVII y XVIII*. 3 vols. Granada: Universidad de Granada, 1998.

López-Morillas, Consuelo. *The Qur'ān in Sixteenth-Century Spain: Six Morisco Versions of Sūra 79*. London: Tamesis, 1982.

Lowenthal, David. "Fabricating Heritage." *History and Memory* 10 (1998): 5–24.

———. *The Heritage Crusade and the Spoils of History*. New York: Viking, 1997.

———. *The Past Is a Foreign Country*. Cambridge: Cambridge University Press, 1985.

Luna, Miguel de. *La verdadera hystoria del rey don Rodrigo en la qual se trata la causa principal de la perdida de España y la conquista que della hizo Miramamolin Almançor rey que fue del África, y de las Arabias compuesta por el sabio Alcayde Abulcacim Tarif Abentarique, de nación Árabe, y natural de Arabia Petrea*. Granada, 1592.

Luque Moreno, Jesús. "Granada en la poesía de Juan de Vilches." In *Clasicismo y humanismo en el Renacimiento granadino*, edited by José González Vázquez, Manuel López Muñoz, and Juan Jesús Valverde Abril, 185–206. Granada: Universidad de Granada, 1996.

———. *Granada en el siglo XVI. Juan de Vilches y otros testimonios de la época*. Granada: Universidad de Granada, 1994.

MacKay, Angus. "Ritual and Propaganda in Fifteenth-Century Castile." *Past and Present* 107 (1985): 3–43.

MacKay, Ruth. *The Limits of Royal Authority: Resistance and Obedience in Seventeenth-Century Castile*. Cambridge: Cambridge University Press, 1999.

Madriz, Francisco de Paula de la. *Sermón en la acción de gracias de la Toma de Granada*. Granada, 1669.

Magnier, Grace. "The Dating of Pedro de Valencia's *Sobre el pergamino y láminas de Granada*." *Sharq al-Andalus* 14–15 (1997–98): 353–73.

Mâle, Émile. *L'art religieux de la fin du XVIe siècle, du XVIIe siècle et du XVIIIe siècle; étude sur l'iconographie après le Concile de Trente*. 2d ed. Paris: Librairie Armand Colin, 1951.

Manca, Gavino. *Relación de la invención de los cuerpos de los santos mártires S. Gavino, san*

Proto, y san Ianuario, patrones de la Yglesia Metropolitana Turritana Sacer en Serdeña, y de otros muchos que se hallaron el año de 1614. Madrid, 1615.

Mansi, J. D. *Sacrorum conciliorum nova et amplissima collectio.* Vol. 2. Florence, 1759.

Manuale sacramentorum secundum consuetudinem sanctae ecclesiae Garnatensis accuratissime emendatum. Granada, 1543.

Maravall, José Antonio. *Culture of the Baroque: Analysis of a Historical Structure.* Translated by Terry Cochran. Minneapolis: University of Minneapolis Press, 1983.

Marcos Martín, Alberto. "Percepciones materiales e imagenario urbano en la España moderna." In *Imágenes de la diversidad. El mundo urbano en la Corona de Castilla (s. XVI–XVIII),* edited by José Ignacio Fortea Pérez, 15–50. Santander: Universidad de Cantabria, 1997.

Marías, Fernando. *El largo siglo XVI. Los usos artísticos del renacimiento español.* Madrid: Taurus, 1989.

Marieta, Juan de. *Catálogo de los obispos y arçobispos de Granada.* Madrid, 1602.

Marín de Rodezno, Francisco. *Decisio Granatensis tribunalis Sancti Oficii in causa famosi libelli, adversus sacrosanctam Iesu Christi legem, & incorruptam Deiparae Virginitatem, perpetuoque florentem pudicitiam publice affixi.* Granada, 1641.

Marín López, Rafael. *El Cabildo de la catedral de Granada en el siglo XVI.* Granada: Universidad de Granada, 1998.

———. "La Iglesia y el encuadramiento religioso." In *Historia del reino de Granada,* vol. 1, *De los orígenes a la época mudéjar (hasta 1502),* edited by Rafael G. Peinado Santaella, 661–86. Granada: Universidad de Granada, Legado Andalusí, 2000.

———. "Un memorial de 1594 del arzobispo de Granada don Pedro de Castro sobre su Iglesia con motivo de la visita *ad limina." Revista del Centro de Estudios Históricos de Granada y su Reino* 7 (1993): 227–306.

Marín Ocete, Antonio. *El arzobispo don Pedro Guerrero y la política conciliar española en el siglo XVI.* Madrid: CSIC, 1970.

———. "El Concilio provincial de Granada en 1565." *Archivo teológico granadino* 25 (1962): 23–95.

———. *Gregorio Silvestre. Estudio biográfico y crítico.* Granada: Facultad de Letras, 1939.

———. *El negro Juan Latino. Ensayo biográfico y crítico.* Granada: Librería Guevara, 1925.

Mármol Carvajal, Luis del. *Historia del rebelión y castigo de los moriscos del reino de Granada.* Málaga, 1600. Reprint. Edited by Ángel Galán. Madrid: Editorial Arguval, 1991.

Marocchi, Massimo. "L'immagine della Chiesa in Carlo Borromeo." In *Carlo Borromeo e l'opera della "grande riforma." Cultura, religione e arti del governo nella Milano del pieno Cinquecento,* edited by Franco Buzzi and Danilo Zardin, 207–30. Milan: Credito Artigiano, 1997.

Márquez Villanueva, Francisco. "La voluntad de leyenda de Miguel de Luna." In *El problema morisco (desde otras laderas),* 45–97. Madrid: Libertarias/Prodhufi, 1991.

Martín Casares, Aurelia. *La esclavitud en la Granada del siglo XVI: género, raza y religión.* Granada: Universidad de Granada, 2000.

Martín Hernández, Francisco. *Un seminario español pretridentino, el Real Colegio Eclesiástico de San Cecilio de Granada (1492–1842).* Valladolid: Universidad de Valladolid, 1960.

Martín Pradas, Antonio, and Inmaculada Carrasco Gómez. "Datos biográficos inéditos so-

bre el Padre Martín de Roa." In *Luis Vélez de Guevara y su época*, edited by Piedad Bolaños Donoso and Marina Martín Ojeda, 379–83. Seville: Fundación El Monte, 1996.

Martinelli, Serena Spanò. "Cultura umanistica, polemica antiprotestante, erudizione sacra
nell 'De probatis Sanctorum historiis' di Lorenzo Surio." In *Raccolte di vite di santi dal
XIII al XVIII secolo. Strutture, messaggi, fruizioni,* edited by Sofia Boesch Gajano, 131–
41. Fasano di Brindisi: Schena, 1990.

Martínez, Sebastián. *Las partidas de la gran ciudad de Granada en metro o en manera de perque
. . . con un villancico.* N.p., 1550.

Martínez de Buendía, Francisco. *Noticia breve de la vida, y hechos del gloriosíssimo S. Gregorio Iliberitano, llamado el Bético, primero de este nombre, en lo primitivo de la Iglesia Católica,
y fundamentos de la immemorial tradición de el patronato que obiene de la ciudad de
Granada, y de las excelencias de el sitio de su iglesia.* Granada, 1693.

Martínez de la Escalera, José. "Jerónimo de la Higuera S.J.: falso cronicones, historia de
Toledo, culto de San Tirso." In *Tolède et l'expansion urbaine en Espagne (1450–1650): actes
du colloque,* 69–97. Madrid: Casa de Velázquez, 1991.

Martínez Medina, Francisco Javier. *Cultura religiosa en la Granada renacentista y barroca. Estudio iconológico.* Granada: Universidad de Granada, 1989.

———. "Los hallazgos del Sacromonte a la luz de la historia de la Iglesia y de la teología
católica." *Al-Qanṭara* 23, no. 2 (2002): 437–75.

———. "La Iglesia." In *Historia del reino de Granada,* vol. 2, *La época morisca y la repoblación,*
edited by Manuel Barrios Aguilera, 251–307. Granada: Universidad de Granada, Legado
Andalusí, 2000.

———. "Los libros plúmbeos del Sacromonte de Granada." In *Jesucristo y el emperador cris-
tiano: catálogo de la exposición celebrada en la catedral de Granada con motivo del año ju-
bilar de la encarnación de Jesucristo y del V centenario del nacimiento del emperador Carlos,*
edited by Francisco Javier Martínez Medina, 619–43. Córdoba: Cajasur, 2000.

———. "El Sacromonte de Granada y los discursos Inmaculistas postridentinos." *Archivo
teológico granadino* 59 (1996): 5–57.

———. "El Sacromonte de Granada, un intento de reinculturación entre la guerra de los
moriscos y su definitiva expulsión," *Chronica Nova* 25 (1998): 349–79.

———. *San Cecilio y San Gregorio. Patronos de Granada.* Granada: Editorial Comares, 2001.

Martínez Ruiz, Emilia. "Fundación y constituciones de la Hermandad del Santo Rosario de
Nuestra Señora del Triunfo de Granada en 1698." *Chronica Nova* 18 (1990): 415–45.

Martínez Ruiz, Juan. "Cartas de Thomas van Erpen (Thomas Erpenius) en un Archivo de
Granada (1623–1624)." *Boletín de la Real Academia Española* 55 (1975): 265–306.

———. "Cartas inéditas de Bernardo J. de Aldrete (1608–1626)." *Boletín de la Real Academia Española* 50 (1970): 77–135, 277–314, 471–515.

Martínez Torres, José Antonio, and Enrique García Ballesteros. "Gregorio López Madera
(1562–1649): un jurista al servicio de la Corona." *Torre de los Lujanes* 37 (1998): 163–78.

Martz, Linda. "Toledanos and the Kingdom of Granada, 1492–1560s." In *Spain, Europe and
the Atlantic World,* edited by Richard L. Kagan and Geoffrey Parker, 103–24. Cambridge:
Cambridge University Press, 1995.

Mateos Royo, José Antonio. "All the Town Is a Stage: Civic Ceremonies and Religious Festivities in Spain during the Golden Age." *Urban History* 26 (1999): 165–89.

Mayáns y Siscár, Gregorio. *Orígenes de la lengua española*. 2 vols. Madrid, 1737.

Medina, Pedro de. *Libro de las grandezas y cosas memorables de España. Libro de la verdad.* Seville, 1548. Reprint. Edited by Ángel González Palencia. Madrid: CSIC, 1944.

Medina Conde, Cristóbal de. *El fingido Dextro convencido de tal por su pluma, o descubierto con su misma mano*. Málaga, 1772.

Melion, Walter S. "*Ad ductum itineris et dispositionem mansionum ostendendam:* Meditation, Vocation, and Sacred History in Abraham Ortelius's *Parergon*." *Journal of the Walters Art Gallery* 57 (1999): 49–72.

Memon, Muhammad Umar. *Ibn Taimīya's Struggle against Popular Religion: With an Annotated Translation of his Kitāb iqtiḍā' aṣ-ṣirāṭ al-mustaquīm mukhālafat aṣḥāb al-jaḥīim*. The Hague: Mouton, 1976.

Memoria de las grandes maravillas que nuestro Redemtor Iesu Christo ha sido servido de descubrir en el termino de la dichosa ciudad de Granada. Baeza, [1595?].

Memorial histórico español. Vol. 19. Madrid: Imprenta Nacional, 1865.

Memorial sumario de algunas relaciones que de varias provincias, ciudades y lugares, se han embiado, en que se refieren algunos escándalos que han passado en defensa de las opiniones de la Concepción de nuestra Señora. N.p., [1616].

Méndez, Francisco. *Noticias sobre la vida, escritos y viajes del rmo. p. mtro, fr. Enrique Florez*. 2d ed. Madrid: Impr. de J. Rodriguez, 1860.

Mendoza, Fernando de. *De confirmando Concilio Illiberitano*. Madrid, 1594.

———. *La defensa y aprovación del Concilio Illiberritano*. Madrid, 1594.

Mendoza, Rocío. "Vecinos del Albaicín rechazan una pintada aparecida ayer contra la nueva mezquita." *El Ideal*, August 19, 2003.

Mendyk, Stan. *Speculum Britanniae: Regional Study, Antiquarianism, and Science in Britain to 1700*. Toronto: University of Toronto, 1989.

Menéndez y Pelayo, Marcelino. *Biblioteca de traductores españoles*. Vol. 1. Edited by Enrique Sánchez Reyes. Santander: Aldus, 1952.

———. *Historia de los heterodoxos españoles*. 4th ed. Vol. 2. Madrid: Biblioteca de Autores Españoles, 1987.

Meseguer Fernández, Juan. "La Real Junta de la Inmaculada Concepción (1616–1817/20)." *Archivo Ibero-Americano* época 2, no. 15 (1955): 3–248.

Middleton, David, and Derek Edwards. Introduction to *Collective Remembering*, edited by David Middleton and Derek Edwards, 1–22. London: Sage Publications, 1990.

Mitchell, Timothy. *Passional Culture: Emotion, Religion, and Society in Southern Spain*. Philadelphia: University of Pennsylvania Press, 1990.

Momigliano, Arnaldo. "Ancient History and the Antiquarian." *Journal of the Warburg and Courtauld Institutes* 13 (1950): 285–315.

Moner, Michael. "Los 'libros plúmbeos' de Granada y su influencia en el *Quijote*." *Ínsula* 538 (1991): 29–30.

Morales, Ambrosio. *La vida, el martyrio, la invención, las grandezas y las translaciones de los . . . niños mártyres San Iusto y Pastor y el solemne triumpho con que fueron recebidas sus santas reliquias en Alcalá de Henares*. Alcalá de Henares, 1568.

Morales Hondonero Castillo y Salazar, Juan de. *Ceremonias que esta ciudad de Granada ha de observar, y guardar en las ocasiones que se le ofrezcan, assí en su sala capitular, como en las funciones públicas*. Granada, 1752.

Moreno Garrido, Antonio. "El grabado en Granada a fines del siglo XVI: los descubrimientos del Sacromonte y su reproducción." *Cuadernos de arte de la Universidad de Granada* 20 (1989): 101–9.

———. "El grabado en Granada durante el siglo XVII. I. La calcografía." *Cuadernos de arte de la Universidad de Granada* 13 (1976).

———. *La iconografía de la Inmaculada en el grabado granadino del siglo XVII.* Madrid: Fundación Universitaria Española, 1986.

———. "La iconografía de la Virgen de la Antigua en el grabado granadino del siglo XVII: una plancha inédita de Ana Heylan." *Cuadernos de arte de la Universidad de Granada* 21 (1990): 205–10.

Moreno Garrido, Antonio, José Manuel Gómez-Moreno Calera, and Rafael López Guzmán. "La Plataforma de Ambrosio de Vico: cronología y gestación." *Arquitectura de Andalucía Oriental* 2 (1984): 6–11.

Moreno Olmedo, María Angustias. *Heráldica y genealogía granadinas.* 2d ed. Granada: Universidad de Granada, 1989.

Morocho Gayo, Gaspar. "Pedro de Valencia en la historia de la traducción del *Pergamino* y *Láminas* de Granada." *Livius* 2 (1992): 107–37.

Muir, Edward. *Civic Ritual in Renaissance Venice.* Princeton, N.J.: Princeton University Press, 1981.

Münzer, Hieronymus. *Viaje por España y Portugal (1494–1495).* Madrid: Ediciones Polifemo, 1991.

Muñoz y Morales, José. *La nombrada y gran ciudad de Granada coronada . . . en su celeberrima Toma.* Murcia, 1780.

Nader, Helen. "'The Greek Commander' Hernán Núñez de Toledo, Spanish Humanist and Civic Leader." *Renaissance Quarterly* 31 (1978): 463–85.

———. *The Mendoza Family in the Spanish Renaissance, 1350 to 1550.* New Brunswick, N.J.: Rutgers University Press, 1979.

Nalle, Sara T. "Catholicism in Comparative Perspective: The View from Spain." Paper presented at the annual meeting of the Sixteenth Century Studies Conference, St. Louis, October 29, 1999.

———. *God in La Mancha: Religious Reform and the People of Cuenca, 1500–1650.* Baltimore: Johns Hopkins University Press, 1992.

———. "A Saint for All Seasons: The Cult of San Julián." In *Culture and Control in Counter-Reformation Spain,* edited by Anne J. Cruz and Mary Elizabeth Perry, 25–50. Minneapolis: University of Minnesota Press, 1992.

Narbona Vizcaíno, Rafael. "El Nueve de Octubre. Reseña histórica de una fiesta valenciana (ss. XIV–XX)." *Revista d'història medieval* 5 (1994): 231–90.

Natalibus, Petrus de. *Catalogus sanctorum et gestorum eorum ex diversis voluminibus collectus.* Lyons, 1519.

Natividad, Juan de la. *Coronada historia, descripción laurada, de el mysterioso genesis, y principio augusto de el eximio portento de la gracia, y admiración de el arte la milagrosa imagen María Santíssima de Gracia.* Granada, 1697.

Natividad, Manuel de la. *Encantos, divinos, y humanos de Granada en su restauración y Toma gloriosa.* N.p., [1701].

Navagicro, Andrea. *Il viaggio fatto in Spagna, et in Francia.* Venice, 1563.

Navas, Gaspar Luis de. *Oración panegyrica, del glorioso mártyr y obispo San Cecilio . . .* Granada, 1728.

Nieto Alcaide, Víctor. "El mito de la arquitectura árabe, lo imaginario y el sueño de la ciudad clásica." *Fragmentos* 8–9 (1986): 132–56.

Nora, Pierre. "Between Memory and History: Les Lieux de Mémoire." *Representations* 26 (1989): 7–25.

———, ed. *Les lieux de mémoire.* 7 vols. Paris: Gallimard, 1984–92.

———, ed. *Realms of Memory: Rethinking the French Past.* 3 vols. English language edition edited by Lawrence D. Kritzman, translated by Arthur Goldhammer. New York: Columbia Press, 1996–98.

North, John David. *Horoscopes and History.* London: Warburg Institute, 1985.

Norton, William. *Explorations in the Understanding of Landscape: A Cultural Geography.* New York: Greenwood Press, 1989.

Nos Don Pedro de Castro . . . Arçobispo de Granada . . . Aviendo tratado de las reliquias . . . fallamos . . . que devemos declarar . . . las dichas reliquias en este proceso contenidas . . . Granada, 1614.

Nuti, Lucia. "The Mapped Views by Georg Hoefnagel: The Merchant's Eye, the Humanist's Eye." *Word and Image* 4, no. 2 (1988): 545–70.

Obra Sierra, Juan María de la. *Mercaderes italianos en Granada, 1508–1512.* Granada: Universidad de Granada, 1992.

———. "Protocolos Notariales. Fuentes para el estudio de la esclavitud: el esclavo extranjero en la Granada de principios del siglo XVI." *Anuario de historia contemporánea* 12 (1985): 5–27.

Officia quae in ecclesia Granatensis, dicenda sunt extra illa quae in Brevario novo continentur. Granada, 1575.

O'Gorman, Edmundo. *The Invention of America: An Inquiry into the Historical Nature of the New World and the Meaning of Its History.* Bloomington: Indiana University Press, 1961.

Olmos y Canalda, Elias. *Los prelados valentinos.* Madrid: CSIC, Instituto Jerónimo Zurita, 1949.

Ollero Pina, José Antonio. "La carrera, los libros y la obsesión del Arzobispo D. Pedro de Castro y Quiñones (1534–1623)." In *De libros y bibliotecas. Homenaje a Rocío Carvajal,* edited by Sonsoles Celestino Angulo, 265–76. Seville: Universidad de Sevilla, 1994.

O'Malley, John W. *Praise and Blame in Renaissance Rome: Rhetoric, Doctrine, and Reform in the Sacred Orators of the Papal Court, c. 1450–1521.* Durham, N.C.: Duke University Press, 1979.

Oracion compuesta por el glorioso apóstol Santiago, patrón de las Españas, la cual traya y se aprobechada de ella en todos sus travajos y adversidades: fue hallada con las reliquias de los santos mártires, sus discípulos, en el Monte Sancto de Granada. [Santiago de Compostela?], 1610.

Ordenanças de la Real Audiencia y Chancillería de Granada. Granada, 1601. Reprint. Granada: Diputación Provincial de Granada, 1997.

Ordenanzas que los muy ilustres, y muy magníficos señores Granada mandaron guardar, para la buena governación de su república, impressas año de 1552. Que se han buelto a imprimir por mandado de los señores presidente, y oydores de la Real Chancillería de esta ciudad de Granada, año 1670. Añadiendo otras que no están impressas. Granada, 1672.

Ordóñez Agulla, Salvador. "El P. Martín de Roa y la historia antigua de Écija." In *Luis Vélez de Guevara y su época,* edited by Piedad Bolaños Donoso and Marina Martín Ojeda, 403–12. Seville: Fundación El Monte, 1996.

Orlandis, José, and Domingo Ramos-Lissón. *Historia de los concilios de la España romana y visigoda.* Pamplona: Ediciones Universidad de Navarra, 1986.

Orozco Díaz, Emilio. *Granada en la poesía barroca. En torno a tres romances inéditos. Comentarios y edición.* Granada: Imprenta Urania, 1963.

———. *El poema "Granada" de Collado del Hierro.* Granada: Patronato de la Alhambra, 1964.

Orozco Pardo, José Luis. *Christianópolis: urbanismo y contrarreforma en la Granada del 600.* Granada: Diputación Provincial de Granada, 1985.

———. "Una fiesta alegórica en Plaza Bibarrambla." *Cuadernos de arte de la Universidad de Granada* 23 (1992): 189–96.

Ortega, Ángel. *La tradición concepcionista en Sevilla, Siglos XVI y XVII: notas histórico-críticas.* Seville: Imprenta San Antonio, 1917.

Orti y Mayor, Joseph Vicente. *Fiestas centenarias, con que la insigne, noble, leal, y coronada ciudad de Valencia celebró en el dia 9 de Octubre de 1738 la quinta centuria de su christiana conquista.* Valencia, 1740.

Ortiz de Zúñiga, Diego. *Anales eclesiásticos y seculares de la muy noble y muy leal ciudad de Sevilla.* Edited by Antonio María Espinosa y Carzel. Madrid, 1796. Reprint. Seville: Guadalquivir Ediciones, 1988.

Osorio Pérez, María José, María Amparo Moreno Trujillo, and Juan María de la Obra Sierra. *Trastiendas de la cultura: librerías y libreros en la Granada del siglo XVI.* Granada: Universidad de Granada, 2001.

Pacheco, Francisco. *Libro de descripción de verdaderos retratos, de ilustres y memorables varones.* Seville, 1599. Reprint. Edited by Pedro M. Piñero Ramírez and Rogelio Reyes Cano. Seville: Diputación Provincial de Sevilla, 1985.

Paracuellos Cabeza de Vaca, Luis. *Triunfales celebraciones, que en aparatos magestuosos consagró religiosa la ciudad de Granada, a honor de la pureza virginal de María Santíssima en sus desagravios, a quien devota las dedica esta ciudad, en todo ilustre, en todo grande.* Granada, 1640.

Parrilla de Torres, Luis. *María desagraviada o oración evangélica contra el libelo que perfidos hereges opusieron a su pureza virginal.* Granada, 1640.

Pasqual y Orbaneja, Gabriel. *Vida de San Indalecio: y Almería ilustrada en su antigüedad, orígen, y grandeza.* Almería, 1699.

Peinado Santaella, Rafael G., ed. *De Ilurco a Pinos Puente. Poblamiento, economía y sociedad de un pueblo de la vega de Granada.* Granada: Diputación Provincial de Granada, 1998.

———. "La sociedad repobladora: el control y la distribución del espacio." In *Historia del reino de Granada,* vol. 1, *De los orígenes a la época mudéjar (hasta 1502),* edited by Rafael G. Peinado Santaella, 477–524. Granada: Universidad de Granada, Legado Andalusí, 2000.

Peinado Santaella, Rafael G., and Enrique Soria Mesa. "Crianza real y clientelismo nobilario: los Bobadilla, una familia de la oligarquía granadina." *Meridies* 1 (1994): 139–60.

Perceval, José María. *Todos son uno. Arquetipos, xenofobia y racismo. La imagen del morisco en la Monarquía Española durante los siglos XVI y XVII.* Almería: Instituto de Estudios Almerienses, 1999.

Perea, Andrés de. *Sermón en común de martyres, y del glorioso San Thesiphon, uno de los tres patronos del Santo Monte de Granada.* Granada, 1610.

Peregrín Pardo, Cristina, and Cristina Viñes Millet, eds. *La imprenta en Granada.* Granada: Universidad de Granada, 1997.

Pérez Boyero, Enrique. "Los mudéjares granadinos: conversiones voluntarias al cristianismo (1482–1499)." In *Actas del II Congreso de Historia de Andalucía. Historia Medieval,* 1:381–92. Córdoba: Junta de Andalucía, Cajasur, 1994.

———. "Los señoríos y el mundo rural." In *Historia del reino de Granada,* vol. 1, *De los orígenes a la época mudéjar (hasta 1502),* edited by Rafael G. Peinado Santaella, 567–610. Granada: Universidad de Granada, Legado Andalusí, 2000.

Pérez de Colosia, María Isabel. "La Inquisición: estructura y actuación." In *Historia del reino de Granada,* vol. 2, *La época morisca y la repoblación,* edited by Manuel Barrios Aguilera, 309–55. Granada: Universidad de Granada, Legado Andalusí, 2000.

Pérez de Hita, Ginés. *Guerras civiles de Granada: Primera Parte.* Zaragoza, 1595. Edited by Shasta M. Bryant. Newark, Del.: Juan de la Cuesta, 1982.

Pérez Moreda, Vicente. "The Plague in Castile at the End of the Sixteenth Century and Its Consequences." In *The Castilian Crisis of the Seventeenth Century: New Perspectives on the Economic and Social History of Seventeenth-Century Spain,* edited by I. A. A. Thompson and Bartolomé Yun Casalilla, 32–59. Cambridge: Cambridge University Press, 1994.

Pérez Pastor, Cristóbal. *Bibliografía madrileña.* Vol. 3. Madrid: Tip. de los Huérfanos, 1907.

Pescador del Hoyo, María del Carmen. "Cómo fué de verdad la toma de Granada, a la luz de un documento inédito." *Al-Andalus* 20 (1955): 283–344.

Phillips, Carla Rahn. *Ciudad Real, 1500–1750: Growth, Crisis, and Readjustment in the Spanish Economy.* Cambridge: Harvard University Press, 1979.

Pike, Ruth. *Aristocrats and Traders: Sevillian Society in the Sixteenth Century.* Ithaca: Cornell University Press, 1972.

Pizaño de Palacios, Álvaro. *Segundo discurso en confirmación de la Concepción Puríssima de la Virgen y Madre de Dios . . .* Seville, 1616.

Polman, Pontien. *L'élément historique dans la controverse religieuse du XVIe siècle.* Gembloux: J. Duculot, 1932.

Porcel y Salablanca, José de. *Gozo, y corona de Granada, en la proclamación solemne, que del rey nuestro señor don Carlos Tercero celebró esta ciudad con la pompa, que se describe, el día 20 de enero de 1760.* Granada, 1760.

Poska, Allyson M. *Regulating the People: The Catholic Reformation in Seventeenth-Century Spain.* Leiden: Brill, 1998.

Pou y Martí, José María. "Embajadas de Felipe III a Roma pidiendo la definición de la Inmaculada Concepción." *Archivo Ibero-Americano* 34 (1931): 371–419, 508–34; 35 (1932): 72–88, 424–34, 481–525; 36 (1933): 5–48.

Pulido Serrano, José Ignacio. "La fe desatada en devoción: proyección pública de la Inquisición en Granada (1640)." *Torre de los Lujanes* 40 (1999): 95–108.

Quesada, Santiago. *La idea de ciudad en la cultura hispana en la edad moderna*. Barcelona: Universitat de Barcelona, 1992.

[Quintanadueñas, Antonio de]. *Gloriosos mártyres de Ossuna, Arcadio, Leon, Donato, Niceforo, Abundancio, y nueve compañeros suyos*. Seville, 1632.

Ramírez Arellano, R. *Ensayo de un catálogo biográfico de los escritores de la provincia y diócesis de Córdoba, con descripción de sus obras*. Vol. 1. Madrid, 1921.

Ramos Gavilán, Esteban. *Oración panegyrica en las memorias que al invicto rey Don Fernando el Católico dedican todos los años los señores del Real Acuerdo, y del tribunal santo de la Inquisición, en la Capilla Real de Granada a 23 de enero, día en que murió*. Granada, 1666.

Ramos López, José de. *Breve reseña de la tradicional capilla denominada la Cárcel de San Cecilio, existente en el Albaicín, y de la reparación del piadoso local, verificada en 1891 por el cura económo de Nuestro Salvador, Don Juan Rivero Palomares*. Granada: Est. Tipográfica de R. Calero, 1897.

———. *El Sacro-Monte de Granada*. Madrid: Imprenta de Fortanet, 1883.

Ranum, Orest, ed. *National Consciousness, History, and Political Culture in Early-Modern Europe*. Baltimore: Johns Hopkins University Press, 1975.

Rapin, René. *Instructions for History: With a Character of the Most Considerable Historians, Ancient and Modern*. Translated by John Davies. London, 1680.

Recibimiento i fiesta que la ciudad de Granada, con sus dos cabildos, corregidor, veyntiquatros, y las demás gente della, hizieron al Illustríssimo señor don Pedro de Castro y Quiñones Arçobispo de Sevilla . . . Sacado de cartas que algunas personas graves de aquella ciudad, escriven a ésta de Sevilla. Seville, 1618.

Recío, Alejandro. "La Inmaculada en la predicación franciscano-española." *Archivo Ibero-Americano* época 2, no. 15 (1955): 105–200.

Reder Gadow, Marion. "¿Conmemoración política o religiosa? La fiesta de San Luis en Málaga." In *Religión y cultura*, vol. 1, edited by Salvador Rodríguez Becerra, 637–46. Seville: Junta de Andalucía, Fundación Machado, 1999.

Redondo, Agustín. "Légendes généalogiques et parentés fictives en Espagne au Siècle d'Or." In *Les parentés fictives en Espagne, XVIe–XVIIe siècles: colloque international, Sorbonne, 15, 16 et 17 mai 1986*, edited by Agustín Redondo, 15–35. Paris: Publications de la Sorbonne, 1988.

Reglas y estatutos de la illustríssima Hermandad de la Maestrança de la ciudad de Granada. Granada, n.d.

Relación breve de las reliquias, que se hallaron en la ciudad de Granada en una torre antiquíssima, y en las cavernas del monte Illipulitano de Valparaíso cerca de Granada: sacado del processo, y averigüaciones, que cerca dello se hizieron. Granada, 1608.

Relación breve de las reliquias que se hallaron en la ciudad de Granada en una torre antiquíssima, y en las cavernas del monte Illipulitano de Valparayso cerca de la ciudad: sacado del processo y averigüaciones, que cerca dello se hizieron. Granada, 1614; Granada, 1617.

Relación cierta y verdadera de la invención de las reliquias y libros que se hallaron en las cavernas del monte de Valparaíso, cerca de la ciudad de Granada, y de las que se hallaron en la torre vieja de la iglesia mayor, sacada del proceso y de las averigüaciones que cerca della se hizieron. Granada, 1598.

Relación de la grande autoridad y certeza de las reliquias del Sacro Monte. N.p., n.d.

Relación de la grandiosa fiesta que hizo la ciudad de Granada, domingo, 13 de mayo de 1640 al desagravio de la limpia, y pura concepción de la sacratíssima Virgen nuestra Señora. Barcelona, 1640.

Relación y memorial sacado de las ynformaciones que se an hecho, acerca de los prodigios, y maravillas que se an visto al pie de la muralla y torres del Alacaçar de la villa de Arjona, diocesis de Iaén, y en los huessos y cenizas que allí se hallaron. Jaén, 1630.

Rey Castelao, Ofelia. *La historiografía del Voto de Santiago. Recopilación crítica de una polémica histórica.* Santiago de Compostela: Universidad de Santiago de Compostela, 1985.

Riding, Alan. "Pride in Spain's Islamic Roots Is Blooming Again." *New York Times,* March 1, 1993, A4.

Riera i Sans, Jaume. "La invenció literària de sant Pere Pasqual." *Caplletra* 1 (1986): 45–60.

Río Barredo, María José del. *Madrid, urbs regia. La capital ceremonial de la Monarquía Católica.* Madrid: Marcial Pons, 2000.

Roa, Martin de. *Flos sanctorum: fiestas, i santos naturales de la ciudad de Córdova.* Seville, 1615.

———. *Málaga su fundación, su antigüedad eclesiástica i seglar, sus santos Ciriaco i Paula mártires: S Luis Obispo, sus patronos.* Málaga, 1622. Reprint. Málaga: El Guadalhorce, 1960.

Roca Roumens, Mercedes, Maria Auxiliadora Moreno Onorato, and Rafael Licano Preste. *El Albaicín y los orígenes de la ciudad de Granada.* Granada: Universidad de Granada, 1988.

Rodríguez Becerra, Salvador. "La toma de Zahara: antropología histórica de una comunidad fronteriza en la baja Edad Media." In *Las tomas: antropología histórica de la ocupación territorial del reino de Granada,* edited by José Antonio González Alcantud and Manuel Barrios Aguilera, 137–57. Granada: Diputación Provincial de Granada.

Rodríguez de Ardila, Pedro. *Las honras que celebró la famosa y gran ciudad de Granada . . . en 13 de octubre de 1611.* Granada, 1612.

Rodríguez Escabias, Gabriel. *Discurso apologético por la verdad en defensa de la antigüedad de Granada.* Granada, 1645.

———. *Exortación al herege que puso en la ciudad de Granada Iueves Santo en la noche cinco de abril del año de mil y seis cientos y quarenta un papel contra nuestra santa fe católica.* Granada, 1640.

Rodríguez Marín, Francisco. *Luis Barahona de Soto. Estudio biográfico, bibliográfico y crítico.* Madrid: Estab. Tip. "Sucesores de Rivadenryra," 1903.

Rodríguez Mediano, Fernando, and Mercedes García-Arenal. "Diego de Urrea y algún traductor más: en torno a las versiones de los 'plomos.'" *Al-Qanṭara* 23, no. 2 (2002): 499–516.

Rojas Villandrando, Agustín de. *El viaje entretenido.* Madrid, 1603. Reprint. Edited by Jacques Joset. Madrid: Espasa-Calpe, 1977.

Roldán Hervás, José Manuel. *Granada romana: el municipio latino de Iliberri*. Granada: Editorial Don Quijote, 1983.

———. *Historia de Granada*. Vol. 1, *De las primeras culturas al Islam*. Granada: Editorial Don Quijote, 1983.

Ron de la Bastida, C. "Manuscritos árabes en la Inquisición granadina (1582)." *Al-Andalus* 23 (1958): 210–13.

Ros, Carlos. *La Inmaculada y Sevilla*. Seville: Editorial Castillejo, 1994.

Rosenthal, Earl E. *The Cathedral of Granada: A Study in the Spanish Renaissance*. Princeton, N.J.: Princeton University Press, 1961.

———. *The Palace of Charles V in Granada*. Princeton, N.J.: Princeton University Press, 1985.

Rothstein, Marian. "Etymology, Genealogy, and the Immutability of Origins." *Renaissance Quarterly* 43, no. 3 (1990): 332–47.

Rowland, Ingrid D. *The Scarith of Scornello: A Tale of Renaissance Forgery*. Chicago: University of Chicago Press, 2004.

Royo Campos, Zótico. *Abades del Sacromonte*. Granada, 1964.

———. *Albores del Sacro Monte, o, vida de San Cecilio*. Granada: Abadía del Sacro-Monte, 1958.

———. *Bellezas sacromontanas*. Granada, 1967.

———. *El Insigne Colegio-Seminario del Sacro-Monte y la Universidad de Granada*. Granada, 1951.

———. *Reliquias martiriales y escudo del Sacromonte*. Granada: Abadía del Sacro-Monte, 1960. Reprint. Edited by Miguel Luis López Muñoz, Granada: Universidad de Granada, 1995.

Rubiera Mata, M. J. "La mesa de Salomón." *Awrāq* 3 (1980): 26–31.

Rubio García, Luis. *La procesión de Corpus en el siglo XV en Murcia*. Murcia: Academia Alfonso X el Sabio, 1987.

Rubio Lapaz, Jesús. *Pablo de Céspedes y su círculo: humanismo y contrarreforma en la cultura andaluza del renacimiento al barroco*. Granada: Universidad de Granada, 1993.

Ruíz, Teófilo. "Unsacred Monarchy: The Kings of Castile in the Late Middle Ages." In *Rites of Power: Symbolism, Ritual and Politics since the Middle Ages*, edited by Sean Wilentz, 109–44. Philadelphia: University of Pennsylvania Press, 1985.

Ruiz Ibáñez, José Javier. *Las dos caras de Jano. Monarquía, ciudad e individuo. Murcia, 1588–1648*. Murcia: Universidad de Murcia, 1995.

Ruiz Martín, Felipe. "Movimientos demográficos y económicos en el reino de Granada durante la segunda mitad del siglo XVI." *Anuario de historia económica y social* 1, no. 1 (1968): 127–83.

Ruiz Povedano, José María. "Las ciudades y el poder municipal." In *Historia del reino de Granada*, vol. 1, *De los orígenes a la época mudéjar (hasta 1502)*, edited by Rafael G. Peinado Santaella, 611–60. Granada: Universidad de Granada, Legado Andalusí, 2000.

———. "Las élites de poder en las ciudades del Reino de Granada." In *Las ciudades andaluzas (siglos XIII–XVI): actas del VI Coloquio Internacional de Historia Medieval de Andalucía*, edited by José E. López de Coca Castañer and Ángel Galán Sánchez, 357–415. Málaga: Universidad de Málaga, 1991.

Ruiz Rodríguez, Antonio Ángel. *La Real Chancillería de Granada en el siglo XVI*. Granada: Diputación Provincial de Granada, 1987.

Rus Puerta, Francisco. *Historia eclesiástica del reino y obispado de Jaen*. *Primera Parte*. Jaén, 1634.

"Rutas por Granada." Guía de Granada, <http://www.moebius.es/ii/granada/rutas1.htm# Pie>, accessed September 15, 1999.

Sahlins, Peter. *Boundaries: The Making of France and Spain in the Pyrenees*. Berkeley: University of California Press, 1989.

Sallman, Jean-Michel. *Naples et ses saints à l'âge baroque (1540–1750)*. Paris: Presses Universitaires de France, 1994.

———. "Il santo patron cittadino nell '600 nel Regno di Napoli e in Sicilia." In *Per la storia sociale e religiosa del Mezzogiorno d'Italia*, edited by Giuseppe Galasso and Carla Russo, 187–211. Naples: Guida Editori, 1982.

San Cecilio, Pedro de. *Annales del orden de Descalzos de Nuestra Señora de la Merced redempción de cautivos christianos*. Barcelona, 1669.

———. *Vida y martyrio de D. Fr. Pedro de Valencia obispo de Jaén del Orden de Merced*. Granada, 1629.

Sánchez Ferro, Pablo. "La ciudad en procesión: estudio sobre traslación de reliquias (Centrado en el ejemplo de San Fructos, patrón de Segovia)." *Espacio, Tiempo y Forma*, Serie IV, Historia moderna, 12 (1999): 47–66.

Sánchez Lucero, Gonzalo. *Dos discursos theológicos en defensa de la Immaculada Concepción de la Virgen Santíssima, Madre de Dios y señora nuestra*. Granada, 1608; Madrid, 1614; Seville, 1617.

Sánchez Moguel, Antonio. "El Arzobispo Vaca de Castro y el Abad Gordillo." *Boletín de la Real Academia de la Historia* 16 (1890): 407–19.

Sánchez Ramos, Valeriano. "El culto a San Tesifón en Berja (Almería)." In *Religión y cultura*, vol. 1, edited by Salvador Rodríguez Becerra, 621–35. Seville: Junta de Andalucía, Fundación Machado, 1999.

Sánchez Rivero, Ángel, and Angela Mariutti de Sánchez Rivero, eds. *Viaje de Cosme de Médicis por España y Portugal (1668–1669)*. Madrid: Junta para Ampliación de Estudios e Investigaciones Cieutíficas, 1933.

Sánchez-Montes González, Francisco. *La población granadina del siglo XVII*. Granada: Universidad de Granada, 1989.

Sánchez-Mesa Martín, Domingo. *Técnica de la escultura policromada granadina*. Granada: Universidad de Granada, 1971.

Santacruz Molina, Gerónimo de. *Copia de las reliquias que atesora la Real Capilla de Granada, sepulchro de los señores Reyes Católicos, don Fernando y doña Ysabel*. Granada, 1631.

Santiago Simón, Emilio de. "Algunos datos sobre la posesión de los bienes raíces moriscos en el lugar de Cenes de la Vega de Granada (1572)." *Miscelánea de estudios árabes y hebraicos* 22 (1973): 153–61.

Santissima Trinidad, Jacinto de la. *Granada rendida a nuestra santa fe, ensalzada y ennoblecida por la mano poderosa de Dios . . . sermón panegyrico-historial en la solemnidad annual de la exaltación de la fe*. Granada, 1764.

Santos Urbina y Desfusa, Cecilio [Luis Francisco de Viana y Bustos]. *Disertación eclesiástica crítico-histórica en que el cathólico reyno de Granada vindica la religiosa piedad de su constante culto, a las sagradas antiquíssimas lypsanas, que se hallaron al fin del siglo XVI en la Torre Turpiana, y en el Sacro Monte; advirtiendo el modo único decoroso de leer la bulla de la santidad de Inocencio XI.* Pamplona, 1752.

Schilling, Heinz. "Urban Architecture and Ritual in Confessional Europe." In *Religious Ceremonials and Images: Power and Social Meaning (1400–1750),* edited by José Pedro Pavia, 7–25. Coimbra: Centro de História da Sociedade e da Cultura, European Science Foundation, 2002.

Schneider, Robert A. *The Ceremonial City: Toulouse Observed, 1738–1780.* Princeton, N.J.: Princeton University Press, 1995.

Schreiner, Klaus. "*Maria Patrona.* La Sainte Vierge comme figure symbolique des villes, territoires et nations à la fin du Moyen Âge et au début des temps modernes." In *Identité régionale et conscience nationale en France et en Allemagne du moyen âge à l'époque moderne,* edited by Rainer Babel and Jean-Marie Moeglin, 133–53. Sigmaringen: J. Thorbecke, 1997.

Schwartz, Barry. "The Social Context of Commemoration: A Study in Collective Memory." *Social Forces* 61 (1982): 374–402.

Sciascia, Leonardo. *The Council of Egypt.* Translated by Adrienne Foulke. Manchester: Carcanet, 1988.

Sebastián, Santiago. *Contrarreforma y barroco. Lecturas iconográficas e iconológicas.* Madrid: Alianza, 1989.

Seco de Lucena Paredes, Luis. *La Granada nazarí del siglo XV.* Granada: Patronato de la Alhambra, 1975.

———. "De toponimia granadina. Sobre el viaje de Ibn Baṭṭūṭa al reino de Granada." *Al-Andalus* 16 (1951): 49–85.

Sentencia con que se autorizaron las reliquias de algunos discípulos del apóstol Santiago, en virtud de las láminas del Santo Monte de Granada. Granada, 1600.

Sentencia con que se calificaron las reliquias de doze martyres, que fueron quemados vivos en el Monte Santo de Granada. N.p., n.d.

Señor. El abad, y cabildo de la insigne Iglesia Colegial de el Sacro Monte de Granada, que está a la real protección de V. Magestad, dize: Que aviéndose llevado a Roma los libros de plomos del Sacro Monte, en virtud de breve de su santidad . . . el año de 1642 . . . ha llegado a su noticia, que su santidad ha expedido decreto, en seis de março, que se publicó en veinte y ocho de setiembre del año passado de 1682 condenado dichos libros . . . N.p., n.d.

Señor. El Patronato del Sacro monte de Granada que fundó el arzobispo don Pedro de Castro de su propia hazienda y patrimonio, es de V. Mag. y en el privilegio de aceptación, que fue servido de otorgar ante Iorge de Tobar a diez de mayo de mil y seiscientos y veinte y uno recibió V. Mag. debaxo de su Real protección . . . aquella Iglesia Colegial, libros, y reliquias . . . y prometió V. Mag. por si, y sus sucessores ampararlos . . . N.p., [1630].

[Serna Cantoral, Diego de la]. *Relación breve de las reliquias que se hallaron en la ciudad de Granada, en una torre antiquíssima y en las cavernas del monte Illipulitano de Valparayso cerca de la ciudad: sacado del processo y averigüaciones que cerca dello se hizieron.* 4 vols. [Lyon, 1706].

Serrano y Ortega, Manuel. *Glorias sevillanas. Noticia histórica de la devoción y culto que la muy noble y muy leal ciudad de Sevilla ha profesado a la Inmaculada Concepción de la Virgen María, desde los tiempos de la antigüedad hasta la presente época.* Seville: Imp. de E. Rasco, 1893.

Shaʿrānī, ʿAbd al-Wahhāb ibn Aḥmad. *Vite e detti di santi musulmani.* Edited by Virginia Vacca. Turin: Unione Tipografico-Editrice Torinese, 1968.

Sieber, Diane E. "The Frontier Ballad and Spanish Golden Age Historiography: Recontextualizing the *Guerras Civiles de Granada.*" *Hispanic Review* 65, no. 3 (1997): 291–306.

Sigüenza, José de. *Historia de la Orden de San Jerónimo.* 2d ed. Vol. 2. Edited by Juan Catalina García. Madrid: Bailly Baillière e Hijos, 1909.

Slater, Candace. *City Steeple, City Streets: Saints' Tales from Granada and a Changing Spain.* Berkeley: University of California Press, 1990.

Sluhovsky, Moshe. *Patroness of Paris: Rituals of Devotion in Early Modern France.* Leiden: Brill, 1998.

Smith, Craig S. "Where the Moors Held Sway, Allah Is Praised Again." *New York Times,* October 21, 2003, A4.

Smith, Hilary Dansey. *Preaching in the Spanish Golden Age: A Study of Some Preachers of the Reign of Philip III.* Oxford: Oxford University Press, 1978.

Sommervogel, Carlos. *Bibliothèque des écrivains de la Compagnie de Jésus.* Vol. 7. Paris, 1846.

Soria Mesa, Enrique. "La asimilación de la élite morisca en la Granada cristiana. El ejemplo de la familia Hermes." In *Mélanges Louis Cardaillac,* vol. 2, edited by Abdeljelil Temini, 649–58. Zaghouan: Fondation Temini pour la Recherche Scientifique et l'Information, 1995.

———. "De la conquista a la asimilación. La integración de la aristocracia nazarí en la oligarquía granadina." *Áreas* 14 (1992): 49–64.

———. "Los judeoconversos granadinos en el siglo XVI. Nuevas fuentes, nuevas perspectivas." In *Estudios sobre Iglesia y sociedad en Andalucía en la edad moderna,* edited by Antonio Luis Cortés Peña and Miguel Luis López-Guadalupe, 101–9. Granada: Universidad de Granada, 1999.

———. "Nobles advenedizos. La nobleza del reino de Granada en el siglo XVI." In *Felipe II y el Mediterráneo,* vol. 2, *Los grupos sociales,* edited by Ernest Belenguer Cebrià, 61–75. Madrid: Sociedad Estatal para la Conmemoración de los Centenarios de Felipe II y Carlos V, 1999.

———. *La venta de señoríos en el reino de Granada bajo los Austrias.* Granada: Universidad de Granada, 1995.

———. "Una version genealógica del ansia integradora de la élite morisca: el *Origen de la Casa de Granada.*" *Sharq al-Andalus* 12 (1995): 213–21.

Soriano, Francisco. *Sermón predicado en el convento de S. Francisco de Granada, en la fiesta de la Inmaculada Concepción de la Virgen Nuestra Señora, en su día.* Granada, 1616.

Sosa, Fernando Alfonso de. *Sermón que predicó el Doctor Don Fernando de Sosa en la Yglesia Mayor de Granada, en dos de enero de 1621 a la solemníssima fiesta por aver entregado los moros esta ciudad al Cathólico Rey don Fernando.* Granada, 1622.

Sot, Michel. "La topographie religieuse et la référence aux origines de l'église de Reims au Xe siècle." In *La religion civique à l'époque médiévale et moderne (chrétienté et islam),* edited by André Vauchez, 9–19. Rome: École Française de Rome, 1995.

Soto de Rojas, Pedro. *Desengaño de amor en rimas*. Madrid, 1623.

Sotomayor y Muro, Manuel. *Cultura y picaresca en la Granada de la ilustración. D. Juan de Flores y Oddouz*. Granada: Universidad de Granada, Centro de Estudios Históricos de Granada y su Reino, 1988.

———. "La Iglesia en la España romana." In *Historia de la Iglesia en España*, vol. 1, *La Iglesia en la España romana y visigoda (siglos I–VIII)*, edited by Ricardo García Villoslada, 7–400. Madrid: Biblioteca de Autores Cristianos, 1979.

Spivakovsky, Erika. "The Jewish Presence in Granada." *Journal of Medieval History* 2 (1976): 215–37.

———. *Son of the Alhambra: Don Diego Hurtado de Mendoza, 1504–1575*. Austin: University of Texas Press, 1970.

Stephens, Walter. *Giants in Those Days: Folklore, Ancient History, and Nationalism*. Lincoln: University of Nebraska Press, 1989.

Stewart, Susan. *Crimes of Writing: Problems in the Containment of Representation*. Oxford: Oxford University Press, 1991.

Stratton, Suzanne L. *The Immaculate Conception in Spanish Art*. Cambridge: Cambridge University Press, 1994.

Suárez, Pedro. *Historia del obispado de Guadix y Baza*. Madrid, 1696. Reprint. Edited by Vicente Castañeda. Madrid: Artes Gráficas Arges, 1944.

Suberbiola Martínez, Jesús. "El ocaso de las mezquitas-catedrales del reino de Granada." *Baética* 18 (1996): 315–30.

———. *Real Patronato de Granada. El arzobispo Talavera, la Iglesia y el Estado Moderno (1486–1516). Estudio y documentos*. Granada: Caja General de Ahorros y Monte de Piedad de Granada, 1985.

Surtz, Ronald E. "Morisco Women, Written Texts, and the Valencia Inquisition." *Sixteenth Century Journal* 32, no. 2 (2001): 421–33.

Szmolka Clares, José. "Cofradías y control eclesiástico en la Granada barroca." *Espacio, tiempo y forma*, Serie IV, Historia Moderna 7 (1994): 377–96.

———. "Iñigo López de Mendoza y el humanismo granadino." In *Clasicismo y humanismo en el renacimiento granadino*, edited by José González Vázquez, Manuel López Muñoz, and Juan Jesús Valverde Abril, 103–18. Granada: Universidad de Granada, 1996.

Tapia Garrido, José A. "La costa de los piratas." *Revista de historia militar* 16 (1972): 73–103.

———. *Historia general de Almería y su provincia*. Vol. 8, *Los almerienses del siglo XVI*. Almería: Cajal, 1989.

Tate, Robert B. "Mythology in Spanish Historiography of the Middle Ages and the Renaissance." *Hispanic Review* 22 (1954): 1–18.

Taylor, Bruce. *Structures of Reform: The Mercedarian Order in the Spanish Golden Age*. Leiden: Brill, 2000.

Taylor, Christopher Schurman. *In the Vicinity of the Righteous: Ziyāra and the Veneration of Muslim Saints in Late Medieval Egypt*. Leiden: Brill, 1999.

Tello de Olivares, Luis. *Ciudad symbólica, de doze piedras preciosas, en la toma, y restauración feliz de Granada*. Granada, 1640.

Terrones, Juan. *Sermón predicado en el convento de San Francisco de Granada en la fiesta de la Immaculada Concepción de la Virgen*. Granada, 1616.

Terrones de Robres, Antonio de. *Vida, martyrio, translación, y milagros de san Euphrasio.* Granada, 1657. Reprint. Granada: Diputación de Granada, 1996.

Terrones del Caño, Francisco. *Obras completas.* Edited by Francisco Javier Fuente Fernández. León: Junta de Castilla y Léon, Universidad de León, 2001.

Thompson, I. A. A. "Castile, Spain and the Monarchy: The Political Community from *Patria Natural* to *Patria Nacional.*" In *Spain, Europe and the Atlantic World: Essays in Honour of John H. Elliott,* edited by Richard L. Kagan and Geoffrey Parker, 125–59. Cambridge: Cambridge University Press, 1995.

Torres-Balbas, L. "Rábitas hispanomusulmanas." *Al-Andalus* 13 (1948): 475–91.

Traslado de las constituciones de la Capilla Real de Granada, que dotaron los Cathólicos Reyes don Fernando y doña Ysabel de gloriosa memoria. Granada, 1583.

Trexler, Richard. *Public Life in Renaissance Florence.* New York: Academic Press, 1980.

Trillo y Figueroa, Francisco. *Apologético historial sobre la antigüedad de Granada* (manuscript, 1672). Edited by Encarnación Almenzar Rodríguez. Memoria de licenciatura, Universidad de Granada, 1960–61.

El triunfo del Ave María: comedia famosa de moros y cristianos. Edited by Francisco de Paula Valladar. Granada: Imprenta de El Defensor de Granada, 1909. Reprint. Granada: Impredisur, 1991.

Tuan, Yi-Fu. *Space and Place: The Perspective of Experience.* Minneapolis: University of Minnesota Press, 1977.

Vaca de Castro y Quiñones, Pedro. *Constituciones de el . . . Colegio de Theólogos del señor San Dionysio Areopagita, sito en el Sacro Monte Ilipulitano Monte Valparyso . . . de Granada.* Granada, 1618.

———. *Gnomon seu gubernandi norma abbati, et canonicis Sacri Montis Illipulitani præscripta.* Granada, 1647.

Valenzuela Márquez, Jaime. *Las liturgias del poder. Celebraciones públicas y estrategias persuasivas en Chile colonial (1609–1709).* Santiago, Chile: Centro de Investigaciones Diego Barros Arana, DIBAM, Ediciones LOM, 2001.

van Koningsveld, P. S., and G. A. Wiegers. "The Parchment of the 'Torre Turpiana': The Original Document and Its Early Interpreters." *Al-Qanṭara* 24, no. 2 (2003): 327–58.

Vander Hammen y León, Lorenzo. *Via sacra, su origen, forma, y disposición, y lo que se deve meditar en ella. Principio, fundación, y antigüedad de la Venerable Orden Tercera de Penitencia del Seráfico P. S. Francisco. Excelencias y prerrogativas suyas. Hijos que ha tenido, y indulgencias de que goza.* Granada, 1656.

Vauchez, André. "Patronage des saints et religion civique dans l'Italie communale à la fin du Moyen Age." In *Patronage and Public in the Trecento. Proceeding of the St. Lambrecht Symposium, Abtei St. Lambrecht, Styria, 16–19 July, 1984,* edited by Vincent Moleta, 59–80. Florence: Olschki, 1986.

Vega, A. C. "La venida de san Pablo a España y los Varones Apostólicos." *Boletín de la Real Academia de Historia* 154 (1964): 7–78.

Velázquez de Echevarría, Juan de. *Paseos por Granada y sus contornos.* Granada, 1764. Reprint. 2 vols. Edited by Cristina Viñes Millet. Granada: Universidad de Granada, 1993.

Vergara Gavira, Miguel de. *Verdadera declaración de las monedas antiguas que se han hallado en un edificio antiguo, que se ha descubierto debaxo de tierra en el Alcazava de Granada, por febrero deste año de 1624.* Madrid, 1624.

Vespertino Rodríguez, Antonio, ed. *Leyendas aljamiadas y moriscas sobre personajes bíblicos.* Madrid: Editorial Gredos, 1983.

V. F. "Vecinos del Albaicín critican la proliferación de pintadas xenófobas." *El Ideal,* September 7, 2003.

Viforcos Marinas, María Isabel, and Jesús Paniagua Pérez. *El leonés don Cristóbal Vaca de Castro. Gobernador y organizador del Perú.* Madrid: S. A. Hullera Vasco-Leonesa, 1991.

Viguera Molíns, María Jesús. "La religión y el derecho." In *El reino nazarí de Granada (1232–1492),* vol. 4, *Sociedad, vida y cultura,* edited by María Jesús Viguera Molíns, 155–90. Madrid: Espasa Calpe, 2000.

Vilar, Jean. "Formes et tendances de l'opposition sous Olivares: Lisón y Viedma, defensor de la patria." *Mélanges de la Casa de Velázquez* 7 (1971): 263–94.

Vilar Sánchez, Juan Antonio. *1526, boda y luna de miel del emperador Carlos V: la visita imperial a Andalucía y el reino de Granada.* Granada: Universidad de Granada, Real Maestranza de Caballería de Granada, 2000.

Villanueva Rico, María del Carmen, ed. *Habices de las mezquitas de la ciudad de Granada y sus alquerías.* Madrid: Instituo Hispano-Árabe de Cultura, 1961.

Villa-Real y Valdivia, Francisco de Paula. *Hernán Pérez del Pulgar y las Guerras de Granada. Ligeros apuntes sobre la vida y hechos hazañosos de este caudillo.* Madrid: Hijos de Manuel Ginés G Hernández, 1893.

Villena Jurado, José. *Málaga en los albores del siglo XVII desde la documentación municipal.* Málaga: Diputación Provincial de Málaga, 1994.

Viñanza, Cipriano Muñoz y Manzano, Conde de la. *Biblioteca histórica de la filología castellana.* Madrid: M. Tello, 1893.

Vincent, Bernard. "El Albaicín de Granada en el siglo XVI (1527–1587)." In *Andalucía en la edad moderna: Economía y sociedad,* 123–62. Granada: Diputación Provincial de Granada, 1985.

———. "50.000 moriscos almerienses" In *Almería entre culturas (siglos XIII–XVI): actas del coloquio; Almería, 19, 20 y 21 de abril de 1990,* 2:489–514. Almería: Instituto de Estudios Almerienses, 1991.

———. "De la Granada mudéjar a la Granada europea." In *La incorporación de Granada a la Corona de Castilla. Actas del Symposium Conmemorativo del Quinto Centenario, Granada, 2 al 5 de diciembre de 1991,* edited by Miguel Ángel Ladero Quesada, 307–19. Granada: Universidad de Granada, 1993.

———. "Economía y sociedad en el reino de Granada en el siglo XVI." In *Historia de Andalucía,* vol. 4, *La Andalucía del Renacimiento,* edited by Antonio Domínguez Ortiz, 160–223. Madrid: CUPSA Editorial; Barcelona: Editorial Planeta, 1980.

———. "Las epidemias en Andalucía durante el siglo XVI," In *Andalucía en la edad moderna: Economía y sociedad,* 39–49. Granada: Diputación Provincial de Granada, 1985.

———. "Et quelques voix de plus: de Francisco Núñez Muley à Fatima Ratal." *Sharq al-Andalus* 12 (1995): 131–45.

———. "La expulsión de los Moriscos del Reino de Granada y su reparto en Castilla."

In *Andalucía en la edad moderna: Economía y sociedad,* 215–66. Granada: Diputación Provincial de Granada, 1985.

———. "Los Moriscos que permanecieron en el reino de Granada después de la expulsión de 1570," In *Andalucía en la edad moderna: Economía y sociedad,* 267–86. Granada: Diputación Provincial de Granada, 1985.

———. "La peste atlántica de 1596–1602." In *Andalucía en la edad moderna: Economía y sociedad,* 51–80. Granada: Diputación Provincial de Granada, 1985.

———. "Les pestes dans le royaume de Granada aux XVIe et XVIIe siècles." *Annales E.S.C.,* 24 année, 6 (1969): 1511–13.

———. "La población de las Alpujarras en el siglo XVI." In *Hombre y territorio en el reino de Granada (1570–1630). Estudios sobre repoblación,* edited by Manuel Barrios Aguilera and Francisco Andújar Castillo, 29–44. Almería: Instituto de Estudios Almerienses, Universidad de Granada, 1995.

———. "La repoblación del reino de Granada. 1570–1580): el origen de los repobladores." In *Hombre y territorio en el reino de Granada (1570–1630). Estudios sobre repoblación,* edited by Manuel Barrios Aguilera and Francisco Andújar Castillo, 45–55. Almería: Instituto de Estudios Almerienses, Universidad de Granada, 1995.

———. "La *toma* de Granada." In *La fiesta, la ceremonia, el rito,* edited by Pierre Córdoba and Jean-Pierre Etienvre, 43–49. Granada: Casa de Velázquez, Universidad de Granada, 1990.

———. "La vision du royaume de Grenade par les voyageurs étrangers au tournant des XVème et XVIème siècles." *Chronica Nova* 15 (1987): 301–12.

Viñes Millet, Cristina. *La Alhambra de Granada: tres siglos de historia.* Córdoba: Monte de Piedad y Caja de Ahorros de Granada, 1982.

———. *Figuras granadinas.* Granada: Legado Andalusí, 1995.

———. *Historia urbana de Granada. Su evolución hasta fines del siglo XIX.* Granada: Centro de Estudios municipales y de cooperación interprovincial, 1987.

Vives, José. *Inscripciones cristianas de la España romana y visigoda.* 2d ed. Barcelona: CSIC, 1969.

———. "Tradición y leyenda en la hagiografía hispánica." *Hispania Sacra* 17 (1964): 495–508.

Voigt, Burkhard. *Juan de Valdés und Bermúdez de Pedraza: zwei spanische Sprachgeschictsschreiber.* Bonn: Bouvier, 1980.

Webb, Diana. *Patrons and Defenders: The Saints in the Italian City-States.* London: I. B. Tauris, 1996.

Wensinck, A. J. "Maryam." *Encyclopaedia of Islam.* CD-ROM ed. Leiden: Brill, 1999.

Westermarck, Edward. *Ritual and Belief in Morocco.* Vol. 1. London: Macmillan, 1926. Reprint. New Hyde Park, N.Y.: University Books, 1968.

Wheare, Degory. *Relectiones hyemales, de ratione et methodo legendi utrasque historias, civiles et ecclesiasticas.* Nuremburg, 1660.

Wiegers, G. A. "The 'Old' or 'Turpiana' Tower in Granada and Its Relics according to Aḥmad b. Qāsim al-Ḥajarī" In *Sites et monuments disparus d'après les témoignages de voyageurs,* edited by Rika Gyselen, 193–207. Bures-sur-Yvette: Groupe pour l'Étude de la Civilisation du Moyen-Orient, 1996.

Wolf, Kenneth Baxter. *Christian Martyrs in Muslim Spain*. Cambridge: Cambridge University Press, 1988.

Wood, David Carrico. "Voting the *millones* in Segovia: Republic, Kingdom, and Conscience in Habsburg Castile, 1590–1621." Ph.D. diss., Johns Hopkins University, 2001.

Worcester, Thomas. *Seventeenth-Century Cultural Discourse: France and the Preaching of Bishop Camus*. New York: Mouton de Gruyter, 1997.

Wright, A. D. *Catholicism and Spanish Society under the Reign of Philip II, 1555–1598, and Philip III, 1598–1621*. Lewiston, N.Y.: Edwin Mellen Press, 1991.

Wright, Elizabeth R. *Pilgrimage to Patronage: Lope de Vega and the Court of Philip III, 1598–1621*. Lewisburg: Bucknell University Press, 2001.

Wulff Alonso, Fernando. "Andalucía antigua en la historiografía española (XVI–XIX)." *Ariadna* 10 (1992): 7–32.

———. *Las esencias patrias. Historiografía e historia antigua en la construcción de la identidad española (siglos XVI–XX)*. Barcelona: Crítica, 2003.

Ximena Jurado, Martín de. *Catálogo de los obispos de las iglesias catedrales de Jaén y anales eclesiásticos de este obispado*. Madrid, 1654. Reprint. Edited by José Rodríguez Molina and María José Osorio Pérez. Granada: Universidad de Granada, 1991.

Ximénez, Andres. *Descripción del real Monasterio de San Lorenzo del Escorial: su magnífico templo, panteón, y palacio*. Madrid, 1764.

Index